RIMFIRE REVOLUTION:

A GUIDE TO MODERN .22 RIFLES

By Michael R. Shea

Published by

Gun Digest® Books, an imprint of Caribou Media
Gun Digest Media, 5600 W. Grande Market Drive, Suite 100
Appleton, WI 54913
www.gundigest.com

To order books or other products call 920.471.4522 ext.104
or visit us online at www.gundigeststore.com

DISCLAIMER: Any and all loading data found in this book or previous editions is to be taken as reference material only. The publishers, editors, authors, contributors, and their entities bear no responsibility for the use by others of the data included in this book or the editions that came before it.

WARNING: For any modern firearm, it is essential that you adhere to the loading recommendations put forth in the reloading manuals of today's components manufacturers, as well as to the owners manual of the maker of your individual firearm (some of today's firearms are so specialized that they will chamber and function reliably only within a very narrow set of criteria in a given caliber range). The potential for things to go wrong is exacerbated in guns long out of production, those chambering obsolete cartridges, and those using cartridges containing black powder or cordite. As a separate caution, you must never fire any cartridge in any gun just because it looks similar to, or has a similar designation to, the cartridge the gun is chambered for. This can be extremely dangerous. Almost is not good enough, so if you are at all uncertain about the proper cartridge, have a competent gunsmith check the bullet diameter and case dimensions and firearms chamber and headspace.

ISBN-13: 978-1-951115-37-1

Edited by Corey Graff
Designed by Jong Cadelina and Gene Coo
Cover photo by Cosmo Genova
All other photos by author unless noted

Printed in the United States of America

10 9 8 7 6 5 4 3 2 1

TABLE OF CONTENTS

For David White

ABOUT THE AUTHOR

Michael R. Shea is a senior editor at Black Rifle Coffee Company, an editor-at-large for *Field & Stream* magazine, and the rimfire contributor for *Gun Digest the Magazine* and *SHOT Business*. A recovering journalist, his work has appeared in *Men's Journal*, *USA Today*, *Popular Science*, *The Week*, *Petersen's Hunting*, *Outdoor Life*, *Game & Fish*, *Ducks Unlimited*, and many more. He holds a master's degree in Nonfiction Writing from Columbia University in the City of New York, where he researched and wrote on the Pacific campaigns of World War II. From March through September, you can find him directing an NRL22 shooting match at his home range in Owego, New York.

ACKNOWLEDGMENTS

Special thanks are due to Ricky King and Will Brantley, whose stories of sniping Eastern gray squirrels at 100 yards with scoped rimfires kicked off this powerful obsession. I'm also grateful to my editor at *Field & Stream*, Dave Hurteau, who encouraged me to dive deep on everything rimfire, as did the notable gun writer and friend David E. Petzal. They provided volumes of advice on writing about shooting.

Special thanks also go to the following, without whom this book wouldn't have come to fruition: Cosmo Genova, Justin Potter, Ryan McCafferty, Tim Bellis, Dave Sweet, Luke Pohlman, and Kenna Milaski.

Finally, I want to thank the board of Tioga County Sportsmen's Association in Owego, New York. When I walked in the door and proposed they commit time and money to the fledgling sport of NRL22, they did not hesitate. These small shooting clubs with public matches like TCSA are keeping the shooting sports alive and well. Particular thanks are due to Robert T. Waite, an enthusiastic supporter of NRL22 and all the rimfire disciplines from our first handshake.

FOREWORD

In 1971, I wrote a modest little book called *The .22 Rifle,* which I intended to guide beginning shooters. That goal was altogether fitting and proper. In those days, we considered rimfires to be starter rifles or something with which you hunted rabbits, shot rats in a dump, or — if you were one of a dedicated handful of competitors — shot in 50-foot competition.

But along with the rest of the shooting industry, rimfires have grown up. They've become diversified to the point that we now use them for purposes that no one dreamed of in 1971. If you're not attuned to all of it, you're missing out.

Mike Shea's book is not modest or little, nor is it intended for beginners. It is sweeping, inclusive, and all-encompassing. By training, Mike is a newspaperman, and he goes at the subject with a good reporter's thoroughness.

He is also a case-hardened hunter and shooter who burns up an estimated 10,000 rounds a year. Mike and I have successfully navigated the horrors of Range Day at the Shot Show, and I can tell you that he knows his stuff. He is also an ultra-long-range rifle shooter. These guys shoot at either 4 miles or 75 miles; I can never remember which. In any event, it's so far away that they have to sight on targets through periscopes that compensate for the extreme holdover necessary, and I believe they also include the rotation of the earth in their firing solutions.

There is a staggering amount of information here. If you digest it, you'll be unlocking a wonderful world where there is no recoil to speak of and very little noise. The ammo is cheap (comparatively), and it's all scaled modestly — making all sorts of shooting available to all kinds of people. Take a look and marvel. If anyone had proposed that this stuff would one day be as common as handheld devices, I would have said, "What in the hell is a handheld device?" — and then suggested that they try on a straitjacket for size.

You do not have this problem. It's all real and waiting for you.

Dave Petzal, Rifles Editor
Field & Stream
October 2020

PREFACE

The diminutive .22 has "killed African lions and Alaskan grizzlies, but they usually account for rabbits and squirrels. They are fired at targets by men of enormous skill, sometimes from rifles that cost hundreds of dollars, but more often they ventilate tin cans." These sentiments are as true today as in 1971 when Dave Petzel penned them in his classic book, *The .22 Rifle* — yet the scale and scope of rimfire rifles have vastly changed.

Over the last 50 years, the shooters have changed, too. Those skilled shots are no longer exclusively men. Some of the very best rimfire shooters in the world are women. The economics are different. A few hundred dollars is still a lot of money, but the very best rimfire rifles cost thousands — in some cases, tens of thousands.

The ammunition is better. The .22 Long Rifle or .22 LR is more refined, consistent, and accurate today than at any point in our history. Shooting sports have evolved, too, particularly here in the United States with the rise of modern precision rifle shooting. Most importantly, for the purview of this book, the rifles have changed — significantly, and for the better.

Computer-driven manufacturing coupled with grassroots demand for insanely accurate, functional rimfire rifles has opened the door to a significant re-thinking of the platform. No longer are .22s miniaturized afterthoughts in walnut and blue. They are precision instruments, as sophisticated in design as their centerfire brethren. Modern precision .22s are capable of Olympic accuracy or ringing steel at 1,200 yards.

A modern precision rifle system by Vudoo Gun Works. Photo: Vudoo Gun Works

Yes, 1,200 yards. That is not a typo. A shot that long in .22 LR requires an astonishing 120 mils of elevation. And it is repeatable.

Make no mistake. We are in the midst of a rimfire revolution. This book aims to chronicle that progress. During my research, as I got deeper into the world of rimfire, it became clear that there was a large data gap between how most Americans thought about .22s — "plinkers," "youth rifles," "squirrel guns" — and what today's new tactical, precision, and long-range shooters were doing. To understand the nuances of how a rifle action works or rimfire ballistic coefficients, I took a deep dive into Internet forums, Facebook groups, and YouTube channels. No published works were explaining, for example, the difference between an Anschütz and a Vudoo, while every shooter thinking of spending serious money on a .22 has undoubtedly asked themselves, *What's the difference between an Anschütz and a Vudoo?* Thanks to my work with *Field & Stream,* I picked up the phone and called these companies and many others, including bleeding edge thought leaders in the rimfire industry. My original intent was to chronicle rifle genealogies, but as with most book projects, it grew into much more.

The challenge of a project like this is keeping the subject accessible for new enthusiasts while not boring the old hands. I've tried to start in the shallow end on each topic, then wade into deeper waters. The book is designed to be read through but could also — I hope — stand as a reference for others.

The book starts by touching on pertinent rimfire history, which is the story of the .22 Short. In the .22 Short, is everything a shooter needs to know about rimfire ammunition and how it works. We then look at modern rimfire ammunition, including the .17s, before pushing off into rifles. To be included in this book, rifles had to meet a minimum consistent standard of 1 MOA accuracy, meaning they had to shoot an approximate 0.500-inch 5-shot group at 50 yards. They also had to innovate within the platform in some way.

Next, we dive into accuracy, cleaning practice and theory, customization and improvements, plus shooting accessories, sports, and technique. A rimfire rifle set up for extreme long range is vastly different than a sporter designed for an NRA postal match. The discipline informs how a rifle system hangs together, what accessories are required, and how you handle it on the firing line. These peculiarities might sound complicated, but it's pretty obvious. You wouldn't shoot Rimfire Challenge with an NRL22 rifle. This section teases out these rifle systems and sport-based nuances.

The last chapter is for readers like me. When I started shooting accurate .22s, I couldn't get enough. This section is for readers who also can't get enough. It begins with raw question-and-answer-style interviews with shooters and thought-leaders pushing the rimfire platform to new heights — including engineers, designers, shooters, and promoters, all accomplished. These discussions are detail-rich, but I hope that a casual reader who's made it through the first two hundred pages can happily follow along. Finally, there's a collection of appendixes for reader reference, other sources to explore, theoretical DOPE charts, an NRL22 gear survey, even a guide to the manufactures mentioned in this book.

At the very least, I hope this book opens the world of modern precision rimfire to new readers and shooters alike, whether a first-time gun owner or a seasoned PRS competitor looking for a .22 trainer. RR

Michael R. Shea
May 2021

1

INTRODUCTION TO RIMFIRES

Allison Zane lay prone behind her rifle, eyeing five targets stretching out over the desert from 100 to 330 yards on a hot Sunday in Las Vegas. The temperature hung around 90, and the 20-mph desert wind gusted to 40. Her dad and fellow competitor, Frank Zane, gave her a wind call. Allison watched the breeze lie down, shook off her dad's effort, then ran her handheld Kestrel wind meter and ballistic problem solver. She set up on the rifle, and in fast succession, sent ten 40-grain bullets of .22 LR downrange, jumping between targets at 100 and 330 yards, plus a few distances in between. She connected on seven of the 10 shots, besting her dad and everyone else at the NRL22 National Championship that day.

By the weekend's close, the 13-year-old eighth-grader from Pennsylvania finished above competitors who've been shooting longer than she's been

Allison Zane shooting at the NRL22 National Match. Photo: ConX Media

The firing line at an NRL22X event. Note the roof pitch barricade. Photo: ConX Media

alive. She easily won the Young Guns division and placed third overall. During the match, National Rifle League executive director Ty Frehner asked Allison how she felt. She just beamed: "I'm having so much fun!"

Fun, says Frehner, is key to the success of NRL22, which has quickly become one of the most popular and fastest-growing shooting sports in the country and around the world. Nearly 90 gun clubs in the U.S. currently hold NRL22 matches, and there are events in England, France, South Africa, New Zealand, and Australia. As long-range centerfire competitions like the Precision Rifle Series have taken off, a growing number of shooters are first learning to go long with a rimfire rifle. Many have found, like Allison, it's just too much fun to give up. It's certainly less expensive than centerfire and more accessible to the average shooter.

Shooting long distance is all the rage these days. But most Americans don't have access to even a 500-yard rifle range, let alone a 1,000-yarder. Yet with a .22, you can have that long-range shooting experience at just 100 yards. A standard-velocity .22 LR round zeroed at 50 yards drops almost 7-1/2 inches at 100. A 10-mph crosswind will move the bullet another 4 inches. That means you have to know your equipment, adjust for the drop, and DOPE the wind to hit, just like shooting longer ranges with a centerfire. By one analysis, the comparator factor between match-speed .22 LR

and most modern precision centerfire cartridges is 25 percent. So, shooting a .22 at 200 yards is roughly equivalent to firing, say, a 6.5 Creedmoor at 800 yards. These parallels are why rimfire training has become a popular low-cost option for tactical precision centerfire competition. The sniper math and shooting technique are mostly the same. It's also why precision rimfire shooting – and the tack-driving .22s required – have grown so popular in their own right.

Frehner and National Rifle League founder Travis Ishida started NRL22 in 2017, figuring it would provide some minor-league fun ahead of his major-league National Rifle League centerfire events. "I was dead wrong," Frehner says. "This rimfire community, these shooters, they're all about .22s. I see some of them at centerfire matches, and they don't have half the money invested in centerfire that they've put into their rimfire guns."

The genesis moment of this burgeoning rimfire revolution, in many ways, can be traced back to the exploding success of NRL22. Part of the appeal of the new sport is the ingenious open-source competition system. Each month, NRL posts a standard course of fire online, and any club or range can run a match. All it takes is a few steel targets and some barricades. NRL22 uses the term "club" loosely. Any group from a sportsman's organization to five guys with a hay-field can download the monthly course of fire, hold a

Modern precision rifles at the NRL22 National Match. Vudoo and CZ make most shown here. Photo: ConX Media

match, and submit scores for national consideration.

Most targets hover around 2 minute of angle, or 2 MOA, in size – roughly 2 inches at 100 yards. (More on MOA, inches, and MILS later.) Sometimes they shrink to 1 MOA or smaller, but rarely. The sport does not require ungodly accuracy, yet that's what its shooters have come to demand of their rifles. Although the scored NRL22 course of fire is always at 100 yards, clubs are encouraged to run bonus stages, often at extended ranges. There are other brand-new rimfire disciplines, such as Extreme Long Range Rimfire or ELR Rimfire, which posts targets beyond 600 yards. NRL22 recently rolled out a longer-range competition as well, with the X series. Match directors set the target distances at their discretion. These larger, regional NRL22X matches have exploded in popularity, with competitors driving for hours to compete, much like centerfire precision shooting events. Many of the targets stand beyond 400 yards. With a modern riflescope, 400 to 500 yards is about the limit of a .22 LR

rifle without special optical equipment, as we'll see.

Still, it takes a certain kind of rifle and excellent ammo to connect that far with .22 LR. Yet, precision rimfire success is not solely about distance. The rifle needs to be durable, handle the rough work of dropping on barricades like ladders and mock rooftops. It needs to run fast, as some stages feature time limits. It requires a great trigger and exceptional ergonomics so that the shooter can build a stable position, whether seated, kneeling, standing, prone, or in some odd contortionist position dreamed up by a sadistic match director. Rolled up together, these are rifle systems, accessories, and shooting techniques pioneered by U.S. military marksmen and snipers as the Global War on Terror shifted the battlespace to urban theaters in Iraq and the mountains of Afghanistan. The grassed-up, hidden-in-the-jungle Vietnam-era sniper work of, say, the great Carlos Hathcock evolved into the build-a-position on a rooftop skillset of Chris Kyle and Craig Harrison. Tactical rifles (tactically "inspired" in most

The first barreled action Vudoo Gun Works showed publicly, in an Accuracy International Chassis. Photo: Mike Bush

Note the serial number: TEST3. Photos: Mike Bush

A lineup of the Vudoo rifles taken to the NRA World Championships at the Peacemaker National Training Center in 2017.

cases) came to dominate the firearms landscape in the early 2000s. But there wasn't a fitting rimfire equivalent until the rise of Vudoo Gun Works of St. George, Utah.

Like NRL22, Vudoo made its debut in 2017 at the NRA World Shooting Championships at the Peacemaker National Training Center in West Virginia. (Peacemaker now holds a summer precision rimfire series, the Lapua Practical Rimfire Challenge.) Paul Parrott, CEO of Vudoo Gun Works, brought the company's brand-new V-22 platform for some of the best hands in precision shooting to try that first day in West Virginia. Veteran competitive shooter Walt Hasser got on the gun, and fellow rifleman Emil Praslick called the wind. Praslick's nickname is the "Wind Whisperer," and he might be the best wind reader in the world. They set up on The Mountain at Peacemaker and spun up the rifle scope to connect on an 18-inch plate at 460 yards. "First shot out, they whacked it," Parrott says. "We were all blown away. In 20 minutes, we had a crowd watching this craziness — a .22 hitting at 460,

shot after shot. Everyone wanted to shoot it."

Mike Bush, a longtime engineer for some of the world's largest firearm companies, designed the V-22 action after years of taking apart and converting old Remington 40x single-shots into repeaters. After the .22 ammunition market settled down from public mass hysteria in the mid-2010s, and PRS shooting was spiking in popularity, Parrott and Bush decided to start Vudoo. Initially, they built the company around the modified 40x action with an innovative Accuracy International Chassis System magazine converted to .22 LR. AICS-patterned magazines were orginally designed to feed .308 Winchester-sized rounds and quickly became the detachable box mag of choice for military, LEO, and civilian sharpshooters. Many stocks and chassis systems now take AICS mags. Bush engineered a feed system for the small .22 LR bullets inside the large .308-sized magazine and departed from the 40x-style bolt to a two-piece control feed system that grabbed and cleanly fed the soft lead bullet into the chamber. The result downrange was world-class groups. "We had no idea it would be so successful," Parrot says.

Besides raw accuracy, the secret to the V-22's early success was scale. Built on a Remington 700 footprint, a Vudoo .22 LR handles like a full-size centerfire and is compatible with the entire world of Model 700 accessories, from stocks and chassis to rails and triggers. At the time, there weren't any full-size or true-to-scale rimfire rifles. These new .22 LRs were often heavier even than the centerfire guns they replicated. Take two barrels of the same length and contour, for example. The tube drilled for .224 is necessarily heavier than the one bored for .30 cal. Vudoo's original idea was to provide a top-end, full-sized replica .22 trainer for centerfire PRS shooters. But just like Frehner and Ishida did with NRL22, Parrot and Bush underestimated the appeal of the .22.

"Rimfire has taken on a life of its own," Parrot says. "There's a whole subset of shooters out there who only use rimfire rifles and who love pushing the limits of what these guns can do."

At a recent ELR rimfire event in Wyoming, organizers set targets from 200 to 600 yards. Shooters later filmed themselves hitting at 750. Competitors like King of Two Mile champ Paul Phillips regularly connect with .22 LR at 1,000 yards. A.J. Stewart, an ELR nut from the same hometown in Alabama as Mike Bush, put repeatable groups on steel at 1,250 yards. There are now copper-solid .22s, long as a .17 HMR, designed for fast-twist barrels to extend that range even farther.

"We're exploring the outer limits, and it's just generally fun, and a little silly, yes. But what's practical about Formula One racing?" Parrot asks. "Practical isn't the point. Formula One is a billion-dollar sport and what's learned there filters down to the rest of us. We're on the fringe, but hunters and shooters are going to benefit down the line from what we're learning and from the ammo, optics, and guns that will come out of it."

Parrot and I had our first version of this conversation in summer 2019. Six months later, at the Shooting,

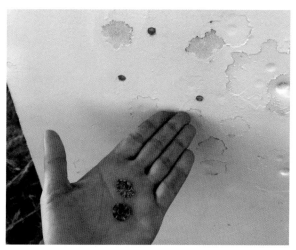
A.J. Stewart showing off three impacts – and two of the found rounds – after connecting at 825 yards with his .22 LR. Photo: Chad Long

Hunting, Outdoor Trade Show (SHOT Show), five other manufacturers displayed Remington 700-footprint .22 rimfire rifles, actions, or action conversions. Half a dozen other new full-sized rifles kitted out for long-range or NRL22 work, many in chassis, were there for evaluation. Such monolithic aluminum stock replacements generally use AR-15-pattern buttstocks and grips and have a wide, flat forend with multiple attachment points for bipods, rail bags, barricades stops, and other accessories. At SHOT 2020, there was a visible uptick in "long-range" branded .22 LR ammunition. There were maybe a dozen new riflescopes, some with 30mm and 34mm tubes with a parallax adjustment down to 25 yards or less. In short, that trickle-down effect Parrot and I discussed had hit the firearms market writ large. At the show, several people commented that I must be happy because, as one friend put it, "the only thing interesting here this year is rimfire."

While Vudoo helped create the modern precision rimfire rifle space, it is certainly not alone. A few years ago, it wasn't Vudoo, but a relatively obscure Australian rifle, a Lithgow Arms LA101, that lit my personal .22 LR fire.

Completely unaware of the Vudoo origin story, I was at Peacemaker on the very same firing line. The Mountain has dozens of targets over a few hundred

The author connecting at 460 yards with a Lithgow rifle and CCI ammo at the Peacemaker National Training Center.

acres at unknown distances past 1,200 yards. We had been shooting 6.5 Creedmoor, and as the day wound down, I took out my Aussie .22 LR. Having never shot the rifle past 100 yards, I put it on a bench and rung steel at 300 in short order. Wade Shambaugh, Peacemaker's lead instructor, suggested I go prone at the 18-inch plate rack. I ranged it at 460 yards. To hit, I needed 94 MOA of elevation. My turret bottomed out at 48 MOA. The reticle gave me another 30. In the ripping 9 o'clock wind, Shambaugh suggested a hold of 8 feet left. I shot with a massive holdover using the base of the post at the very bottom of my field of view. I saw a dust cloud downrange. Way low. I cut the wind hold to about 5 feet and held higher. I missed just a touch left and adjusted. With that third shot, I heard the distant ring of steel.

"Impact!" Wade hollered.

I shot again.

"Impact!"

Five of my ten shots connected. You couldn't slap the smile off my face. If we put that much dope into our 6.5s, we'd have needed a target at 1,830 yards.

"Not too long ago, most people would say a shot like that is impossible with a .22," Shambaugh said.

Well, not anymore. And thanks to impressive advancements in rimfire ammunition, it doesn't take expensive or obscure rifles to do it, either.

A few weeks after the Peacemaker event, I watched a guy set a 200-yard stage on fire with a Ruger American and inexpensive scope at my first precision rimfire match. I went in confident, shooting 3/4-inch groups at 100 yards with my Lithgow. But until that point, I'd only ever practiced from a bench or prone. One stage had us crammed into a sewer pipe. At another, we balanced on top of an overturned barrel. At a third, we knelt against a flexible 1-inch sapling. The guys who shot well knew how to build a stable position on unfamiliar objects. I realized — painfully, I might add — that if you don't have positional fundamentals drilled into your bones, you won't get very far in precision shooting. The guy with the Ruger American and cheap scope cleaned my clock. The rifle platform mattered so much less than fundamental shooting skills. I fell deeper down the rabbit hole.

Taken together, this is modern precision rimfire shooting — a functional blend of purpose-built rifles and positional shooting skills. This book hopes to explore aspects of both, from $300 rifles to $3,000 barreled actions, from shooting form and competition shooting to chilly September mornings in the squirrel woods. I hope readers will find, like I have, the excitement of this exploding precision rimfire world. Hitting tiny targets a long way off with minuscule bullets is immensely gratifying and, like Allison Zane said, just downright fun.

When the NRL22 National Championships wrapped up in Las Vegas, Open-Division winner Paul Dallin stood at the prize table next to Allison. In front of them were two Vudoo rifles, one red and one blue. Dallin asked the Young Gun winner which she liked best. She said red, so he took the blue one. Up to that point, Allison had been sharing a rifle with her dad — but not anymore. Suppose you sign up for an NRL22X match in Western Pennsylvania or eastern Ohio. In that case, you'll probably see her, cleaning stages with her red rifle — a living example of the future of shooting, ringing steel from a very long way away, with a humble, almost antique, 40-grain slug of lead. RR

2
RIMFIRE HISTORY

There's a cartoon floating around online called "The Invention of Archery." Three guys are standing beside each other. The first guy says *I want to stab that guy, but he's way over there.*

Firearms were likely dreamt up along the same lines. Someone hit upon the idea that blackpowder stuffed down a tube, topped with a projectile, and touched off with fire, did spectacular damage downrange. *Man, I want to knock that castle down, but it's way over there.*

In Europe, cannons showed up in Italy around 1320. For the next 200 years, firearms were essentially hand cannons — short, stout barrels loaded with blackpowder, then packed with rocks, pebbles, and sometimes arrows. You jabbed a hole in the barrel's top or side with a smoldering stick or hot iron. Firing

it was a two-person job. One soldier would hold the hand cannon (while presumably saying his prayers), and a second would grace the touch hole with the red poker. Anyone who's seen a small wheel-mounted cannon go off — the type that shoots golf balls and is popular at sportsmen's clubs in the country on chicken barbeque weekends — can imagine the thrill of holding such a device under one's arm. Hand cannons weren't particularly safe or accurate, but when they worked, lookout.

By the 15th Century, the matchlock came along. A lever, and later a trigger, was added under the barrel. When pulled, the "lock" dropped a lit cord or match into the flash pan and started the ignition process. There was a painful time delay between pulling the trigger, the lock dropping the match into a flash pan that ignited a sprinkle of powder, and the main charge in the barrel going off. Today, engineers still work to reduce that "lock time" between trigger pull and ignition, but now they're shaving fractions

the invention of archery
I really wanna stab that guy, but he's way over there.

ifunny.co

The Internet gets it right, again. Photo: Public domain

A replica matchlock. Note the long-burning cord. It would stay lit over many shots. Photo: Kathy Rittyrats

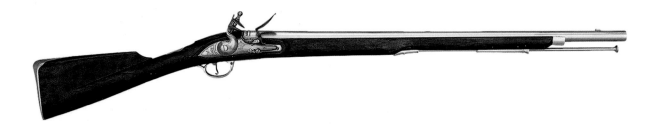

A replica Brown Bess flintlock by Davide Pedersoli. Gunsmiths converted many of the early rifles to percussion caps through the 1800s. Photo: Pedersoli

A big rimfire: The Spencer rifle of the American Civil War proved a deciding mechanical advantage for the North.

of milliseconds. In contrast, a 1400s French *arquebus* could have taken several seconds to go off.

It's worth noting, early firearms weren't more accurate or deadlier than archery tackle, but they were faster to reload than a crossbow and less expensive and time-consuming to manufacture. Firearms flattened the training curve, too. An illiterate peasant with a matchlock and some instruction could knock a mounted knight off his horse in short order. Proficiency with lance or sword or bow could take years of training. Firearms democratized combat in the Middle Ages.

The matchlock evolved into the wheel lock, dog lock, and eventually the flintlock. Instead of a smoldering match dropped in the flash pan, a piece of flint struck steel sending a shower of sparks toward the blackpowder. Flintlocks didn't require an always-smoldering length of cord, but they still had issues. The powder in the pan sent up a noxious yellow smoke cloud before the bullet took off that would

often eclipse the target, affecting accuracy and spook game animals.

In 1800, British chemist Edward Charles Howard discovered fulminates — chemical compounds that exploded on impact. This discovery forever changed firearms for the better. A few years later, a Presbyterian minister in Scotland — annoyed that birds would flush as powder smoked in the pan of his flintlock — adopted fast-acting fulminates to his shotgun lock. British gunsmith Joseph Manton invited a cap-like system in 1814. Still, it took an American artist in Philadelphia, Joshua Shaw, to develop the sealed copper cup laden with fulminates, which we know today as the percussion cap.

Like the M1819 Hall Rifle and the British Brown Bess, many early percussion muskets were flintlock conversions. The flash pan was tossed, replaced with a metal "nipple" connected to the chamber's powder by a small tube. Copper and sometimes brass percussion caps shaped like miniature top hats sat over the head of the exposed nipple. When you pulled the trigger, a heavy hammer dropped on the percussion cap, detonating the fulminates, which sent sparks to the powder in the barrel, and away the lead ball went. An infantryman armed with a percussion musket or rifle would carry a pouch of caps and another of paper cartridges. To load, he'd rip open the powder-end of the cartridge with his teeth, spill the pre-measured slug of blackpowder down his musket barrel, seat the lead ball by hand, then use a ramrod to get the whole package snug at the bottom of the barrel. Musket shouldered, on went the percussion cap. After the first volley, it took a well-trained soldier 20 to 30 seconds to reload. A fighting regiment could get off three volleys a minute.

Throughout the 1800s, firearms development coincided with cartridge development. Engineers, inventors, gunsmiths, and crackpots tried various ways to speed reloads by integrating fulminate primer, powder, and bullet into a single package — then they built guns around their idea.

In 1808, the Swiss gunsmith Jean Samuel Pauly developed a self-contained paper cartridge with primer snugged behind the bullet. You loaded this gun from the breech end, much like a modern break-action shotgun. When you pulled the trigger, a needle struck through the paper and detonated the primer. Frenchman Casimir Lefaucheux took this idea and replaced the paper for brass to develop the pinfire cartridge. Each round had a firing pin that jutted off the cartridge's side at a 90-degree angle. Trip the trigger on an early pinfire, and the hammer dropped, striking the integrated pin, detonating the primer. Then around 1845, another Frenchman, Louis-Nicolas Flobert, created the first modern firearm cartridge.

The Parisian Flobert took a simple copper cup, loaded it with fulminate primer compound, and topped it with a round ball — essentially a bullet crimped to a percussion cap. There was no real rim or flange at a 90-degree angle in his first designs. The case head had a taper that wedged the cartridge in the cham-

Smith & Wesson's early variation on the Flobert design. Note there is no real rim. The first designs taper fit to the chamber.

ber. There was no powder in the case, only the primer and the lead ball. Flobert's rifles and revolvers were designed for indoor parlor shooting or whacking a troublesome rodent in the pantry. They were gallery guns, designed to punch paper or tip over little tin animals at a few steps, much like gallery shooting games prevalent at American carnivals and country fairs until recent times. The early Flobert designs had heavy hammers that crushed the primer side of the self-contained metallic cartridge. In later versions, he added a firing pin to the action.

At the London Exposition of 1851, Flobert exhibited his small .22-caliber rifle. Attending were two Americans, Horace Smith, and Daniel Wesson. They were impressed, and by 1857 they had developed a new cartridge of similar design, the .22 Short, for the new Smith & Wesson Model 1 revolver. They patented the cartridge on April 17, 1860, as the "S&W .22 Rim Fire."

This new metallic cartridge had a straight case and hollow rim — a first in the United States. The hollow rim allowed Smith & Wesson to use a wet priming mixture, spun to the rim's edge, and dried. You could then add the powder to the case without mixing it with powdered primer — a problem that led to constant misfires in the duo's other post-London designs. Smith & Wesson loaded its first .22s with 4 grains of fine blackpowder. The powder sat atop a perforated-paper wad to further prevent the dried primer from mixing with the powder. (Later, as S&W perfected the wet-primer process, it dropped the paper disc.) The

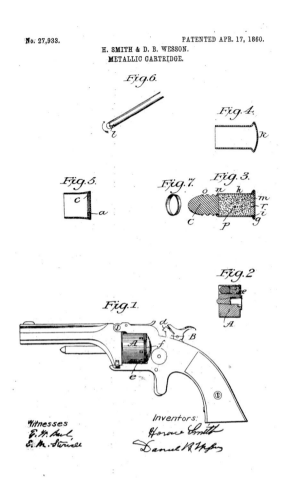

No. 27,933. PATENTED APR. 17, 1860.
H. SMITH & D. B. WESSON.
METALLIC CARTRIDGE.

Fig.6.

Fig.4.

Fig.5.

Fig.7. Fig.3.

Fig.2.

Fig.1.

Witnesses Inventors:

Smith & Wesson's .22 Short patent illustration shows a clear rim and convex case head it believed led to better primer ignition. The firm patented the Short along with the Model 1 revolver that fired it.

head of the case was convex or dished out, not flat like modern rimfire ammo. There was no headstamp. Smith & Wesson thought the dished head helped more evenly distribute the primer around the rim. Pull the trigger, and a firing pin stabbed the brass case's rim, igniting the primer.

Like today, yesteryear's ammo makers loaded the first .22 Shorts with a 29-grain lead round-nose bullet. The bullet had a tapered heel that reduced the backside of its diameter so it would fit in the case. This design became known as a "heeled" or "outside lubricated" design. You applied wax or grease to the bullet outside the case to prevent lead buildup in the bore. (All .22 rimfire bullets are still heeled and outside lubricated except for the .22 Winchester Magnum Rimfire.) Smith & Wesson's 1860 patent shows three

lubrication grooves, or cannelure, along the bullet's diameter. The cartridge case had a light crimp on the bottommost cannelure to secure the bullet in place. With this design, the diameter of the brass case matched the outside caliber diameter of the bullet. The bullet base was convex or dished as if you pressed a BB into the lead — a likely design holdover from the caseless Volcanic and Rocket Ball cartridges that were cutting edge in their day. Modern bullet and cartridge designs have abandoned most of these principles, but you could never call these features unsuccessful. The .22 rimfires are still the most widely produced arms and ammo in the world. The antique .22 Short remained an Olympian as the official round for international rapid-fire pistol competition until 2004, when the .22 LR replaced it.

While underpowered by today's standards, the Model 1 in .22 Short became a popular compact self-defense revolver with soldiers on both sides of the Civil War. Smith & Wesson's first pistol and cartridge were a major early financial success, too, thanks mainly to the rimfire manufacturing process it developed. Like copper and copper-alloys like brass, soft metal could be rolled into thin sheet metal, then punched into small discs. These discs were then "drawn" into little tubes with one end closed. A rim was "bumped" into the head, much like how a handloader uses a re-sizing die to shape centerfire brass. The malleable metal didn't tear or split through the forming process. Hundreds of these little cups could be drawn and bumped in a single pass of a 19th-Century machine press. This process made ammunition for the Model 1 widely available and affordable. Several U.S. manufacturers started producing the easy-to-make ".22 Rim Fire." Overseas, Eley of England manufactured it as the .230 Rimfire. By 1871, annual round production hit 30 million.

Flobert's cartridge developed more of a rim and became known as the .22 BB Cap. The BB stands for "bullet breech," a reference to the breech-end loading in Flobert rifles and pistols. (Later came the .22

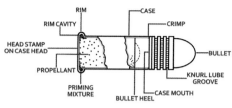

RIMFIRE

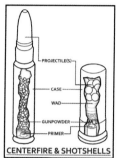

An early Flobert design. The trigger pull drops a heavy hammer that slams a short, squat firing pin into the back of the round. These guns were popular in the United States until the start of World War II. Flobert manufactured this rifle in 1933.

CB for Conical Bullet.) When multiple variations on the Smith & Wesson cartridge appeared in the 1870s, including the .22 Long in 1871, the firm renamed it the .22 Short.

The hollow rim and wet-priming process pioneered by Smith & Wesson did several things very well. First, the rim of a rimfire held the cartridge securely in the breechface. A closed action effectively clamped the round in place. (Many of the early Flobert actions didn't even lock. A stout mainspring held tight

enough.) Second, the ammunition was relatively weather-sealed with the bullet pressed in place surrounded by a copper case — a dramatic improvement over loose powder and paper cartridges. Third, the malleable copper case created a seal at the breech end and further expanded to the chamber on detonation, so all the toxic fulminate gases and blackpowder smoke went down the barrel and away from the shooter's face. Four, the rim provided an excellent gripping surface for reliable extraction and ejection.

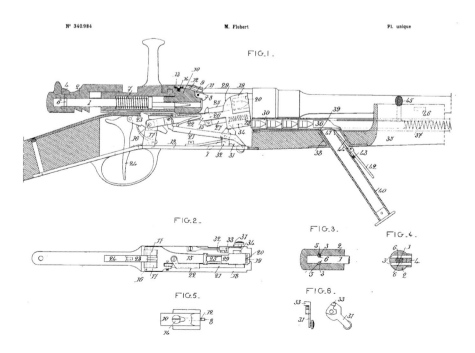

This 1904 patent by Flobert demonstrates the giant mechanical leaps it quickly made. Note the magazine, turn bolt, tube magazine, and firing pin and mainspring within the bolt.

(Extraction and ejection issues plagued early needle-fires and pinfires). Five, the rim provided an effective way to measure and build proper headspace into bolts and barrels, which helped make the round accurate. Headspace is the distance between the bolt face and the chamber's part that prevents the case from moving forward. With a rimfire, the headspace takes up the rim thickness, sandwiched between the bolt face and the breech.

Inventors flooded patent offices in the U.S. and Europe with rimfire designs between the 1860s and 1890s. There were many new but inconsequential .22s developed, but most were much larger.

In 1860, B. Tyler Henry patented a rimfire repeater with a cartridge called the .44 Henry Flat. By 1865, repeating carbines utilizing .56- and .58-caliber rimfire cartridges like the Sharps and the Spencer outmatched all muzzleloading small arms on the battlefield and helped the North win the Civil War. The U.S. Army reportedly resisted the Spencer rifle, chambered in .56-56 Spencer, but after President Abraham Lincoln shot a Spencer himself in 1863, he insisted a large order get placed. After the war, the Winchester 1866 "yellow boy" in .44 Rimfire went on to win the West — and Winchester the imaginations of shooters everywhere. By 1880, a catalog for Union Metallic Cartridge Company listed 40 rimfire cartridges for sale. Only two were .22s. More than half ranged between the Colt .41 and .58 Joslyn.

Rimmed big-bore cartridges dominated small arms until the advent of smokeless powder required cartridges to handle high pressures. Like the French Poudre B, early smokeless powders proved three times more potent than blackpowder by weight and produced much less smoke. Rimfire cases by design straddled the pressure curve from the very beginning. The brass case had to be soft enough for a firing pin to depress the rim and ignite the primer and strong enough not to blow out the case head or split the case in the chamber. In small doses, smokeless worked well in rimfire cartridges, but the brass of big bores like the .44 Henry pushed a 200-grain bullet with 28 grains of blackpowder and could not handle the equivalent weight of smokeless or semi-smokeless. One of the largest rimfires ever developed, the .58 Miller, sent a 500-grain bullet downrange pushed by 60 grains of blackpowder. The smokeless powder had much different pressure demands and quickly ushered the development of centerfire priming and beefed-up case heads.

Around 1887, .22 Shorts hit the market loaded with semi-smokeless and smokeless powder. This development brought together all the features of modern rimfire ammunition into a single package — all of which persist today. The brass case had a hollow rim spun full of wet primer. The heeled, outside-lubricated lead bullet matched the diameter of the case. Makers loaded the self-contained little rimfire cartridge with smokeless powder. Many iterations of these features would come and go, but none would take over like the world-famous .22 Long Rifle — by far the most widely produced small arms cartridge the world has ever seen. **RR**

3

MODERN RIMFIRE AMMUNITION

It's tempting to think an inventor can bring a new ammo, action, or other world-changing creation into existence by penciling a schematic on the back of a napkin. It rarely works like that. Successful design is most often a drawn-out process of incremental change. Rimfire ammo is no different. All the ingredients for the .22 LR were on the table in 1887. But gradual changes over the last 130 years — from priming and powder chemistry and the geometry of case and bullet to refinements of the manufacturing process — have brought us to where we stand today, with the very best small arms ammunition ever developed. Rimfire or centerfire, ammunition has never been better, whether for hunting, plinking, competition, or long-range shooting. Ammo isn't like automobiles, where you can make a reasoned argument that they made them better back in the day without the innovations of plastics and computer-

A pile of ELEY Match ammo with the telltale 'E' headstamp.

CCI Quite-22, a modern subsonic .22 LR load.

CCI Pistol Match.

CCI Clean-22 is designed to produce less fouling and works as advertised. It's especially less dirty on suppressors.

Lapua Center-X, the gold standard for most serious precision rimfire competitors.

Lapua Midas+ is the same ammo as Center-X but has been lot tested by Lapua and proven more consistent round to round.

ELEY Tenex, designed for 50-meter competitions, has won more gold medals and World Cup titles than any .22 LR ammo on earth.

controlled emissions. Ammunition is the best it's ever been, even the inexpensive stuff.

Four facilities in the United States currently produce modern rimfire ammunition: CCI in Lewiston, Idaho; Federal in Anoka, Minnesota; Remington in Lonoke, Arkansas; and Winchester in Oxford, Mississippi. Vista Outdoors owns Federal, CCI, and Remington. CCI makes Hornady-branded rimfire ammunition. CCI is widely considered the best of the American manufactures. By that, I mean they make the cleanest loads that shoot the most consistently in the broadest array of rifles. (More on this in the chapter, *Precision & Accuracy*.)

Nevertheless, American rimfire manufacturers tool up for quantity — not quality. They measure success in production output and sales, not gold medals as in Europe. This standard may be changing.

Boutique Pennsylvania manufacturer Cutting Edge

ELEY Semi-Auto Benchrest Outlaw is Tenex but with a lube designed for magazine-fed rifles.

Bullets makes .22 rimfire copper solids for extreme long-range shooting that could revolutionize .22 LR performance, as does South Dakota copper bullet maker Badlands Precision. Oklahoma's Choctaw Nation is building out a rimfire production line through

Brand new .22 LR coming off the line at Federal.

A hopper of copper-plated Federal bullets awaits the loading line.

A handful of Federal brass before priming and loading.

its manufacturing subsidiary Choctaw Defense. CCI and Federal continue to refine their production lines, too, as shooters now demand super-accurate offerings. Still, for the time being, proper match-quality ammunition comes only from Europe.

ELEY Ammunition has a factory in Birmingham, England; Lapua in Schönebeck, Germany; and RWS in Fürth-Stadlen, Germany. Lapua, a Finnish company, had made rimfire in Finland until the mid-2000s. ELEY also produces WOLF Match Target and Match Extra .22 LR. Lapua makes SK-branded ammunition, and RWS, through its parent company RUAG, makes Geco and Norma. The sub-brands like WOLF, SK, and Geco, are a means for the elite European rimfire manufacturers to offer less expensive options to the broader market. In the case of Lapua, one side of the factory makes

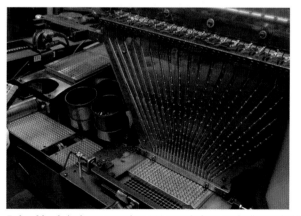

Federal loads its brass cases into 300-round plates at the "waterfall."

Lapua, the other SK. Many of these sub-brands shoot very well. In some cases, the same ammunition is simply repackaged under different brand names, as is the case with several SKUs from Geco and Norma.

Rimfire ammo for the American market is also made

A .22 LR Stinger, left, next to a standard .22 LR. Note the case length difference.

in Brazil by Magtech and in Mexico by Aguila. Aguila does interesting things, from a 60-grain .22 LR subsonic to primer-only .22 BB Cap-like Colibri.

Rimfire Ammo Production

On a macro level, rimfire ammo is all generally made the same way. I saw the process firsthand at the Federal plant in Anoka. It's a fascinating process to watch: raw billets of lead and spools of brass come in one end of the factory, are transformed by fire and force, then stacked on a shipping dock in pallets of ready-to-sell ammunition on the other end of the facility.

Watching so much ammunition made so quickly, it still amazed me that rimfire ammo is as inexpensive as it is — there are so many people, steps, and raw materials required for that $20 bulk pack. It also drove home the scale of the public's appetite for .22 LR. The rimfire operation at Federal can run 24 hours a day, seven days a week, 365 days a year, and still not catch consumer demand.

The .22 LR manufacturing process starts with the cases. Brass is an alloy of copper and zinc with small

A .22 LR Stinger, left, next to a nickel-plated .22 LR Federal Hunter Match, RWS 50, Lapua Center-X, and ELEY Tenex.

percentages of tin, lead, and other elements. It arrives at Federal in large spools like jumbo-sized rolls of duct tape. (Other manufactures process brass sheets.) The brass is cold rolled and punched into discs drawn out into roughly 1/2-inch length cups or blanks for .22 LR. Machine operators seal one end, which will become the rimmed case head. The other end is open where the bullet crimps.

Brass waste material from the punched sheeting or "webbing" is recycled off-site into more case material. The blanks are annealed or heat-treated to alleviate the metal stresses resulting from the cold punch and

A pallet of ELEY ammunition ready for shipping. Photo: ELEY

draw process. They're washed and dried on a tinker table that violently shakes off the water before a conveyor belt takes them to an oven for more drying. The blanks are moved to a press that draws them to the finished diameter and length before cycling them back through another anneal, wash, and dry cycle. The blanks then move to a header machine where they're picked up by a mandrel and pressed into a die that forms the hollow rim and marks the headstamp. Finished cases drop away into huge, wheeled totes that employees roll to the loading line.

The smelter melts raw lead into cylindrical billets in hot-tub-sized melting pots. The billets are then extruded into lead wire a touch larger than the diameter of the finished bullet. Giant spools wind the wire, while a cutting machine lops off bullet-length lead slugs from the tag end. The slugs are lubricated, then swaged or machine-hammer molded into a bullet or bullet-core form. A color sprayer coats raw lead bullets. An electrochemical bath washes copper-plated bullets and lays down a few thousandths of an inch jacket.

Cases and bullets come together across the factory

floor on an assembly line of conveyor belts, loaders, presses, ovens, sorters, and crimpers. The serpentine production line takes up a few hundred square feet but if laid out straight in a line, it would run more than 100 yards. These machine lines are costly to build out, which is why .22 LR is prone to sell out whenever panic buying takes over the firearms market, even with machines running around the clock. Building new rimfire lines are so expensive that even substantial and successful companies hesitate to do it because the return on investment for such an inexpensive product as rimfire ammo takes years and years to recoup. It boils down to millions of dollars to build machines that print fractions of a penny. And, when panic buying isn't running rampant, there's enough rimfire production capacity to meet the world demand.

This return-on-investment factor is also why the American manufacturers do not make real match ammunition. Sure, some label their better stuff "match," but this is still not the same thing as what comes out of Europe. Yet, it is easy to understand why American companies are not interested in the elite world of

ELEY brass is cleaned and tumbled before loading. Photos: ELEY

Tenex on the line before packaging into a "brick" of 10 boxes.

Olympic-quality ammunition. The match market is difficult to penetrate with national teams and NCAA schools loyal (or contractually bound) to the Europeans. But as one American rimfire maker told me, the price to convert its existing rimfire tooling to match equipment would start at $8 million. And that's just one line. Suppose this new match ammo sold for $20 a box — a price very difficult for most American rimfire shooters to swallow. It would take 400,000 boxes sold to hit that $8 million mark. Considering the cost of producing that new match ammo on a new line, it would probably need to double that to recoup the expense. Is there a market in the U.S. for 800,000 new $20 boxes of .22 LR? There isn't. At least not yet.

On Federal's assembly line, cases go into a hopper that feeds them to a "waterfall," which orients and drops the individual brass into 300-round plates. An employee observes this process, ensuring everything lines up and there are no gaps in the plates. From there, the plates travel by conveyor belt to the priming room. The bulk primers are highly explosive, so the room is separate from the rest of the floor, isolated by heavy block walls. Inside this blast house, an employee paints a frame with a thin coat of wet primer. He uses a large scraper to run the primer across the frame — a tool like a wide putty knife or drywall tap-

ing knife. As the 300-case plates feed under the frame, he closes the frame over the plate, gives it a knock, and 300 dots of primer drop in the cases. The thickness of the frame and plates determines the weight of the primer dot.

The conveyor belt transports the primed case plates from the block primer room to a spinner, which picks up the individual base cases from the plate and spins them to ensure the primer covers the entire inside case head. It then re-plates them. An employee inspects the plates as they move toward a forced-air oven that dries the primer to the inside rim edge. Out of the oven, the plates move under a powder dropper. The powder magazine that feeds the dropper is armored, much like the primer room.

Not all rimfire manufacturers prime their cases the same way. ELEY has a patented ELEY Priming System, which used to be advertised right on the box, i.e., ELEY Match EPS, Tenex EPS, etc. Designed originally

A loading plate at Lapua in Germany. Photos: Capstone Precision

to be a safer method of loading as it does not require spinning and drying, the ELEY system is generally considered the most consistent priming rimfire technology. At ELEY, a dry primer is dropped into the case and tamped into the rim with a rod. A drop of liquid activates the compound. ELEY has sold this technology to other companies, which is why, at one time, Aguila advertised its ammo as "ELEY Prime" while still loading it in Mexico.

After Federal primes and dries the cases, the brass continues down the line by conveyor belt. Bullets enter the system from a large hopper. They go to a second waterfall that sorts them heel down for loading. Rollers ensure everything is aligned and the bullets are dropped into the charged cases 20 at a time. The loaded cartridges move to a series of presses that seat and crimp the bullets. The completed rounds filter out in a single file to a wheeled tote where an employee moves them to a different station to be lubed and packaged.

At the European manufacturers, priming technology isn't the only difference. Surgical-like conditions produce match-grade ammo in rooms that are temperature and humidity-controlled. Aspects of the machines are different, too, and the runs are much smaller. Components and finished ammo aren't bulk transported in totes, which can off-size brass cases and nick soft lead bullets. The components are babied, frankly, through the entirety of the process. One lot at an

Lapua bullets dropped on each primed and loaded case.

Each bullet nose is carefully protected from deformation.

American ammo maker may exceed 250,000 rounds, whereas ELEY caps it at 30,000. The Europeans also have more rigorous quality control standards, from chemically testing powder and primer compounds before turned over to production, to lot sorting and lot testing finished rounds. Lot testing largely determines velocity variance round to round — calculated either as "extreme spread" or "standard deviation," which we'll dive into later. The lots with the smallest variance in velocity often make up the more premium brands. For example, Lapua Center-X, Midas+, and X-ACT are the same case, bullet, primer, and powder, loaded on the same machines by the same employees. The lot that will become X-ACT has shown through testing to be more consistent round to round than the lot that will become Center-X. When shooting rimfire ammo farther than 200 yards, standard deviation or extreme spread is often a more telling indicator of success than group size at 50 or 100 yards. (More in the chapter *Precision & Accuracy*.)

At Federal, a single plate from start to finish takes a few minutes to run the loading line. Dozens of plates are on the line at the same time. Three to half-a-dozen lines are up at any given time, depending on the manufacturer, in nine major factories worldwide. These machines run nearly 24 hours a day, seven days a week. Each line is capable of hundreds of thousands of rounds a day. The total daily world output of rimfire boggles the mind. Annually, it's in the billions.

Shooters like to band about statistics like ".22 LR is the most common firearm in the world," or "56 percent of all firearms are .22s," or "300 million rounds are made every day," but the truth is no one knows. In 2016, Federal publicly stated there are 50 to 80 million Americans who own .22s. But let's be clear: a dataset with a swing of 30 million can also be called a wild-ass guess. Federal did say at that time that they're working toward 10 million rounds of .22 LR a day. Seeing the works, I don't doubt this one bit and suspect it has surpassed that significantly now with the most recent national ammunition shortage. The National

Shooting Sports Foundation (NSSF) tracks industry data and estimates total rimfire ammo consumption in the U.S. at 4.1 billion in 2018, down from 5.4 billion in 2015. You can bet your face mask 2020 far surpassed 2018. NSSF stresses that these are just estimates.

Finding data on firearms by caliber is even trickier. The FBI National Instant Criminal Background Check System data does not report calibers. The ATF, which tracks U.S. firearm production, doesn't document caliber, either. Neither does the U.S. International Trade Commission or USITC, which documents firearms imports.

What's safe to say when it comes to rimfire figures is flatly this: there's a damned lot, tens of millions of firearms in the U.S. alone, with billions of rounds produced every year.

With all that production capacity, hoarding ammo may make as much sense as hoarding toilet paper. Ammo demand in the U.S. often out-strips supply in politically uncertain times, as we've seen. Also, as we'll see, the very best shooters test and buy ammunition by the lot. They'll find a lot of ammo that works well in their gun and buy

Some 6mm Flobert blanks. Photo: Cosmo Genova

5,000 rounds, or 10,000 rounds, or the entire lot of 20,000 to 30,000. That might sound excessive, but a competitive shooter can burn up 10,000 rounds a year, and rimfire ammo doesn't expire.

In this day and age, if you find ammo that sings in your rifle — and later we'll see how to determine what ammo is the best for your rifle — no one will fault you for buying a case or five. That's true whether you're a competition shooter, a small game hunter, or just want to be prepared for a zombie squirrel apocalypse.

The question remains: what kind of rimfire ammunition is available today? There is a dizzying amount of rimfire calibers and loads on the market. There are half a dozen types of .22 LR alone over as many manufacturers, each with a laundry list of product lines. To make sense of it all, a short overview of current production rimfire ammo by caliber, including relevant history and application, follows. We'll take a deeper dive on finding the right ammo for your particular

The Caps, or 6mm Flobert

	.22 BB Cap	.22 CB Cap
Designer	Flobert, 1845	Flobert, 1888
Parent case	Tapered percussion cap	.22 BB
Case type	Rimmed, straight	Rimmed, straight
Bullet diameter	.222 in. (5.6mm)	.222 in. (5.6mm)
Neck diameter	.224 in. (5.7mm)	.225 in. (5.7mm)
Base diameter	.224 in. (5.7mm)	.225 in. (5.7mm)
Rim diameter	.270 in. (6.9mm)	.271 in. (6.9mm)
Rim thickness	.040 in. (1.0mm)	.040 in. (1.0mm)
Case length	.284 in. (7.2mm)	.284 in. (7.2mm)
Overall length	.343 in. (8.7mm)	.520 in. (13.2mm)
Bullet weights	17 gr.	17 gr.
Powder weight	N/A	N/A
Twist	1:16 in.	1:16 in.
Velocity Range	~ 400 fps	~ 700 fps

A pre-war smoothbore Anschütz garden gun chambered for 6mm Flobert. Photo: Cosmo Genova

From left to right: a 6mm Flobert blank, a .22 Short Blank, a .22 Short CB, .22 Shot, .17 HM2, .22 LR, .22 LR Stinger, .22 WRF, .17 HMR, .22 WMR., 5mm Remington, .17 WSM.

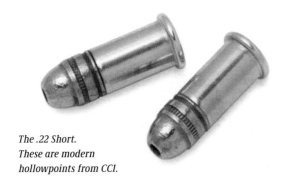

The .22 Short.
These are modern
hollowpoints from CCI.

rifle and ways to improve its accuracy through practices like lot testing and sorting in the chapter *Precision & Accuracy*. This overview is designed to prime the well for a more in-depth discussion on rifles, how they work, accuracy, plus hunting and competition considerations.

The Caps — or 6mm Floberts, as they're known in Europe — are not suitable for anything save the niche circumstance of target shooting in a confined indoor space. Pistol shooters relegated to practice in a cramped basement, maybe. The Caps are capable of dispatching small critters at close range. Garden guns in 6mm Flobert were somewhat popular in the middle of the last century to stone rabbits across small allotments or dust mice in the pantry. These guns were often smoothbore and loaded with a BB Cap-type round topped with a tiny payload of No. 12 shot. The actual diameter of all the Caps and 6mm Flobert rounds is .222 inch or 5.6mm. It's unclear how it earned the misleading 6mm name.

The .22 BB is the closest thing to Flobert's original design — a lead ball fixed to a percussion cap; no powder added. The .22 CB Cap adds the powder. Flobert initially loaded a 29-grain round nose and 1.5 grains of blackpowder. Cartridge buffs describe it as a cross between the .22 BB Cap and the .22 Short. The CB stands for "conical ball." Early examples can be spotted across a French parlor by their pointed, triangular bullets. First manufactured in 1888, many hoped the CBs would maintain the accuracy of the .22 Short, but with reduced noise. They didn't do either.

The .22 BB Cap was popular in the U.S. through World War II as it sold for less than .22 Shorts, but after the war, they were largely discontinued. RWS in Germany still manufactures BBs and CBs. Czech producer Sellier & Bellot makes them, too, as well as the oddball 4mm Flobert. Umarex and Fiocchi load the larger brass-cased shotgun cartridge 9mm Flobert with No. 8s and 9s.

The enduring production of this ammo in Europe is thanks to gun laws. For example, Flobert rifles are in the same legal category as air rifles in the Czech Republic, requiring less red tape to own and shoot. Additionally, many antique rifles chambered for blackpowder .22 Shorts and .22 Longs can safely fire 6mm Flobert ammo.

CCI still loads a 29-grain "CB .22 Short" for pest control with the same dimensions as its .22 Short, but with reduced charges. Advertised velocity is 710 fps compared to 1,080 fps with the regular Shorts. While it fits some Flobert chambers in my experience, it should be considered a low-powered .22 Short and not sent through old guns ill-equipped for smokeless powder and modern pressure curves.

Aguila loads CB Caps in its Colibri line at an advertised 375 fps and Super Colibri at 500 fps. They have the same case length and rough overall length as the outdated .22 Long, but Aguila designed them as reduced noise offerings for modern .22 LRs.

Confused? The takeaway is this: You should not fire modern CCI and Aguila ammo in antique Flobert rifles or garden guns. If you must shoot relics, get ammo from RWS and Sellier & Bellot. Stock up if you can stomach the higher prices as it's getting harder to find. (It's hard not to believe the Caps will go the way of the dodo in our lifetime, at least here in the U.S.) Rifles chambered for .22 LR can shoot the CCI and Aguila ammo, but the shortened cases create terrible fouling in the long rifle chamber. Mostly these rounds are oddities and should be treated as such. Back away slowly.

The .22 Short

.22 Short	
Designer	Smith & Wesson, 1857
Parent case	.22 BB
Case type	Rimmed, straight
Bullet diameter	.222 in. (5.6mm)
Neck diameter	.226 in. (5.7mm)
Base diameter	.226 in. (5.7mm)
Rim diameter	.278 in. (7.1mm)
Rim thickness	.043 in. (1.1mm)
Case length	.421 in. (10.7mm)
Overall length	.695 in. (17.7mm)
Bullet weights	27 or 29 gr.
Powder weight	~ .5 gr
Twist	1:24 in.
Velocity Range	800 to 1,100 fps

As noted, the .22 Short is the oldest American self-contained metallic cartridge and the granddaddy of all rimfire ammunition. We have Smith & Wesson to thank for it, with a hat tip to that surly French gunsmith Flobert.

Aguila, CCI, Remington, and Winchester still load it, though, for hunting and target shooting, it does nothing the .22 LR doesn't do better. It is accurate and quiet, but many of today's .22 LR loads are more accurate and make less noise. (That could not be said a decade ago.) Bullet choices are the 29-grain round noses and a single 27-grain hollowpoint offering from CCI. The Short still warrants production mainly because it was so popular in its day. There are many firearms in circulation chambered for it, from relics to more modern competition pistols. It was the round of choice for international pistol shooting through the late 1990s. The sole use I've found for .22 Shorts is in a pistol kept in my shop next to our chicken coop. They're deadly on weasels.

I hope that this American original stays in production forever, but in reality, Shorts do nothing modern subsonic .22 LR ammo doesn't do better.

The .22 Long

.22 Long	
Designer	Unknown, 1871
Parent case	.22 Short
Case type	Rimmed, straight
Bullet diameter	.222 in. (5.6mm)
Neck diameter	.226 in. (5.7mm)
Base diameter	.226 in. (5.7mm)
Rim diameter	.278 in. (7.1mm)
Rim thickness	.043 in. (1.1mm)
Case length	.613 in. (15.6mm)
Overall length	.888 in. (22.6mm)
Bullet weight	29 gr.
Powder weight	1,100 to 1,200 fps
Twist	1:16 in.
Velocity Range	1,200 fps

Bigger is not always better. That was the lesson of the .22 Long. It came about in 1871 with a case length 5 millimeters longer than the popular .22 Short. The initial load was 5 grains of blackpowder, 25 percent more than the 4-grain Short. The intention was to produce greater velocities than the Short, which it did, but at the cost of accuracy. CCI stills loads a .22 Long for shooters with older guns. It shoots okay from .22 LR chambers.

We may see a renaissance in .22 Long in the next few years — or at least in the idea that inspired it. In the search for all things self-defense, ballisticians have determined that the best-penetrating .22 LR loads use a hyper-velocity powder charge under light bullets. These new .22 LR self-defense loads visually look like .22 Longs — long case, little bullet — but operate at modern pressures. You won't use these bullets for old

.22 Long firearms, only deep concealment pistols in .22 LR. How they'll do in rifles is yet to be seen, but a lighter, faster version of a CCI Velocitor HP could find a home in the squirrel woods. Maybe it's a stretch to lump these into the .22 Long category, as they will not be and should not be used in the .22 Long-chambered firearms, though it's nice to know the original inventors weren't all wrong. After all, ammo companies

A .22 Long Rifle round with a lead round-nose bullet. Photo: Vista Outdoors

The .22 Long Rifles

	.22 Long Rifle, Std. or Match	.22 Long Rifle, Subsonic	.22 Long Rifle, High Velocity	Hyper Velocity (Stingers, etc.)
Designer	Stevens & UMC, 1884	Stevens & UMC, 1884	Stevens & UMC, 1884	CCI, 1970
Parent case	.22 Long	.22 Long	.22 Long	.22 Long
Case type	Rimmed, straight	Rimmed, straight	Rimmed, straight	Rimmed, straight
Bullet diameter	.223 in. (5.7mm)	0.223 in. (5.7mm)	0.223 in. (5.7mm)	.223 in. (5.7mm)
Neck diameter	.226 in. (5.7mm)	.226 in. (5.7mm)	.226 in. (5.7mm)	.226 in. (5.7mm)
Base diameter	.226 in. (5.7mm)	.226 in. (5.7mm)	.226 in. (5.7mm)	.226 in. (5.7mm)
Rim diameter	.278 in. (7.1mm)	.278 in. (7.1mm)	.278 in. (7.1mm)	.278 in. (7.1mm)
Rim thickness	.043 in. (1.1mm)	.043 in. (1.1mm)	.043 in. (1.1mm)	.043 in. (1.1mm)
Case length	.613 in. (15.6mm)	.613 in. (15.6mm)	.613 in. (15.6mm)	.613 in. (15.6mm) to .710 in. (18mm)
Overall length	1.000 in. (25.4mm)	1.000 in. (25.4mm)	1.000 in. (25.4mm)	1.000 in. (25.4mm)
Bullet weight	40 gr.	40 to 60 gr.	32 to 40 gr.	26 to 36 gr.
Powder weight	~ 1 gr.		1 to 2 gr.	2+ gr.
Twist	1:16 in.	1:16 in. or 1:9 in. for the 60s	1:16 in.	1:16 in.
Velocity Range	980 to 1,080 fps	540 to 1,080 fps	1,150 to 1,400 fps	1,400 to 1,640 fps

developed the Long as a self-defense load for small revolvers, not tack-driving rifles, and 150 years later, the best ballistic thinking has proven those old ideas sound.

Following the Long came the now-extinct .22 Extra Long in 1880, with a case length of .750 inch. The Extra Long bears remembering because it was the first use of the 40-grain lead round nose — the heeled and outside-lubricated bullet that would go on to .22 Long Rifle fame. Many considered the .22 Extra Long to be a

self-defense round for small revolvers. In rifles, it gave unacceptable accuracy and poor feeding in repeaters. It did not survive the transition from blackpowder to smokeless. Ammo companies discontinued it in 1935.

The .22 LR is probably the most successful small arms caliber of all time. In terms of raw production or just the sheer number of bullets made, it certainly is the most widely and mass-produced ammo ever. Yet how it came to be isn't exactly clear.

Joshua Stevens of the J. Stevens Arm & Tool Company long held the credit for this 1887 cartridge. Yet diligent researchers have shown it was a joint venture between Stevens and W. M. Thomas of Union Metallic Cartridge Company, Peters Cartridge Company assisting, which provided the early powders. Peters also first manufactured the round. I've mentioned other prominent names in early firearm design in its development. So, it's most likely that a joint committee of various ammunition and firearm companies created the .22 LR. It was no "back of the napkin" stroke of genius.

Early accuracy reports were not good. This new cartridge combined the 40-grain Extra Long bullet in a .22 Long case and 5 grains of blackpowder. It was tested through the 1:20 twist .22 Short barrels of the day and proved a dull performer until the committee landed on the 1:16 twist rate. (The twist rate indicates how much spin a rifled barrel imparts on a bullet.) A barrel that is a 1:16 twist means that the rifling will spin the bullet one revolution in 16 inches. The lower the twist, the faster the bullet will spin. That is, a 1:12 puts more revolutions on the bullet than a 1:16. Bullet type, length, and velocity all factor into the correct twist rate for a particular cartridge. When correct, the bullet will fly like a well-thrown spiral football. When the twist rate doesn't match the load, the bullet wobbles, like that time Aunt Susan wanted to quarterback the Thanksgiving Day touch football game. 1:16 proved ideal for the 40-grain .22 LR, yet soon after, many rifles were also designed with a "three in one" chamber to shoot .22 Short, .22 Long, and .22 LR. Early examples of these guns typically had a 1:17 twist as a compromise between the Short and the Long Rifle.

When ammo developers combined the .22 Long case, the bullet of the .22 Extra Long, and the 1:16 twist, they made history. The cartridge gained traction just as small arms transitioned from blackpowder to semi-smokeless and ultimately smokeless. Colonel Townsend Whelen wrote in the 1930s of an accurate Winchester load of 85 percent blackpowder and 15 percent smokeless. Target shooters loved it, and ev-

.22 Long Rifle with a copper-alloy hollowpoint bullet.
Photos: Vista Outdoors

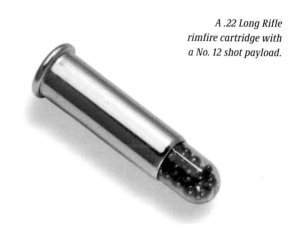

A .22 Long Rifle rimfire cartridge with a No. 12 shot payload.

erything else about .22 LR. It proved spectacularly accurate out to 200 yards. Yet even with a touch of smokeless added, blackpowder was a mess, leaving residue in chambers and down barrels that required regular cleaning. Pure smokeless loads solved some of this, but early primers weren't much better. They sent a nasty rust-promoting chemical wash down barrels every time you pulled the trigger.

Early primer compounds generated a salt-like potassium chloride gas that would coat barrels and attracted moisture that promoted rust. If you've ever looked down the barrel of an antique wall hanger to find a red bloom of fuzz like shag carpet, you can thank early primers.

Remington solved for primer fouling in 1927 with Kleanbore — a brand name still alive today in its muzzleloader line. Kleanbore was a huge success, and Remington followed it up in 1930 with the first high-velocity loads that pushed 40-grain bullets to 1,375 fps. New powders gave the load more juice, but containing that heat was only possible because Remington updated the metallic case material.

Since the days of Flobert, most rimfire cases were copper or soft "yellow brass" alloys. Remington was the first to use a stronger, more resilient brass alloy, which allowed for higher chamber pressures while remaining pliable enough for solid primer strikes. (The .17 WSM is a testament that you cannot easily achieve this balance.) Standard-velocity .22 LR of the day had a chamber pressure of around 12,000 psi. Remington's high-velocity load in a beefier case safely doubled that to 25,000 psi.

For the next 40 years, manufacturers refined primer compounds and powders for faster and more accurate ammunition. CCI provided the next major innovation in 1977 with the first hyper-velocity round, the .22 Stinger. CCI extended the case length from .613 to .710 inch, filled it with a slow-burning powder, and topped it with a light 32-grain bullet. The result was a 30 percent increase in muzzle velocity over standard loads and a 25 percent increase in muzzle energy. Stingers break the 1,600-fps barrier, and the two Remington hyper-velocity rounds that came out shortly after that — the Yellow Jacket and Viper — break 1,400 fps without the extended case length.

*Copper-plated hollowpoint
.22 LRs from CCI. An excellent
hunting option.*

High-velocity and hyper-velocity loads produce a flatter trajectory. The bullet travels faster, so it drops less over a given distance, making it ideal for small game hunting where you engage critters at unknown or ballparked distances. If you guess 40 yards, but it's 50, it's still a dead cottontail with a flat trajectory. Fast-velocity .22 loads are not match accurate, at least on the hair-splitting level by which you measure .22s. Yet they are minute of squirrel to 100 yards all day long. Though I don't recommend Stingers for auto-loaders like the ubiquitous 10/22, Yellow Jackets and Vipers cycle smoothly through them.

Match quality and extreme long-range accuracy come at velocities under 1,125 fps, which is the speed of sound. Funny things happen to projectiles when they cross over the sound barrier or "go transonic." The best way I've heard this explained is to imagine a powerboat. Going full speed hydroplaning down the lake life is good, but what happens if you throttle back? The wake catches the back of the boat, and you're rolling in some self-made seas. When bullets come out of supersonic flight and cross the sound barrier, this happens to them. They begin to pitch and yaw in their self-generated hyper-velocity air currents, much like that powerboat that abruptly slowed down on the lake — caught by its wake. The bullet's center-of-gravity will shift during its flight, and backpressure or turbulent air from behind makes it wobble.

The best solution for beating this effect in rimfire is never to cross the sound barrier in the first place. Target loads rarely run faster than 1,100 fps. Lapua and ELEY advertise most match offerings at speeds close to 1,080 fps. If you learn how to read lot numbers, you can figure the exact velocity in meters per second of those lots as tested in the factory. (More in *Precision & Accuracy*.) But ambient temperature, barrel length, and a host of other factors affect real-world bullet velocities. Some companies, like Lapua, plan for this. Lapua Polar Biathlon has a higher speed than Midas+ because Biathlon shooting usually occurs in below-freezing conditions that slow velocities.

Real match ammo (left to right): RWS 50, Lapua Center-X, ELEY Tenex.

Often, rimfire ammo chronographs faster than what manufacturers print on the box. This discrepancy is because Sporting Arms and Ammunition Manufacturers' Institute or SAAMI uses test barrel lengths of 24 inches for published velocity figures. With .22 LR, between 16 and 17 inches of barrel length, bullet velocities begin to drop, albeit not much. The barrel imparts "drag" on the bullet that hurts speed but can help accuracy — to a point. So, if Ammo X measures its velocity from a 24-inch barrel, but your .22 has a more typical 16-, 18-, or 20-inch barrel, it makes sense that you'll see Ammo X chrono speeds faster than advertised. The ammo companies know this and do a good job keeping standard and match velocities away from that dreaded sound barrier — and high-velocity rounds well over it.

In the last 10 years, the American ammo makers have spent more time working on slow ammunition than fast. Standard-velocity rounds are technically subsonic, and some "subsonic" ammo lines are simply standard-velocity loads rebranded with cool new marketing. But there are also new school subsonic loads that undercut standard velocity figures by several hundred feet per second. Most loads fly between 900 and 700 fps, yet a few outliers are as slow as 540 fps. These rounds are designed for no-noise applications and shoot virtually silent when suppressed.

To call a suppressed .22 LR rifle shooting subsonic ammo "silent" is not an overstatement. The loudest noise from a suppressed Volquartsen Summit I used for a spell was the sharp *clink* of the firing pin hitting the case head and a quick *pfft* of air, like an air gun, or a sharp, angry burst of flatulence after a decadent dessert. I know of USDA wildlife agents who've eradicated invasive swans with suppressed Anschütz rifles shooting subsonic loads under night vision. Suppressed rimfires shooting subsonic loads are tailor-made for this kind of black ops work. They're also damn fun.

I've fired many firearms in all calibers, from big-bore African dangerous game rifles to belt-fed machine guns, but nothing made me smile more than a suppressed full-auto 10/22.

The .22 LR is something special. No cartridge in the world can do so much, from recoil-free plinking with children to Olympic gold medals, to light loads that whisper in the night, to fast loads that can dent the eye of a tree squirrel at 75 yards. The .22 LR is here to stay, and as we'll see, it's only getting better.

The Magnums

.22 Winchester Magnum Rimfire (.22 WMR) with a copper-plated hollowpoint bullet. Photo: Vista Outdoors

	.22 Winchester Rimfire	.22 Winchester Magnum Rimfire	5mm Remington Rimfire Magnum
Designer	Winchester, 1890	Winchester, 1959	Remington, 1969
Parent case	none	.22 WRF	none
Case type	Rimmed, straight	Rimmed, straight	Rimfire, shouldered
Bullet diameter	.224 in. (5.7mm)	.224 in. (5.7mm)	.204 in. (5.2mm)
Neck diameter	.242 in. (6.1mm)	.242 in. (6.1mm)	.225 in. (5.7mm)
Base diameter	.242 in. (6.1mm)	.242 in. (6.1mm)	.259 in. (6.6mm)
Rim diameter	.294 in. (7.5mm)	.294 in. (7.5mm)	.325 in. (8.3mm)
Rim thickness	.050 in. (1.3mm)	.050 in. (1.3mm)	.050 in. (1.3mm)
Case length	.965 in. (24.5mm)	1.055 in. (26.8mm)	1.020 in. (25.9mm)
Overall length	1.180 in. (30.0mm)	1.350 in. (34.3mm)	1.30 in. (33mm)
Bullet weight	45 gr.	30 to 50 gr.	30 gr.
Powder weight		5 to 7.5 gr.	
Twist	1:14 in.	1:14 in. to 1:16 in.	1:12 in.
Velocity Range	1,300 fps	1,800 to 2,200 fps	2,200 fps

It's hard to call .22 Winchester Rimfire "modern," but like the Caps and the .22 Long, it is still in production thanks to CCI. Developed in 1890 specifically for the John Browning-designed Winchester 1890M slide rifle, it was the first significant improvement in killing power over the .22 LR and the first of the .22 rimfires to use a modern flat-base, inside-lubricated bullet. It proved an accurate and effective hunting cartridge but never really caught on like the Long Rifle. Gun writers have suspected that's because it was relatively expensive compared to .22 LR, and there wasn't ever a wide array of bullet options. Remington did make its version of the round, the extinct .22 Remington Special, topped with a round-nose bullet, but it wasn't enough to save it.

Rifle makers haven't chambered for .22 WRF since the 1950s, but .22 Winchester Magnum Rimfire guns can shoot it fine. The reverse is not true. Today, the .22 WRF is loaded by CCI with a copper-plated 45-grain hollowpoint to 1,300 fps. (Winchester did a limited run several years ago, too.) CCI says explicitly not to shoot it through revolvers as the tighter pistol bores don't respond well to the copper plating.

The big four (left to right): .17 HM2, .22 LR, .17 HMR, .22 WMR. These are the most common rimfire rounds.

In 1959, Winchester updated the .22 WRF with the .22 Winchester Magnum Rimfire, known everywhere as the .22 Magnum. The Magnum remains the most powerful .22-caliber rimfire cartridge in the world, sending 30- and 40-grain bullets downrange above 2,000 fps.

The .22 Mag. earned an early reputation for poor accuracy. There are multiple reasons for this. First, in the 1960s, it was chambered only in revolvers and a few low-end rifles. Things improved with better guns hitting the market in the 1970s from Remington and Anschütz. However, underlying accuracy issues still existed thanks mainly to the original, sloppy chamber dimensions and shoddy bullets. Neither is conducive to the hyper-accurate shooting of today's standards. Since the development of better .22-caliber bullets, like the Hornady V-MAX, gunsmiths and custom rifle builders have caught on and cut better chambers into their guns with more dramatic angles. (*For more on this, see the Q&A with the great Dave Emary in the Interviews chapter.*)

I have an old Ruger 77/22 sporter in .22 Magnum with a pencil barrel that Randy at Connecticut Precision Chambering re-chambered, set back, headspaced, re-crowned, and lapped. It is a sub-MOA rifle. Likewise, Mike Bush at Vudoo Gun Works knows how to make the .22 magnums sing. I have a V-22 Magnum sporter that shoots sub-MOA at 100 all day long with

	.17 Hornady Magnum Rimfire	17 Hornady Mach 2	.17 Winchester Super Magnum
Designer	Hornady, 2002	Hornady & CCI, 2004	Winchester, 2012
Parent case	.22 WMR	.22 Long Rifle	.27-caliber nail gun blank
Case type	Rimmed, shouldered	Rimmed, shouldered	Rimmed, shouldered
Bullet diameter	.172 in. (4.4mm)	.172 in. (4.4mm)	.172 in. (4.4mm)
Neck diameter	.190 in. (4.8mm)	.180 in. (4.6mm)	.197 in. (5.0mm)
Shoulder diameter	.238 in. (6.0mm)	.226 in. (5.7mm)	.269 in. (6.8mm)
Base diameter	.238 in. (6.0mm)	.226 in. (5.7mm)	.269 in. (6.8mm)
Rim diameter	.286 in. (7.3mm)	.275 in. (7.0mm)	.333 in. (8.5mm)
Rim thickness	.05 in. (1.3mm)	.043 in. (1.1mm)	.066 in. (1.7mm)
Case length	1.058 in. (26.9mm)	.714 in. (18.1mm)	1.200 in. (30.5mm)
Overall length	1.349 in. (34.3mm)	1.00 in. (25mm)	1.440 in. (36.58mm) to 1.590 in. (40.39mm)
Bullet weights	15.5 to 20 gr.	15.5 or 17 gr.	15, 20, or 25 gr.
Powder weight	~ 5 gr.	2.7 gr.	
Twist	1:9 in.	1:9 in.	1:8 in. or 1:9 in.
Velocity Range	2,000 to 2,650 fps	~ 2,000 fps	2,600 to 3,000 fps

CCI V-MAX and VNT ammo. For comparison, I have a Savage-Anschutz 1516 from the 1980s that, while a beautiful rifle, can't shoot better than 1.5 inches at 100 yards no matter the load. If and when it gets a better chamber, I'm confident those groups will shrink. The takeaway: You can make the .22 Mag. tack-sharp accurate with a little know-how.

Finally, of the magnums, there remains the oddball 5mm Remington Rimfire Magnum. This round was long dead until Aguila released two new loads in 2019. In the day, 5mm Remington represented an improvement over the .22 WMR, but modern .22 bullets eroded that position. The latest run of bottleneck cartridges come with either a semi-jacketed or full-jacketed 30-grain .204-caliber hollowpoint at an advertised velocity of 2,200 fps. The 5mm Remington didn't catch on when Remington Arms Company first released it in 1969, and it hasn't caught on now. By 1974, Remington discontinued the only two rifles it

The .17 Mach 2 loaded with a Hornady V-MAX bullet. Photo: Vista Outdoors

chambered for the round. No companies have stepped up to make new rifles for it, either. (There were rumors of a handgun from Taurus for some time.) Standard rimfire calibers have all but vanished during the current ammunition shortage, yet you can still find Aguila 5mm Remington everywhere. The challenge with this cartridge is finding a gun to shoot it.

The .17s

The biggest thing to happen in rimfire in the last few decades is the ascent of the .17 caliber. There are three that matter: the .17 Hornady Magnum Rimfire, a necked-down .22 magnum; the .17 Hornady Mach 2, a necked-down CCI Stinger; and the .17 Winchester Super Magnum, a necked-down .27-caliber nail gun blank with a mixed track record. The .17 PMC, or .17 Aguila, or .17 High Standard, or whatever you want to call it, is a necked-down .22 LR and is irrelevant with the development of the Mach 2. Only High Standard ever chambered it. The ammo is no longer in production, but you can still find it in many places because no one ever bought it. You can shoot it from a .17 Mach 2 chamber, but I don't advise attempting the opposite.

The .17 HMR is easily the most successful new rimfire cartridge since the .22 WMR of 1959. If not for the 6.5 Creedmoor, it'd likely be the most successful small arms cartridge of the last 50 years. (Dave Emary, the former senior ballistician at Hornady, is mainly responsible for both.) Federal and Winchester had played with the idea of necking down the .22 WMR to a .17 in the 1980s, but powder chemistry wasn't sophisticated enough to make it happen. In the late 1990s, Emary, unaware of the work Federal and Winchester had done, considered the project for a low-to-no-recoil varmint rig for his ailing dad. Powders like the hot and fast Lil' Gun had come along to provide enough juice to make it happen. Developed in conjunction with CCI, the .17 HMR flattened the trajectory of the .22 WMR by almost 10 inches at 200 yards and bucked the wind better.

There seems to be a popular misconception that .17-caliber bullets perform worse than .22-caliber bullets in the wind. Comparing .17 HMR to .22 WMR or .17 HM2 to .22 LR in a ballistics calculator, it's clear the .17 calibers do better, much better than the .22s. For example, a 17-grain V-MAX from a .17 HMR sent at 2,550 fps will drift 11.4 inches at 200 yards in a 10-mph crosswind. A 30-grain V-MAX from a .22 WMR running 2,200 fps will drift 19.4 inches — almost twice as much. You can expect the same performance gain from the .17 Mach 2 over the .22 Long Rifle of any velocity.

Why does this myth persist? Until .17 HMR, many shooters were not sending rimfire bullets much past 100 yards. Suddenly, with a round that could connect comfortably on a prairie dog at 200 yards, shooters took more long-range shots with rimfires, and wind effects became more noticeable at these distances. It is safe to say that the little .17s aren't great in the wind, but they're a lot better than the .22s. The truth

A .17 Hornady Magnum Rimfire with a V-MAX load.

The .17s (left to right): .17 Mach 2, .17 Hornady Magnum Rimfire, and .17 Winchester Super Magnum.

Squrriel hunter and outdoor writer Will Brantley takes aim in the Kentucky hardwoods.

is that no rimfire round is effective in the wind, making it excellent as a practice tool for centerfire shooting. But of the rimfire rounds, the .17s buck the wind best.

The .17 HMR is potent on small game like ground squirrels, tree squirrels, prairie dogs, crows, and even fox. I've seen it stone a coyote firsthand — a 175-yard shot, the bullet placed right between the eyes — but it is generally too light to kill 'yotes except in rare cases, like the lucky shot I witnessed. It's marginal on woodchucks as they tend to go in their hole and die with a body hit, but headshots stop them cold. Such shots are possible because the .17 HMR is a wildly accurate cartridge. Even inexpensive factory rifles can drive MOA groups with this one. Good rifles with sorted ammo, which we'll explore later, can drive one-hole groups at 50 yards most of the day.

The .17 HMR was a wild success, so the following year Hornady and CCI unveiled the .17 Mach 2, a necked-down CCI Stinger .22 LR. The intention was to release a .17 rimfire cartridge that would work well in autoloading rifles like the Ruger 10/22. The .17 HMR

had too dramatic a pressure curve for the blow-back semi-autos, and, it turned out, so did the Mach 2. Nevertheless, the result was a .17 that fit in .22 LR actions and magazines — the only change in most cases is a barrel — but with double the velocity of match-speed .22s and more than 500 fps over the Stingers. At 2,100 fps, the little bullet ran *flat.* This attribute meant long shots did not require oodles of drop compensation that .22 LR distance shooters must learn. Like the .17 HMR, there was no rainbow trajectory with this little .17. For hunting, that translates to head-only holds on squirrels at 150 yards with an HMR and 100 yards with the Mach 2. It's hard to stress how revolutionary this was for many a squirrel hunter.

A few years after its introduction, the Mach 2 cemented a niche position as the best rimfire round for taking squirrel-sized game inside 100 yards. Many die-hard squirrel shooters considered the more expensive and more potent .17 HMR overkill. But then came the ammo shortage of the mid-2000s. Consumer panic resulted in a shortage of .22 LR on the market, and ammo makers couldn't produce plinking rounds fast enough. Ammo factories made Mach 2 on the same factory lines as .22 LR, so they switched all lines to .22 LR. Mach 2 ammo dried to nothing. Bricks of ammo that retailed under $60 sold for hundreds in online auctions.

In 2018, that changed. The Mach 2 legend among squirrel hunters only grew in those ammo-thin times. Hornady and CCI brought it back with three loads. Savage and Volquartsen put out new rifles in the caliber. The Anschütz North America Custom Shop started pumping them out again, many with stainless Lilja barrels. Barrel makers started making drop-ins for new, modern .22s like the CZ 455/457 and the Tikka T1x. Vudoo Gun Works now makes a Mach 2.

Not to be left behind, Winchester launched its .17 magnum cartridge in 2013, the .17 Winchester Super Magnum. Available in 20- and 25-grain bullet loads, the 20 grainers break 3,000 fps and hold the speed record for rimfire. To get such velocity requires lots of powder and high pressures, over 33,000 psi. That's 9,000 psi more than the .22 WMR and 7,000 psi more than the .17 HMR.

Winchester used a larger and thicker .27-caliber nail gun blank for the brass to get the powder capacity and prevent high-pressure case blowouts. The case wall is thicker by half than the .22 WMR or .17 HMR. This thickness makes the roaring 3,000 fps possible without case head blowouts, but this is not without issues. Because the brass is thicker, it requires a heavy firing pin strike. Heavy springs are needed in the action to get that strike, which in turn requires a stout trigger system. By the cartridge design, it's not conducive to light, crisp trigger pulls. Mike Bush of Vudoo Gun Works, who helped design the original .17 WSM rifle for Savage, has said this is why Vudoo has stayed away from the cartridge, as have other rifle companies. The Savage B-Series and a few limited Ruger 77/17s are the only bolt guns chambered for it. The Ruger 77/17 is a great rifle, but for a precision-minded shooter, it needs a trigger job — and pushed too far, trigger work can affect mechanical reliability in a way that is not so with the .17 HMR or .22s.

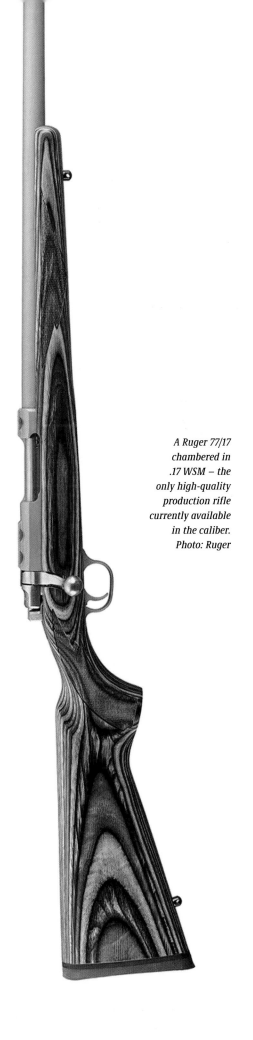

A Ruger 77/17 chambered in .17 WSM – the only high-quality production rifle currently available in the caliber. Photo: Ruger

Volquartsen discontinued its autoloader in .17 WSM, but there are AR-15-pattern semi-auto options from Jard and Franklin Armory. High-volume prairie dog and ground squirrel hunters love this cartridge because it stays accurate and retains varmint-level killing power at 300 yards. Even though the ammo is expensive for rimfire, it's cheaper than reloading the pipsqueak centerfires like .17 Hornet — never mind all the time that you save.

The life expectancy of .17 WSM, like my personal favorite, the .17 Mach 2, is unclear. Unlike the Mach 2, there are no real high-end or tinkerer's rifles for the caliber. It will be a shame if it goes the way of the 5mm Remington, but every year that looks more and more likely.

Volquartsen brought renewed excitement to the round when it announced in January 2020 that it was chambering the round in its excellent Summit bolt-action platform. Yet, despite high demand, the project stopped 10 months later. To put it bluntly, Volquartsen cited piss-poor quality control by the ammo manufacturer, Winchester.

In an email to customers, Scott Volquartsen wrote:

"The .17 WSM is an awesome concept with ballistics unmatched by any other rimfire cartridge. A rimfire cartridge generating over 3,000 fps at the muzzle is no small feat. Without a doubt, the engineers behind this round had to think outside the box in order to accomplish these velocities from a rimfire round.

"The downside of this round is that the variance from one round to the next, in particular in the rim dimensions. We have tried to overcome this issue in a multitude of ways and design changes. After testing our most recent design changes, we thought we had the answer. As our testing continued from one lot of ammunition to the next, our excitement was short-lived. Upon changing from one lot of ammunition to the next, the issues we had been working hard to correct soon resurfaced.

"Initially, we thought maybe something had changed within the rifle itself. However, after switching back to the previous lot of ammunition, the problems disappeared. Unfortunately, this process has repeated itself more times than we would care to count." RR

4

MODERN RIMFIRE RIFLES

It is crucial to grasp how rifles work to fully understand why the modern precision rimfires are so significant in the recent history of firearms and what makes them so accurate. There are several types of rifle actions, from single shot to lever action to fully automatic. Only two are relevant in tactical-style precision shooting: the bolt action and the semi-automatic or autoloader.

These rifle actions both perform six basics steps:

1. Feeding — a cartridge is pushed up from the magazine by spring pressure and moved forward into the barrel chamber by the bolt;

2. Locking — the cartridge is locked in the chamber under bolt pressure;

3. Firing — a striker or firing pin under spring pressure within the bolt detonates the primer when the trigger is pulled;

4. Extracting — one or two hook-like devices on the bolt face pull the fired brass case clear of the chamber as the bolt cycles rearward;

5. Ejecting — the case is flipped clear of the rifle as the bolt goes back;

6. Cocking — the striker and spring are armed for the next shot.

These steps are the stuff of an introductory Hunter Education course. But to fully understand the

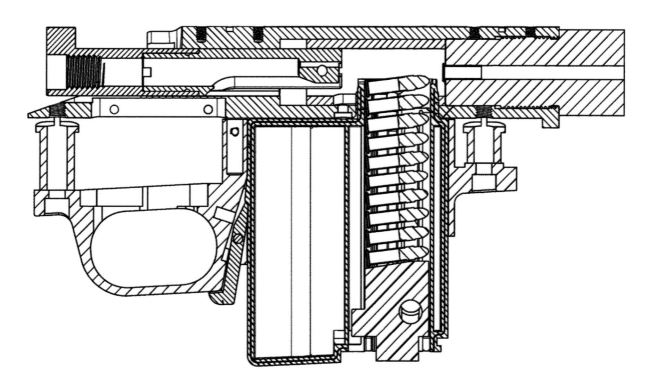

Illustration by Kenna Milaski

nuances of rifle models, it pays to dive in a little deeper. Let's start with the semi-automatic.

Semi-Autos

With a round in the chamber, a full magazine, and the safety off, the semi-auto rifle is ready to fire. The striker or firing pin is held back in the bolt under spring tension when cocked. A sear or sharp notched bar in the trigger mechanism holds the striker and spring in place under tension. When you pull the trigger blade, the sear moves out of its notched position, releasing that spring tension, which throws the firing pin forward, striking the primer in the chambered round.

When the primer detonates, it ignites the gun powder, which generates hot gases that rapidly expand and "push" the bullet down the barrel. This process isn't technically an explosion — it's a rapid expansion of gases. The chamber contains the cartridge case at the shooter's end of the rifle. Therefore, the only direction for the gas to go is down and out the barrel. Some of that gas pushes the firing pin and spring rearward until the sear grabs it and is held in place again or re-cocked. The bolt conceals the spring and striker and uses the hooks on the bolt face to extract and eject the case while traveling backward. Ammunition in the magazine is pushed upward into the action, so when the bolt ejects the spent case, a fresh round is drawn up and fills the action gap. When the bolt closes again, it seats and locks this new round in the chamber.

In a piston system, like an AK-47, gases from cartridge ignition that push the bullet down the barrel are siphoned off through a tube above the barrel, which cycles a piston, forcing the bolt back — restarting the loading process. An M4 or AR-15 with a "direct impingement" system does the same thing but without a piston. The gas itself creates enough pressure to move the bolt. With semi-automatic rimfires, the same principle applies, but there is no siphoning of gases in most cases. These are called "direct blow-back" and sometimes the modified "delayed blow-back" actions. The mainspring or recoil spring holds the bolt against the breech face. When the round ignites, most of the gases expand forward, launching the bullet, while some of the gas directly blows back the bolt against mainspring pressure and cycles the action.

There's a hammer in the trigger system in many semi-auto action designs, like the Ruger 10/22.. Pull the trigger. The sear disengages and drops a spring-tension hammer — the hammer strikes the back of the firing pin, which hits and detonates the cartridge primer. As the gas pushes the bolt back under mainspring tension, it re-arms or tensions the hammer, spring, and sear. This concert of motion is called "timing."

Bolt Actions

A bolt action works the same way, but rather than gas expansion cycling the bolt, the shooter manually does it in four motions. First, lift the bolt handle and draw it back, which extracts and ejects the spent case. Then push the bolt forward, which loads a new round into the chamber. Rotate the bolt handle downward — locking it in place. In most cases, rimfire actions use the base of the bolt handle as a locking lug. With this system, no expanding gases travel backward. This system often aids higher and more consistent muzzle velocities or the speed at which the bullet leaves the barrel. As we'll see, constant velocity is a centerpiece to an accurate rifle system. That said, some semi-automatic builders and gunsmiths have taken those platforms to shocking degrees of consistency when it comes to velocity.

Whatever the action, the time between pulling the trigger and the striker detonating the primer is called "lock time." We measure lock time in milliseconds. The faster, the better. Fast lock time gives the shooter less time to wiggle and twitch off target. The cartridge rim is sandwiched between the breech face or flat end face of the barrel and the bolt with a rimfire.

A Ruger 10/22 converted to .17 HM2 demonstrates the violent blowback that extracts, ejects and chambers a round in a semi-automatic action.

The distance between the two, taken up by the thickness of the rim, is called "headspace." The technical definition of headspace is "the distance measured from the face of the bolt to the mechanical feature of the firing chamber that stops forward motion of the cartridge," according to SAAMI This dimension is the distance between the bolt face and breech face and, in the best case, matches the thickness of the ammunition rim within .001 inch. Changing the headspace or making the bolt/rim/breech fit tighter or looser can profoundly affect ignition consistency and, therefore, downrange accuracy. The dimensions of the chamber the ammunition sits in or chamber geometry can also have a profound effect. Of utmost importance is the quality of the barrel itself.

Rimfire Rifle Barrels

Rifle barrels are, well, rifled. The tube is not straight-walled, but grooves are cut, pressed, or hammered in the steel that imparts a spiral motion on the bullet as it travels down the bore. "Lands" and "grooves" create this spiral pattern. The lands are the elevated ridges. The grooves are the recesses. How much the lands and grooves twist in the bore is noted as "twist rate." The most common twist rate for .22 LR for almost 130 years has been 1:16, which means the .22-caliber bullet does one full rotation over 16 inches of barrel. However, that's changing with modern bullets and shooters wanting to hit targets from very far away. Extreme long-range or ELR is the bleeding edge of rimfire right now: shooters send 30- and 40-grain projectiles beyond 500 yards. They're finding that 1:12 or even 1:9 twist rates in longer barrel lengths may be advantageous to hitting way out. A faster twist puts more spin on the bullet. The barrel's end, or the last point of contact between the barrel and the bullet, is called the "muzzle." The shape and cut of the face of the muzzle are the "crown." Well-made barrels have a bore cut concentric to the receiver and bolt, with a well-cut chamber and crown to protect the muzzle.

A functional and accurate rifle system does all these things well. It feeds reliably, has a tight lock up, and a smooth, crisp trigger system. When fired, the lock time is fast. The headspace is ideal and set to the thickness of the cartridge rim within .001 inch. The chamber is of accurate design. The barrel is high qual-

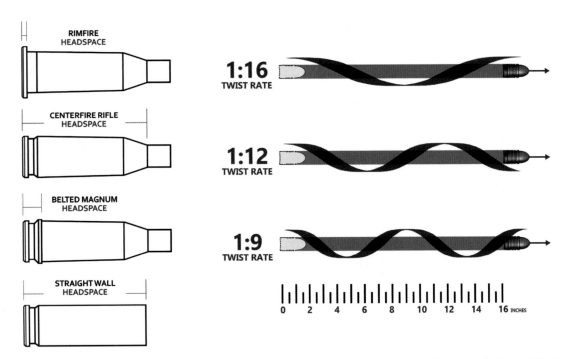

RIMFIRE
HEADSPACE

CENTERFIRE RIFLE
HEADSPACE

BELTED MAGNUM
HEADSPACE

STRAIGHT WALL
HEADSPACE

1:16
TWIST RATE

1:12
TWIST RATE

1:9
TWIST RATE

0 2 4 6 8 10 12 14 16 INCHES

Illustration by Kenna Milaski

ity, with polished and concentric lands and grooves without deviation down the bore's length. (Maybe. More about this in the chapter on Precision & Accuracy.) The crown is precisely cut. The bolt effortlessly extracts the spent case and ejects it clear of the rifle. The magazine sends up the next round without issue, and at a proper angle, so the bolt cleanly loads it into the chamber without scuffing, marring, or deforming the bullet nose against the breech face or chamber walls.

Easy, right?

Anschütz

"It's attention to detail." – Steve Boelter, president of Anschütz North America

Genealogists had traced the Anschütz surname to firearm construction and gunsmithing as far back as 1606 when Jacob Anschütz established a gun shop near the city of Suhl in what later became East Germany.

The modern firm JG Anschütz GmbH & Co. KG traces its roots to Julius Gottfried Anschütz and his shop's founding in the same region in 1856. Anschütz spe-

cialized in Flobert and other pocket pistols along with hunting guns like shotguns and *teschings* rifles. In 1896, the company had 76 employees and moved from a small workshop to its first factory in Zella-Mehlis, Thuringia, north of Suhl.

The City of Suhl is notable in firearms history as the cradle of the Germanic arms industry. Suhl foundries produced some of the earliest guns in Europe and fed the Nazi war machine through the Second World War. After 1940, the Nazis moved an estimated 10,000 forced laborers to the city to increase weapons production. The U.S. Army liberated Suhl in April 1945, but the town fell into Soviet hands when Europe split east and west. Suhl would remain a hotbed of arms innovation and production under the Soviets. Suhl smallbore trainers and positional rifles are still renowned for their build quality and accuracy. Rimfire benchrest shooters, in particular, still build guns on Cold War-era Suhl actions.

The Treaty of Versailles signed after the First World War limited German arms production, but smallbore rifles were mostly exempt. By 1935, Anschütz grew to its largest size, 550 employees, manufacturing training and parlor rifles, including guns chambered in the short 4mm RF cartridge, among other metal goods. Anschütz made training rifles during the war, but when the Soviets took over, the factory was confiscated and dismantled. The Soviets forced Rudolf Charles Anschütz to work as a woodcutter. A bleak future ahead of them, the Anschütz family fled to Ulm in West Germany.

Founded in 1950, the new JG Anschütz GmbH company in Ulm had seven employees and 20 machines. It first made air pistols, carried out firearm repairs, then added Flobert and target rifles to the program. In 1954, it debuted the now famous three-lug Match 54 action with its 53.5-degree bolt lift. Olympic positional rifle shooters immediately loved the design. You could cycle it with less physical movement within their shooting position than the Winchester 52 and other target turn bolts that dominated the day.

Anschütz rifles earned their first gold medals in the 1960 Olympics. Dieter Anschütz, the long-time chief executive, took the helm in 1968. He worked directly with Lones Wigger — gold medalist and member of the U.S. Army Marksmanship Unit — to improve the rifle further. By the 1972 Summer Games in Munich, most of the smallbore Olympic competitors were shooting Anschütz, including Team USA members John Writer and Lanny Bassham, who earned gold and silver, respectively. German as the rifles were, it was their Olympic successes that brought notoriety. In the hands of Team USA medal winners and world record holders like Wigger, Writer, Bassham, Gary Anderson, and Margaret Murdock in the late 1960s and 1970s, international acclaim built its well-earned reputation for next-level accuracy.

Anschütz dominance in three-position and prone shooting has eroded mainly to other European manufacturers like Bleiker, Walther, and Grünig & Elmiger. Still, its 1827 F Biathlon Rifle with the straight-pull Fortner action remains the only competitive biathlon rifle on the world stage. Dieter Anschütz, in part, is responsible for biathlon moving from centerfire to

The Anschütz 1827 F Bionic.

Germania-Block-Teschings mit Ganzschaft.

System ähnlich wie Keßler, alles maschinell
hergestellt, billigste Blockbüchse.

Nr. 1302. Kal. 6, 7 und 9 mm, fein gezogen, mit Stecher, Schraubvisier, Korn mit Perle, Pistolen-
griff, eingesetzte Garnitur, Schiene guillochiert . . . . Mk. 34.50
„ 1303. Desgl. Kal. 22 Winchester (Vierlingbüchse) . . . . „ 37.15
„ 1304. Desgl. für Messinghülsen Kal. Z 6x17 mm, Z 7x23 mm und P 7,3×40 mm . . . . „ 39.—
Nr. 1302–1304 mit Schweizer-Diopter erhöht den Preis um Mk. 4.50
„ 1302–1304 mit Steig-Diopter erhöht den Preis um Mk. 6.—

Germania Block Teschings with one-piece stock

Barreled action similar to Keßler, everything made on machines, very inexpensive block rifle.

No. 1302. Cal. 6, 7 and 9 mm, nicely rifled, with double-set trigger, screwed sight, pearl sight, pistol grip,
           inserted system, engine-turned tail   marks 34.50
No. 1303. Dto., Cal. 22 Winchester (four-barrel receiver)   marks 37.15
No. 1304. Dto., for brass receivers cal. Z 6x17 mm, Z 7x25 mm and P7.3 x 40 mm   marks 39.00
           No. 1302-1304 with Swiss sight for an extra charge of marks 4.50
           No. 1302-1304 with vertically adjustable sight for an extra charge of marks 6.00

An Anschütz *"block" shotgun manufactured from 1900 to 1920.*
Photos: Anschütz

Anschütz *built its new factory in the Danube Valley in Ulm in 1950.*

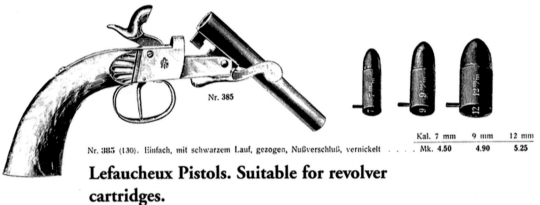

Lefaucheux-Pistolen. Für Revolver-Patronen passend.

Nr. 385

Kal. 7 mm   9 mm   12 mm

Nr. 385 (130). Einfach, mit schwarzem Lauf, gezogen, Nußverschluß, vernickelt . . . . Mk. 4.50   4.90   5.25

Lefaucheux Pistols. Suitable for revolver cartridges.

No. 385 (130)   Simple, with black barrel, rifled, nut action, nickel-plated.

An early pinfire pistol made by Anschütz.

The Anschütz *1710 HB G TAC. All rifle photos here by Anschutz*

rimfire. He petitioned the International Olympic Committee for the change to .22 LR. It was a sharp move not just for his company but for the sport. Shooting at 50 meters rather than 300 meant biathlon events could be safely held in a stadium with competitors skiing laps, then dropping out and hitting targets off to one side. While biathlon hasn't taken hold in the U.S., in Europe, the world cup events have Super Bowl vibes — huge stadiums, roaring fans, international media coverage. Anschütz rifles dominate. At the last few Winter Olympics, every single biathlon competitor, man or woman, shot an Anschütz. Like much American-style precision shooting, biathlon requires a varied skillset of endurance, speed, and accuracy. Curiously, the rifles haven't gained more traction stateside in modern precision shooting like NRL22. Part of that certainly is the price.

In 2006, Anschütz celebrated its 150th anniversary. At the time, Dieter Anschütz told Shooting Sports USA, "Our plans for the future are the production and further development of the world's best target rifles." From its headquarters in Ulm, Anschütz is a truly global company, with distributors in 90 countries, including Anschütz North America in Trussville, Alabama, and a Custom Shop in Las Vegas, Nevada.

Anschütz Rifles

	1710 D HB	1761 MPR	1827 F
Action	54	1761	Fortner
Bolt Type	Three lugs, 53.5°	Three lugs, 60°	Straight pull
Stock Type	Sporter	MPR	Biathalon
Stock Material	Walnut	Hardwood	Hardwood
Total Weight	7 lbs. 15 oz.	7 lbs. 11 oz.	8 lbs. 6 oz.
Barrel Type	Heavy contour	Medium contour	Biathalon
Barrel Length	23 in.	21 in.	21.6 in.
Trigger	Single-stage	5061 Two-stage	Various
Trigger Weight	2 lbs.	2 lbs.	1.1 lbs.
Mag. Capacity	5 or 10	5	5
Calibers	.22 LR	.22 LR	.22 LR
MSRP	$2,295	$1,995	$3,995

If we awarded a prize to a gun company for the most opaque, hard-to-track system of model names, it would go to Anschütz every time. Over the years, it has changed the naming scheme, too, which makes things more confusing. A spreadsheet of all rifles by numerical model name runs hundreds of guns deep without precise rhythm or reason. These muddied waters would not be such an issue if the rifles weren't so damn good. For example, the aftermarket for Anschütz rifles is booming. A 54.18 MSR from 1986, for example, is still capable of dominating a precision shooting match in a good shooter's hands. Many shooters got into Anschütz through the vibrant used market, but it takes a deep dive at places like rimfire-central.com to sort out older Anschütz model names, features, and resale values. The *Blue Book of Gun Values* and the *Standard Catalog of Firearms* are great resources. Still, the listed values are universally low, what with the surge of American interest in smallbore shooting.

Considering current production rifles, Anschütz slices its lineup in three ways: Hunting or Sporting, Target, and Biathlon. Sporting lineup variations through Anschütz North America include the Meister Grade Series with premium walnut stocks and the Canyon Creek Series with super-premium walnut. These rifles are largely magazine-fed repeaters. The Target rifles are geared toward Olympic-style positional shooting and benchrest and are primarily single shots. Anschütz has been slow to move into the NRL22-style precision market. Still, there are Custom Shop options — magazine-fed trainers available in laminated GRS stocks and a Rimfire Trainer Series in an XLR chassis. Think of Anschütz in broad categories of Sporting, Hunting, and Biathlon, but the real differentiator model to model is the action.

Anschütz has five primary rifle actions: the foundational Match 54; the variant 54.30; the practical and recently discontinued 64; the new swap-barrel 1761; and the straight-pull Fortner biathlon action. Anschütz has been deliberate over the years in its designs. Each action serves a purpose and serves it well.

54 Action

The Model 54 is effectively a three-lug design with a bank vault-strong lock up. There are two rear locking lugs on the solid steel bolt, plus the bolt handle's lapped base that acts as the third lug. There is a short 53.5-degree bolt lift with a famously glass-slick race-

way. The light firing pin travels less than 2 centimeters, which gives the 54 one of the fastest lock times in rimfire. The receiver is thicker and heavier than other actions in the Anschütz line and most rimfire actions in general, at least until the recent rise of centerfire-inspired Remington 700-footprint actions. This oversize makes a good support for heavy contour barrels. Most barrels are press fit with a dual retaining pin.

There are repeater and single-shot versions of the 54 action. The repeater magazines are a curved single-stack similar to a CZ mag. There are several trigger options, but the benchrest-quality two-stage 5018 is perhaps best regarded. It's fully adjustable with a pull weight range of 2.1 to 8.6 ounces. I suspect the Model 54 with 5018 trigger is the winningest match receiver/action combo in smallbore history due to its long dominance across multiple disciplines. (The Winchester 52 may be close due to its long successful run. I have no data to support this either way.) But it is undoubtedly true that the 54 action and its excellent triggers put the Winchester and Remington 40x out of business at the elite shooting level almost overnight. The short bolt lift, lock up, lock time, and premium Anschütz barrels came to define peak rimfire accuracy.

Current production 54 action rifles include the single-shot 1907, 1913, and 2013 match rifles. You can think of the 1907 barreled action as a lighter version of the 1913 with a slightly smaller barrel diameter. The 2013 action is an updated variant of the Match 54 single shot with an extended and squared bedding area and clamp-style barrel attachment. Anschütz uses the

The Anschütz 1710 DB Classic.

Anschütz 1727 F in a German-style walnut stock.

Anschütz 1761 HB MSR—the go-to Annie for many modern percision shooters.

54 action in the 1710 and 1712 sporter rifles. For silhouette and modern precision, shooting the 17xx line is the most widely used of the 54s.

54.30 Action

In 2015, Anschütz updated the single-shot 54 action with the 54.30. It moved the loading port rearward 30 millimeters, hence the 54.30, which reduced the overall action length by 18 percent. This change made the action stiffer and lessened the movement required by positional shooters to cycle it. The revision further lightened the firing pin for an even faster lock time. The 54.30 also has a threaded receiver and barrel connection, and it cut barrels with a new-to-2015 proprietary Anschütz match chamber. Not only that, the rounded footprint matches that of the 1907 and 1913. Depending on the stock, these positional rifles run between $4,700 and $5,500. That

is a lot of money but represents almost a bargain compared to Bleiker, Feinwekbau, and other exalted European rifle makers, which can cost two or three times as much.

64 Action

The 64 action rifles are what most Americans think of when they think of Anschütz. For a long time, Savage imported them as Savage-Anschütz, and they're all over the used market in .22 LR and .22 WMR. Newer version 64s — not imported by Savage — can be found on the used market in .17 HM2 and .17 HMR. The rifle that kicked off my obsession with rimfire was an Anschütz 1502 with the 64 action in .17 Mach 2. (You could blame this whole book on that rifle.) Anschütz discontinued the 64 in favor of the newer 1761 action. According to Steve Boelter, president of Anschütz North America, it received the last U.S. shipments of

The Anschütz 54.30 in the 1907 walnut stock.

Another Anschütz 54.30 in the 1914 walnut stock.

The Anschütz 54.30 in the BR-50 walnut stock.

guns and service parts in December 2020. Shooters with 64s should not worry about future parts availability. "We have enough ejectors and firing pins to last a century," he told me.

The 64 action is a scaled-down lightweight version of the 54, which suits sporter rifles and small game guns. The one-piece solid steel bolt body has no lugs. The locking surface is the base of the bolt handle. The 64 has a different trigger system, and while there are many good ones — Anschütz does not make a lousy trigger — there is no trigger model for the 64 that equals the two-stage 5018. The 64 and 54 are two different footprints, so stocks and triggers are not interchangeable between the two actions. The 64 barrels are press fit with one horizontal locking pin. The magazine release is less than ideal for position or bench shooting, but there are extended aftermarket options available to correct that. There was also a run in the 2000s where every new 64 seemed to have ejection issues. The case would eject slowly and often tumbled into the open receiver port. Engineers corrected this with a new ejector, and for a while, Anschütz sent them out for free or did the work themselves if you mailed them the bolt.

People ask, "What is more accurate, the 54 or the 64?" Mechanically, the 54 may have more accuracy potential with its heavy-duty build, locking lugs, and faster lock time. It certainly requires more hand finishing work and is a premium action. The barrels are made the same way, on the same machines, of the same or similar contours, with the same chambers. The 54 is a more sophisticated and expensive action, but to call it more accurate? Well, it depends. There are less-than-perfect 54s and barn-burner 64s, as is the nature of factory-built rifles. On average, the 54 series is more so a precision instrument. It has more potential as an accurate rifle system, but I've yet to shoot a 64 or know anyone who has one and complains about poor accuracy. The universal question on rimfire forums is always, "Is this rifle more accurate than that rifle?" The answer is almost always, "It depends."

1761

The newest Anschütz action, the 1761, has a host of modern features and has been designed to replace the 64 as a light, all-purpose, and relatively cost-effective platform. What started as a rework for the 1710 and 1712 Match 54 repeaters became a total redesign. As Anschütz put it in a good explainer on its North American website:

Anschütz 64 Biathlon Sprint.

The Anschütz 1761 MPR.

"...we opted to slightly increase the bolt lift from 53 to 60 degrees as a trade-off in order to move the locking lugs from the rear to the middle of the bolt. The lugs were switched from smaller eccentric lugs to a much more robust set of three lugs and evenly spaced these around the bolt. This allowed us to move from a long dual-spring firing pin to a very short, light firing pin and single-spring striker system. The new spring and striker mechanism was moved to the rear half of the bolt. This change also made the bolt much shorter in overall length."

The bolt's back is a roller bearing, making the opening motion smoother with less required force. The dual ejector system borrows from the single-shot Match 54. Ejectors are held in place by plunger and spring rather than c-clamp.

The smooth barrel tenon slip fits in the receiver like a CZ, but with one key difference: Rather than grub screws directly tensioning the tenon, there are two small v-blocks that Anschütz says more evenly distribute pressure and don't mar the tenon. Shilen, Lilja, Lothar Walther, and other quality barrel makers produce drop-ins.

The steel billet receiver is CNC machined with an integral recoil lug and square bottom bedding surface.

The action has square lines, not the rounded body of more traditional Anschütz actions. It is 4 centimeters shorter than the Match 54 action (read: very rigid) and held down in the stock with two action screws. There is an 11mm dovetail rail on top. Anschütz opted not to tap it, which is a mistake. (The best Anschütz rings, according to many, including me, are the one-piece Talley rings and bases for the tapped receiver, not the more common 11mm dovetail clamp-style rings.)

The magazine is a steel and poly combo. As of early 2021, there were only 5-rounders, though a 10-round prototype has moved toward production. The small radiused hinge release button is behind the magazine and accessed through a cutout in the triggerguard. You can drop the mag with a forward slap of the trigger finger. The triggerguard is an unfortunate plastic, but steel models are available on the aftermarket. Calibers include .22 LR, .17 HMR and .22 WMR.

Fortner Action

Peter Fortner invented the straight-pull action that bears his name, and he still manufactures them in a small shop in Rohrdorf, Germany. Under a licensing agreement, his entire run of rimfire actions goes to Anschütz, which builds them into its flagship biathlon guns and the 1727 F line of sporting rifles in .22 LR, .17 HMR, and .17 Mach 2. Fortner also designed a center-fire equivalent for German rifle builder Heym. Boelter likens the Fortner relationship with Anschütz like a speed shop within an auto manufacturer, AMG within Mercedes.

Straight pulls operate faster than classic turn bolts, with less motion required to cycle them. Rather than the four movements of lifting the bolt, pulling it back, and pushing it forward, then pushing it back down again, there are just two motions to a straight pull: rearward and forward. Shooters typically run them with their thumb on the back of the bolt.

After the shot, the trigger finger comes up and cycles the bolt rearward. Then the thumb pushes it home on the fresh round. Much of Europe has out-lawed semi-automatics, so when speed is needed, as in biathlon events or boar hunting dense forest with centerfires, straight pulls have proven fast and accurate. That explains why Anschütz, Heym, Blaser, and others have cultivated the design. Straight-pull actions have mostly gone unnoticed in the US of A. That's because 1. we have all the guns, and 2. the cost. Straight pulls are necessarily complicated and expensive to make. The exceptions on this side of the pond are the Browning T-bolt and the Savage Impulse.

The Fortner action uses seven ball bearings that act like rear locking lugs. The action works very much like a hydraulic tractor hose or an air tool connection. When you put pressure on the bolt handle, it relieves stress on the bearings that sit within the sleeved bolt. This movement withdraws the ball bearings into the bolt, and you can cycle the action. The handle is spring-assisted, so the balls extend out and into the re-cesses in the receiver body and lock up when it snaps forward. This design allows for a linear rather than a rotating bolt action. Pulling the handle acts like pulling the collar on a quick-connect hydraulic line. It retracts the bearings and breaks the connection. Compared to a semi-automatic rimfire, this creates a stronger lockup. Advocates say they can run the bolt accurately almost as fast, too. Well, maybe. What is certain is the design is effortless to run. A broken-in Fortner seemingly wants to cycle itself with just some encouragement from forefinger and thumb. The Fort-ner action is rounded with a floating ring recoil lug and press-fit, two-pin barrel connection and comes with the world-class 5020 two-stage trigger with a pull weight range of 3.1 ounces to 1.375 pounds. Bi-athlon rifles come set at the required 500 grams or 1.1 pounds. The total package is a remarkable feat of firearm engineering.

Anschütz Barrels

Anschütz barrels are made in-house in Germany. It processes about 50 tons of steel into barrels per year. The company makes most of its barrels of 4000 series

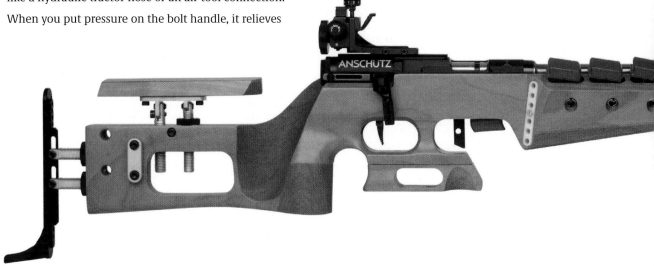

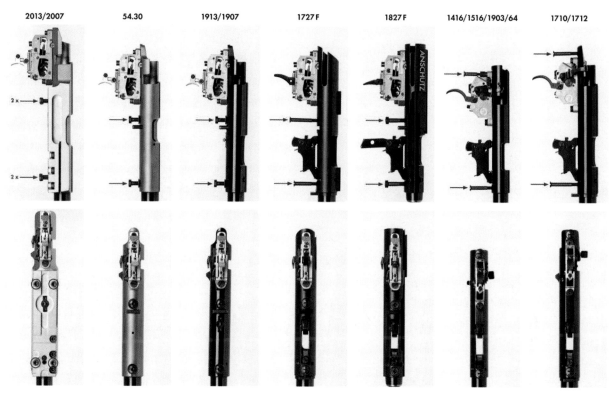

| 2013/2007 | 54.30 | 1913/1907 | 1727 F | 1827 F | 1416/1516/1903/64 | 1710/1712 |

A comparison of the current Anschütz action footprints.

Chromoly, and it does offer some stainless models. Anschütz also makes a propriety steel alloy barrel designed just for biathlon rifles. The metal resists cold temps and big temperature swings. Anschütz knows this for sure. It has a test range in Ulm, where the mercury can drop to -20° Celsius (-4°F). Biathlon rifle materials and barreled actions are tested for accuracy and point-of-aim shift over a wide swath of temperatures.

The barrel-making process begins with circular steel blanks. They are cut to length, chamfered, and drilled with a bore smaller than the finished caliber. The bore is then ground in four stages and honed. Finally, it is button-rifled — pulling an oversized button through the barrel. Compressing the metal impresses the rifle grooves into the bore. The barrels are then stress relieved, contoured on a CNC lathe, chambered, and hand-finished with a file as needed. After barrel completion and rifle assembly, it's test range time. Testers fire 10 rounds from a vise, and if the group size is more than 18mm or 0.70 inch at 50 meters, they rework the rifle until it meets that standard. These benchmarks are not arbitrary figures. The scoring ring on a biathlon target is 45mm at 50 meters. Accuracy in the 15 to 18mm range gives athletes a decent degree of forgiveness for racing heart, burning lungs, and blurry eyes through iron sights.

Anschütz 1827 F Comfort.

Common Anschütz Abbreviations

Anschütz feature abbreviations have changed over the years, with some added and others dropped, but these are the most common ones found on the company's current rifles and older but still popular models.

D = Single-stage trigger

F = Fortner straight-pull action

G = Heavy, threaded barrel 1/2x20 Metric

HB = Heavy barrel

HMR = Chambered .17 HMR

HW = Hardwood

KL = Traditional folding leaf rear sight

L = Left-handed

R = Repeater

AV = American Varminter 18 in. threaded 1/2x28

MC = Monte Carlo

MP = Multi-Purpose

SA = Savage Anschütz

SS= Stainless steel barrel

S BR = Sporter benchrest

W = Walnut

Example: The 1727 F G is a Fortner action gun with a heavy contour threaded barrel. The 1761 D HB is a 1761 action with a single-stage trigger and heavy barrel.

Anschütz barrels are renowned for accuracy. A few are in the Top 10 most accurate rifles at the ELEY test tunnel in Texas and the Lapua test tunnels in Arizona and Ohio. There is no magic fairy dust they sprinkle on barrels or rifles, says Boelter. "It's attention to detail. The barrels are made in-house. Nothing is outsourced. For a long time, we had a machine that made screws. We made our own screws. Outsourcing, you're at an immediate quality disadvantage because you're relying on the other guy. We do it all every step of the way."

Anschütz Pros and Cons

Anschütz has been slow to respond to the burgeoning tactical precision rimfire market. For example, the 1761 came without a 10-round magazine, which is essential for any NRL22 or Rimfire PRS course of fire. It does have Match 54s for sale through the Custom Shop with the GRS and XLR chassis. These are excellent rifles even with the $2,500 price tag. But with an Anschütz, you lose the wide world of aftermarket support that comes with the Rugers, CZs, and Remington 700 platform rifles. Straight from the box, no Ruger or

The author's current Annies: a 1502 chambered in .17 Mach 2 and a 1516 Savage-Anschütz in .22 WMR.

The Bergara B-14R – R for Rimfire, of course.

CZ is remotely on the same level as a Match 54, but it is possible to make them just as accurate with custom barrels, trigger swaps, and some work. In a way, this is very much like buying a Porsche and being done with it or purchasing a Ford and building it up in your home garage. They're two very different animals.

Another drawback is the price. German precision does not come cheap. Europe is also filthy with taxes and export tariffs that affect the cost to consumers in export markets. These costs affect parts, which are generally pricey. J&P Custom Products, DIP, Inc., and Nordic Marksmen in Canada, among others, sell screws, springs, strikers, bases, triggerguards, and everything else needed to rehab a used gun. If the bore is clean and well cared for, most old Anschütz rifles can hang with new rifles produced today.

If biathlon is your game, or walnut and blued steel your fancy, Anschütz makes the best factory rimfire rifles in the world. You don't often meet an unhappy Anschütz owner.

Bergara

"You absolutely must start with a good barrel. Then it's all about mechanical repeatability." – Dan Haus, Director of Technical Development, Bergara

If you were to reduce Bergara to a math equation, it would look like this: (Spanish Steel + American Process) x the United States Marine Corps = Accurate Rifles.

Bergara Barrels started in 2006, named after the town it calls home in the Basque Country of northern Spain. The hills there are quite literally made of iron. There's a centuries-old tradition of sword and knife-making in the region. *Ezpata dantza*, or the "sword dance," is one of the Basque Country's oldest tradition-al dances. The raw minerals that make high-quality Spanish steels are mined and forged in the region and have been for centuries.

The American process comes from legendary barrel maker and Benchrest Hall of Famer Ed Shilen. The Spaniard-owned Dikar Corp. controls Lawrenceville, Ga.-based BPI Outdoors, which purchased Connecticut Valley Arms Co., a small maker of affordable muzzle-loaders, in 1999. BPI executives very quickly realized that third-party barrel suppliers hamstrung CVA. Barrel demand outstripped supply, and makers of quality barrels could effectively name their price. The BPI team approached Dikar, which owned a manufacturing facility in Spain, and inquired about making its barrels. Dikar went for it, and the team quickly recruited Shilen as a consultant to show them his process for making record-setting customs.

Their shared goal was not modest. The new company wanted to build a system to manufacture the most accurate factory barrels in the world.

The difference between a custom and factory barrel is time and touch. More time goes into a custom blank. There's more hands-on labor cost, from properly setting the barrels in CNC fixtures to ensure concentricity to hand lapping for accuracy and reflecting an internal mirror finish. Shilen showed the team in Spain how to keep tolerances from stacking, and the team invested in state-of-the-art CNC machines.

When Bergara branched from barrels into custom rifles, the barrel manufacturing process it worked out instantly gave its centerfires an immediate reputation for incredible out-of-the-box accuracy. That process starts when the 4140-series or stainless steel is brought to the factory and checked for straightness.

Bergara inspects the cylindrical steel bars to ensure there's no more than 0.004 inch of deviation over the bar's length. If it's off-spec, gunsmiths straighten the steel in a press before moving on.

The steel bar moves to a four-spindle deep-hole drilling machine that bores through the bar's length. Bergara then uses three separate honing spindles that utilize diamond-tipped bits. These bits polish the bore's interior surface to a mirror-like finish. Bergara says this is what separates its barrels from most other gun companies "because it avoids reaming, which has the potential of leaving tool marks inside the barrel,

Dan Hanus, Bergara's technical lead and former USMC precision weapons specialist.

causing an obstruction and decreased life-span."

The next step is button rifling with a groove diameter deviation of less than 0.0002 inch. Unlike cutting rifling, a grooved button is pulled through the bore, compressing the grooves into the steel. This process induces stress in the steel, which is relieved in the final process by heat treatment. The closely guarded secret works by getting the barrel hot enough to realign the steel molecules to ensure the finished barrel is stress-free, will not warp when cut, and is ready to shoot.

Centerfire or rimfire, every Bergara barrel blank is made this way. The barrel stock is then sent to the United States, where it is contoured and built into the Premiere series or the BXR 10/22 clone rifles. The B-14 series of rifles are machined and constructed from start to finish in Spain.

The Marine Corps Way

Barrels make accurate rifles, but a rifle is more than a barrel. When Bergara branched out into custom rifle manufacturing in Lawrenceville, it hired Dan Hanus, a 22-year Marine Corps veteran who was Production Chief and Chief Instructor for the Marines' Precision Weapons Section at Quantico, Virginia.

The Corps PWS team builds and maintains the M40 series sniper rifles for the Reconnaissance Marines and the Scout Sniper programs. They made and maintained the National Match M16s for the Corps and the National Match .45s and 9mms. PWS is effectively a 45-employee special operations unit of armorers and gunsmiths, with its school, practices, and protocols, with the singular focus of building the most accurate combat and target rifles in the world. In Hanus, Bergara snagged one of the U.S. military's best 'smiths.

The Fort Dodge, Iowa native, enlisted in the Corps at 18 years old. As a small arms repair specialist, he helped keep the Corps' M4s in good working order. Throughout his time, he'd bump into the gunsmiths from PWS. They had a separate room and separate machines behind closed doors. They weren't hostile but didn't mingle with the other armors, either. "One day, I cornered a guy and asked him just what they do," Hanus remembered. They specialized in extreme accuracy, and Hanus wanted in.

He applied three times, and PWS denied him three times — as is expected in the most elite military schools. When his enlistment was up, he re-enlisted as a recruitment officer for the Marines, which came with a big perk. After a tour in recruiting, he could pick his next assignment. He did, and into the PWS pipeline he went. One of the first tests was to make a perfect 1x1-inch aluminum square with just a file and hacksaw. He did. For the next test, they had to make all their gunsmithing tools. "The program turns you into a basic machinist," he said.

He served with the First Recon Battalion, building and maintaining the rifles for its sniper school. He deployed to Iraq multiple times and, at the Marines' request on the ground, modified their M40/M40A5 rifles for detachable magazines, among other battlefield improvements. He went on to teach at the PWS school, and after 22 years of service, it was time for Hanus to retire or re-up.

Bergara BXR

It was 2010, and the Marine Corps was going through a downsizing. The Corps offered him a promotion to stay on, but that meant moving his family from Quantico to Camp Lejeune, North Carolina, to take a job as Ordnance Chief for the 2nd Marine Division. A big job, but the division was fast approaching a scheduled 15-month deployment in Afghanistan. "I had just gotten back from more or less three years in Iraq, and when I mentioned the new assignment to my wife and moving the family to North Carolina, she said I could have fun down there by myself," he remembered with a laugh. "She wasn't moving to North Carolina."

As a backup plan, he worked up a civilian resume and went to a gunsmith seminar and job fair at Brownells back in his home state of Iowa. He met Mark Hendricks, Vice President of Technical Development at BPI, and the rest is history.

With high-quality Spanish steel on hand, a benchrest-proven barrel-making process from Shilen, and now an elite Marine Corps rifle builder, Bergara launched custom rifles in 2012. It built its first on Stiller

	Bergara BXR	Bergara B14-R	Bergara BMR
Action	10/22 clone	B-14R	BMR
Bolt Type	N/A	Two lugs, 90°	Two lugs, 90°
Stock Type	Sporter, polymer molded	HMR	Sporter, polymer
Stock Material	Polymer molded	Polymer molded, aluminum block	Polymer molded
Cheek Riser	No	Adjustable	No
Total Weight	4.75 to 5.2 lbs.	8.1 lbs.	5 to 5.4 lbs.
Overall Length	34.5 in.	38 in.	36 in. or 38 in.
Barrel Type	4140 CrMo Fluted steel	No. 6 Taper carbon fiber or steel	No. 6 Taper carbon fiber or steel
Barrel Length	16.5 in.	18 in.	18 in.
Trigger	Bergara	Bergara Performance, Rem 700 compatible	Bergara Performance, Rem 700 compatible
Trigger Weight	3.5 lbs.	2 lbs.	2 lbs.
Mag. Capacity	10	10, ACIS-pattern	10, slim fit
Calibers	.22 LR	.22 LR, .17 HMR, .22 WMR	.22 LR, .17 HMR, .22 WMR
MSRP	$565	$1,150 or $1,245	$565 or $659

The Bergara BXR—one of the most innovative 10/22 clones to date. Photo: Bergara.

actions, then its own in-house Remington 700 clone with an extended collar and integral recoil lug.

In 2014, it developed a production rifle with the B-14. Bergara added rimfire to its catalog, with the Made in the USA 10/22 clone, the BXR, and the Remington 700 footprint turn-bolt B-14R, made in Spain.

"We became sponsors of the Precision Rifle Series, and attending those matches, we heard all this buzz around NRL22," Hanus said. "Everyone said, 'This thing is going to be big.' You can effectively run a match on a 100-yard range. So, we kind of dove in deep in the technical development and worked feverishly on developing a .22. We came up with two. I'd say they've been well received. We can't make them fast enough."

One of the best custom 10/22 builders in the country once told me that making Ruger's famous design accurate comes down to three things: the barrel, the barrel, and the barrel. That's one of the many reasons the rimfire world has been excited about Bergara's entry into the 10/22 market.

The BXR comes in two configurations: The base model sports a 4140 fluted steel barrel with a black Cerakote finish to match the receiver. The upgraded model has a carbon-fiber barrel. Both are 16.5-inches long and threaded at the muzzle for a brake or suppressor, with Bentz chamber on the backside and more threading. Like most other Ruger clones, Bergara threads barrels to the receiver rather than holding them with a v-block.

This does not close off the world of aftermarket 10/22 barrels for the Bergara receiver. The receiver also accepts traditional slip-fit barrels with a v-block. Though, KIDD, Volquartsen, and 10/22 experts like gunsmith Joe Charon will tell you there's no accuracy advantage to threading over a v-block. I believe them because if threading were some secret sauce, they'd all be doing it. Threading still might have some advantages, though, from banging rifles around to idiot-proofing the barrel swap process. (My guess is most home-built 10/22s have overtightened v-block screws.) The threaded receiver was a bold move on Bergara's part and could hint at a real sea change in the world of 10/22s. The patent design works in a way that the receiver can take non-threaded barrels, too.

Additionally, the BXR's receiver comes with an integral 30 MOA Pic rail and a cleaning hole. There are three holes drilled into the end of the receiver, in addition to the cleaning hole for future rear tang integration.

The HMR-like stock has a single sling stud in the front and the buttstock, plus forward and aft flush-mount QD cups. The buttstock has a lovely hand hook and extra texturing at the touchpoints. There are dimples in the buttstock to mark drilling locations for a Karsten-style cheek riser, which hints at a bright and features-rich future for the BXR line. Bergara has stated multiple times it is all-in on rimfire, and if you look at this rifle hard enough, you can see where it's going.

Bergara B-14R and BMR

Bergara's first bolt-action rimfire, the B-14R, is built on a full-sized Remington 700 footprint, so it's com-

US 20200333097A1

(19) **United States**

(12) **Patent Application Publication** (10) Pub. No.: **US 2020/0333097 A1**

HENDRICKS et al. (43) Pub. Date: **Oct. 22, 2020**

(54) **FIREARM WITH INTERCHANGEABLE THREADED AND NON-THREADED BARREL - RECEIVER CONNECTION**

(71) Applicant: **BLACKPOWDER PRODUCTS, INC.**, Lawrenceville, GA (US)

(72) Inventors: **Mark D. HENDRICKS**, Duluth, GA (US); **George A. HAWTHORN**, Kalispell, MT (US)

(73) Assignee: **BLACKPOWDER PRODUCTS, INC.**, Lawrenceville, GA (US)

(21) Appl. No.: **16/390,395**

(22) Filed: **Apr. 22, 2019**

Publication Classification

(51) **Int. Cl.**
    F41A 21/48   (2006.01)
(52) **U.S. Cl.**
    CPC *F41A 21/485* (2013.01); *F41A 21/487* (2013.01); *F41A 21/482* (2013.01)

(57)   **ABSTRACT**

A firearm having a threaded barrel-receiver connection, with a threaded receiver opening for cooperative engagement with a threaded barrel. The receiver is also compatible with a clamping system for engagement of an unthreaded barrel, so that threaded and unthreaded barrels may be used interchangeably. The threads of the receiver may have a flat crested thread profile for sliding engagement upon installation of an unthreaded barrel.

The unique BXR receiver allows for threaded Bergara barrels or standard slip-fit 10/22 aftermarket barrels.

patible with the vast universe of Model 700 triggers, stocks, chassis, and bases. The rifle sits in the company's excellent, fully adjustable HMR stock with an integral aluminum bedding rail and takes a Bergara-designed ACIS-pattern magazine converted to .22 LR. The rifle also feeds well from similar Vudoo and RimX magazines. The BMR, or Bergara Micro Rimfire, is nearly identical, except it takes smaller traditionally sized magazines.

Bergara cuts the first-class Spanish-made button barrels with a "proprietary match chamber." It's tight and engraves bullets from ELEY, Lapua, and CCI deeply. The two-piece, two-lug floating bolt could be mistaken for a Ruger 77/22. DIY headspace adjustment

is possible by shimming the bolt, which often requires lathe work on most rimfires. The B-14R comes in two models, one with a 4140-steel barrel, the other with a lightweight carbon-wrapped tube.

The action shares the Remington 700's footprint, but like Bergara's centerfires, it has several improvements over the original Ilion design. An extended collar incorporates and conceals the recoil lug. The B-14R has a full-sized recoil lug, unlike actions from Vudoo and RimX, which both have short and slender integrated lugs. The Bergara has an 8 1/16-inch overall length, just like the centerfire short-action and the same 90-degree throw. Hanus said their goal was to make a trainer in .22 LR that matched Bergara's cen-

The Bergara BXR Carbon Fiber model shaves ounces, and maintains .22 LR precision.

The Bergara B-14R bolt next to a Ruger 77/71 bolt, which informs its bolt nose design.

terfire rifles, and that's 100 percent what they did.

Full rifles and barreled actions come with either Bergara's No. 6 (heavy) profile 18-inch, 4140 Chromoly steel barrel or a No. 5 profile 18-inch carbon-fiber barrel. Both have CIP "match" chambers — not SAAMI — as the rifles are built and proven in Spain. They're both threaded 1/2-28 for a suppressor or muzzle device with European-style metric M27x3 threads on the barrel shank. BPI is working with several premium barrel manufacturers to get drop-in options in the U.S. market.

The bolt design is not original. Of the several variants tested by Bergara, the Ruger-style two-piece design worked the best with its action and ACIS-patterned magazine, Hanus said. The mid-lug lockup provided ample space for the .22 LR round and high magazine feed lips to line up with the chamber. The

bolt's front half has wings that slot into the raceway and do not rotate when you cycle the bolt. What looks like two pinned extractors on the bolt face are an extractor and a tensioner that grab the rim of a .22 LR cartridge from the magazine and slot it into the chamber. Bergara calls this a push-feed system, but it's much more akin to a control feed as the bolt grabs and holds positive control of the round from about the halfway point between magazine and chamber. The bolt doesn't appear to have the grabbing power of a Vudoo or a RimX, but it is not a flimsy push-feed design, either.

The bolt separates behind the wings and before the lugs, so it's possible to add shims to tighten up the headspace. This feature lets users optimize headspace at home. It also helps make factory rifles more accurate by making up for slight variances in barrel seating depth and extractor cut timing with a little handwork on the bolt. TriggerShims.com sells a kit for the Bergara bolt. The rim's recesses in the bolt face measure a slim 0.030 inch, so a few thousandths of the needed 0.039- to 0.043-inch headspace is taken up between the action and barrel fit.

The bolt breaks down quickly. Remove the bolt from the rifle. Cock it. Near the front of the shroud, near the bottom edge, you'll see a square cut slot through the shroud. Slide a 0.050-inch Allen wrench through the space to capture the firing spring. Next, unscrew the bolt shroud and remove the cocking mechanism. To separate the bolt body, drive out the small pin near the recoil lugs. The shims sit between the mid-body lugs and the winged front section. It's bone simple and much easier to break down than a traditional Remington 700 bolt, as with Bergara's centerfire rifles.

The total package is remarkably accurate out of the box, quickly laying down sub-MOA groups at 50 yards, and in the case of my B-14R at 100 with Lapua Center-X. It's possible to bleed more accuracy from this system with a little work, such as a better trigger and bedding, but that is the case with nearly every factory rifle.

What Bergara has done here cannot be understated. Until it came along, the only Remington 700 footprint, full-sized .22 LR trainers ran well north of $2,000. You can find this rifle for half of that. The barreled action sells for less than $600. That puts this platform in the hands of many. Most of my friends have a $1,000 rifle or two in their gun safe. Very few own a $2,000 gun. Bergara is giving us a grown-up rimfire we can afford.

CZ

"From the start, we wanted to build a culture of promoting and encouraging modularity and aftermarket support." – Zachary Hein, CZ-USA

Spend any time among smallbore competitors or serious squirrel hunters, and you'll bump into *Česká zbrojovka Uherský Brod* or CZ — widely considered the best value in rimfire rifles. You just get more for your

money with a CZ. To fully understand why, it's best to consider the history.

The earliest Czech firearms trace back to the 1370s, but like so much of modern European manufacturing, the most relevant threads spin out of Nazi Germany and the political fallout of World War II. In October 1918, the Czech and Slovak people declared their independence from the Austro-Hungarian Empire and established Czechoslovakia's new state. The new government created the national *Československá Zbrojovka* or "Czechoslovakian Armory" in the city of Brno.

After the Treaty of Versailles disarmed Germany, *Československá Zbrojovka* and *Zbrojovka Brno* or the "Weapons Factory of Brno" began production of Mauser and Mannlicher rifles. In the mid-1920s, a new factory in Brno brought automobile production lines under the roof and the expanded bolt-action rifle and machine gun production. In the 1930s, it diversified further with Remington-licensed typewriters and tractors.

In 1936, Adolf Hitler openly rejected Versailles' terms with Western Germany's re-militarization along the French border. As the specter of war re-emerged on the continent, *Československá Zbrojovka* opened a new weapons factory in Uherský Brod in eastern Czechoslovakia — far away from the German border. Early production focused on military arms, particularly aircraft machine guns, military pistols, and smallbore rifles. Two years later, the Nazis annexed the Czech-controlled Sudetenland before pushing into historically Czech lands in March 1939. With the Czechoslovakian government in exile, the Germans took the territory, managed under various sham governments, but all as part of the Third Reich.

When the victorious Allies divided Europe at the end of the war, the Czech and Slovak people landed in Soviet hands. Czechoslovakia, along with its highly regarded manufacturing facilities Zbrojovka Brno and Uherský Brod, went communist.

The *Wehrmacht* and the Communists both wanted a quality .22 LR military training rifle, an inexpensive, mass-produced firearm to train marksmanship on the cheap. In 1943 or 1944, at the occupying Germans' request, Zbrojovka Brno developed what became known as the BRNO Model 1. In 1947, the Model 1 was mass-produced for export, and in 1954 a parallel model was released, as the BRNO Model 2, stamped ZKM-452 — an acronym for *Zbrojovka* (for the national arsenal), *Koucký* (for the rifle's designer, Josef Koucký) and *Malorážka* (literally «small arms» in Czech.) I suspect the «52» in the model name 452 comes from its development year or when development started. CZ-USA says this is plausible but could not confirm it.

Allied bombing destroyed Zbrojovka Brno at the end of the war, and most Česká Zbrojovka arms production continued at Uherský Brod, known now by its initials CZUB. The communist Ministry of Foreign Trade and Czechoslovak Proof Authority soon after decided any rifle built for export would bear the name Brno, as it had greater international name recognition. (Zbrojovka Brno was rebuilt and continued to make BRNO rifles into the 1970s.) In 1989, after the Velvet Revolution, the one-party communist system collapsed, and in 1993 Czechoslovakia amicably split into two countries, the Czech Republic and Slovakia.

CZUB was privatized during that political transition from communism to democracy — and one country to two. Over the decades, the Uherský Brod facility has expanded with the factory walls built out to the city streets on all sides. Today, it's the largest small arms facility globally, as measured by square footage under roof, and employs more than 1,800 people.

In 1997, the subsidiary CZ-USA established itself to import small arms into the U.S. BRNO Model rifles, widely known for their accuracy and affordability, had trickled into the U.S. through the 1960s, 70s, and 80s, under various exporter/importer agreements. Still, with CZ-USA, the door blew wide open. The wide availability of the popular Czech military trainer, the CZ 452, hit North America.

Old School: The Model 2 to the 452

Compared to the Model 1, the Model 2 had a rear sliding tangent sight marked off from 25 to 200 meters. (For collectors, this is the fastest way to identify them.) The Model 2 also came with an improved Winchester Model 70-style trigger, vent holes in the bolt, a narrower crescent-shaped ejection port, and a Mauser-like perpendicular top safety, and there were various other BRNO rimfire models (Model 2E, 3, 3S, etc.). Still, the Model 2 in its proper "military trainer" style was

The author's new squirrel rifle: a CZ 457 Premium with a Lilja .17 HM2 barrel and Maven optic.

the most produced. CZ keeps production numbers close to the chest, but collectors believe about 140,000 Model 2s were manufactured, compared to around 7,000 of the target-specific Model 3. Collectors have also figured out how to identify Brno-made Model 2s versus those produced in Uherský Brod and prefer the Brno models.

The cold hammer-forged carbon steel barrels were central to these early rifles' success — a process still used in part today. It began by "seasoning" the steel, leaving it outside and exposed to the elements for at least one year, forcing the metal through several natural freeze/thaw cycles. "It's a little science and a lot of tradition," says Zachary Hein, Marketing Communications Manager for CZ-USA, who traveled to the Brno workshop to watch the 452 Grand Finale rifles built on the original machines. Blanks are drilled with a bore diameter greater than .22 and then fed into a cold hammer forge, a machine which Hein says is about "the size of a semi-tractor." The barrel steel is drawn over a .22-caliber mandrel as the forge's giant circular hammer slams down around it, molding the rifling into the barrel by brute force. This method is the "cold hammer forge" process.

Barrels are lapped and threaded at the tenon (except in .17 HM2 rifles where gunsmiths pinned barrels to the receiver). "They screwed the barrel onto the receiver, then [the builders] physically used their hip. Literally, they put their body weight into the breaker bar to make sure it was tight," Hein remembers. "It was incredibly old school, but that's the way they used to build them." This method effectively sets the headspace by feel.

On gun store shelves, consumers couldn't necessarily spot the old-world build techniques, but they could spot the stocks in a hot second. What set the 452s apart from so many other .22s was the wood. In the 1990s and early 2000s, many rifles, especially inexpensive ones, moved away from walnut to polymer and synthetic stocks. CZ shelved a few synthetics but never slowed down on more classic styles in American and Turkish walnut, along with less expensive models in beechwood. The stock lines and handling of many of its designs were true sporters — nimble, quick pointing. Some of the walnut ones even had excellent figuring, which no one expected then or now from a $500 rifle. CZ fans refer to these specimens as "hitting the wood lottery." Even today, order a walnut-stocked CZ, and you might get one consistent with the price, or you may get something many degrees greater.

The Model 2/452 design ran in regular production from 1954 to 2011, when CZ updated it to the 455. There was also briefly a 453 with a French-style set trigger. Diehard 452 fans collectively groaned when CZ discontinued the rifle — or rather, replaced it by the switch barrel 455. CZ-USA spearheaded a final run of 452 Grand Finale edition rifles as a final goodbye: a premium build with a walnut and ebony stock, hand-engraved metalwork, and a jeweled bolt. It would be a fitting end for a design birthed in conflict. It outlived Nazism and communism — and found widespread success in the land of the free and the home of the brave.

New School: The 455 and 457

It is not easy to own a gun in Europe, which is why switch-barrel rifles, where the shooter can swap vari-

*The heavy-barreled
CZ 452 Varmint.*

ous caliber barrels — and multi-barreled firearms, like drillings — are so popular across the pond. Legally, it's one gun. When the Czechs planned the updated 455 with a switch barrel, the Americans at CZ-USA enthusiastically supported it. "From the start, we wanted to build a culture of promoting and encouraging modularity and aftermarket support," Hein said. "When they talked up the new design, we were like, 'Heck yeah!' We looked at it like the AR-15 model."

With the 452, different calibers had different bottom metals and various stock inlets, with the 455 all standardized. CZ upgraded the machinery that made the new receivers. While the 452 was a milled receiver, CNC machine tools cut the 455 to much tighter tolerances.

By standardizing the receiver mounts, footprint, barrels, and triggers across the lineup, it created a kind of swap ability and aftermarket of custom options that the rimfire world had only then seen with Ruger's 10/22. But this was a bolt-action. A parent could buy their kid a CZ 455 Scout, with a short iron-sighted barrel and youth-sized stock, and swap it for a full-sized stock with a longer barrel and optics as the child grew up. Or, more likely, a serious rifle shooter could build a full-sized .22 LR that replicated the look and feel of their centerfire precision rifle.

As the 455s came into the U.S. in late 2010 and early 2011, CZ-USA cultivated the idea of a serious .22 LR for a serious shooter. On gun sites like Sniper's Hide, shooters and tinkerers were already building full-sized "replicas" of their centerfire guns in .22 LR for low cost, no recoil training. CZ-USA partnered with Boyd's and rolled out a model in the "Tacticool" stock (now called the Pro Varmint) with a tactical-inspired

vertical grip, raised Monte Carlo cheekpiece, and a butt hook for shooting off bags. Suddenly, there was a "sniper-style" .22 LR on the market for around $500. Chambered in .17 HMR, it quickly proved an excellent and affordable varmint rig, and hunters jumped on board.

CZ also partnered with fellow Kansas City business, Manners Composite Stocks, and rolled out the CZ 455 Varmint Precision Trainer in .22 LR. As long-range PRS-style shooting skyrocketed in popularity, competition rifle shooters started requesting factory "trainers" for low-cost, low-recoil practice. This sentiment was very much the same ask militaries had in World War II and the post-war years. Fundamentals of hitting what you aim at do not change, whether it's a .22 LR or .416 Barrett. With the 457 Varmint Precision Trainer, shooters running a 6.5 Creedmoor in a Manners at a weekend match now had a weekday trainer that could safely spit .22 LRs at steel targets off the back deck. Make those steel targets less than an inch wide, and suddenly it's possible to drill positional shooting like kneeling, sitting, or shooting off a barricade at 25 or 50 yards — skills that translate when shooting larger calibers at long distances. This info is all old news now, but CZ was the first prominent manufacturer to get behind the precision shooting community in this way, and the community responded big time.

The 455 was a huge success, but there were many things that the European design didn't get correct for an American market. CZ corrected these in the 2019 update with the Model 457 by swapping the stamped bottom metal for a sculpted two-piece system. Instead of the "backward" European version on the 455 and its predecessors, it installed a push-to-fire safety. The bolt rotation was tweaked from 90 degrees to 60, so big scopes can be mounted lower, and the action can be run faster with one hand while in the firing position. CZ also lightened the firing pin for faster strikes and further improved lock time by cutting almost an inch off the overall action length. CZ slab-sided it to make it as trim and lightweight as possible. The ho-hum 455 triggers, which needed aftermarket springs to sing or a full-custom replacement like a BScar Trigger, were switched out for a fully adjustable model with a pull weight reduced to nothing right out of the box.

The 2019 rollout of the 457 was a big deal in the rimfire world, with nine models ranging from a new Manners-stocked Varmint Precision Trainer to the traditional sporter American and the youth Scout. In 2020, CZ updated the series with a 457 Varmint Precision Chassis model. It sported a CZ-USA-designed billet aluminum chassis with a Luth-AR buttstock and a very European Hogsback 457 Jaguar with a 28.5-inch iron-sighted barrel. But what set the 455 and now the 457 apart was the thriving aftermarket. It was now possible not just to buy a quality, affordable, accurate .22 LR bolt-action but to take that rifle and make it your own.

The "Custom" 457

When it comes to rimfire rifles, there are generally two schools of thought. I consider the Savage approach — making a rifle that shoots great and is affordable, with a great price vs. performance ratio. The second is the Ruger approach — create a rifle that's affordable and modular, then support and encourage an aftermarket, so shooters can make them as accurate as they want on their dime. CZ straddles these two schools of thought. On the one hand, you can find a CZ 457 American Combo with a .22 LR and .17 HMR barrel set online for less than $500. They shoot incredibly well right out of the box. Half-inch groups at 50 yards (or very close to it) should be expected from the entire 457 lineup with a factory barrel and match ammo. But the 457 platform also provides for the tinkerer who wants to work their rifle to the next level.

There are stock and chassis options from all the great builders such as Manners, MDT, and Masterpiece Arms. There are barrels from Proof and Lilja, among others. I've switched a CZ Varmint Precision Chassis to a Proof that's among my go-to NRL22 rigs. My new squirrel gun of choice is a 457 with a limited-run Lilja

	457 American	457 Varmint MTR	457 Varmint Precision Chassis	457 Varmint Precision Trainer
Action	457	457	457	457
Bolt Type	Three lugs, 60°	Three lugs, 60°	Three lugs, 60°	three lugs, 60°
Stock Type	American-style sport	One-piece, target style	Precision chassis	Manners composite
Stock Material	Turkish walnut	Turkish walnut	Aluminum chassis	fiberglass
Cheek Riser	No	No	No	no
Total Weight	6.17 lbs.	7.5 lbs.	7.65 lbs.	7.1 lbs
Barrel Type	Cold hammer-forged	Cold hammer-forged	Heavy tapered cold hammer-forged	heavy tapered cold hammer forged
Barrel Length	24.8 in.	20.5 in.	16.5 in.	16.5"
Trigger	457	457	457	457
Trigger Weight	2.5 lbs.	2.5 lbs.	2.5 lbs.	2.5 lbs
Mag. Capacity	5 or 10	5 or 10	5 or 10	5 or 10
Calibers	.22 LR, .17 HMR, .22 WMR	.22 LR	.22 LR	.22 LR
MSRP	$515	$785	$1,039	$1,189

.17 HM2 stainless tube. There are trigger springs and kits from YoDave and BScar, plus a drop-in trigger from Timney. From muzzle to buttpad, there are options to make the CZ more accurate and make it your own. (For a deep dive on upgrading CZs, see the chapter Custom Shop.)

Or you can take it straight from the box, never touch it, and still have an excellent rifle.

The current vogue in precision rimfire is Remington 700 everything. Vudoo, RimX, Bergara, and Ultimatum all have near custom-level .22 LR actions that fit a Model 700 footprint, opening the wide world of aftermarket Remington stocks, triggers, and accessories to small-bore. You can't say the same of the 457, but what the CZ has that the others lack is the performance at a price point most shooters can justify. It's a good rifle as sold but can expand as a shooter's interest does. This versatility should not be understated.

There's also something to be said for *not* having an oversized ACIS-pattern magazine that Vudoo invented and those we're now seeing in RimX, Bergara, and other rifles. Like fellow European Anschütz, the .22 LR magazines from CZ just work. You don't have to pay special attention to how you load them; they feed well, don't often mar bullets, are inexpensive, and from a pure rimfire shooter perspective, they're not clunky. Some have said larger ACIS mags are easier to handle, but I fumble the big magazines more than the little jobs you can insert with two fingers.

I run a small monthly NRL22 match, and the question new shooters always ask me is, 'What rifle should I get?' I send them what's become a form e-mail, linked out to a few different write-ups, with options ranging from $300 Savages to $3,000 Vudoos. Nine times out of ten, these new shooters come back with a CZ. Why? Because when you do your homework, there isn't a better deal in bolt-action rimfire rifles. There are more expensive rifles. There are more accurate rifles. But with CZ, you get every nickel worth, and then some.

The Ruger 10/22

"To be the leading provider of quality products for the shooting, hunting, and rugged outdoor enthusiast."

William Batterman Ruger was born in Brooklyn, New York, in 1916. His mother was from a wealthy family of department store magnates. As R. L. Wilson writes in *Ruger and His Guns: A History of the Man, the Company & Their Firearms:*

"Adolph Ruger was a fairly successful trial lawyer who became a heavy drinker when he started having

CZ-USA partnered with Boyd's and rolled out a model in the "Tacticool" stock (now called the Pro Varmint) with a tactical-inspired vertical grip, raised Monte Carlo cheekpiece, and a butt hook for shooting off bags.

The classy-looking CZ 457 American.

The long-barreled CZ Jaguar R.

problems in his law practice. In 1918 he moved with his family to a house in Albemarle Terrace, in the then-fashionable Flatbush section of Brooklyn. He also purchased a farm farther out on Long Island, where the family stayed off and on. Inevitably, however, his alcoholism had a terrible effect on his finances, and when the economy sagged, on the eve of the Great Depression, Adolph was unable to keep up with payments on an office building he had financed with his brother and law partner, Julius. His home was also heavily mortgaged, and the bank foreclosed. When his parents' marriage ended, Bill and his mother moved into his grandfather Karl William Batterman's comfortable house, also in Brooklyn, where he spent the remainder of his childhood."

Adolph's son Bill would start the largest firearm manufacturer in the United States and one of the world's largest. Notably, Sturm, Ruger & Company would remain financially solvent through its more than 70 years and counting without ever leaning on foreign ownership or management. That's no small feat in the volatile world of firearms, where many big companies have fought rounds of bankruptcies, restructures, and foreign sales. Lessons Ruger learned by watching his father's plight, he learned well.

Bill Ruger grew up in New York City in the 1920s

and 1930s. Life was vastly different back then. Ruger and his friends set up a basement range in a Brooklyn apartment building where they practiced with a Remington Model 12 pump-action .22 — a gift to Bill from his father on Bill's 12th birthday. They shot a Spanish-American War surplus .30-.40 Krag ordered from the back of *Popular Mechanics* at the end of the Fulton Street rail line not far from present-day JFK International Airport.

In 1938, as a college student at the University of North Carolina, Chapel Hill, Bill Ruger converted an empty room in his dormitory into a machine shop. He designed his first firearm, an innovative light machine gun for the military. U.S. Army Ordinance saw so much promise it hired him as a gun designer at the government-run Springfield Armory.

After two years he left, to work again on his machine gun design, yet at the outbreak of World War II, he took a job with Auto-Ordinance, where he spent the war in a prototype shop. He struck out on his own again and, in 1949, entered into a partnership with Alexander McCormick Sturm. The .22 LR Ruger Standard Model pistol came out that year. The pistol, and the partnership, would go on to change the American firearms industry forever.

Sturm died in 1951, but not before designing the famous eagle crest that would identify Ruger firearms worldwide. In 1953, Bill Ruger developed a precision investment casting method for gun parts — often called "lost wax" casting — creating an impression in the mold filled with molten alloyed metal. It is a low-cost, high-volume production process that allowed

the young company to scale quickly and beat many of its competitors on price.

10/22 History and Development

Bill Ruger's boyhood rifle, and his first successful firearm design, the Ruger Standard pistol, were both .22 LRs. In many respects, the company was founded on and built by rimfire. But no one, Bill Ruger included, could have predicted the success of its modular autoloader, the Ruger 10/22. As of 2015, the company has sold more than 7 million of them.

According to Wilson, the design was a joint project between Harry Sefried, Bill Ruger, and Doug McClenahan, with plans forming as early as the late 1950s. The rotary magazine was inspired by one of Bill's favorite hunting rifles, the Savage Model 99. Long before anyone spoke much of "training rifles" or complimentary centerfire and rimfire rifles, Ruger's goal was to build a .22 LR carbine with the fit and feel of his .44 Magnum Model 44 Carbine. (The Model 44, and the 10/22 that would follow, had the lines and barrel band of the famous M1 Carbine.) A Ruger ad from the early 1960s promotes the two rifles as a pair, "the ultimate .22 RF self-loader" next to "the perfect brush country deer rifle." The 10/22 first sold for $54.50, the Ruger 44 for $108.

As Walt Kuleck writes in his excellent book, *The Ruger 10/22 Complete Owner's and Assembly Guide,* the magic of the 10/22 stems from three creative innovations: the barrel block, the rotary magazine, and the bolt.

"Today's 10/22 owner can be forgiven if she or he

CZ's Model 457 Varmint Precision Chassis model.

The CZ 457 Action.

assumes that the barrel block or v-block mounting of the 10/22's barrel was arranged so as to make barrel swapping easy," *Kuleck writes.* "Well, that it does, but the reason is not ease of barrel removal; the reason is ease of barrel installation."

Mating the steel barrel to the cast aluminum receiver proved difficult. In the 1960s, after Ruger fitted a barrel to a receiver, a metal finish like bluing was applied. A steel barrel and aluminum receiver required two different finishes — bluing for the barrel and a hardcoat anodizing process for the receiver. The parts needed to be finished separately before assembly. Screwing the barrel into the receiver, which Ruger experimented with, required a rigid clamp that blemished the finished surfaces. Dovetailing the underside of the barrel shank and securing with a v-block kept the cosmetics clean and proved faster and more cost-effective.

Rimfire rifles before the 10/22 all had tube magazines, like a Marlin Model 60 or the lever guns of the American West. Arthur Savage pioneer the detachable rotary box magazine with his Model 99, yet the idea had been in the air with similar patents popping up in Europe around the same time. Bill Ruger immediately saw the benefits of the rotary box magazine design for rimfires. First, it simplified the action. Unlike a lever gun with a tube magazine, the cartridge does not have to move backward and upward, then forward into the chamber. With a box mag, the round needed to elevate and line up with the chamber.

The rotary design provided additional benefits. A single-stack box mag feeds rounds up with spring tension. That tension changes depending on how many rounds are in the magazine. One round loaded, the spring is relatively extended and doesn't apply much pressure on the cartridge. The tenth round can be quite different. This varied amount of spring pressure on the rounds can change the angle at which the bullet feeds into the chamber on inexpensive magazines. You can see this in some mags with the naked eye. The first and last round present extreme angles, and the intermediate rounds are something in between. The different angles can cause jams or scrape and deform soft lead .22 bullets as they enter the chamber, which is detrimental to accurate shooting. It's also possible to interlock rimfire rims within a magazine

and cause a jam. If a cartridge's rim lies behind the rim under it in a box magazine, neither round will feed. (This is a known issue — or known user error in loading — with some of the newer ACIS-patterned .22 LR magazine rifles.) The rotary design cures both ailments. The feed angle is consistent round to round, and it's impossible to interlock the cartridge rims while loading.

"The third innovation that has contributed to the 10/22's success is its 'breechblock decelerator,' again from Ruger's Harry Sefried," *Kuleck writes*. "One of the challenges faced by the designers of semiauto (and full-auto) firearms is that of balancing bolt cycle speed and magazine cycle speed, thus ensuring that there is sufficient time for the magazine to present each cartridge in front of the bolt in time for the bolt to 'pick up' the cartridge."

This decelerator is how the cutout in the bolt's back meets the buffer that runs crosswise through the action's rear. The circular cutout does not squarely match the circular buffer. It's a touch low, so when the bolt travels back and connects with the buffer, the back end lifts a hair upward, puts the bolt's nose down, and slows the bolt speed. It mechanically forces the bolt to cam down just enough to slow down yet still have enough juice to pick up and chamber the

next round.

"By simply giving the bolt a bit of cam action, he created a semiautomatic .22LR rifle which, as tested by *Guns & Ammo* in 1964, exhibited the second slowest cyclic rate of the thirteen rifles tested, at 945 rounds per minute (rpm),» *Kuleck notes.* "The slowest was the Stevens 87J, at 860 rpm, followed by the Ruger at 945 rpm. The two fastest were the Remington Nylon 66 at 1560 rpm and the Mossberg 351C at an astounding 1600 rpm. Harry was certainly successful keeping the 10/22's cyclic rate reined in, contributing to the reliability and durability of the little rifle."

The 10/22 would go on to be one of the most successful rifle designs of all time. Thousands of adolescents first learned to shoot on the Ruger 10/22. It has ventilated and recycled more tin cans than the foundries of Asia. It's responsible for untold millions of squirrels and rabbits at the hands of small game hunters. The suppressed Military and Special Purpose model with a custom folding stock saw service in the Vietnam War with the U.S. Navy SEALs. It is reportedly still in service with the French and Israeli militaries. Simple, inexpensive to make, and deadly accurate with a little work, the 10/22 is a rimfire rifle for the ages.

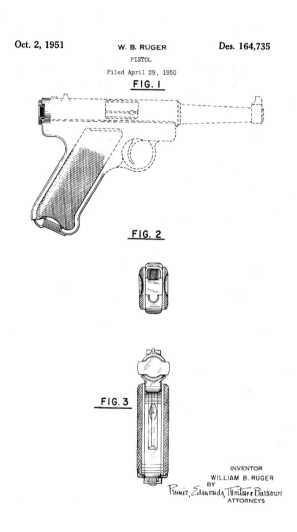

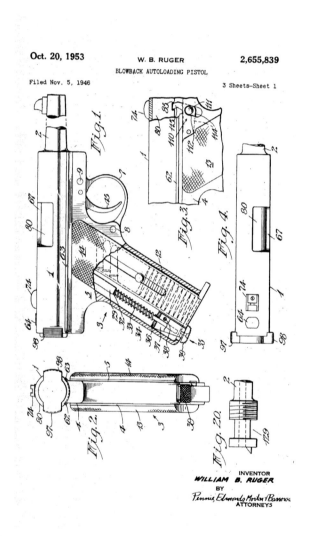

The patent illustration of Ruger's first pistol, the .22 LR Standard Model.

Modern Precision 10/22s

A utility patent in the United States generally runs for 20 years. Yet entire rifles are not often patented, rather distinguishing innovative new features are protected, like Ruger's v-block, rotary magazine, and bolt design. Also, patent holders don't always file the collection of patents that make up a rifle system together simultaneously. Copyrights, trademarks, and "likenesses" can also be protected. So, while the bulk of the 10/22 patent protections expired in the 1980s, that has not stopped Ruger from going after competitors like Rock Island Armory and Smith & Wesson for selling 10/22 clones.

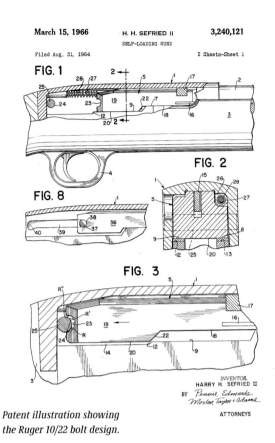

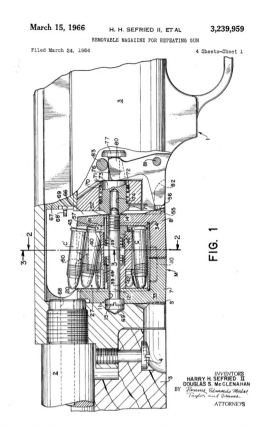

*Patent illustration showing
the Ruger 10/22 bolt design.*

The 10/22 rotary magazine was inspired by the famous Savage 99.

Ruger has filed actions against companies making low-cost alternatives to its bread-and-butter budget rifles. The high-end 10/22 builders have mainly been left alone. This strategy by Ruger — and a smart one at that — helped usher in a wave of super-premium 10/22 clones, like those from KIDD Innovative Design and Volquartsen. Ruger has not abandoned the performance market, either. In recent years, more and more tack-driving 10/22 models have come out of Newport, New Hampshire. This diversity of buying options, plus the modularity that allows any handy person to build one at home (see the chapter, Custom Shop), puts the 10/22 in the rarified air of the AR-15 — not so much a rifle model but a fully-realized weapons platform.

Ruger makes dozens of 10/22 variants. For precision shooters, only two categories are worth consideration: The Target series and the Competition series. There are two to half a dozen Target models in production at any given time, many offered as distributor exclusives.

Generally, these come in laminate hardwood stocks, with upgraded BX-Trigger groups and .920-inch straight-contour bull barrels.

Barrels are made in-house as of the early 1990s with a cold hammer-forged process. Machine operators drill a barrel blank larger than the finished bore size, then a rifled mandrel is inserted. They run a blank and mandrel through a power hammer machine that exerts 80 to 140 *tons* of force at a rate of up to 1,200 hammer strokes per minute. The entire rifling process takes about 2.5 minutes. The rifled blanks are cut to length and finished. Ruger makes its ultralight bull barrels this way, but the barrel itself is a thin length of 4140 tensioned in a .920-inch aluminum alloy barrel sleeve.

The Ruger Custom Shop builds the Competition series rifles. Ruger gears these rifles to speed matches, like Steel Challenge. It tunes others like the Model 31120 and 31127 for NRL22-style precision shooting. By most reports, they're competitive with the more expensive boutique 10/22s.

The Ruger 10/22 Target model.

Ruger 10/22 Competition model from the Custom Shop.

Gunsmiths at the Custom Shop upgrade the standard Ruger 10/22 receiver for the Competition series rifles, with many add-ons shooters developed a taste for in the aftermarket. The new receiver is CNC machined 6061-T6511 aluminum − not cast − with a rear bedding lug that better secures the receiver to the stock. The 30 MOA Pic rail isn't bolted on but is machined. (There is a cleaning hole on the backside.) The barrel gets a proprietary chamber tighter than the traditional .22 Sporting used on most 10/22s.

Of non-Ruger 10/22-style rifles, the Bergara BXR, Thompson Center (Smith & Wesson) TC/R22, Tactical Solutions, and Magnum Research are popular options. All have CNC machined receivers and many of the features found in the Ruger Competition lineup. Magnum Research rifles are available in magnum calibers. KIDD and Volquartsen make up the top-tier of 10/22 clones.

At the NRL22 National Match in 2019, six of the 10/22s shot were KIDDs, three were from Ruger, one was from Tactical Solutions, and one built on a Brownell's receiver. No one shot semi-autos at the 2020 nationals. With that match postponed due to COVID-19 and the resulting limited participation, that is not an indictment of the platform.

Of the top-tier 10/22s, perhaps the KIDD Supergrade is the most interesting. The unique barrel system has an extra-long barrel extension of 1 7/8 inches in length, compared to the standard 3/4 inch. You can also remove the rifle's barrel without taking the action out of the stock if bedded in the KIDD custom version of the Magpul X-22 stock. They also can be made with a rear tang for a second action screw behind the receiver. This revision corrects what many perceive − though they haven't proven − to be the loose or tippy one-screw married action and stock. The Supergrade also has all the bells and whistles that have earned KIDD its sterling reputation, from the radius, jeweled, and trued bolt to the great two-stage trigger.

Ruger Bolt-Action Rimfires

In May 1983, at the NRA show in Phoenix, Ruger unveiled its bolt-action Model 77/22 originally in .22 LR, and eventually in .22 WMR and the centerfire .22 Hornet. Only the Hornet is still in production among the .22s, along with the 77/17 version in .17 WSM and .17 Hornet. Ruger deserves great credit for this, as the 77/17 is one of only two .17 WSM bolt rifles on the market. (The other is the Savage B.MAG.)

Ruger designed the 77 Series as a rimfire version of the centerfire Ruger M77 − a modernized Mauser 98

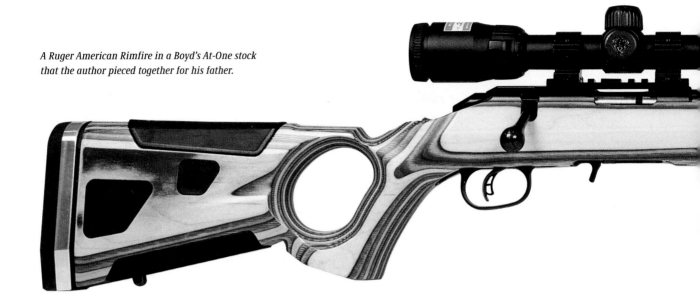

A Ruger American Rimfire in a Boyd's At-One stock that the author pieced together for his father.

design with a three-position lever safety. Centerfire or rimfire, the 77s have a two-part bolt design with a winged front half that does not rotate and a two-lug back half that rotates and cocks the striker at 90 degrees. It's a straightforward and practical design recently adopted by Bergara in its B-14R rimfire trainer.

The detachable rotary box magazine works very much like the 10/22 magazine, but they are not identical. The BX mag of the 10/22 has a rounded bottom. The JX mag of the 77/22 in .22 LR is flat. This difference seems only cosmetic as both magazines run in both guns fine.

Ruger rifles' downside is that some make it out of the factory in less than perfect order. Correcting issues with Rugers has become a specialized industry.

A noted African hand told me you'd often see PHs in Zimbabwe shooting Ruger big bores. The reason is, American hunters would show up without checking to see if their rifles worked. When they'd fail to feed and scare the living snot out of the hunter, the hunters would gift the guns to the PH, "who would take them to a gunsmith in Bulawayo who specialized in making Rugers work." The rimfires are no different.

Connecticut Precision Chamber (CPC) has built a very nice business of making Ruger rifles sing. My first 77/22 was a Gunbroker find in .22 WMR. Nice rifle, it fed fine, but it wasn't laying down the groups

I wanted. The trigger felt like how dropping a rotten melon on pavement sounds. Randy at CPC re-pinned, squared and headspaced the bolt. He set back the barrel and rechambered it. He did a trigger job. Now that old used 77/22 with the pencil barrel is among my very favorite personal rifles. It's lighter, handier, and shoots better than my much more expensive Anschütz in .22 Magnum. It shoots better groups before the barrel gets hot, too. These nuances show the upside and downside of Ruger: The rifles are fantastic, handy, well-designed, gimmick-free, classic. They're real shooters. But, it takes some occasional gunsmithing to bring all that to the surface.

Ruger Precision Rimfire (RPR)

Designers at Ruger have paid close attention to the new precision rimfire revolution and were among the first to offer a dedicated, affordable, precision .22 LR. The Ruger Precision Rimfire is a companion trainer to the larger centerfire Ruger Precision Rifle. The rimfire version is 6.8 pounds with a 35-inch overall length. The centerfire in short-action is 10.7 pounds and 43.25 inches long. Ruger builds the rimfire RPR on a polymer chassis with integral buttstock and an AR-15-style free-floated aluminum handguard. Under the handguard is AR-inspired. The barrel is a slip-fit design like a 10/22 but with a threaded barrel nut that holds it in

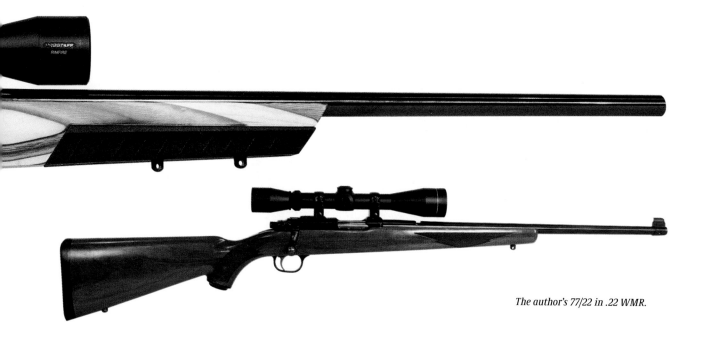

The author's 77/22 in .22 WMR.

place. The nut and barrel come off with an armorer's wrench, just like an AR barrel but easier. There are aftermarket RPR rimfire barrels from all the big players, including Shilen, Lilja, IBI, and Green Mountain.

It takes AR-15-type grips. There is an AR-style switch safety. The trigger is Ruger's take on the AccuTrigger — the Ruger Marksman, adjustable from 2.25 to 5 pounds. It's possible to modify these triggers by removing or replacing springs. This mod tends to make them an exceptional 1-pound kill switch. A 30 MOA Pic rail sits atop the receiver, and the bolt locks up at the

base of the oversized bolt handle. The throw is 90 degrees, and it draws 1.5 inches, or you can set it to pull 3 inches by removing a c-clip — the same as a short-action centerfire. It takes 10/22 magazines and comes with a 15-round BX-15 or a standard 10 rounder. For shooters with the centerfire version, the Precision Rimfire is a no-brainer. It's also a remarkably durable rifle with the AR foregrip and integrated buttstock. Accuracy reports are hit and miss, with some getting absolute barn burners. Others have had to swap barrels for peak performance.

*The Ruger
Precision Rimfire.*

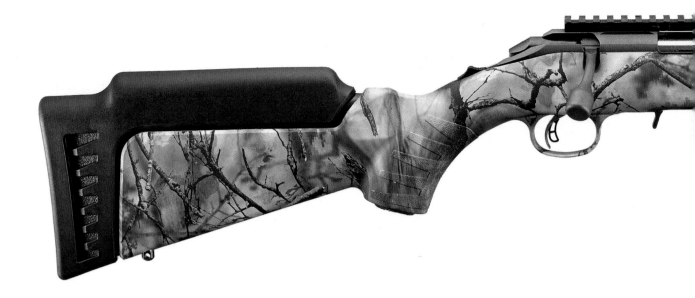

Ruger American Rimfire

Disclosure: I have a soft spot for the Ruger American Rimfire. It is the same action as the Precision Rimfire but in a sporter stock. A good friend and squirrel hunter has one he bought used for $200 in .22 WMR, and the joke is the rifle has an auto-targeting system. Point the rifle in the general direction of a squirrel, pull the trigger, and the bushy tail will die of a gunshot wound to the head. It's a deadly little rifle.

Likewise, with some work on an inexpensive sport

	Ruger Precision Rimfire	Ruger American Rimfire Long-Range Target	Ruger 77/17	Ruger 10/22 Competition
Action	American action	American action	Model 77	blowback semi
Bolt Type	Three lugs, 60°	Three lugs, 60°	three lugs, 60°	10/22-
Stock Type	Ruger Precision	M4-style precision	heavy sporter	one-piece
Stock Material	Polymer/aluminum	Polymer molded	laminate	laminate
Cheek Riser	Yes	Yes	no	yes
Total Weight	6.8 lbs.	5.9 lbs.	7 lbs	6 lbs
Overall Length	35.13 in. to 38.63 in.	38.37 in.	37.75"	36"
Barrel Type	Threaded cold hammer-forged 1137 alloy steel	Threaded cold hammer-forged 0.860 in. bull barrel	threaded cold hammer-forged 1137 alloy steel	threaded cold hammer-forged 1137 alloy steel
Barrel Length	18 in.	18 in.	18.50 in	16.12"
Trigger	Ruger American	Ruger American	Model 77	Ruger BX
Mag. Capacity	10 or 15, Ruger BX	10, Ruger BX	6 rounds	10 round, Ruger BX
Calibers	.22 LR, .17 HMR	.22 LR, .17 HMR, .22 WMR	.17 WSM, 22 hornet	.22 LR
MSRP	$529	$469	$1,069	$899

The Ruger American Rimfire.

.22 LR kit version, we got my dad's Ruger American spitting dime-sized groups at 50 yards with CCI Mini Mags. The affordable factory sporter stock is relatively rigid and comes with brass pillars installed. This good bedding is a contributing factor as to why they shoot so well. The barrel contacted the forend, but I quickly floated it by sanding out the channel. There is zero doubt in my mind it's the best of the inexpensive polymer factory stocks.

For dedicated precision shooting, pay attention to the Target and Long-Range Target rifles. As with the 10/22s, the Target line is mainly heavy barreled rifles in laminate wood stocks. The Ruger American Long-Range Target Rimfire is a beautiful total precision package that you can get at a street price of around $500. The synthetic stock calls to mind the famous A4 with a more vertical grip than standard, adjustable comb riser, and forend lines that run parallel to the barrel. There's a hand hook in the buttstock and flush-mount QD cups forward and aft, and it has the same excellent brass bedding block system as the sporter. This rifle is a direct attack on the NRL22 base class with all the features needed to perform at a fantastic price.

Sako/Tikka

100 years of accuracy and counting.

The Finnish people have long been precision-minded. Much of that bore from historical and geographical necessity. A country about the size of New Mexico, Finland shares an 832-mile border with Russia. That has led to many conflicts over the generations and a mid-20th-century need for accurate shooting. This is the legacy of Sako, Tikka, and Lapua.

From the middle ages, the Catholic and crusading Kingdom of Sweden dominated the Finn lands until the 1809 Finnish War when most of the Finnish-speaking landmass ceded to the Russian Empire. Under the Russians, the Tikkakoski factory was established in 1893 in the northern city of Jyväskylä to produce sewing machines and other household goods. Very quickly after Finland declared independence in 1917, the factory converted its production lines to gun parts. Sako — an acronym for *Suojeluskuntain Ase-ja Konepaja Osakeyhtiö* that translates to "Firearms and Machine workshop of the Civil Guard" — was established in 1921 to build rifles for the new and independent country.

During World War II, Finland fought a series of wars against the Soviets and the Germans, armed mostly with updated and improved Mosin-Nagant rifles from Tikkakoski and Sako. During the 105-day Winter War of 1939 and 1940, they beat back the Russians with a fraction of the troops, tanks, or air support of their numerically superior rival. The Finns took 70,000 casualties to the Soviets' estimated 320,000 or more. Much of that success was due to the Finns' guerrilla tactics, dividing the Soviet lines, then picking them apart with

sniper fire in the frigid below-zero conditions. (In early January, temperatures on the battlefield dipped below -45 degrees.) The Finns knew their country, how to stay warm, and often skied into position through the thick snow-strewn woodlands to strike, then vanish back into the trees. The Sako bolt-action rifle dealt more death than the young country's ineffective fleet of tanks and airplanes.

The Finnish sniper Simo Häyhä, nicknamed "The White Death," killed between 505 and 542 Russian soldiers with his Sako-produced Mosin-Nagant. The Model M/28-30 shot the accurized Finnish variant 7.62x53mmR and was widely used for target shooting before the war by the Civilian Guard. It had iron sights with a rear micrometer marked from 150 to 2,000 meters. Much later, Lapua's radar trajectory tested the

round and the sight markings. It found it remarkably accurate at all distances. Many remember Häyhä as the deadliest sniper in world history — a distinction almost lost to time. Decades after the war, someone discovered his journals hidden in an old drawing box and only then did the full scale of his remarkable war record fully come to light.

Accurate rifles kept modern Finland independent. After the Winter War, the Russians came at the Finns again, with the Continuation War of 1941 to 1944. Unfortunately, Finland was helped considerably by Nazi Germany this time before turning on the Germans in the Lapland War of 1944 and 1945. During this highly volatile time in Europe, Finland is something of a wonder. Russians were pressing in from the East, Germans from the North through occupied Norway, yet

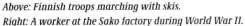

Above: Finnish troops marching with skis.
Right: A worker at the Sako factory during World War II.

The Tikka T1x Ultimate Precision Rifle (UPR).

neither occupied Finland. The country wasn't taken over or complicit in Nazi war production, like Sweden who's iron ore fields fed German foundries. The Fins held their land from all-comers with skis and bolt-action rifles. Look at a list of the most deaths by the percentage of the population in World War II by country, and Finland doesn't even make the top 20 — and unlike most other countries, it shared long, hostile borders with Soviet Russia and the Third Reich.

After the war, the arms factory Tikkakoski was considered a German-owned company by the Allied Powers. Its assets were confiscated for the Soviet Union in 1947, discontinuing firearms production and focusing again on sewing machines. Sako remained independent after the war, owned by the Finnish Red Cross. Finnish businesspeople bought Tikka from the Soviets in 1957; in 1962, they sold it into private hands. Rifle production continued, and in 1983 Sako bought Tikka.

In 1986, the arms manufacturing division of the government-owned Valmet conglomerate purchased the combined company. The state relinquished ownership in a 2000 sale to the Italians, Beretta Holdings Group.

Sniper rifles during WWII or precision rimfires today, the Finns extrude accuracy. It says something, too, that in a world market where firearms manufacturers try to do everything — hunting rifles, ARs, shotguns, pistols, ammunition, optics — Sako and Tikka only do one thing. They make accurate bolt-action rifles.

Sako Quad

Finland might be the best place in Europe to own a gun. About 12 percent of the population owns firearms, yet every gun purchase requires a license and registration, which must state the intended use, i.e., hunting, target shooting, etc. Finns can use firearms outside that use, say a hunting rifle for target shoot-

The first-ever Tikkakoski factory was established in 1893 in Jyväskylä, Finland. Photo: Sako/Tikka

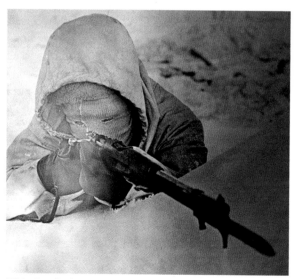

White Death, Simo Häyhä, is credited with the most sniper kills in combat ever recorded. Most of them unfolded over the 10-month Winter War.

The SAKO Quad Range.
Photos: Sako/Tikka

SAKO Finnfire Hunter.

The SAKO
Finnfire Varmint.

ing, which is why switch-barrel rifles have become so popular there and in the rest of Europe.

In rimfire, the Sako Quad modernized the switch-barrel idea in the early 2000s. With the Quad, a shooter had one rifle, one set of paperwork, but four barrels in four calibers — .17 HM2, .22 LR, .17 HMR, and .22 WMR. The Quad was equally at home in a smallbore match or a small game hunt.

Swapping a barrel takes less than 20 seconds. Insert the provided hex-wrench barrel tool into the locking bolt and unscrew it. Then rotate the barrel and lift it forward. The barrels are color-coded — blue is .17 Mach 2, red is .17 HMR, green is .22 LR, and yellow is .22 WMR. Of course, the point of impact will change caliber to caliber, but the lockup is so tight that the rifle returns to zero within a click or two when taking off and reinstalling the same barrel.

For example, sight in the .22 LR barrel, remove it, shoot the .17 HMR, then put the .22 LR back on and reshoot it. If you didn't touch your optic when shooting the .17 HMR, that .22 LR would still hold after the swap. This repeatability, coupled with the speed of changing barrels, is what makes the system so noteworthy. (Some centerfire precision rifles have gone this route, too. Such as the Accuracy International AX Multi-Caliber, which has deployed with U.S. special operators.)

For a spell, Burris had a color-coded rifle scope for the Quad with different turret rings for various calibers, mostly unnecessary. A competent rifle shot will quickly learn, say, when they zero the rifle at 50 yards in .22 LR, the .17 HMR point of impact at 100 is X number of clicks up and Y number of clicks left. This correlation is not difficult to keep track of over multiple calibers.

Modern ballistic apps like the Kestrel 5700 Elite even have a Zero Height (elevation) and Zero Offset (windage) feature to correct known point of impact changes within the ballistic calculation. With this, a shooter theoretically doesn't need to re-zero the rifle, only dope the scope with the provided solution for the target at a distance. Would I switch barrels and let electronics tell me where my point of impact lays without taking confirmation shots before a match or a hunting trip? Of course not, but it speaks to the sophistication and repeatability of these systems that this workflow is even possible.

The Sako hammer-forged barrels are free-floated in all the various Quad stocks, so the receiver bedding is not affected by the barrel switch. The barrel is held to the receiver only by the locking lugs and a single barrel bolt, accessible from the stocked rifle's underside in front of the triggerguard — without removing the barreled action from the stock. In the receiver is a spring-loaded plate at 6 o'clock that captures the barrel shank and correctly indexes it with a 12 o'clock lug in the receiver. As you push the barrel home and twist, it snaps into place.

The Quad's 5- and 10-round box magazines are the same for all four calibers. Sako includes a spacer for the shorter .22 LR and .17 HM2 rounds. The .17 HMR/.22 WMR does not have one. Spacers can be removed or added to mags as needed.

The two-locking-lug bolt has a 50-degree lift and a 1.60-inch throw, reminiscent of the Anschütz 54. The short, fast-firing pin travels 0.20-inch for a speedy lock time. The single-stage trigger, as with all Sako and Tikka triggers, is excellent. It's crisp, with zero creep, and breaks over with a sharp crack. There is little overtravel. The factory trigger pull weight is 2 to 4 pounds, but it's possible to get it much lighter.

The Quad comes in five models. Four of them are barrel and stock variations. The Hunter Pro and Varmint have lovely walnut stocks. The Synthetic and Heavy Barrel have polymer stocks. The Hunter Pro and Synthetic have iron-sighted sporter contour barrels, the Varmint and Heavy Barrel sport a heavier straight-contoured target-style barrel. The Quad Range is in a European-style silhouette or biathlon-inspired stock. It's very modern-looking and impossible to find secondhand because everyone who has one loves it.

In the United States, it's hard to fathom the need for a switch-barrel beyond wanting to upgrade to a better barrel at home easily. If we want another caliber, most of us have the luxury of buying another rifle. But the Quad stands to prove a point that the switch-barrel isn't just an accurate shooter but can also be a high-quality, high-end firearm.

	Sako Quad	Sako Finnfire II	Tikka T1x MTR	Tikka T1x UPR
Bolt Type	Two lugs, 50°	Three lugs, 60°	Three lugs, 60°	Three lugs, 60°
Stock Type	Various	Sporter	Sporter	Precision sporter
Stock Material	Various	Walnut	Synthetic	Fiberglass
Cheek Riser	No	No	No	Yes
Total Weight	5.75 lbs.	6.2 lbs.	6.5 lbs.	5.7 lbs.
Overall Length	39.8 in.	40.35 in.	33.7 in.	33.7 in.
Barrel Type	Medium contour	Medium contour	Medium contour	Medium contour
Barrel Length	22 in.	22 in.	16 in.	16 in.
Trigger	Sako single-stage	Sako single-stage	Tikka single-stage	Tikka single-stage
Mag. Capacity	5	5	10	10
Calibers	.22 LR, .22 WMR, .17 HMR, .17 HM2	.22 LR, .17 HMR	.22 LR, .17 HMR	.22 LR, .17 HMR

Sako Finnfire II

If the Quad is the epitome of new school rimfire rifle design, the Finnfire is its classy, traditionalist brother. The original Finnfire, released in the 1990s, came in three variations. The sporter-barreled hunter, the Varmint with a 24-inch heavy barrel, and the Range with a current match stock.

The Varmint proved the most popular, so when Sako updated the line in 2014, the Finnfire II mirrored it, but with a 22-inch barrel chambered in .22 LR or .17 HMR. It sits in a gorgeous Turkish walnut stock. It's worth noting that before anyone was chattering online about full-sized .22 LR "trainers," the Finnfires were on the market, and they're full-sized Sako 75s in the rimfire calibers.

The two-lug bolt is like the Quad with a 50-degree lift and short throw with a fast lock time. Unlike the Quad (and like the Tikka below), the magazine well and triggerguard is plastic. Sako/Tikka does factory synthetics better than anyone. Its fiberglass-infused stocks and bottom plastics are crowbar ridged and tough. Even still, actual bottom-metal should be required kit on a rifle this nice and not using it was a misstep. (DIP, Inc. makes metal replacement parts for these rifles if the plastic aggravates your OCD, as it does mine.)

The Finnfire II is a modern classic, a step-up from the comparable CZs and very much on par with the Anschütz 64 sporters. Finland is a country of hunters and riflemen, and this classic rimfire hunter is a fitting homage.

Tikka T1x MTR and UPR

This full-sized .22 LR trainer from Tikka set the Internet on fire three times. First, excitement: it has the same footprint as the T3 centerfire, so all the available T3 stocks and chassis fit it. Second, with anger: as its import to the U.S. was delayed, importers grossly underestimated demand, and many distributors got caught holding customer pre-order dollars for months on end while rifles sat in Finland or with customs. Then, third: excitement again, as reports of the T1x's outstanding accuracy trickled in — all at a street price well under $500.

For an affordable, light, fast-pointing .22 LR or .17 HMR equally at home in the squirrel woods as on the match line, I don't think there's a better rimfire rifle on the market.

Consider the NRL22 base class, where the combined cost of rifle and scope cannot exceed $1,050. In 2019, at the National Match, Savage dominated with its Mark II and B22 rifles. In 2020, the winning rifle was a Tikka T1x. Shooters competed with several T1xs in open class at the National Match, fitted in chassis from KRG, MDT, Onyx, and XLR. There are others, should you want to customize your rifle or match it to a T3 centerfire.

The stainless steel bolt has a rear locking lug at the handle with a short 45-degree lift, 1.5-inch long throw. Tikka achieved this while maintaining the centerfire footprint by extending the receiver's bottom edge past the barrel connection by about 1.5 inches. This extended lip or tongue runs past the chamber like

Tikka T1x Multi-Task Rifle (MTR).

The Tikka T1x barreled action. Note the extended lip on the reciever under the barrel to accommadate T3 footprint stocks.
Photos: Cosmo Genova

a runway for the otherwise free-floated barrel. This design caps the maximum barrel diameter at 0.890 inch. The bolt has a single extractor and a 12 o'clock firing pin that tapers down to a radiused point for tight, concentrated impacts. In this way, it's very much like an Anschütz in how it handles brass. It's a push feed with little positive control over the round as it journeys from the magazine to chamber, but the geometry is good with no discernable bullet markings, no matter the action torque. (Some push feeds, like the Savages, can get wonky feeds if over-torqued.) The polymer magazine loads easily. It's impossible to stack rounds into it willy dilly and cross rims. The 10-rounder is not a double stack or a single stack but staggers the rounds like a SIG P365 pistol mag. The magazine's bottom does not sit flush with the factory stock's bottom with an odd − or "modern" − shark fin-esque bump. The magazine release button, which sits in front of the magazine, is small but perfectly acceptable for most applications. There are extended aftermarket options for race gun builds.

The barrel is also swappable, though Tikka hasn't much advertised this point. It is tension fit and glued, then secured with three T15 Torx screws. It's an incredibly secure design, much more so than the CZ

The extended receiver. Three Torx screws clamp the barrel to the action.

slip fit or even the very best 10/22 receivers. Currently, Lothar Walther and International Barrels make drop-ins. "Drop-in" might be the wrong word. The fit is so tight many have required gunsmiths to break the Torx screws and get the original barrel out. DIY'ers, be warned.

Only match shooters or ELR nuts wanting a premium barrel should consider a barrel change in my estimation. For most of us, the medium contour or heavy sporter stock barrels, available in 16 and 20 inches, do remarkably well out of the box. I have not yet encountered a Tikka that is not *sub-MOA at 100 yards*, in .22 LR or .17 HMR with match ammo. The Tikka barrels are the very same made by Sako through a cold hammer-forged process. The only difference between the T1x barrel and the much more expensive Quad barrel system is how it attaches to the receiver.

RIMFIRE REVOLUTION

Tikka makes the synthetic stock of the MTR (Multi-Task Rifle) of 35 percent fiberglass, so it's rigid — the most rigid "plastic" stock I've put my hands on — and incredibly light. The newer updated model UPR (Ultimate Precision Rifle) comes with a full fiberglass stock, with carbon-fiber bedding surfaces along the receiver inlet. It has an adjustable cheekpiece, butt hook, adjustable length of pull via spacers, and tacti-

cal-style vertical grip, and dual forward and aft flush-cup QD mounts. UPR bottom metal and a barrel channel insert for the T1x are available, too, so if a shooter bought a centerfire T3 UPR, they could drop a T1x in the same stock and get shooting. While there are multiple chassis options, it's tough to beat the affordable KRG Bravo for the Tikka, with its full-length aluminum bedding rail and over-molded polymer furniture. It's

comfortable, accurate, and has a host of add-on features for whatever you need the rifle to do. The MTR stock is excellent for general purpose work, though a glass and pillar bedding job with DIP, Inc. bottom metal does improve it. It's a shame Tikka doesn't offer a model in really nice walnut for the old-school squirrel hunters among us.

The Sako/Tikka single-stage trigger is excellent. I've been able to turn them down to about 1.5 pounds, despite claims that it only goes as low as 2 pounds. It's possible to get it as low as 10 ounces with a Yo Dave spring kit. An aftermarket Bix'n Andy T3 Precision Trigger fits the T1x — a trigger that costs more than the entire rifle. That said, because of the speed, smoothness, and trouble-free function of the Tikka action, I wouldn't fault the shooter that wants to go all-in and custom barrel this rifle, drop in a Bix'n Andy and put it in an MPA or MDT chassis. All dressed up or bone stock, it's an incredible gun.

Savage Arms

"Our company's founders didn't mess around, and their spirit of American, get-it-done ingenuity has always been Savage Arms' driving force."

Arthur Savage organized The Savage Arms Company in Utica, New York, in 1894. The 37-year-old had already lived a full life, but his contributions to firearms were just beginning. Born in Kingston, Jamaica, his father was a Welsh politician remembered for setting up an educational system for emancipated British colony slaves in 1834 — almost 30 years before the American Civil War. In the late 1870s, while living in London, Savage heard a lecture on the splendor of the natural world by Charles Darwin and convinced an uncle to buy him passage to Australia. He searched for gold and opals with three companions and soon joined up with a band of Aborigines, with whom he lived for two years, moving across the Outback. In 1876, Savage returned to British colonial society, working for periods as a sheep shearer, doctor's assistant, hotel bouncer, and cattle rancher. He met his wife Anne, fathered four of eight children, moved back to London, and in 1886 took a job managing a coffee and banana plantation in Jamaica. In 1892, always restless, Savage moved to New York and got a part-time apprenticeship at the Utica Hammer Magazine Company. It's unclear if the coffee business failed, or he simply decided to liquidate and head to America.

Two years into gun building, he formed Savage Arms to mass-produce his Model 95 centerfire rifle — a direct predecessor of the Savage Model 99. A hammerless, lever-action design with a rotary box magazine, the 95 and 99 were immediately distinguishable from their peers. The rifle could shoot spitzers or spire-point bullets, unlike other lever actions with tubular magazines. (A spitzer in a tube mag, where

Savage B-22 Precision.
Photo: Savage

An early advertisement for the Savage 99.

One of the few surviving photographs of Arthur Savage.

bullets line up end to end, meant the pointed tip of one bullet touched the primer of the round ahead of it and risked accidental ignition.) Savage solved for this, and big game hunters loved him for it. The 99 earned a reputation as a handy and accurate big woods rifle.

During the world wars, Savage produced small arms for American troops and our Allies. Savage made 1.4 million Thompson submachine guns by one account and more than a million No. 4 Enfield rifles during WWII, averaging 55,000 guns per month. The company acquired Stevens Arms and shotgun maker A.H. Fox in the 1920s, but its modern rimfire lineup didn't take shape until a 1993 acquisition of Ontario, Canada-based Lakefield Arms.

Canada never had much of a firearm manufacturing base, but one company left an indelible mark on the country — the H. W. Cooey Machine & Arms Company. During the First World War in 1903, on the corner of Queen Street and Spadina Avenue in Toronto, the machine and tool shop made small rifle parts, like folding peep sights for the Canadian Ross rifle. After the war in 1919, Cooey debuted its first full rifle, a single-shot .22 bolt action — the Cooey Canuck. It was an immediate hit in Canada and around the world. As Daniel Fritter wrote in *Calibre, The Canadian Firearms Magazine*:

"The first of Cooey's designs, this single-shot action that seems so rudimentary today was quite innovative when new, due in large part to the unique automatic half-cock

safety. Billed as a "patent-pending system" (although there is no evidence of patents having ever been filed), this system employed a two-part bolt that used a half-cock notch on the striker assembly to retain the striker behind the bolt face when the bolt was closed but did not bring the action to a fully cocked position. To do that, the shooter would have to grasp the closed bolt's tail and pull rearward. This engaged the striker upon the sear and completed the task of readying the rifle for firing.

Nearly all the major firearm companies use this two-part, two-step bolt design for youth-sized single-shot rimfire rifles in the U.S., Canada, and Europe through the 20th century. Go to any pawnshop with a wall of guns, and you'll likely find an old .22 that works this way, but true Cooey Canucks have become more rarified collectors' items. Model names also included the Model 39, the Ace, the Bisley Sport, the Model 75, and others. Many were made by Cooey and stamped with other manufacturers and even department store names.

Cooey developed the single-shot action into a tube-fed repeater in 1939, with what would become the Model 60 and Model 600. The bolt worked much like the Canuck, but the striker cocked fully on the bolt close.

In 1961, with the untimely death of H. W. Cooey's son, Hubert, the company sold to the Olin Corporation

The H.W. Cooey Machine Shop in Toronto, to which many of Savage's modern rimfire designs trace.

The last Cooey factory, in Cobourg, Ontario, Canada.

that year. Winchester launched the Cooey-designed semi-automatic Model 64 three years later under its Winchester-Western brand — the same year Ruger debuted the 10/22. In 1970, Winchester moved the Cooey plant and updated it to German tooling aimed at a 2,000 guns per day production cycle. By 1979, the operation ran into insolvency thanks to poor financial planning, labor strife, and a touch of Canadian gun politics. Lakefield Arms in Lakefield, Ontario, bought its designs and tooling.

Lakefield opened in 1969 after a boat manufacturer in town went out of business, and the owners felt the workforce could apply their talent to smallbore rifles. It developed the Mark II bolt-action repeater and the Model 64-like Mark III semi-auto — both of which are still among Savage's best-selling rifles today. In 1993, Savage bought Lakefield, and in 1994 it became Savage Canada. Savage makes all of its rimfire rifles in Canada, except for the .17 WSM B.MAG and the A-17 and A-22 magnums produced at Savage headquarters in Westfield, Mass.

Savage Esoterica

Savage offers many different rifle configurations — almost 160 rimfires alone at last count. To manage this, it has a rather byzantine naming system. This cheat sheet can help make sense of all the available options.

Model Names:

Mark II – bolt action, box magazine, .22 LR, .17 HM2

93 – bolt action, box magazine, .17 HMR, .22 WMR

B Series – bolt action, rotary, all calibers

64 – semi-automatic, box magazine, .22 LR

A Series – semi-automatic, rotary magazine, all calibers except .17 WSM

Rascal – single shot, youth rifle, .22 LR

Model Codes:

AK - Adjustable Muzzle Brake

B - Laminate Stock

BT - Laminated Thumbhole Stock

C - Clip (Detachable Box Magazine)

F - Synthetic Stock

EV – Evolution Stock

G - Hardwood Stock

H - Hinged Floorplate

L - Left hand

ML - Muzzleloader

NS - No Sights

P – Police

SR - Suppressor-Ready barrel (threaded)

SS - Stainless Steel

T - Rimfire Peep Sights

V - Heavy Varmint Barrel

XP - Package Gun

Y - Youth model

Examples: The "93R17 GV LEFT HAND" is a bolt-action .17 HMR with a box magazine in a wood stock with a heavy varmint barrel, left-handed. The "MARK II FV-SR GATOR CAMO" is a bolt-action .22 LR in a synthetic stock (with the gator camo pattern) and a heavy varmint barrel threaded for a suppressor.

Note: "Precision" in the Savage rimfire world denotes an MDT-made aluminum chassis. The laminate stocks are Boyd's stocks — and have much accuracy potential with a proper glass bedding job. The "Minimalist" stocks are a newly designed lightweight laminate stock.

The Savage Rimfire Rifles

	B-Series Precision	A-Series Precision	Model 93R17 FV-SR	Mark II TRR-SR
Action	B receiver	Delayed blowback semi-automatic	E receiver	Savage E receiver
Bolt Type	Single lug, 90°	N/A	Single lug, 90°	single lug, 90°
Stock Type	MDT chassis	MDT chassis	Sporter	precision, Tactical
Stock Material	Aluminum	Aluminum	Wood-laminated	hardwood
LOP	12.75 to 13.75 in.	12.75 to 13.75 in.	13.75 in.	13.75"
Cheek Riser	Yes	Yes		yes
Total Weight	7.38 lbs.	7.278 lbs.	5.5 lbs.	7.85 lbs
Overall Length	36.625 in.	37.25 in.	37 in.	39.5"
Barrel Type	Carbon steel	Carbon steel	Carbon steel	carbon steel
Barrel Length	18 in.	18 in.	16.5 in.	21"
Trigger	AccuTrigger	AccuTrigger	AccuTrigger	AccuTrigger
Trigger Weight	1.5 to 5 lbs.	1.5 to 5 lbs.	2.5 to 6 lbs.	2.5 to 6 lbs.
Mag. Capacity	10, rotary	10, rotary	5, box	10 round, box
Calibers	.22 LR, .17 HMR, .22 WMR	.22 LR, .17 HMR, .22 WMR	.17 HMR, .22 WMR	.22LR
MSRP	$599	$599	$345	$645

There are nearly 13 dozen Savage rimfire rifle configurations. Yet, they all stem from two foundational bolt actions and two semi-auto actions, plus the Rascal line of single-shot youth rifles.

The Mark II action (for .22 LR-sized cartridges) and the Model 93 (for magnum-sized rimfire cartridges) are the original bolt-action design. The B Series is the other. The blowback Model 64 comes from the Cooey-designed semi-auto action of the same name. The A-Series is a modernized delayed blowback semi-auto capable of handling .22 WMR and .17 HMR and .22 LR and .17 HM2. The Mark II, Model 93, and Model 64 have barrels pinned to the receiver. Savage threads the B Series and A Series with its barrel nut system.

The Mark II & 93 Rifles

The early Savage rimfires looked much like the early Cooey and Lakefield rifles until the 2007 advent of the updated Mark II and 93 rifle actions. It was dubbed the "E" receiver in-house at Savage with the "E" standing for "everything," as the action could handle the four dominate rimfire calibers with just a bolt and barrel change. The E receiver made possible hundreds, if not thousands, of different rifle configurations off the same tooling and design. From a manufacturing perspective, this took the 58 rifle SKUs made by Lakefield and streamlined them down to eight. "It was a tremendous advance," says Terry McCullough, Vice President and General Manager of Savage Canada. "It streamlined our whole manufacturing process."

Thanks to its button-rifled barrels, Savage has long been known for excellent accuracy. When quizzed, McCullough points to Savage's standardized manufacturing process, from the same Pratt & Whitney gun drills used for the centerfire bores in Westfield to a protocol on how often to sharpen its tools to the talented workforce. Take a "cheap" Savage .22 LR, set it up correctly and break it in, then shoot match ammunition, and it will hit way above its price class. The rifles remain competitively accurate at every price point, but especially so in the sub-$500 bracket where they mostly exist.

When *Outdoor Life* first tested the new Mark II with a heavy stainless barrel in a laminate varmint stock in 2008, it won both the Best Buy and Editor's

Choice award — a first in that magazine's decades of gun testing. The writers were so impressed, they cast shade on Anschütz, the long-time gold standard in accurate rimfires. "The Savage MK II .22 RF we tested proved to be not just the most accurate rimfire we tested this year, but the most accurate rimfire we've ever tested, including some high-dollar rifles of exalted European origin," they wrote. Gun writers testing accuracy is highly problematic, as we'll dive into in the chapter Precision & Accuracy. Still, the review

The author toured the Savage factory to see the barrel-making process. Here, bundles of barrel steel for A-Series rimfire rifles lay on racks before the machining process.

The drilling machines have sliding doors to cut down on flying steel chips.

Drilled blanks are staged in carts that move to the next step in the process.

Barrels are contoured in a CNC turning center.

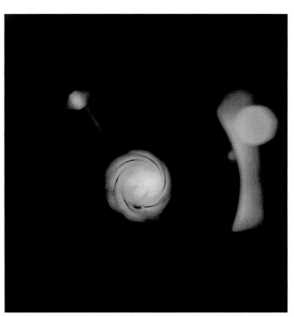

A finished barrel is checked with a borescope. This barrel shows no curved shadows or dark spots, so it is straight.

showed the world that the E receiver could make the foundation for a great shooting rifle.

The Mark II and 93 ships with bladed two-stage Savage AccuTriggers, and you can turn these down on some models under 1.5 lb. (Savage claims 1.5 lb. as the bottom limit.) Note: not all AccuTriggers are created equal. The triggers in the A-Series magnums, for example, tend to be heavy and crunchy, and overall, just not good, though they are labeled "AccuTriggers" nonetheless. This sad fact is inevitable thanks to lawyers and the real fear of possible double taps in the higher-pressure, fast-cycling semi-auto actions. The AccuTrigger's advantage is not just pull weight, but it is easily adjustable and serviceable at home. It has a fast lock time in the E receivers, which favors accurate shooting.

Mark II feed issues are common. The problems have been traced back to the 10-round box magazines. New stainless mags often correct the problem, as does working on wonky mags by tweaking the feed lips. It's a straightforward fix.

Still, the Mark II generally remains as accurate today as when it launched. It's become a staple of NRL22 base class shooters. At the 2019 NRL22 National Match, the first-place winner shot a Mark II and three of the remaining Top Five shot Savage B Series rifles. The Mark II TRR-SR is the current tactically styled precision version, with a 22-inch heavy carbon steel barrel and a threaded muzzle in a black hardwood stock. You can find synthetic-stocked heavy-barreled models at around $200. It is easily the least expensive of the popular modern precision rimfire rifles, yet you can make it shoot like rifles that cost four times as much.

The Savage Mark II.

The 2008 Outdoor Life Review of the Savage Mark II

June 6, 2008, might as well have been centuries ago in the rimfire world, but this famous write up still holds water and goes to show how accurate factory Savage rifles can be. Savage included it in presentations and press materials for the longest time, as they should have. They make damn accurate rifles.

Savage Mark II Price: $421

Editor's Choice & Great Buy

For the first time since we began doing our annual gun test, a single rifle has won both the Editor's Choice and Great Buy awards. So how did it do it? With its gleaming stainless-steel action and barrel and a laminated hardwood stock that echoes the sculpting of legendary stock-stylist Reinhart Fajen, the MK II certainly looks considerably more upscale than its price tag indicates. But good value alone doesn't win Outdoor Life's top award. To do so, a firearm must exhibit a level of performance consistently better than that of other guns in its class. The Savage MK II .22 RF we tested proved to be not just the most accurate

rimfire we tested this year but the most accurate rimfire we've ever tested, including some high-dollar rifles of exalted European origin. After the gun was sighted-in at 50 yards in a test tunnel, the first four 5-shot groups measured .191, .202, .263, and .260 inches, for an average of .229 inches. Yep, that's less than a quarter-inch! More remarkable is the fact that these tiny groups were fired with standard Remington/Eley ammo and an old lot of CCI Green Tag, neither of which are considered the ne plus ultra by accuracy fanatics. The smallest group of all was fired by team member Sam Arnett, who demonstrated his award-winning benchrest technique with a barely measurable .109 inches. By comparison, an eighth of an inch equals .125 inches, so go figure. Aside from its obviously super-accurate barrel, much of the MK II's shootability was credited to its weight and the solid way the contoured stock rides the bags.

Testers' Comments: Incredible value; can›t beat the price for this kind of accuracy; Trigger pull could be better; A tack driver; Savage can be proud of this firearm; Aesthetically very pleasing overall; a damned fine .22 rifle; I'll buy it.

Savage B-22 Precision.

The B Series

Released in 2017, the B Series is a modern iteration of the E receiver. The two-piece bolt body locks at the handle's base like the Mark II, rather than with lugs. (The B.MAG is a variant of the B Series chambered in .17 WSM and has rear locking lugs to contain the higher pressures.) There are two extractors on the counterbored bolt face at 3 and 9 o'clock with a rectangular striker at 12. The bottom half of the bolt face is machined, so the rotary magazine-fed rounds pick up under the extractors with a positive grip.

The 10-round rotary mag has a metal backplate and synthetic housing. The Savage mag is not quite the marvel of Ruger's, but you can tune it by removing some plastic around the edges closest to the soft lead nose of a .22 LR bullet to prevent scraping. All the B Mags I've shot have been very sensitive to torque, too. Finding the sweet spot generally makes feed issues go away and minimizes scraping. The AccuTrigger is user-adjustable to less than 1.5 lbs. in some cases. Savage threads the barrel to the receiver with a cone-style breech face that eliminates the need for extractor cuts.

The B22 Precision is the flagship B Series rifle and comes in a solid aluminum billet chassis. Savage worked with British Columbia-based Modular Driven Technologies, MDT, to develop a chassis for this action. The chassis is one-piece machined aluminum, from buttstock to forend. There are no swapping buttstocks like MDT's other designs. A spacer system allows length-of-pull adjustments from 12.75 to 13.75 inches, and there's an adjustable cheek riser. There are four M-LOK slots on the forend at 3, 6, and 9 o'clock.

There are a forward sling stud and an M-LOK slot in the buttstock for a rear sling attachment, monopod, or bag rider. The rifle comes with an angled MDT grip with large palm swell and takes AR-patterned grips should the shooter want to swap them.

Chassis to barreled action fit is exceptional. Torqued down, there is zero wiggle or flex, and the barrel centers perfectly in the channel. MDT recommends 65 in/lbs. To ensure magazine fit, do this with a magazine in the rifle and apply some rearward pressure on the barreled action while torquing it down.

Savage positioned this rifle squarely at NRL22 base class with an MSRP of $599. Mine has reliably shot 1 MOA groups. That accuracy coupled with the trigger, chassis, and price quickly put it among the best one-stop-shop for a budget-conscious precision rimfire shooter.

The A-Series

Thanks to its innovative delayed blowback action, Savage has succeeded in autoloading .17 HMRs and .22 WMRs where others have failed. Rather than pressure from a fired round, throwing the bolt directly back and chambering a new round, the Savage bolt has a top lug that locks the bolt in place. Firing delays the blowback a few milliseconds while pressure cams the lug down before sending the bolt back, ejecting the spent shell, and loading a new round. These events create enough delay for the higher magnum pressures to drop off for safe and reliable semi-auto cycling. Some companies like Volquartsen, JARD, and Magnum Research have successfully modified the 10/22

Savage A-22 Precision.

platform for magnum rimfire calibers. Still, none have reached the level of acceptance — and market penetration — as the A-Series from Savage.

The A-Series magnums can also produce great accuracy results. By bedding the factory laminate stock and swapping the trigger group for a light aftermarket JARD, mine averages just over 1 MOA. Individual shooter and rifle data are highly variable, but in my mind, it goes to show if you take a project-minded approach to these rifles, they can sing. There is no better non-custom, low-price, high-volume magnum rimfire for varmint shooting on the market.

Savage rifles are not perfect, but they may be as close to perfect as possible for a $200 to $400 rifle. Drawbacks lay mainly with aftermarket support. There just isn't a wide selection of components and accessories to tweak Savages like there are with Ruger or the Remington 700 platform rifles from Bergara and Vudoo. There are some chassis options available, from the likes of MDT and others, and Rifle Basix makes an excellent Savage trigger should the Accu-Trigger not prove smooth enough, but this pales compared to the diversity of options available for other platforms. They're not rifles for tinkerers.

Less expensive models also suffer from price-point fluctuations, like flexible and poorly fitting synthetic stocks, bolt timing problems, and feed issues that require some know-how to iron out. None of this is insurmountable if peak accuracy is the goal — you can stiffen and bed stocks and tweak magazines to improve functionality.

Also, Savage rimfires are not full-sized rifles. While the bolt actions have a long tubular receiver, barrel contours — even heavy or target-taper barrels — don't often exceed 0.820 inch. They sit in 3/4-sized stocks and chassis. For the plinker and small game hunter, this is generally a non-issue, but for precision shooters who want a replica of their centerfire rifle, Savage has no current option.

As Savage's centerfire lineup leans into the precision shooting world through recent collaborations with players like PROOF Research, it's only a matter of time before these ideas trickle down to the rimfires. The threaded receiver and barrel nut system to adjust headspace poise the B Series for the barrel-swap mania taking over pretty much every other rimfire brand. As it is, the B Series Precision in the MDT chassis is the most feature-rich .22 LR out there for NRL or PRS shooting at a street price under $500.

Volquartsen

"Every gun we make is built from start to finish by a single craftsman, who not only hand-selects his raw materials but also test-fires each gun before it's ready to ship. Each product is a promise — and we take that very seriously." – Scott Volquartsen

In the early 1970s, Tom Volquartsen could be found in the basement of his small home in Carroll, Iowa, tinkering away on guns. Word got out, and soon he was re-bluing a shotgun for a friend, refinishing an old hunting rifle, improving the trigger on a bullseye pistol. Nights and weekends grew busy for the full-time tax collector.

Ten years in, with the support of Iowans like Bob Brownell, Volquartsen established a reputation for quality work on a wide variety of firearms. The family moved to some acres with an existing outbuilding. The new digs gave Volquartsen the room he needed to move from a benchtop lathe and mill to heavier duty equipment. Soon after, with the support of his wife and four kids, he transitioned to full-time gun-smithing, and the media quickly took notice. Firearms magazines "discovered" Volquartsen in the late 1980s, including a 1989 cover of *American Handgunner*, which kicked off a demand that would forever change the small family business.

"Up until that point, Dad had spent his time work-ing on all makes and models of firearms," wrote son Scott Volquartsen on the 45th anniversary of the busi-ness and his dad's 70th birthday. "Everything from re-bluing shotguns to customizing Lugers and every-thing in between." With just two employees — mom in the front office, dad in the shop — it had become too much. Volquartsen decided to focus on the world

of rimfire. "It may seem hard to believe to younger shooters, but the 10/22 market was not always what it is today. It wasn't common to invest money in sig-nificant parts upgrades for a rifle that, back then, cost under $100," Scott wrote.

Giving tinkerers what they wanted was an uphill battle. Barrel makers didn't want to run small batches of barrels to Volquartsen specs as they saw no upside. When he found a small-scale barrel maker to work with, his dealers and distributors pushed back. Over and over again, he heard, "No one is going to pay to upgrade an inexpensive .22."

Scott wrote, "There are a lot of adjectives that can be used to describe Dad, but one that fits him best might be stubborn."

Eventually, the world caught up with Volquartsen's vision of a vibrant rimfire aftermarket. Soon he was building among the very best 10/22s on the planet, and customers were happily spending 5x and 6x the price of a bone stock Ruger on one of his custom rifles. Or they were paying for Volquartsen parts to make that bone stock Ruger shoot better.

"Quality is quintessential" is part of Volquartsen's mission statement. That isn't corporate b.s. You feel the quality in its rifles, as you do when you pick up an Anschütz or a Vudoo.

The Volquartsen Summit in .17 Mach 2.
All rifle photos here by Volquartsen.

The Volquartsen Inferno.

My introduction to Volquartsen came by way of the .17 Mach 2 when a friend brought over a Deluxe he had bought online chambered for that smallest of rimfire cartridges. The Volquartsen cycled flawlessly, which you cannot say of most Mach 2 semi-autos, and drove groups at 50 yards we could cover with a dime.

Volquartsen is most known for its rimfire race guns — speed guns, tuned for Rimfire Challenge and USPSA Steel Challenge like its Black Mamba pistol or 10/22-style carbines. It also makes a host of parts for Ruger, Remington, and Smith & Wesson firearms. (The fastest and least expensive way to make a stock 10/22 trigger sing is to get the Target Hammer pack.) What's less known is it makes a heck of a precision rifle with the toggle-bolt Summit action.

Designed originally by Primary Weapons Systems, the Summit action uses a straight-pull toggle-bolt system rather than the traditional blowback design of a 10/22 or turn-bolt of nearly every other bolt action on the market. Other than the receiver and bolt, all aftermarket 10/22 magazines, stocks, triggers, and barrels fit the system. The outside dimensions and receiver footprint are that of a 10/22. Volquartsen makes its receiver from hard-anodized 6061-T6 aluminum with a machined-in Picatinny rail with 20 MOA of taper with

	Deluxe	Inferno	Summit
Action	10/22 clone	10/22 clone	Straight pull
Stock Type	Sporter	Chassis	Magpul Hunter
Stock Material	Various	Aluminum	Polymer
Cheek Riser	No	Yes	No
Barrel Type	Various	Various	Carbon tensioned
Barrel Length	Various	Various	16.5 in.
Trigger	TG2000	TG2000	TG2000
Trigger Weight	2.25 lbs.	2.25 lbs.	1.75 lbs.
Mag. Capacity	10, Ruger BX	10, Ruger BX	10, Ruger BX
Calibers	.22 LR	.22 LR	.22 LR, .17 HM2
MSRP	Approx. $1,900	$2,274	Approx. $1,300

a stainless bolt that operates via linkage.

The bolt moves forward and back in a straight line, similar to a Browning T-bolt or Anschütz Fortner action. Straight pulls are faster to operate than turn-bolts, which is why they've come to dominate biathlon shooting. Like turn-bolts, they have better lockup than a semi-auto, which uses rearward escaping gases from ignition to cycle the bolt. In the Summit's aluminum receiver, a toggle handle rotates around an integral pin machined into the steel bolt. The bolt runs along a steel guide. When you push the handle forward, the linkage forms a straight line and locks the bolt into the breech face. You unlock the action by pulling back on the bolt handle, causing the linkage to cam around the pivot pin in the top of the bolt. In this way, it's more akin to the T-bolt with its series of levers compared to the Fortners, which use steel ball bearings as locking lugs.

Volquartsen sells actions and complete rifles, including a Summit in .17 HM2, which fast became my favorite small game rifle. It's virtually weatherproof in the Magpul Hunter stock and, with scope and sling, weighs just a shade over 6.5 pounds thanks to Volquartsen's carbon-tensioned barrel.

The thin 416 stainless steel barrel is fitted with a .920-inch bull barrel diameter carbon-fiber tensioned sleeve that adds stiffness while keeping things lightweight — Volquartsen threads its barrel for a suppressor, which is really where the Summit shines. A suppressed 10/22, even shooting subsonic, isn't silent as the bolt slams back and forth between buffer and breech with every shot. The Summit makes the platform virtually silent.

The action/barrel combination uses shims to ensure perfect headspace and a tight lockup. The inside bolt face recess measures 0.041 inch, and you can adjust that headspace and the tension on the toggle-bolt linkage using the four shims provided by Volquartsen with the action. With the right .22 LR barrel of which Volquartsen makes many, the Summit could be a barn-burner at a precision rimfire match. It's a fast,

The Summit is made for squirrel hunting.

accurate, and innovative system. No surprise, as it's a Volquartsen.

Vudoo Gun Works

"Envision and create the exceptional."

No company has done more to spur the modern rimfire revolution than Vudoo Gun Works of St. George, Utah. The Vudoo V-22 repeater stands as the first full-sized rimfire rifle on the Remington 700 footprint and has set off an arms race among firearm manufacturers looking to harness some of that true-to-scale magic and market share.

Before Vudoo, there were zero current production rimfires with the weight, length, and overall fit of a centerfire precision rifle. After Vudoo, there are no less than five and counting. Vudoo, and notably its co-founder and lead engineer Mike Bush, took a hard-core group of shooters on the Internet seriously. First, Bush converted single-shot Remington 40x actions for them. Then he built the rifle they wanted from the ground up, the heart of which is the V-22 action. In conjunction with the birth and raging success of

The author bushy tail hunting with a Summit in .17 HM2.

A Vudoo V-22 repeater in MPA BA Comp chassis with Nightforce Optic and MDT Ckye-Pod bipod. This setup is a typical high-end NRL22 build. Photo: Vudoo Gun Works

NRL22, a new kind of rimfire rifle, shooter, and match developed. At the highest levels of precision rimfire shooting today, the Vudoo is something like the standard kit. At the 2020 NRL22 National Match, 21 of the 71 shooters surveyed shot a Vudoo, including 8 of the top 10 finishers.

Full-sized, heavy-weight rimfire rifles are not new. The classic Winchester 52 target rifle ran 45-inches long in most configurations and weighed 9 to 13 pounds without an optic. Shooting rimfire rifles at long ranges is not new: 200- and 300-meter competitions were popular from the turn of the century through the advent of World War II. Yet in the post-war years, except for a small handful of European companies, manufacturing efficiencies and price-point designs trumped quality (and accuracy) for most firearm builders. Rimfire rifles got smaller and less expensive. Rimfires were a volume play. The goal was not winning medals, as it had been before the war, but selling an inexpensive child-sized rifle to every household in America. This aspiration was not all bad. It gave us the 10/22 and the Cooey-designed Savage

*Winchester 52 Target.
Photo: Rock Island Auction Company*

bolt guns. Yet, it left out many serious shooters hungry for a more sophisticated rimfire rifle platform.

Mike Bush grew up in Mobile, Alabama, on the floor of his father's diesel engine shop. He joined the Federal Bureau of Investigation in a technical role as a young man, serving from 1991 to 2001. Afterward, he cast around. Bush became a pilot and flew helicopters, but he always returned to working on guns, like he had done growing up in his father's shop in the South. He came to work closely with custom action builder Defiance Machine of Columbia Falls, Montana. He earned a reputation as a "rescue man" within the firearms industry — called in to consult on floundering firearm and ammunition designs. He worked with Remington on a rimless automatic shotgun shell that never got off the ground. He also worked with the Turkish manufacture Canik to design the well-regarded TP9-SFx polymer pistol. Bush later took a job at Savage Arms as director of engineering, but all the while, he refined personal projects in his home machine shop in Connecticut. He spent a lot of time online on the various firearm forums, reading, learning, providing an engineer's insight to the endless stream of questions people ask on the Internet.

In real life, Bush is quiet, reserved. Yet when he speaks, he does so in a matter-of-fact manner. The man likes to listen. He prides himself on this, and it has served him well. As he puts it, "I tend to be good at paying attention."

The Vudoo Apperition in a JP-APAC chassis is an ideal ELR22 rig.

Snipershide.com, started by former Marine Corps Scout Sniper Frank Gali, is a motley lot of the most serious shooters on the Internet, if not the world. As with all public forums, where anyone can post topics and offer advice, there's a healthy dose of unsubstantiated opinion. But get out your muck boots and start digging through the threads, and there's absolute gold to find if you're into precision shooting.

Sniper's Hide fast became a clearinghouse for the latest ideas on precision shooting through the middle 2000s. Bush watched this and became an active and informative participant under his screen name Ravage. A group of shooters out of Colorado that dubbed themselves "The 40x Mafia" intrigued him. These centerfire PRS shooters took old single-shot Remington 40x rifles and ran them in the manner of precision rifle series competition — shooting long, fast, and accurate. For many, .22 LR offered a low-cost alternative to train for centerfire events. Without recoil, rimfire was an ideal platform on which to practice. Plus, it was less expensive to shoot and didn't suck up weeknights at the reloading bench. Bush started converting Remington's 40x actions to repeaters. His first insight was that a full-sized action needed a full-sized magazine.

"A small form-factor magazine married to large form-factor receiver doesn't work," he says. "For vari-

The three common Vudoo barrel contours.

Poor action timing leads to bullets deforming as they're fed into the chamber, as seen here.

ous reasons, we needed to put a proper form-factor magazine in that 1.350 diameter Remington action."

Rimfire rifles are more complex than centerfires. For one thing, .22 LR bullets have a soft lead nose that easily deforms when contacted by the chamber walls when feeding. Rimfire bolts mostly don't work with forward locking lugs, as is the gold standard in centerfire. Large lugs forward create issues when picking up and feeding the small .22 LR round. That's why most rimfire designs lock up at the bolt handle with rear lugs or with a "winged" bolt like the Ruger 77/22. Bush puzzled over this. He wanted a strong lockup but didn't want to replicate what Ruger invented in the 1980s. What he landed on is well explained in the V-22 receiver patent, awarded on Feb. 14, 2019:

"A less common, but more desired design, are mid lockup receivers: the locking lugs on the bolt are located midway through the receiver. Forward of the bolt body is a bolt nose that remains stationary to the turning of the bolt body. Although the mid lockup arrangement is preferred for rifle accuracy, it has generally been avoided because the design is more difficult and costly to manufacture. In addition, available manufacturing process dictates the lug ways run the full length of the receiver without terminating at the abutments. This produces a less rigid receiver and minimal support for the bolt nose, which adversely affects rifle accuracy.

"Prior art examples of mid lockup receivers are the Remington 40x 22LR, Kelbly Swindlehurst, and Stiller Lonestar. It should be appreciated that only the Stiller Lonestar remains in production. Production of these receivers was short-lived because of their high manufacturing cost. In the case of the Kelbly and Stiller receivers, potential customers balked at purchasing them because of their perceived accuracy disadvantage resulting from them have lug ways continuing forward of the abutments."

In other words, mid lockup receivers are considered a more accurate design, but until this point, the lug ways — or the path inside the receiver where the lugs travel as you cycled the bolt — crippled them since they had to run the full length of the action. This design flaw meant the receiver wasn't as rigid as it could be, and the bolt nose would effectively "float" in the receiver as the lugs stopped midway with no material to fill the open lug ways forward of the lugs.

Bush came up with an innovative solution: a two-part receiver with the main receiver body and an in-

ternal sleeve forward of the lugs that manages to stop and lock the lugs. This feature captures and secures the non-rotating bolt nose. It proved the best of both worlds: a mid-lock-up bolt with a beefed-up receiver forend to hold the bolt nose tight.

Now, let's reconsider the magazine, which Bush created first and considers primary importance to an accurate repeating rifle action. As described, the bolt can grab the rimfire case head cleanly between extractors and feed it into the chamber without the soft lead bullet running afoul of the chamber walls. But the bolt also needs to "pick up" that round success-

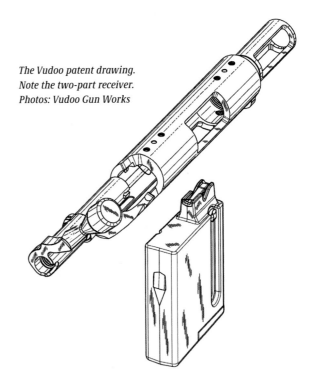

The Vudoo patent drawing. Note the two-part receiver. Photos: Vudoo Gun Works

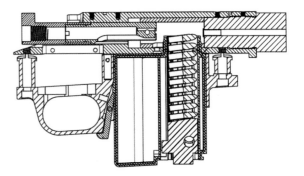

A side shot of the Vudoo receiver as shown in the February 2019 patent.

fully from the magazine. The cartridge needs to travel up the mag under spring pressure without the bullet nose compressing against the magazine or other rounds. At the top of the stack, the bullet needs to lift high enough at the nose so that it doesn't scrape on a feed lip or ramp, while the back end of the case is exposed enough for the bolt to grab it. This arrangement is a four-dimensional geometry problem. The dimensions at the top of the magazine, bolt face, and breech need to align so the bullet isn't scuffed. And it needs to do so throughout the bolt cycling forward in the action. Getting this geometry and timing right is not unique to Vudoo. Every bolt-action rifle must do it, though some are more successful than others. This operation is what gun engineers mean when they talk of action timing.

To dramatically illustrate this, take any .22 LR rifle and torque the barreled action into the stock just enough so the magazine won't drop out. Cycle a live round. One of two things will likely happen. The round will either nosedive and jam into the magazine's front or angle up and jam into the breech face out of alignment with the chamber. The magazine height and bolt timing are off, so the rifle jams. Of course, use a proper torque on any rifle, and it will mostly correct this, but often not perfect. Grab a well-used factory .22 LR rifle and look at the magazine. Odds are you will find a light gray marking like a sil-

ver Sharpie along the feed lip. This spot is where the bullet scraps its way toward the chamber. For plinking, hunting, even the accuracy required to succeed at a 100-yard precision match like NRL22, this is not the end of the world. But that was not enough for a guy like Mike Bush. His new action needed to feed rounds with zero bullet contact.

For these reasons, it bothers Bush and the folks at Vudoo when their work is reduced to "just" a Remington 40x repeater. The 40x used Ithaca and Marlin magazines and was so expensive to make and riddled with feed issues that Remington never made a full production run. While the old 40x and the Vudoo share the same exterior dimensions that open the world of Remington 700 components to the action, internally, it's a very different animal. The last bit of "Remington DNA," as Bush describes, has been extracted with its latest action, the 60-degree bolt throw Three 60.

Just like the founders of NRL22, Bush and Vudoo partners Paul and Jill Parrott thought their rifles would occupy the niche world of centerfire shooters wanting a rimfire replica of their bigger bore guns. When they took the first guns (serial number #0003) to the NRA World Shooting Championships at the Peacemaker National Training Center in West Virginia in 2017 and watched accomplished shooters light up a plate at 460 yards, a light bulb went on. The 6.5s and .30 cals stayed on the bench the rest of that afternoon as a

Note the silver coloring on the feed lips, indicating bullet scrape while feeding. Photo: Cosmo Genova

crowd formed to watch this long-range .22 LR do its magic. Paul Parrott, an industry veteran of Springfield Armory, Surgeon Rifles, McMillan, Armalite, PMC Ammunition, and FN America, had a saying that genuinely accurate rifle systems were a mix of science and "a little bit of voodoo." That day they realized, with the V-22 action, they had found their Vudoo.

Going long in the desert. Photo: Vudoo Gun Works

Vudoo Gun Works Rifles

No rifle system is perfect. The very first Vudoos shipped with Winchester 52D match chambers — a chamber renowned for accuracy but so short in length that those early rifles would not extract a live round. Competition shooters that loaded a single round, but didn't pull the trigger, weren't thrilled to pull a jackknife from their pocket to dig out a cartridge. Vudoo now uses its own "22LR Ravage" chamber that solved the live round extraction problem. Vudoo's new crescent-shaped firing pin, which strikes below the cartridge rim for more consistent ignition, has led to occasional no-fires in some rifles. The issue there was an outside supplier making parts off-spec. Bush personally deburred 600 strikers to make the problem right. (See the Q&A with Bush in the back pages for a deep dive on how the company innovates.) There were hang-ups, too, with some magazines fitting some chassis and stocks. The fast solution there was half a strip of Velcro on the front edge of the magazine. This issue is caused mostly by shooters building their rifles with Vudoo barreled actions. Also, it's possible to load the magazines incorrectly, leading to rim lock or the top round locking behind the round under it — mainly a user error. Vudoo put out a video to show knuckle-draggers (like me) how to load it properly.

Such shenanigans all could understandably drive someone who just spent $3,000 on a rifle into fits of rage. But Vudoo has developed a level of world-class transparency and customer service that makes it all seem okay. I've yet to find a human in real life, or online, who will bitch about how Vudoo treats its customers. When you buy a Vudoo, not only are you purchasing support for the life of the rifle, but you're buying into the bleeding edge of precision rimfire. Vudoo innovates in real-time and lets its customers in on the action. In this regard, I think of it as a tech company with the mantra, "move fast and break things." As the magazine fit or crescent pin situation unfolded, Bush took to Sniper's Hide to set the record straight. Owners having those issues chipped in with intel. To this day, Bush actively posts developments on his various projects to the forums. He answers customer questions in real-time for all his core customers to see. It's exciting to watch, frankly. With what other company can you post an anonymous question on the Internet and get a direct response from the inventor?

Vudoo rifles are custom built for each customer. You can't find them new on the rack at the local gun store. There is a build sheet with options posted on its website. Vudoo takes online orders but always completes the process with a phone call. The lead time has slowly ticked down from a few months to two weeks, only to push back to four to six weeks since the COVID-19 pandemic, which, if anything, has boosted sales. (A friend joked with me when his stimulus check arrived: "I finally got some Vudoo money!") Vudoo is expanding now faster than it ever has but still can't keep pace with the market it created. Paul Parrott, the CEO, told me they were frankly caught flat-footed by the rapid demand from the very beginning, and the demand hasn't stopped.

Vudoos are available as barreled actions or full builds. All Vudoo-designed barrels are cut-rifled by Ace Barrels, which now only does runs for Vudoo. Vudoo designed the Ravage chamber for Lapua ammunition. It headspaced the rifles at or just below the .043-inch rim thickness of the Lapua family of ammo. Vudoo does not sell actions only and actively discourages shooters from re-barreling them. The single shot is an exception: It's available with an Ace or Shilen Ratchet. The company works with other premium barrel makers on a more limited basis. What's available and when requires a phone call. Expected soon is a line of pre-fits from Josh Kunz at Patriot Valley Arms. These barrels will thread and time directly to any existing Vudoo action.

Of the full rifle builds, five variants are on the three repeater actions: the .22 LR and .17 HM2 V-22 action, the new Gen 3 Three 60 with a three-lug 60-degree bolt throw in the same calibers, and the V-22m in .17 HMR and .22 WMR.

The sporter Raven and Crow rifles sit in a Grayboe outlander stock with a "Spector" light contour barrel.

The Crow is youth-sized. The Sinister rifle is similar but in a beefier M40-like Grayboe Terrain stock.

The Ravage is Vudoo's most premium-stocked rifle. It is available in the Grayboe Renegade, Ridgeback, plus any McMillian, Manners, Foundation, or other Remington 700 footprint stock the customer so desires.

The Apparition is the chassis version, available in all the popular Remington 700 chassis stocks from Masterpiece Arms, JP Rifles, MDT, and many others.

The Conjour is a sporter rifle with an integrally suppressed 20-inch Ace barrel, the suppression work done by KGM Technology.

You can fit any Remington 700 trigger to a Vudoo, but as a company, it has a special relationship with — and often recommends — Timney. All rifles are available right- or left-handed.

The Raven.

A Ravage in a Manners PRS stock.

A Ravage rifle in a Grayboe stock.

An Apparition rifle in an MPA BA Comp chassis.

The Vudoo Flavio Fare 90-degree trigger.

Vudoo designed its Single Shot action for benchrest and f-class competition. It is available right bolt left port, right bolt right port, left bolt right port, or left bolt left port. Bush worked with Italian trigger maker Flavio Fare to design a unique trigger for the action. It has a 90-degree sear face and spins down to a 2-ounce pull weight. The new bolt has a 6 o'clock firing pin, and the angled extractor cuts at something close to 2 and 10 o'clock. The three-lug design has a 60-degree lift. There are a new vertical side bolt release and a unique feed tray for straight-in loading. Vudoo Ace 22BR and Shilen Ratchet barrels that come fitted to the action contour from 1.20 inches at the breech cylinder down to a straight-taper .900 inch.

The newest Gen 3 repeater action, the Three 60, is like a love child between the Gen 2 repeater and ground-up single-shot design. With Gen 2, Bush redesigned the fire control system and took Gen 3 a step

Vudoo single-shot rifle.

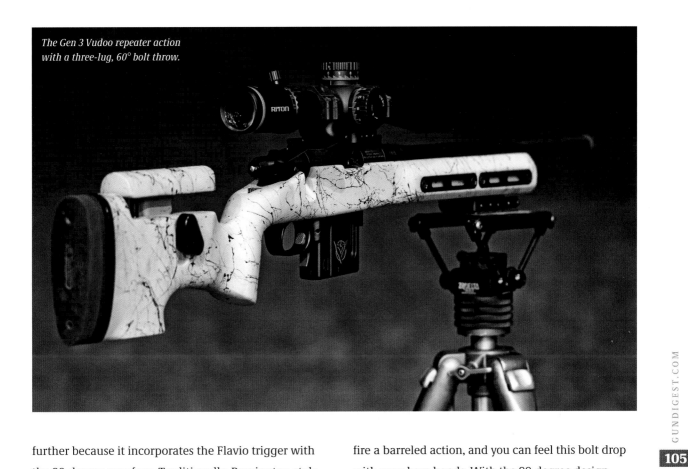

The Gen 3 Vudoo repeater action with a three-lug, 60° bolt throw.

further because it incorporates the Flavio trigger with the 90-degree sear face. Traditionally, Remington-style triggers have all had a 60-degree sear face, which puts upward pressure on the bolt until it's dropped. Dry-fire a barreled action, and you can feel this bolt drop with your bare hands. With the 90-degree design, there is no upward pressure, so the striker isn't moving down, then forward. It just goes forward, so more

	Vudoo Apparition	Vudoo Single Shot	Vudoo Crow
Action	Gen 2 V-22	V-22S	Gen3 V-22
Bolt Throw	Two lugs, 90°	Three lugs, 60°	Three lugs, 60°
Stock Type	Various	McMillan Kestros	Sporter
Stock Material	Chassis	Fiberglass composite	Composite
Cheek Riser	Various	No	No
Total Weight	9 to 12 lbs.		Approx. 7.75 lbs.
Barrel Type	416R stainless	416R stainless Ace	416R stainless
Barrel Length	16.6 in., 18 in., 20 in., or 22 in.	Up to 22 in.	16.6 in., 18 in., 20 in., or 22 in.
Trigger	Timney 510v2	Vudoo Flavio 90° Sear	Timney 510v2
Trigger Weight	2 lbs.	2 oz.	2 lbs.
Mag. Capacity	10	Single shot	10
Calibers	.22 LR, .17 HM2, .22 WMR, .17 HMR	.22 LR	.22 LR, .17 HM2, .22 WMR, .17 HMR
MSRP	$2,395 +	$2,800-$3,450	$2,395

consistent primer strikes, more consistent ignition. The Flavio triggers' lack of upward pressure makes the 60-degree bolt throw remarkably light. Typically, 60-degree throws require more downward force when locking the bolt than 90-degree throws as you're doing the same work of cocking the bolt in less distance. Bush says his prototype Gen 3 with the Flavio and a 13-pound firing spring is the lightest 60-degree action ever made. The bolt keeps the 12 o'clock ignition from Gen 2. The Gen 3 bolt is effectively a Vudoo single-shot bolt body with a Gen 2 bolt head.

Vudoo is easily one of the most exciting firearms companies operating today. Mike Bush has told me his design workflow runs many years out. While there are four generations of actions on the market, several others are finished and more in development. Most recently, the company is testing fast-twist barrels like 1:9 and 1:12 for extreme long-range work. Early results show the extra twist does not seem to hamper accuracy inside 200 yards and increases it well beyond that with barrels at least 22 inches long. Pro shooter Daniel Horner has been demoing the prototype in a sniper class he teaches. Early reports sound almost too good to be true.

Vudoo is also looking at international shooting — the highly specialized world of European race guns for Olympic-style games. "The V-22 is the only modern American gun that has met Team U.S.A. accuracy standards," Paul Parrott told me. "It's still a way down the road, but I can see a day when the American Olympic team is shooting American rifles."

It's hard not to talk to these guys or shoot their outstanding rifles and not get excited about the future of American-made smallbore precision rifles.

Zermatt

"A true-to-scale Remington 700 footprint rimfire action designed for training and competition."

A few years ago, there was only one bolt-action rimfire rifle action on the Remington 700 footprint. Now there are five. The RimX from Zermatt Arms stands as the first real custom .22 LR Remmy 700 since the Vudoo and remains Vudoo's chief competitor.

RimX's roots trace to AJ Goddard of Bighorn Arms, who has long been making some of the world's hottest precision centerfire actions. His flagship TL3 centerfire action incorporates the best of Remington and Savage designs with a Rem. 700 footprint and fire control system, along with a floating bolt head and action threads for Savage small shank pre-fits. This configuration makes swapping barrels relatively easy with his centerfire action — all that's needed is a vise and an action wrench.

A few years ago, Goddard partnered with the team at Bennet, Nebraska-based Zermatt Arms, notably Ray Heusinkvelt and Aaron Tritsch. The intent was to scale up production of the popular Bighorn centerfire actions, and from that mind-meld came something new — an innovative rimfire action with some Bighorn DNA.

The RimX action has an interchangeable bolt head system so that shooters can swap heads from a .22 LR/.17 HM2 to the larger .22 WMR/.17 HMR pattern. The bolt body remains identical, like with a Savage centerfire. A full bolt replacement is also available for .17 WSM. The action has a threaded tenon print, so barrel swaps are a breeze. Caliber change is as easy as bolt or bolt head replacement and a barrel swap. Like the TL3, it takes the best from Remington and Savage DNA.

The innovative flush-faced extractor system means there are no extractor cuts in the breechface. The recess sets headspace in the bolt face, spacers, and barrel depth. The timed threads set the barrel depth on the

RimX*	
Action	RimX - Remington 700 footprint
Bolt Type	Two lugs, 90°
Mag. Capacity	10
Calibers	.22 LR, .17 Mach 2, .17 HR, .17 WSM
MSRP	$1,150
	* Sold as action only

RimX Build: 16-inch PROOF Sendero carbon-fiber barrel, Timney The Hit Trigger, Grayboe Ridgeback stock, Atlas PSR bipod, and Vortex Strike Eagle.

tenon and in the receiver, so swapping out barrels is a matter of buying a pre-fit and torquing it. (Zermatt sells no-go gauges to double-check headspace.) The bolt is headspaced at 0.039 inch or the rim thickness of ELEY ammo, but it also chambers and shoots Lapua ammo exceedingly well. When I emailed Heusinkvelt and asked him what ammo it likes before shooting, he said as much. I didn't believe him. Then I shot it. There's no appreciable accuracy difference that I can tell between the Lapua family of Center-X/Midas+ and ELEY Match/Tenex, at least in my PROOF-barreled tester.

With most major barrel manufacturers now making pre-fits for the RimX action, this is remarkably easier — and less expensive — than buying a blank and having a gunsmith chamber and fit it. There are no v-blocks like a 10/22 or grub screws like a CZ.

Two things quickly distinguish the RimX from its peers, including Vudoo and Bergara. Those two things are the bolt and the magazine.

The bolt is straightforward to break down. Twist the bolt nose and pull. Nose off, grab the bolt handle, twist the shroud clockwise, and separate from the handle. It makes cleaning a breeze. The heavy-duty stainless firing pin is tapered and stepped down to a narrow rectangle of a striking surface that marks cases cleanly at the rim edge. The firing pin connects to the shroud with a metal clip, and you can easily pull it and replace it if damaged. The firing pin sits at the 6 o'clock position, meaning it strikes the ammunition case low-center at 6 o'clock. Custom rimfire actions

from the benchrest world mostly moved the firing pin to 6 o'clock, based on smallbore pioneer Bill Calfee's work in the book, *The Art of Rimfire Accuracy*. (More in the chapter Precision & Accuracy.) The ignition is more consistent with a 6 o'clock impact as primer burns upward and therefore more constantly and thoroughly — though there is little besides anecdotal testing to confirm this. (Many tack-driving Olympic-level European rifles do not have 6 o'clock firing pins.) Still, it is widely considered a gold standard among the accuracy-obsessed world of benchrest and certainly does not hurt. Tritsch, who spearheaded the design for Zermatt, was smart to include it. The two-lug bolt is a mid-lock design with a "winged" bolt nose like the Ruger 77/22 and the Bergara B-14R that followed it.

With the RimX, perhaps even more innovative is the completely flush extraction and ejection system — the bolt face itself is completely flat. With a round chambered, the cartridge rim snugs against the breechface, as with any rimfire firearm. What's different here is the bolt completely encapsulates 45 degrees of the case head when the bolt is closed. There are no relief cuts in the breechface for extractors, creating a 360-degree pressure seal. A spring-tensioned ejector captures the case rim and applies enough pressure to snug the round into the flat extractor. It produces 100 percent positive control of the shell from the magazine to the chamber, holding the cartridge by the rim securely in the bolt face. A small set screw holds the stainless extractor plate and the ejector with a spring

The flush-faced extractor and ejector of the Zermatt RimX have such positive control over the round you can load the rifle sideways or upside down with zero bullet deformation.

The face of a RimX bolt. Note the flush-fit replaceable extractor. There is no stronger system in rimfire.

plunger. Should something break, both can easily be swapped out with minimal tools and just a few small parts. It's hard to convey how elegant this flat-faced system looks and how strong it holds a cartridge. Just for kicks, I secured a live shell in the bolt nose and dropped it on my office carpet. Three out of four times, the round didn't pop out. There is zero chance, in my mind, that the system will not extract short of ripping the brass apart. It is undoubtedly the strongest extraction system ever put into a rimfire rifle.

The only drawback of this design is that you cannot load a single round into the action through the side port. It requires feeding from the magazine and a slot in the bolt face to close. For some, this may be a deal-breaker. There are certainly times in NRL22-style matches when I've mistakenly ejected a live round and have had to stuff that 10th shot in the action to complete a stage of fire, often on the clock. The solution is to pack a second magazine and ready it. Nothing in life comes free, and this is the tradeoff for such a dynamite extraction system.

Every RimX action ships with a 10-round AICS-patterned 7075 aluminum magazine. The RimX mags are very similar to the single-stack design created by Mike Bush at Vudoo, but with a few innovative improvements. The mag is held together with screws at the four corners so you can disassemble it for parts replacement, cleaning, or repair. There's an adjustable magazine catch on the rear of the mag. Adjust the

set screw, and you can move the catch up or down to tweak the height at which the mag sits. This design ensures compatibility with Remington 700 stocks and chassis and is a must-do step when building a RimX rifle to ensure proper timing.

Additionally, the magazine's bottom plate slides off to get at the spring and the follower without disassembling the entire thing. Overall, it's simple, tunable, and a very impressive total package — as it should be with a retail price for extra mags running $125. After shooting it all summer, the magazine on my test rifle is scuffed and scarred from NRL22 battle — a testament to how well it fits.

Zermatt is *not* selling barreled actions. It's on the consumer to pick out the best barrel for their use case and build the rifle themselves or seek out one of the many custom builders now working with the RimX platform. (South Dakota-based gunsmith TS Customs and Primal Rights are putting together some real stunners.) My tester came with a 16.5-inch PROOF barrel in the Sendero contour. For a trigger, I installed The Hit from Timney, adjusted it down to 12 ounces, and sat it in a Grayboe Ridgeback with Grayboe bottom metal. The action arrived with a pinned 30 MOA Pic rail, to which I installed a new 5-25x56 Vortex Strike Eagle in Vortex rings. With an Atlas PSR bipod and Armageddon Gear Game Changer rear bag, it very quickly connected on an 18 by 24-inch IPSC target at 500 yards with Lapua Center X. It seemed unfair,

Bleiker Challenger II. Photo: Bleiker

frankly, to put the rifle together in a rush and push it to 500 yards on the first outing. Still, after easy connections at 100 and 325 yards, 500 felt plausible despite an unbroken-in rifle. It has since seen about 1,000 rounds, including a summer of NRL22 matches. The nitride-coated action runs slick as snot. In all those rounds fired, there has not been a single marred bullet, misfire, failure to feed, failure to eject, or any issue whatsoever. The action has run flawlessly.

PROOF will not say how it chambers its .22 LR barrels but does recommend CCI Standard for a low-dollar ammo choice and Lapua Center-X for a few dollars more. (Retailers have posted online that PROOF uses a Bentz chamber for its .22 LRs, but the company will not confirm or deny this.) I've found this rifle shoots *everything* well. When it comes to good match ammo, it shows no real preference for Lapua over ELEY.

The beauty of the RimX is that you can build it with whatever barrel you want, in whatever rimfire caliber you like. It is a customizable platform. It should be no surprise that when centerfire über rifle builder Gunwerks made a limited run of .22 LR trainers dubbed the Rim Reaper, they used RimX actions and magazines — topped with a Gunwerks Revic PMR 428 Smart Rifle Scope, the rifles sold for $9,975 with 1,000 rounds of ELEY Tenex. Even at that eye-watering price, they sold out in less than a day.

The RimX pushes the precision rimfire envelope with incredible, user-friendly actions, worthy of the very best rimfire builds out there. It is the first legit precision centerfire action builder, schooled on PRS and centerfire NRL competition, to enter this new rimfire landscape.

I suspect it won't be the last.

Other Notable Rifles

Several other manufactures make rimfire rifles that are or could be considered precision shooting instruments. However, none of the rifles here have deeply penetrated the American market. For most, that's due to design. Four of the rifles listed below are European race guns built for Olympic-style competition. Some are sporter rifles but have suffered from poor distribution, while others still are niche custom small game rifles. None of these guns are inexpensive. The American rimfire market is changing, but the price is still a significant factor in most shooters' buying decisions. It's hard to sell all but the most dedicated on a walnut and blued Austrian rifle, for example, when they can get a proven German gun for the same money or a comparable Czech rifle for half the price.

Bleiker Challenger II

The Bleiker is what a $10,000 single-shot rimfire rifle looks like. Bleiker designed the Challenger II series for three position and prone Olympic-style shooting. It comes in five models, the major difference being the five stock/chassis designs. All Bleiker rifles use Lilja Precision Rifle Barrels made in Montana. The action is notable for its extremely short bolt design, which brings the receiver closer to the shooter and requires less overall movement to reload and a lightning-fast lock time. For example, some shooters can cycle the action in a prone position without lifting their elbows off the ground. Gold medalist Ginny Thrasher — interviewed later in this book — shoots a Bleiker and says positional shooting is about cultivating stillness. The action-back Bleiker design and short bolt throw promote stillness. The Swiss company brought home 13 gold, 14 silver, and nine bronze medals in the 2014 World Cup and five medals and four new Olympic records at the 2016 games in Rio. It continues to excel in international competition, eclipsing most others. For several years, a Bleiker held the record for the most accurate rifle tunnel tested by ELEY in England.

Christensen Arms Ranger 22

The Ranger 22 brings a rimfire back to this Gunnison, Utah high-end rifle builder's lineup. The Ranger takes 10/22 mags and comes with a TriggerTech Remington 700-style trigger. It is not a Remington-700 footprint, nor is it a "full-sized" rimfire trainer, like other Remington-based hybrids. Instead, this Frankenstein of a sporter is a high-quality small game rifle with a carbon-fiber stock and a carbon-fiber tension barrel. It's light, handy, and because it's a Christensen, you can reckon it drives tacks. It comes with a sub-MOA guarantee and weighs just 5.1 lbs.

Cooper Firearms Model 57M Jackson Squirrel

Founded in 1990, Cooper Firearms of Montana makes modern bespoke rifles with classic good looks. The Model 57 was added to the lineup in 1999 and evolved by 2001 into the model 57M Jackson Squirrel rifle, which many consider the Holy Grail of small game rimfire rifles. Cooper guarantees sub-MOA, but most rifles come with test targets that show much tinier groups nowhere near MOA. The barrel is 24 inches and stainless and comes in .22 LR, .17 HMR, and .22 WMR. The stock is a work of art in AAA claro walnut with a rollover cheekpiece, semi-beavertail forearm, and hand-checkered grip in a cross-over multi-point pattern. They run around $3,000.

Feinwerkbau KK 2800

Released in 2018, the KK 2800 is among the newest of the Olympic discipline Euro race guns on the market. Made in Germany, the action has been moved rearward like its competitors for less motion while cycling the action and a rear-from-center balance point. Like the Walther that came first, the bolt can be switched from left- to right-handed without tools. There are wood and aluminum stock models.

Christensen Arms Ranger 22. Photo: Christensen Arms

Cooper Firearms Model 57M Jackson Squirrel. Photo: Cooper Arms

Feinwerkbau KK 2800. Photo: FWB

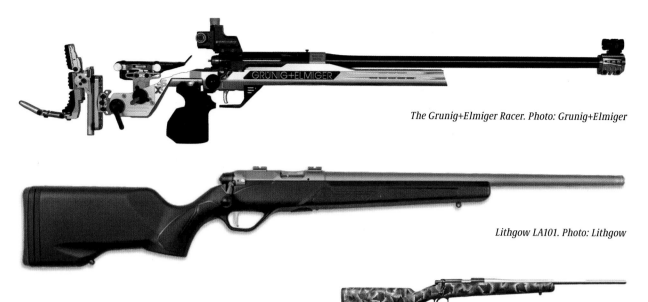

The Grunig+Elmiger Racer. Photo: Grunig+Elmiger

Lithgow LA101. Photo: Lithgow

New Ultra Light Arms Model 20 Rimfire. Photo: New Ultra Light Arms

Grunig+Elmiger Racer

Swiss G+E has been making target rifles since the 1930s. The R3 Racer is its signature series smallbore positional rifle. The endlessly adjustable aluminum chassis looks like a space gun, a rifle decades ahead of its time. It's aptly named but is rare stateside with no real distribution. They're Bleiker-level expensive.

Lithgow LA101

I have a soft spot for the Australian-made Lithgow LA101, imported to the U.S. by Legacy Sports, until recently. It might be the most accurate .22 LR available at a street price under $1,000. Maybe. Or at least mine is. (It's the most accurate rifle I've ever owned at that price point.) This full-sized rifle feels and runs very much like a Tikka T1x. The solid three-lug, rear-locking bolt with a 60-degree throw runs like glass. It's available in right- or left-handed models with a hammer-forged, free-floated, medium-contour varmint barrel. The synthetic stock isn't cheap Tupperware material, but it is not as ridged as the comparable Tikka. It takes CZ magazines. The trigger is nothing to call home about, but for $15, you can get a spring set from Lumley Arms, which brought mine down to a pleasing 1.5 pounds. The problem with the Lithgow is the utter lack of aftermarket support in the United States. There are no stocks, chassis, triggers, or anything else to tinker with or personalize a precision rifle system. BScar makes a 25 MOA Pic rail for it. (The prototype

volunteered for that rail was my rifle, and I'm grateful he took the time to do the work.) They're shooters with Australian-made medium contour button-rifled barrels. It's well under sub-MOA, and on my first ELR outing, it handled 460 yards like it was no big deal.

New Ultra Light Arms Model 20 Rimfire

Melvin Forbes is a living legend, and every rifleman in American should know his name. He pioneered the now-ubiquitous ultra-light mountain rifle in the 1980s, building Kevlar and carbon-fiber stocks with custom-barreled actions that all hung together well under 5 lbs. The Model 20 Rimfire with the repeating action is squirrel hunter's dream rifle, but he also makes single shots in benchrest stocks — so accurate is his work.

Steyr Zephyr II

This flashy Austrian rifle is tailor-made for the squirrel woods but has mostly not caught on in the United States. Part of that could be its old school meets new school European looks. The walnut stock has a classic Schnabel forend with deep-cut modern fish-scale checkering. The bolt handle is a long, thin, butter knife design. The 18.7-inch medium weight cold hammer-forged barrel has eight-groove rifling and

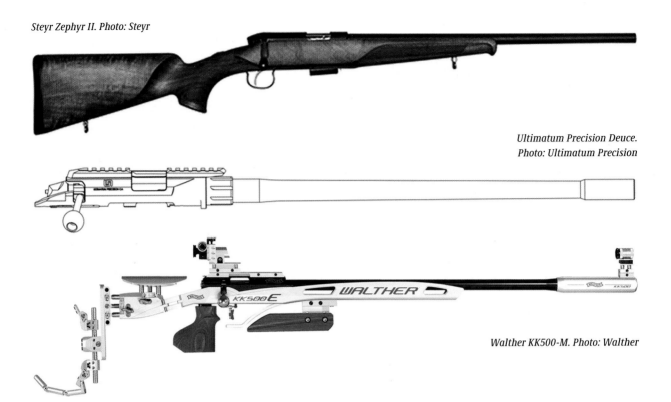

Steyr Zephyr II. Photo: Steyr

*Ultimatum Precision Deuce.
Photo: Ultimatum Precision*

Walther KK500-M. Photo: Walther

a 1:15.75 twist. The outside of the barrel has a hammered-in spiral design. It's unique. By all accounts, it's a shooter out of the box. Distribution stateside has not been good, making it not as widely available as comparable Anschütz, Sako, and CZ rifles. The comparatively priced Anschütz and Sako rifles have a much longer track record of good shooting, and you can get the CZs for about half the price. There is not a real aftermarket for upgrades and accessories. This state of affairs is all a shame because, at 5.8 pounds, it could be an ideal bushy tail or ground squirrel rig.

Ultimatum Precision Deuce

British Columbia shop Ultimatum Precision is betting on a pair of 2s with the Deuce, its slick new contender in the rapidly expanding world of custom rimfire bolt actions. The Deuce is a three-lug design with a 60-degree bolt throw and integrated lug. It takes Vudoo magazines. The action will sell alone, or with an International Barrels matched tube as a barreled action. Ultimatum designed the extractor for an inverted cone breech. It removed metal in the barrel breach around the chamber so the firing pin

will never strike barrel steel. The lack of extractor cuts in the barrel, plus the action's Savage-style barrel nut, means a shooter can headspace their rifle to whatever the rifle likes best. You can expect an aftermarket of other barrels from which to choose. This design is sort of like a three-way lovechild between CZ, Vudoo, and Savage. Delays through all of 2020 have hampered production. As of this writing, I'm uncertain if they yet exist outside of prototypes and in-house testers.

Walther KK500-M

Made in Germany for positional and prone Olympic-style shooting, the KK500-M is an extension and upgrade over Walther's popular KK300 series rifles. The short receiver minimizes motion. You can switch the new three-lug bolt from left- to right-handed without tools. It has a 6 o'clock firing pin and comes with a mechanical or electronic trigger. It's available in an aluminum chassis or laminate 3-position stock. The rifle came out in 2016, and despite an initial parts shortage, it has been well received in international competition with medals to prove it. Now, if we could just talk Walther into making a repeater again. **RR**

5

OPTICS & ACCESSORIES

The biggest hurdle for new shooters interested in precision rimfire always seems to involve optics. There are turrets, and parallax, and complicated reticles, and debates over MOA vs. MILs. Coming from a hunting background or another discipline like silhouette where you held the crosshairs on the target, a more complicated aiming system can feel overwhelming.

It does not help that "rimfire" + "scope" just meant crappy for the longest time. The glass was inferior. The adjustments were spotty. Drop one or get it wet, and the scope was toast. Here's the thing: you don't need a "rimfire" scope for a "rimfire" rifle. Whether you need an optic for competition or hunting, most quality centerfire scopes will do the job, yet some are better suited for smallbore work than others.

Optics on the line at the NRL22 National Match. Photo: Conx Media

Tricked out and ready to party. A precision rifle on the line at an NRL22X match in January 2020. Conx Media

Shooters define riflescopes by tube diameter. One inch is the classic and most common diameter and is still great for small game rigs. 30mm is the new standard for tactical and match shooting. 34mm is the super-sized big brother and best-suited for extreme long-range work. There are now even 36mm beasts like the Zero Compromise optics and 40mm digital range-finding scopes like the Swarovski dS Gen II. The fatter the scope, the more room for elevation adjustment, thus the more you can spin that turret for a dead-on hold way downrange.

Consider this example. The 30mm Vortex Diamondback Tactical 6-24x50 FFP — a popular base-class NRL22 optic — has 19 MRAD or MILs max elevation adjustment. That means if you zero the scope at the bottommost point, you can compensate for 19 MILs of bullet drop. With match-speed .22 LR and the scope zeroed at 50 yards, that's enough reach to connect to about 350 yards. The Vortex Strike Eagle 5-25x56 FFP with a 34mm tube brings 31 MILs of max elevation adjustment. That equates roughly to 470 yards of possibility. Keep in mind, this is theoretical as it's difficult to zero scopes at their lowest elevation setting, and the equation changes with tapered rails and scope rings, as we'll soon see. This example demonstrates the leap in max range one gets with a 34mm tube over 30mm. Compared to a classic 1-inch scope, the difference is planetary.

MOA vs. MILs

You make riflescope elevation and windage adjustments in minutes-of-angle (MOA) or milliradians

(MILs). To make things confusing, MILs are often also abbreviated as MRAD. They are the same thing for practical purposes. MOA and MILs or MRAD are angular measurements over a given distance rather than a linear distance. With a linear measurement, an inch is an inch. With angular, the value changes based on distance. I visualize this like a laser beam shooting directly from my barrel's bore through targets from 100 to 1,000 yards. If I change the degree of that beam to mark a spot 1 foot over the target at 100 yards, it will put the beam dozens of feet over the target at 1,000 yards. MOA and MILs are units that measure how much I'm moving that laser beam at the rifle to determine where it will hit at various targets downrange.

One MOA equals 1.047 inches at 100 yards and 10.47 inches at 1,000 yards — not 1 inch and 10 inches, as many wrongly believe. (This difference of 0.047 inch matters at distance, especially with rimfire where the elevation drops quickly.) One MIL equals 3.6 inches at 100 yards, which equates to 36 inches or 1 yard at 1,000 yards. Scope adjustments in MOA are usually 1/4 MOA per "click." MILs are often .1 or .2 MILs per click or less. Some wrongly conclude that MOA has more subtle adjustment than MILs, but it's a toss-up. A typical one-click adjustment in MOA is 0.25 inch at 100 yards, whereas MILs can go as low as 0.18 inch at 100.

You can convert an MOA value to MILs by dividing it by 3.43, a MIL to MOA by multiplying it by 3.43.

So, which is better?

Neither system is inherently better or worse. A shooter with experience who understands one approach over the other should stick with what they know. But new shooters, or shooters who want to dive down the long-range rabbit hole, should lean toward MILs. MILs are the standard measure for the U.S. military and are used worldwide, unlike MOA that is only used in a handful of civilian markets — and is rapidly going out of style. Reasons for that are multiple, but at its root, if you learn both systems, you'll see that computing MILs quickly in your head is generally faster than MOA. MILs "click," at least for me, in a way that MOA struggles, mainly because in MIL calculations, it's possible a lot of times to move the decimal place.

To learn the precision shooting language of MILs, I strongly recommend Ryan Cleckner's *Long Range Shooting Handbook: The Complete Beginner's Guide to Precision Rifle Shooting.*

MILs is the language of most precision shooters. You're more likely to talk shop and get help in MILs at a match than MOA. Also, when using ballistics programs to solve long-range shooting problems, MOA can create issues. Some optics manufacturers have incorrectly set MOA on their scopes for 1 inch at 100 yards instead of 1.047 inches. If your ballistics program

Are MILs or MOA turrets and reticles right for you? Use what you already know, but if you're starting new, the author recommends MILs.

is calculating based on 1 MOA = 1.047 inches, but your optic is adjusting 1 MOA = 1 inch, you could miss the target. That's especially true in long-distance rimfire shooting, where you need to make significant scope adjustments at not-so-big distances. A 0.047-inch error can compound very quickly in .22 LR. It's also a challenge to figure out if an MOA riflescope uses 1.047- or 1-inch adjustments. Nikon always used 1.047 for MOA, but Vortex uses 1 inch. If you go MOA over MILs in precision optics, you may have to call customer service to get the numbers straight. If, as I did, you shoot both Nikon and Vortex MOA optics, you need to make sure you change the MOA value in your ballistics program to get accurate results for each rifle system.

MILs being universal avoid all this rigmarole.

With scope size determined and the MOA vs. MILs argument decided, there are five factors to consider when settling on a precision optic for rimfire: parallax, focal plane, reticle design, turrets, and magnification power. Let's look at them:

Adjustable Parallax

If you've ever seen the reticle (crosshairs) of your

scope float or come in and out of focus while on target, you've probably noticed the phenomenon of parallax. The reticle and the target are no longer on the same focal plane within the scope's main tube. The difference between focal planes becomes exaggerated at extremely close and far target distances — decreasing accuracy and obscuring the reticle. Some scopes allow you to manually adjust for this and bring everything into focus at specified target distances, while others have fixed parallax at a specific range.

Most centerfire scopes with fixed parallax are factory-focused, around 150 to 175 yards — too far for typical rimfire applications. Manufacturers set fixed parallax rimfire scopes at 50 or 60 yards, which can work fine for small game hunting but make 20- or 25-yard shots — standard in many smallbore sports — a blurry mess. For any precision smallbore match scope and most hunting scenarios, I recommend an adjustable parallax down to at least 25 yards.

Most tactical-inspired and long-range centerfire scopes have a side knob for parallax adjustment, sometimes called "side focus." Bench shooting target scopes often have the parallax control built into the objective bell, called "Adjustable Objective" or AO. Side controls are easier to run when jumping between near and far targets within the same shot string in a match. AO controls work fine when you have plenty of time. For match shooting, I highly recommend adjustable parallax via a side focus knob.

Focal Plane

There are two locations within the tube where makers install the reticle. If the reticle goes in toward the objective lens (the front of the tube), that's called first focal plane (FFP). If it goes in near the ocular lens or the back of the tube, that's called second focal plane (SFP). When dialing up the magnification on a FFP scope, the reticle will grow larger. In SFP scopes, the reticle will appear the same size no matter the magnification. There are pros and cons to each.

Many long-range shooters and hunters have migrated to FFP scopes because reticle holdover values don't change with the scope power. In other words, if every hash mark along the vertical stadia (the main crosshair line) represents 1 MOA at the lowest power, they still equal 1 MOA at the highest magnification. The second hash under the central crosshair equals 1 MOA drop at 4x power and 16x power. FFP scopes are a significant advantage in some precision matches where single-stage targets may be from 20 to 100 yards or beyond, and the shooter must change scope magnification and holdover within the shot string. An FFP optic's drawback is that the reticle can be small and hard to see at the power range's low end. In my NRL22 matches, many older shooters struggle

The Athlon Argos BTR is a first focal plane (FFP) optic.

to see the FFP reticles when turned down to 4x and 6x or even 8x. FFP systems are not for older eyes. Hard-to-see reticles also don't work well while hunting, where you might have to tease out a squirrel head in a tangle of branches and leaves. Fat, clear, stadia work much better.

Second focal plane scopes work well in these situations, and old or bad eyes can usually find the mark quickly. The classic duplex reticle draws the eye to the center and makes for high-speed target acquisition. SFP scopes also tend to be less expensive than FFPs, but the former can cause trouble when you use the reticles for drop compensation.

Several years ago, I was on a pronghorn hunt in Wyoming. I had a .25-06 with me and tagged out on the first morning. A friend had long wanted a .25-06, and as we talked about it, I suggested he borrow my rifle to get his goat. Taped to the stock's side was the bullet drop for that SFP reticle when at the full 16x power. My friend came back after that first day discouraged. He had missed a shot at 400 yards — sailing the bullet over the old buck's back. The animal was grazing broadside. He had a steady rest and decades of Western hunting experience that made this shot — he thought — a layup. He had used my DOPE chart on the side of the stock, and when he shot, the scope was at 14x. At that magnification power, my chart was worthless. That's a rare situation, but it goes to show how "off" a reticle can be within an SFP scope if you don't pay careful attention to magnification. In the

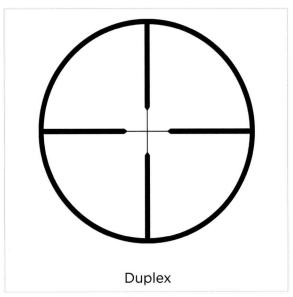

Duplex

A classic duplex reticle.

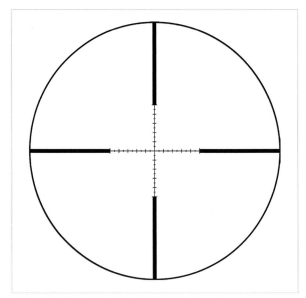

A clean duplex-style reticle with MOA hash marks.

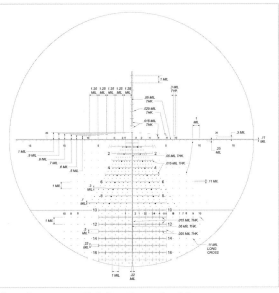

The tech specs on a Nightforce Tremor3 reticle.

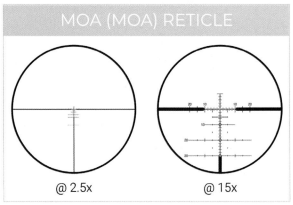

MOA (MOA) RETICLE

@ 2.5x | @ 15x

A Maven MOA reticle in an FFP scope, as seen at 2.5x and 15x. Note the size difference.

more likely event of moving fast through a competition stage, running different targets at different scope powers could be a real liability.

Reticle Design

In the last few years, no part of the riflescope has been designed and redesigned more than the reticle or aiming point. For hunting with laser-flat .17 calibers, it's hard to beat a simple duplex crosshair. Developed in the 1960s by Leupold, the duplex uses four heavy crosshair lines that taper down to fine lines where they meet in the center. This design makes placing the crosshairs on a target fast, and it always provides a clean sight picture. When shooting slow rimfire loads like .22 LR, bullet drop is more of an issue. For hunting work, .22 LR Ballistic Drop Compensating (BDC) reticles, like those in the now-discontinued Nikon Prostaff Rimfire series, can work very well. Tract Optics and Hawke Optics have picked up the slack, producing dedicated rimfire BDC scopes that are not junk like many "rimfire" scopes. BDC optics have reticles with hash marks tuned to either standard-velocity .22 LR, high-velocity .22 LR, or .17 HMR, indicating where the bullet will impact at longer ranges. It takes some trial and error to figure exactly

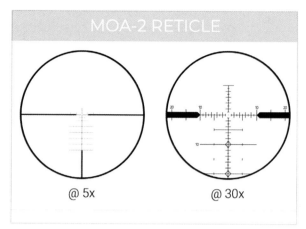

@ 5x   @ 30x

A Maven FFP at 5x and 30x.

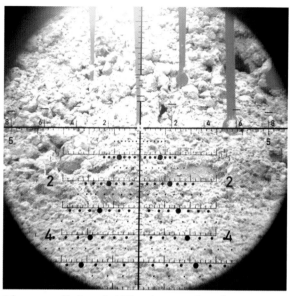

A know-your-limits rack at 50 yards as seen through a Nightforce. Photo: Greg Hamilton

The stock turrets on the Maven scope.

where the hash marks and downrange impacts line up, but once you figure it out, it's a fast and elegant solution for a hunting or plinking rifle.

Competition reticles can quickly become complicated. Rather than hash marks indicating likely holdovers by caliber, each line may represent a certain number of MOA or MILs. The sub-tensions or white space between the hashes all have a set value, too. The finer these marks are, the more precise the measurement, theoretically. But too many marks can quickly clutter the sight picture, particularly for a shooter who has spent their life using a duplex. That is especially the case with FFP scopes on low magnification, where a complicated reticle can look like smudged ink. But, when lying prone 100 yards or more from your target with match .22 LR ammo that drops like a brick, all those hash marks become very handy.

Different optics companies run various reticles, but there are a few standards. The Horus H59 started a revolution of "Christmas tree-style" reticles and quickly became the standard for many elite marksmen. Below the centerline is a grid laid out in 0.2-MIL increments that make for exact drop calculations and fast follow-up shots. It's clear to see where the first shot landed, then hold that spot in the reticle for the second shot. At first blush, a system like the H59 and the many similar reticles it spawned can look like a complex geometry problem but spend some

time with them on the range, and it comes together quickly. Like understanding MILs, these reticles make good sense with a little time spent behind the trigger.

Turrets

For the most part, there are two kinds of turrets available on riflescopes. You can get either exposed turrets, which allow for manual adjustments in the field, or capped turrets usually adjusted once when zeroing a rifle, then left alone. Most precision shooters use adjustable turrets, which allow you to dial-in precision shots for a given range.

For a .22 LR with a 50-yard zero, the crosshair center is still an accurate hold from 20 to 60 yards or

Dialing elevation with turrets is easy and more accurate for most shooters than using a reticle. Photo: Mike Semanoff

more, depending on ammo velocity. Push out beyond 60 or 70 yards, and the shooter has a decision to make: Use the hash marks on the reticle to hold over the target, or spin up the turret and hold the center. In a PRS-style rimfire match, if the stage involves shooting a close target, at say 30 yards, then jumping to a 100-yard plate, most shooters use the reticle. If target distances are fixed at 65 yards or more, dialing the turrets is a more elegant solution. However, for extended-distance rimfire shooting, like the developing sport of Extreme Long Range rimfire — or when clipping varmints across the plains — adjustable turrets are necessary.

I'm partial to turrets that lock. To spin them, you pull up on the turret, which lets it click free. Push the turret down, and it won't move on you. Many less expensive tactical scopes don't have locking turrets, which strikes me as a risk while afield.

When you're in the woods chasing squirrels or rabbits, all turrets tend to just get in the way. Most of the shots taken at small game are inside 60 yards, anyway. I've played with optics with complicated reticles and turrets on hunting rifles and have migrated away from them. Duplex reticles and capped adjustments work for me in the hunting woods, complicated reticles and big locking turrets for competition rigs.

Magnification Power

Magnification is useful, and it's the first thing many people consider when buying optics, but it's probably the least important feature when hunting or competing in a rimfire match. Sure, when shooting from a rock-solid rest at a tiny target 1,000 yards away, 35x magnification is handy, but in most cases, that's not the situation.

Match shooting like in NRL or PRS is often done from compromised and unsteady shooting positions at reasonable-for-caliber distances. The targets are rarely less than 1 MOA in size. Significant magnification can amplify wobbles and shakes and hurt the shot from unsteady rests. Unless you're going long on a varmint or ground squirrel hunt, magnification is even less critical when hunting small game. It's hard to beat 3-9x or 4-16x for a hunting setup. One of the killingest bushy tail hunters I know spent most of his career behind a fixed 4x scope. Many run larger scopes with power ranges from 4x to 5x on the low end to 25x or 35x on the high end for match shooting. But all those shooters will tell you most of the time they live in the middle band of that power range. A superior-quality scope with less power than you think you need is often a better call than a lower-quality scope with a massive high-end zoom.

Recommended Optics

What is the best optic for your rifle? That's a hard question to answer, and as we'll see later, it is highly dependent on your end-use. As mentioned, I prefer MILs over MOA. I like 1-inch optics without turrets for hunting rimfires because they're lighter and look better on a sporter rifle. For varmint hunting and traditional 100-yard NRL22 competition, I lean toward 30mm optics with locking turrets for the added adjustment and security in rough and tumble stages. For ELR, I like 34mm. Considering these features, I then look at the price. As a general rule, I want the MSRP of the riflescope to match *or exceed* the MSRP of the rifle. In many shooting situations, especially NRL22, the optic is more important than the gun. Repeat: *the optic is more important than the gun.* That's because even low-end factory rifles have enough raw accuracy to be competitive at NRL22 — or snipe a squirrel at 100 yards — but you cannot say the same about low-end optics.

Some optic manufacturers are ahead of others when it comes to precision. Look at the gear survey from the 2020 NRL22 National Match, included in the back of this book, and you'll get an idea of who is leading the charge. Of the 68 shooters surveyed, 30 chose Vortex, 11 Athlon, and 9 ran Nightforce. If you consider high-end optics (read: expensive), you could add Kahles, US Optics, Zero Compromise, and Trijicon to that Nightforce in a "money is no object" class of the best riflescopes.

What follows is a roundup of some of the better general interest match and hunting optics, whatever the budget. I've personally shot all these on rimfire rifles and will vouch for them. Optics makers introduce new scopes every year that push the performance level, so this list is by no means exclusive. There are some great scopes not included here. A savvy buyer looking for a competition optic will track what the pros are using in their shooting discipline of choice, such as through the posted National Rifle League gear surveys. You can also follow the very excellent Precision Rifle Blog or track the various benchrest or other shooting organizations in which they compete — most publish extensive winning gear lists.

Athlon Ares ETR 4.5-30x56 FFP
34mm; $1,499

The Athlon Ares ETR 4.5-30x56 FFP scope is a beast. There are no two ways about it. It weighs 2.2 pounds, and the 34mm tube is more than 15 inches long with big exposed locking turrets and a 56mm bell. For a pure precision match rifle, where more weight is generally better, the Ares ETR shines in the heft department. The 30x magnification makes 100-yard NRL22 targets look gigantic. The illuminated APRS1 reticle shows 6 MILs of drop at 30x and the full 10 MILs at 16x — the magnification power I tend to run most. On a course of fire that has me jumping between various

target distances, I can keep the power at 16x, use the 25-yard to infinity side focus to pick up targets clearly from 20 yards to well beyond 100, then make the shots using the corresponding hashmark in the reticle for those distances. With a 25 MOA Pic rail under the scope, plus Burris XTR Signature Rings with another 5 MOA drop, this scope can zero my match ammo at 50 yards, then provide a ridiculous 24 MILs of come-ups in the turret for an accurate hold to 420 yards.

Athlon Argos BTR, 6-24x50 FFP
30mm; $449

Athlon Optics has quietly built a reputation for making quality, well-priced tactical scopes geared toward precision shooting. The Argos BTR, which you can find for under $400 (and sometimes almost half that on sale), is a strong example. It's one of the most popular base-class optics in NRL22 competition, where the combined rifle and scope MSRP can't exceed $1,050. The scope has a 30mm tube with FFP guts; repeatable, positive MOA or MIL turrets; side focus from 10 yards to infinity; and an illuminated reticle. The 6-24x50 is Athlon's most popular competition configuration, but 8-34x56 and 10-40x56 models are available if you're looking for high-level magnification on a budget.

Athlon Cronus BTR 4.5-29x56 FFP
34mm; $1,999

Don't let the MSRP of this monster scope from Athlon deter you. While the MSRP looks high, you can

Athlon Cronus BTR 4.5-29x56 FFP.

The Bushnell Match Pro 6-24x50mm FFP.

find it online for half that. Athlon's business model works something like this: build a great scope, put a high MSRP on it, slash the price by 40 percent or more online. So, you can find this listed $1,999 scope in many places for $1,200 or better. The Japanese-made Cronus BTR is a good PRS scope. When shopping for "a sky's the limit" optic for a Vudoo in a JP APAC chassis strictly for ELR work, it was my choice. With the Nightforce ATACR (listed below), it's possible to get more top-end magnification and maybe the best glass on planet earth. But is the Nightforce three times better than the Cronus BTR? No way. The Athlon is a do-it-all precision riflescope worthy of the very best rifle builds, and compared to the competition, it'll save you at least a grand in the process.

Bushnell Forge 4.5-27x50 FFP or SFP Deploy MOA
30mm; $500 to $949

For a reach-out-and-touch-them rimfire rifle built for varmint hunting or extreme long-range target work, it's hard to beat the big Forge 4.5-27x50 scope from Bushnell. The FFP version runs almost $1,000, but you can pick up the SFP model for around $500 with a little Internet sleuthing. Bushnell's Deploy reticle is among the simplest of the hash mark-heavy options out there, and 4.5x to 27x power provides ridiculous versatility, whether plinking at long-range or cleaning up prairie dogs. This scope was my first choice for a Savage A17 build. With a 50-yard zero, I can spin up enough elevation for a dead-nuts hold at 360 yards — a long but plausible shot with the .17 HMR. It's a fun combination on steel at 400 yards.

Bushnell Match Pro 6-24x50 FFP
30mm; $449

Bushnell is the new title optics sponsor for NRL22, and much of the marketing push centers around its Bushnell Match Pro 6-24x50 FFP. The 30mm tube has 18 MILs of windage and elevation, so with a 30 MOA rail (see below), it makes a fine extreme long-range optic, with enough guts to hit with a .22 LR to about 400 yards. The Christmas tree-style Deploy MIL reticle is first-rate, with heavier stadia lines that older eyes might like.

Hawke Vantage 30 WA SF IR 4-16x50 Rimfire .17 HMR and .22 Subsonic
30mm; $399

After Nikon left the riflescope market — and took with it a popular lineup of .22 LR BDC tubes — Fort Wayne, Indiana-based Hawke Optics has doubled down on rimfire. The side-focused parallax adjustment on its Vantage 30 WA SF IR 4-16x50 runs from 10 yards to infinity, and the exposed ¼ MOA locking turrets have the excellent, positive "click" of a well-made scope. But what sets these scopes apart are the BDC reticles set for .17 HMR and subsonic .22 LR. Hawke calibrated the .22 reticle for 1,050 fps ammo, unlike most others on the market that are set for 1,600 fps and only work well when tuned to CCI Stingers. Zero the Hawke .22 LR scope at 50 yards with standard-velocity hollowpoints and 16x hash marks in the scope show where to hold 200 yards in 25-yard increments. The .17 reticle was pre-calculated to 2,500 fps ammo and worked well with CCI A17s. It shows hold points to 300 yards in 50-yard increments when zeroed at 100 yards.

Maven RS.1 2.5-15x44
30mm; $1,200

The 6x multiplier in the Maven RS.1 2.5-15x44 allows for more magnification in a smaller package or six times the power at the top end. Suddenly, a scope that's the same size as a traditional 2.5-10x jumps to 2.5-15x. These scopes command serious money and rarely go on sale, but they bring an attractive do-it-all quality to a rifle build. The RS.1 is perfect for hunting. The 44mm bell gathers more than enough light for clear shots a half-hour before sunrise and after sunset, and it's become one of my favorite squirrel optics. Caps cover the windage and elevation dials — they're not exposed turrets like tactical scopes — so even if they do snag on shrubs or trees in the woods, you don't have to worry about your point of impact changing. The side focus runs 10 yards to infinity, and the clean SFP reticle means even at 2.5x you can find your crosshairs easily, which can't be said for all FFP scopes with such low-end magnification. For close shots at squirrels, you have that 2.5x low end. For 80-plus-yard headshots, you get a crystal-clear top end at 15x. That's versatility that's hard to beat. You pay for it, but it's worth it.

Maven RS.3 5-30x56 FFP
30mm; $1,600

Maven built its brand on direct-to-consumer hunting optics with an incredible price vs. performance

ratio. The RS.3 does exactly that, with a high-wattage 30x magnification on the top end in an impressively compact package. (At 13 inches long at 26 ounces, it might be the most compact 30x scope out there.) Because of its size, I put it atop a CZ 457 Premium re-barreled with a stainless Lilja in .17 Mach 2. It may be the deadliest sniper of tree squirrels ever created — not that I'm biased or anything. Maven also has a 34mm version of this scope, the RS.4, which does everything this hunter does with the edge for long-distance shooting. It's not cheap, but on a go-for-broke small game rig, it is excellent.

Tract Optics 22 FIRE 3-9X40 BDC or T-Plex
1-inch; $174

In December 2015, two former Nikon employees started Tract Optics, a direct-to-consumer manufacturer, to provide better-quality glass for the money by cutting out the middleman. Tract's rimfire-specific 22 FIRE does just that. There's more value for the money than other .22 LR scopes on the market. The parallax on the 22 FIRE is fixed at 50 yards. The windage and elevation adjustments are ¼-inch at 50 yards with extremely good spring-loaded zero resets on both dials. The model I tested had highly repeatable adjustments with positive clicks. The 22 FIRE is available with a T-Plex reticle or a BDC optimized for high-velocity ammo like CCI Stingers. Zero with Stingers or similar 1,400 to 1,600+ fps loads at 50 yards with the BDC version and the reticle's dots show where to aim to 150 yards in 25-yard increments. An accurate rifle, plus Stingers, plus the 22 FIRE adds up to a very deadly small game setup.

Vortex Optics Diamondback Tactical 6-24x50
30mm; $499

Another winning base-class NRL22 optic, the Diamondback Tactical from Vortex, has a cult following and comes with Vortex's unlimited, unconditional, no-questions-asked lifetime warranty. I've put this scope on a Ruger American Rimfire in .22 LR as a base-class NRL22 rig, and it makes for an accurate, repeatable, and affordable precision rimfire package. I have another one on a chassis-bound Savage B-Series Precision .22 LR. This FFP optic is available with MRAD or MOA turrets and reticles, and it has 19 MILs or 65 MOA of adjustment in windage and elevation — more than similar 30mm scopes in this price range. It has a wider field of view than many of its price-point peers and is more than clear enough for a daytime shooting match. I've come to like the intuitive EBR-2C (MRAD) reticle, which packs a lot of information into a clean sight picture. The number one question people ask me as an NRL22 match director is, "What scope should I put on my new rifle?" and this Diamondback Tactical from Vortex is my No. 1 answer.

Vortex Strike Eagle 5-25x56 FFP
34mm; $799

Calling this optic from Vortex "budget" or a "price point" scope will make many people groan. After all, $800 is no small sum. But what Vortex has done is pack features found in scopes that cost two and three times as much and made it accessible to the rest of us. The Strike Eagle is the best 34mm optic out there for less than a grand. You get good glass, 25x magnification, the famous Vortex warranty, and a crazy 31 MILs of elevation adjustment. With the right rail and some know-how, you can get on steel with a .22 LR to 500 yards with this sucker. I topped a RimX, PROOF, Timney, Grayboe build with this optic, and it's a real ELR performer.

The Nightforce ATACR is not inexpensive, but if you need one of the best, this is it. Photo: Mike Semanoff

Nightforce ATACR 7-35x56 F1
34mm; $3,600

If you want the best in a long-range precision optic, budget be damned, then this is your scope. At

The Vortex Diamondback Tactical is the one the author most often recommends to new shooters. They aren't disappointed.

The Nightforce NX8 2.5-20x50 is a high-end scope that's ideal for precision rimfire. It hurts the wallet less than the ATACR.

the 2020 NRL22 Nationals, three of the top five shooters ran this optic, less than the five of the top seven that used it in 2019. Still, paired with a Vudoo rifle, the winningest rifle/scope combination in the National Match two years in a row was by far this combination. Sure, a $3,600 scope on a $3,600 .22 LR rifle sounds extreme, but if you're this deep into this book, you're probably no moderate.

Nightforce NX8 2.5-20x50 F1
30mm; $1,950

The Nightforce NX8 2.5-20x50 F1 scope from Nightforce represents the state-of-the-art in precision optics. The 8x erector allows for an incredible 2.5x to 20x magnification window, making it ideal for a price-is-no-concern small game platform or a compact competition package. And compact it is. With a 30mm tube, the NX8 measures 12 inches long and weighs just 28 ounces. Thanks to the wizards at Nightforce, you're not losing any real elevation in that 30mm tube compared to most larger 34mm scopes and it far exceeds adjustments of more mundane 30mms. The NX8 has 32 MILs of elevation adjustment. There is a first focal plan model, the F1, and a second focal model, the F2, which older eyes can appreciate. Nightforce made its name by pushing optics innovation forward. The NX8 keeps that tradition alive and well.

Mounting Systems

A good scope is worth little if it has a poor connection to the rifle. Accuracy issues traced back to scopes are often problems with the rings and bases. If you go all-in on a precision rifle and optic and fix the two together with $9.99 rings made in China from Amazon, you're asking for trouble. Don't skimp on rings or bases.

Earlier, we discussed internal max elevation adjustment in riflescopes, with 34mm tubes providing the most and 1-inch providing the least. 32 MILs of elevation from the latest-greatest 34mm scope is excellent but rarely translates to 32 MILs of usable elevation on target. That spec is the entire elevation range. When zeroed at 50 yards (or centerfire rifles when zeroed at 100 yards), most rimfire rifles live in the bottom center of the elevation range, but this is caliber dependent. Half of 32 is 16 or 17 MILs of usable elevation. You can cheat that with a tapered scope base or rail. That effectively pushes the 50-yard .22 LR zero farther up the scope's elevation range by tilting the scope, so it points a few degrees down. This setup is ideal for long-range shooting, but keep in mind an optic typically has the best clarity or image sharpness through the center of its elevation and windage range. It's wise only to build in as much taper as you think you'll need.

Tapered scope bases or Picatinny rails have been around forever. They're commonplace in the precision shooting world, yet they mystify many new rimfire shooters. Indeed, they're a departure from the traditional rimfire scope mount of 11mm dovetail rings clamped directly to the receiver. Today, companies like dipproducts.com and egwguns.com make Picatinny rails for all major rimfire receivers. Remington 700-style actions from Vudoo, Bergara, and RimX can use Remington 700-style rails, of which there are dozens.

If you plan to shoot your rimfire beyond 200 yards, it makes sense to get a tapered Pic rail. They come with anywhere from 20 to 60 MOA of baked-in elevation — the rail slants forward, so the optic isn't entirely parallel to the receiver. This way, the 50-yard zero we first discussed gets "pushed" up to the top of the elevation range inside the scope. That means instead of 16 or 17 MILs of real-world change (a little more than half of 32 MILs in our example), you're looking at 25 MILs or more. The zero point sits higher in the optic's internal elevation range. That is how ELR rimfire shooters get their .22s to hit at 500 yards without additional gadgetry.

Another option, though less widely used, is to shim the scope rings. Shimming can be as simple as placing a few aluminum soda can pieces on the bottom side of the rear scope ring. Old-timers will remember this was about the only way to get a 50-yard zero with a .22 LR and *cheapo* centerfire scope back in the day. The Burris XTR Signature Rings work on this same principle as soda can shims, but appreciably better. The rings ship with plastic shims that can add up to 40 extra MOA of elevation. They work well, hold firm, and, combined with a canted pic rail, can squeeze the maximum elevation from your rig to bottom out a scope zero.

How much taper should you get in your Picatinny rail? If you plan to shoot NRL22 or a similar precision rimfire match, you'll need to engage targets as close as 25 yards. You can do that without adjustment from a 50-yard zero. I have achieved that on most of my rimfire rifles with a 40 MOA rail using a 34mm optic. That said, a more typical setup is 20, 25, or 30 MOA rails with a 30mm optic. Baked-in canted Pic rails on quality 10/22 receivers, for example, are typically 20 or 30 MOA. With drop compensation in the reticle, it will provide enough adjustment to connect 400 yards with

A heavy-duty Spuhr unimount.

A Vudoo shooter with a Riton optic—another high-quality manufacturer worth considering. Photo: Mike Semanoff.

match speed .22s. To get beyond that, you enter the specialized world of adjustable mounts and prisms, which we'll discuss later in the section on Extreme Long Range rimfire shooting.

What about Weaver? In the precision centerfire world, the Weaver-style bases have lost the war to the much more common Picatinny rail. They're not as relevant in the rimfire world because receivers like those from CZ, Tikka, and Anschütz have built-in 11mm dovetail rails and don't require bases. For these rifles, a tapered Pic rail is an unnecessary addition in most cases unless you want to shoot very long range. You only need 11mm dovetail rings to mount a scope on these actions. Of course, you can put Weaver bases on a Remington 700-style receiver and many of the Ruger receivers, among others. Weaver-style bases are still an excellent option for shooters who want a low-profile mount, especially in a two-piece system. That is, without a monolithic rail running the top length of the action. They do well on lightweight sporter builds.

Finally, unimounts or one-piece scope rings like those from Spuhr, Badger Ordnance, and others are widely considered more secure than the traditional two-piece ring system. In the no-recoil world of precision .22 LR shooting, I don't think this much matters, though. They provide a built-in taper that you can't get in rings alone, save from the Burris system. Second, they let you remove and reinstall the scope with a minimal change of zero. On the downside, they generally don't provide as much flexibility in scope position on the receiver compared to two rings on a Pic rail.

There are many quality manufacturers of rails, rings, and unimounts. I tend to prefer Pic rails from DIP Inc. and EGW with rings mostly from Warne and sometimes Burris when more taper is needed. Vortex rings are good, as are Nightforce, Badger Ordnance, Hawkins, Iota, and the old classic, Leupold. For hunting rimfires and direct attachments to 11mm receivers, I'm partial to Talley. All of my Anschütz rifles are tapped and run Talley integral mounts. I've also used 11mm rings from BLK without issue on several CZ rifles. The key is not to buy junk. Rings and rails are not where to cheap-out on a rifle platform. They matter in a big way.

Accessories

A precision rifle system is not complete with just a gun, scope, and rings. There's a deep well of aftermarket accessories to make your rifle shoot better and, frankly, to look cooler. Coolness factor aside, there are three essential accessories for precision rimfire shooting: A bipod, bags, and a sling. Yet even these three aren't law. As with selecting a rifle and optic, let your shooting or hunting discipline guide you. A bushy tail rifle probably does not need a bipod, but it needs a sling. An ELR rig doesn't need a sling, but the bipod is as vital as the optic. An NRL22 gun needs all three; a rimfire challenge rifle, none of them.

What follows is a roundup of the most common shooting accessories. For deeply sport-specific add-ons, we'll get detailed in those sport-specific sections. Listed here are the basic extras that many precision shooters already have, and new shooters should consider when lining out their first precision rimfire build. This list is not inclusive but a top-level overview of the most common makes and manufacturers.

Bipods

Tactical and long-range shooting — plus most lazy weekends at the range — always includes shooting prone. NRL22, for example, has two prone stages in every month's course of fire. It's a foundational position, the most solid of all shooting positions, and every rifleman needs to learn how to shoot prone well.

There are many good bipods on the market. The most popular in the precision shooting world, whether rimfire or centerfire, are B&T Industries' ATLAS bipods, the Ckye-Pod from MDT, Evolution, Accu-Tac, and the old school but much-loved Harris.

The Harris design is by far the most widely copied, and you can get inexpensive knockoffs for little

Shooting bags are essential in the run-and-gun Precision Rifle Series-style of rimfire competition. Photo: Mike Semanoff

An Atlas PSR bipod with Area 451 ARCA rail clamp. Photo: Mike Semanoff

money online. But you get what you pay for, and none of the cheap Chinese versions match the quality of the 100-percent made in the USA Harris. There are several versions of the Harris, but the differences boil down to leg length and type. The most common Harris bipod leg length is 6 to 9 inches as that lets average-sized shooters get lowest on the deck — and the lower you are, the more stable you are. The standard legs adjust to any length within that range and are pressure-tightened to length, sort of like camera tripod legs. The M series has notched legs that better control the height and adjust fast on the fly.

For ELR shooting, ATLAS Bipods is the current leader in the space with the new BT72-NC Super CAL. Designed for .50-caliber centerfire rifles, it's heavy-duty throughout yet folds down like a traditional bipod and does not exceed 8 inches wide, per new centerfire King of Two Miles rules. Hook this beast to a .22, and you have about the most stable prone bipod platform money can buy. Is it overkill? Yes, but it's fun. The

The very excellent MDT Cyke Pod. Photo: Mike Semanoff

Vudoo tricked out in a JP APAC chassis on the cover of this book sits on a BT72-NC. Other "overkill but fun" bipods for rimfires include Elite Iron and Phoenix Precision models. The Phoenix, at its lowest setting, has a leg spread of almost 20 inches.

Maybe the most common bipod seen at rimfire matches after the Harris is the popular ATLAS Precision Sniper Rifle BT46-NC or the PSR. Developed for

A shooter using a Webie Fortune Cookie bag to get stable on a metal barricade. Photo: ConX Media.

and selected by the United States Special Operations Command, the PSR has non-rotational legs and a limiting locking system for stopping fore and aft movement. The head pans and cants to 30 degrees, and the five-position legs lockout at zero, 45, 90, 135, and 180 degrees. ATLAS also has a more budget-conscious version in the BT10 V8 with the same basic features, such as the built-in pan and cant and five-position locking legs.

Like the Harris, there are various adaptors to get the ATLAS on your rifle, whether you have a sling stud, Pic rail, ARCA rail, or MLOK attachment point.

For 99.9 percent of precision rimfire shooting, it's hard to beat the ATLAS or a more traditional Harris.

Shooting Bags

Front and rear shooting bags help you achieve the most stability possible, from a bench or otherwise. A rear bag with a bipod is the standard setup when shooting prone.

The Gamechanger series of bags from Armageddon Gear can function as a front bag on obstacles that don't play well with bipods, like barricades, fence posts, or any other irregular surface. It also serves as a rear bag for when you use a bipod. This rugged bag holds nearly five pounds of pelletized-polymer fill that gives it enough weight to conform to the shape of supporting objects and provide rock-solid rifle support. Handles on both ends make it easy to grab, and removable Velcro-lined straps across the top let you affix it to the barrel or forend when moving stage to stage. It's available in various sizes and fill weights. It was by far the most popular shooting bag in NRL22 Nationals in 2019 and 2020, with almost half the competitors running it.

Wiebad and Short Action Precision make a variety of high-quality bags. Caldwell makes excellent bags, too. So does your sock draw, with a little help from your kid's sandbox.

You can easily make a rear squeeze bag from an old gym sock. These work remarkably well, as any Marine Scout Sniper will tell you. To make a squeeze bag, get your sock and some filler material. Sandbox sand, rice, and plastic beads sold at crafting stores all work great. Get two thin plastic bags like the kind in the produce section at the grocery store generally

The Short Action Precision rifle sling.

used for bagging wet broccoli. One bag will work, but two will postpone the enviable leakage. Shoot long enough, and your bags will leak filler, no matter who makes them.

Put 2 or 3 cups of filler material in the doubled-up plastic bags and knead, working all the air out. Put the plastic-bagged filler material in your sock and test it out with your rifle. Add or remove filler as needed, then tie off or sew shut the end of the sock. Squeeze bag socks work well, but you can also tweak the design as far as your imagination — and sewing talent — allows. One of the better shooters at my regular NRL22 match uses a homemade bag his wife sewed up. It's roughly a 4x12-inch rectangle, 2 inches thick, and filled with sand. It works great as a rear bag and over barricades.

Slings

You don't just use slings for shouldering rifles. As many riflemen know, they're great for firming up shooting positions, particularly when standing, kneeling, or sitting. I'm partial to the inexpensive and straightforward RLS or Rifleman Loop Sling from Magpul for hunting rifles. It combines the best features of a Rhodesian and a 1907 match sling. It's long enough that you can run the sling over your back and tension the rifle to hand. Or you can use the plastic sling keeper to make an upper loop and tension the hold with your support arm. I've shot many squirrels looped up this way.

The RLS or the various MS-series slings from Magpul all work well, but precision rifle shooting has spawned a relatively new design, the cuff sling. Short Action Precision, TAB Gear, Armageddon, Rifles Only, and others make this style. There's a learning curve, but it's a much more solid system in awkward positions than the traditional sling design.

A Good Case

Steve Boelter of Anschütz has a funny story about a customer who bought an expensive custom shop rifle. The rifle wouldn't group. There were trigger problems. That made little sense to Steve as he built the gun himself and knew it was a barn burner. He asked the customer to ship it back, and it arrived in a hard plastic gun case that "looked like a cat slept in it."

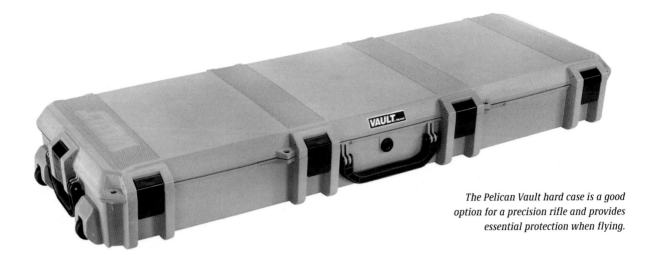

The Pelican Vault hard case is a good option for a precision rifle and provides essential protection when flying.

Pet fur clung to rifle and case alike. Steve cleaned the gun, including the gummed-up trigger. After that, it proved as accurate as the day it first left the custom shop.

Precision instruments need precision treatment, especially in transit. A cheap, flimsy gun case that doesn't seal well is probably not ideal for a ground squirrel rifle that rides in the back of a pickup down dusty Western roads. Pelican cases are excellent but heavy. They're necessary if flying with a gun. For local range trips in a truck cab, a soft case is perfectly acceptable. Just don't let your cat sleep in it.

Chronographs

It's a stretch to call a chronograph basic kit, but it is almost required if you want to send .22 LR rounds past 200 yards. Beg, borrow or steal one from a buddy or your local sportsmen's club to understand what your favorite ammo is doing in your favorite rifle. (Don't steal one.)

In the last few years, the Labradar chronograph system has become the darling of gun writers everywhere because it lets the shooter send groups downrange and capture velocity data simultaneously. There is no more waiting for a bright, sunny day to set up a tripod in a limited shooting window. Say goodbye to barrel contact that can affect harmonics and group size.

Labradar is a contactless, mostly set-and-forget system. It works thanks to the magic of Doppler radar.

The Labradar projects a mini radar array and picks up the bullet traveling through it. It's expensive, especially compared to the older-style, light-based chronographs that cost less than $100. But it works in all light conditions and cuts the pain-in-the-ass factor of traditional chronos down by several orders of magnitude. There's also no risk of shooting it by accident, which does happen — don't ask me how I know. At a recent shooting event with an instructor for the US Navy SEALs, a retired Team 3 guy himself, he described ammo testing .300 PRC and .300 Norma Magnum side by side, with two LabRadars on each gun. They found the two LabRadars only differed occasionally in clocked speeds, and when they did it was only by 1 or 2 fps. That's an accurate system.

The Labradar chronograph system.

A LabRadar at work during an NRL22X competition. Photo: ConX Media

There are some drawbacks. The radar array only works outdoors. It has a preference, too, for wide-open spaces, so threading bullets to a target through the trees doesn't work so well. It can be difficult to aim and get that first string operational when shooting small targets or distances past 100 yards. The Labradar operates by first recording the sound of the firearm report. With low-noise .22 LRs and suppressors, it requires an additional microphone unit and harness. But when set up and running well, it's a thing of wonder.

Clock the snail slow sub-sonic .22 LR in the "handgun" fps range. So long as you space them 2 seconds apart, every shot is captured and written to a .CSV or spreadsheet file on the unit's hard drive or a user-provided SD card. It documents average velocity over the entire shot string, the highest velocity, lowest, plus extreme spread, and standard deviation. It records speed and kinetic energy (based on user-inputted bullet weight) at the muzzle and five preset distances. Since I do most of my testing at my home 50-yard range, I set this up for muzzle to 50 yards in 10-yard increments. Labradar is a painless and passive way to collect a lot of information quickly.

The barrel-mounted MagnetoSpeed chronograph is probably more the industry standard within the precision shooting community as it has a longer track record. Some new mounting systems attach to a rifle or chassis' ARCA rail and get the MagnetoSpeed into position without barrel contact.

Ballistic Calculators, Weather Meters & Other Gadgetry

When shooting long, you need a ballistic problem solver and useful weather data. These can be as

The Kestrel 5700 Elite.

simple as a pair of apps on your smartphone. Strelok Pro, Hornady 4DOF, Geoballistics, and Applied Ballistics Mobile are all trusted apps. I'm most familiar with Ballistic AE and use it frequently. There are pros and cons to each. For weather, there are hundreds of apps from which to choose. I use The Weather Channel and Dark Sky most because they show hour-by-hour wind speed and direction.

The go-to standalone ballistics tool for most precision shooters is the Kestrel Ballistics Wind Meter. Several models range from under $200 to almost $600. The most significant advantage I've found to the flagship Elite 5700 Series is storing 30 rifle and load combinations. If you have one or two precision rifles, this is unnecessary, but it quickly becomes worth the money if you have more.

The higher-end Kestrels don't just read the wind direction and speed. They also measure temperature, humidity, altitude, and pressure, among 9 or 10 other environmental variables. In real-time, the unit then crunches those numbers against information on the rifle and the load via the onboard Applied Ballistics Elite ballistic calculator. The result is precise hold data for the next shot at whatever distance, with environmental conditions considered — something devices without climate meters just can't do. With the 30 firearm profiles, there's plenty of space to log not only your favorite precision rimfire but also your centerfire match gun, and deer gun, and AR, and all the various ammo you like to put through those guns. The upgrade 5700 also has LiNK Bluetooth connectivity to communicate with the SIG Sauer BDX family of scopes and rangefinders, among a few others. That can quickly escalate into a mesh of connected shooting technology. It's all very cool, and the future of shooting, and fun to nerd out on, but not at the expense of dry-fire training. Technology is fantastic, and we should welcome it with open arms, but even the best digital kit is no match for practice, practice, practice. RR

6

PRECISION & ACCURACY

P recision and accuracy are not the same things. *Precision* is the spread of individual shots. When you measure group size, you measure precision or how well the shots cluster together — also called "dispersion." *Accuracy* is a measure of how centered those shots are on a specific target. A bullseye hit is an accurate shot. The bullet went where you aimed. Likewise, five shots spaced around a bullseye at the same distance is an accurate group. A tight cluster of shots in the bullseye, or the "one ragged hole" we all chase, is both precise and accurate.

Precision is inherent to a rifle system. For our purposes, a rifle system is a combination of rifle, optic, mounts, ammunition, and the shooter. You derive precision from the quality of components. As we've

Going long with a V-22 in a JP APAC topped with an Athlon BTR optic. Photo: Cosmo Genova

Tiny groups on paper targets make good photos but don't provide much information outside that specific rifle system.

learned, match ammunition is more precise because of primer, powder, bullet, and brass quality and how manufacturers assemble them. Likewise, you can make a rifle more or less precise through gunsmithing or by adding higher-quality components. For example, when you swap a factory sporter 10/22 barrel for a premium hand-lapped drop-in, you hope it shrinks your groups. You can adjust accuracy through more straightforward means. By spinning the elevation or windage turrets in a riflescope, you can change the point of aim, thereby making the system more accurate — or more likely to hit the target. When those shots cluster tightly in the bullseye, the system is both precise and accurate. You may have gotten this far and wondered, *Why so few target photos in this book?* After all, it is commonplace for gun writers to test a rifle and show off the teeny tiny groups they've inflicted on paper. The assumption is that if Joe Gun Writer can lay down ¼-inch groups with Rifle ABC, then Rifle ABC is a quarter-minute gun, and you, the reader, should buy it. Frankly, this is malarkey. I'm guilty of it myself, reviewing rifles and publishing show-stopper groups, then generalizing on the precision and accuracy of some new rifle. Why is this problematic? Because it is a sample size of one. The reviewer may have had a gem or a lemon. It may have been a prototype, or the tester happened to shoot the rifle with the one lot of

ammunition that sang in that barrel.

Furthermore, the shooter is an integral part of a rifle system. Am I a better shooter than you? Was I shooting off a bipod in the desert with a 20 mile per hour crosswind? Was I shooting indoors? In a tunnel? Off a machine rest? I used to think if I shot several hundred rounds with various ammunition in 5-shot groups and measured and averaged them all, I could get to some general accuracy conclusion about that rifle. With a well-tuned, sophisticated rifle, I also believed that I could shoot and measure different ammunition and make broad claims about which manufacturers have more or less accurate offerings. The deeper down the rabbit hole I've gone, the less I believe either of these things is true.

As you'll see later in this chapter, I took four very nice rifles to the Lapua Rimfire Performance Center in Marengo, Ohio. At this 100-meter test tunnel, I tested eight lots of Center-X and eight lots of Midas+ ammo in all four rifles, with the guns in a vise and the test center manager on the trigger — a four-time NCAA All-American rimfire shooter. One rifle, a CZ 457 with an aftermarket 20-inch PROOF carbon-fiber barrel, stood out. Adjusting from millimeters to inches and meters to yards (more on that later), the CZ laid down the equivalent of a 10-shot 100-yard group just .825-inch center-to-center. That's ten shots at 100 yards!

This 50-yard group was shot with CCI Standard in a Savage B22 Precision.

With a different lot of the same Center-X ammo, it also put down a 3.5-inch group — the worst of all rifles and lots tested by a factor of two. No other rifle or ammo combination was even half that bad.

Is the CZ a sub-MOA barn burner or a dud?

The average group size of the CZ at the (adjusted) 100 yards of all ammo shot that day was 1.438 inches. The median group size was 1.035 inches. Cal Zant of the Precision Rifle Blog has an excellent series on statistics for shooters. In it, he describes the difference between average and median group sets, quoting *Naked Statistics* by Charles Wheelan:

"10 guys are sitting in a middle-class bar in Seattle, and each of them earns $35,000 a year. That means the average annual income for the group is $35,000. Bill Gates then walks into the bar, and let's say his annual income is $1 billion. When Bill sits down on the 11th stool, the average income rises to around $91 million. The original ten drinkers aren't any richer. If we described this bar's patrons as having an average annual income of $91 million, that statement would be statistically correct and grossly misleading. That isn't a bar where multimillionaires hang out; it's a bar where guys with relatively low incomes happen to be sitting next to Bill Gates."

Averages are powerfully affected by outliers. A median is the number that divides a data set in half, so in the Bill Gates example, the drinkers' median income is $35,000. As Zant concludes, "If you had to bet $100 on what the income was of the very next guy who walked in the door, would $35,000 or $91 million be more likely? When we're talking about what is most likely to happen in the future, the median can often be a better choice than the average."

That much should be clear. By testing ammo and measuring groups, you're trying to predict the future or know with certainty how that rifle and ammo will behave in the future to make a successful winning shot on a target in a match or a critter in the woods.

Now, let's go back to my CZ. In lot testing rimfire ammo, *we were looking for outliers*. I wanted to find the lot of ammo that shot the smallest groups. Lots are production runs of ammunition. So, if the loading

The test tunnel at Lapua is a must-stop for rimfire accuracy freaks.

The author tested two Vudoos, in addition to a RimX and a CZ 457, with 16 total ammo lots.

A RimX action in a Remington 700 footprint fixture made for Lapua by Vudoo Gun Works.

machines at Lapua, or ELEY, or CCI, are loaded with ammo components, the lot starts when the operators turn on the loading machines and end when they turn them off. That can be as little as 15,000 total rounds for match ammunition but is more typically 20,000 to 30,000. (At CCI, Federal, Winchester, it may be a lot of 100,000 to 250,000 rounds.) One of the quirks of rimfire is that every ammo lot — always made of the same primer, powder, bullet, brass, and on the same machines — tests *vastly different* from one another, even within the same rifle. When pressed, accuracy-obsessed rimfire shooters will tell you it's impossible even to say this rifle likes Brand X ammunition best. A gun may seem to prefer Brand X ammunition but could shoot one lot very poorly and set world records with the next. The poor lot of Brand X may also shoot worse than an average lot of Brand Y.

If your head is spinning, welcome to rimfire.

By testing lots, you're matching ammunition to the rifle and barrel. By testing lots of lots, we obtained an average and median figure of how well my CZ generally shot Center-X, but this is meaningless, too. If I plan to buy cases (or the entire lot) of the ammunition that shot the best, the average or mean performer of many lots isn't helpful. Lot 23 proved the best in the CZ during my time at Lapua, so I wanted to focus on that. We got 100-yard equivalents of 1.142, 1.145, and

Test protocol: one 10-shot group. If that shows promise, test two or three more 10-shot groups of that ammo lot.

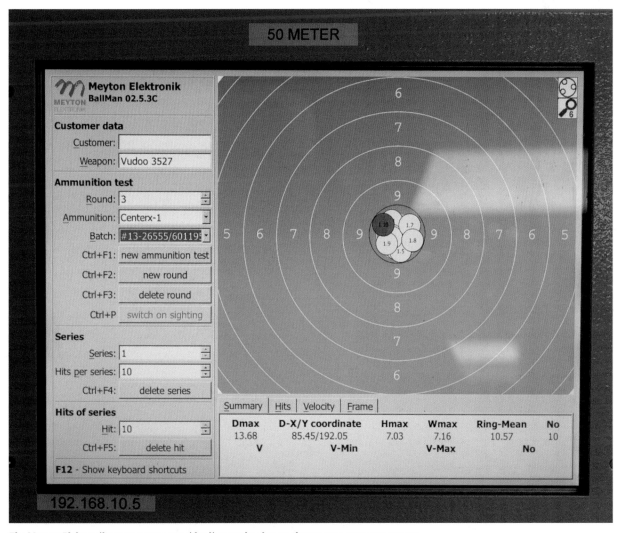

The Meyton Elektronik range system provides live results shot-to-shot on two computer screens.

another fish-stank 3.511-inch group — taken with 0.825 inch that gave us a lot average of 1.656 inches and a median of 1.144 inches. Why is this rifle throwing the occasional flyer that was ruining my numbers? That could be an issue with the ammo, or it could — more likely, I think — be a mechanical issue in the fire control system. Still, Lot 23 proved the best in the CZ and one of my Vudoos. At this point, knowing the mean of that lot can be very helpful in predicting future outcomes. You might be thinking you should find Lot 23 of Lapua Center-X. Well, you can't. I bought the whole lot.

That is what's interesting, maddening, exciting, and futile with publishing rimfire targets and generalizing those conclusions:

The accuracy data only speak to a particular rifle system at one moment in time, and;

It's not helpful to anyone other than that rifle's owner because if he or she discovers a magic lot, it's sold out before any reader ever hears about it, and;

Even if you managed to get a case of that lot, there's no promise it will perform the same way in your rifle.

So, to maximize precision and accuracy in a rifle, you must test lots of lots of ammunition. But how does this help someone looking to buy a new rimfire rifle? Can we make any generalizations about precision and accuracy over a design or factory run of guns?

What I took away from my time at Lapua was discovering a single lot of ammunition that performed best across a few of my rifles and a potential mechanical issue to dig into on my CZ. For me, the big takeaway was a belief that the rifles I tested and the ammunition I found will make a good foundation of a rifle system I want to develop further for NRL- and ELR-style shooting. If my accuracy goals were competitive benchrest shooting, I would have left Ohio underwhelmed. That said, to say my rifle shoots 10-shot .825-inch groups at 100 yards is not false, but it is misleading. It did that once. If it did that with every 10-shot group, I reckon it would be a benchrest contender.

For this book, I've highlighted rifles that I've shot firsthand or seen shot that, like my CZ, are worth working with further. The rifles covered in the earlier chapters can all make the foundation of an accurate, tactical, precision rifle system. That means that they can shoot ½-inch 5-shot groups at 50 yards easily with match ammunition. (Most of them can shoot much better than that.) That is not one group. I shoot at least ten 5-shot groups, measure the outside group diameter, subtract .224 (the diameter of a .22 LR bullet), then compute the average and the median. When those figures are below a ½-inch, I tend to relax. That said, there are many other ways to measure groups that may be better than this. More critical to group size, in my thinking, is understanding how a rifle action works. Focusing on the action opens the door to improvements, so for example, when my CZ throws flyers, I'm not too concerned because I'm confident I can break down the system, work on it, and improve the overall precision.

It's also worth noting that precision in rifles generally — unfortunately — tracks to price. As Dan Killough of Killough Shooting Sports in Winter Park, Texas, who runs ELEY USA's test tunnel, told me, "Mechanical accuracy can be bought." More expensive rifles generally use higher-quality materials and more hands-on care of assembly. That is not to say CZs or Rugers or Savages don't exist that can outshoot the Vudoos and Anschützes of the world, but on the whole, you are much less likely to find a barn-burning $500 rifle than you are to find one in the $2,000 category. How much is that expensive rifle compared to a less expensive one? Again, no easy answers. As Killough put it:

"Say you spend $500 on a baseline CZ 457 rifle or Tikka T1x. Very accurate, very nice rifles. Can we get you something better? Yes. But now we're talking another $700 to step up to an Anschütz if we're considering factory rifles. So that means the price has more than doubled. But that does not mean the accuracy has doubled ... say you're at a ½ inch, and you spend that $1,200 on a new rifle, you may go from .500 inch

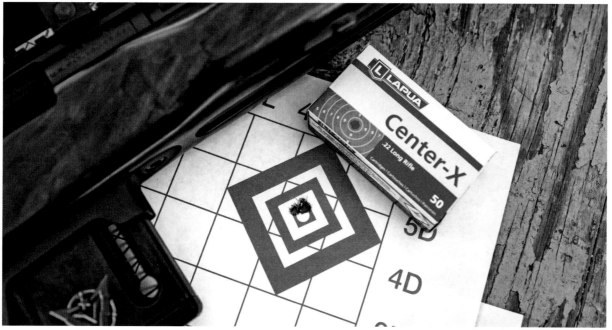

This is the kind of 50-yard group all shooters seek, as shown in this promotional image from Vudoo.

to .400 inch. Then, say you jump up to custom action, custom barrel, custom everything. You spend $3,500, and you went from .400 to .350. Yes, you're more accurate, but each tenth of an inch gets increasingly expensive as you get smaller and smaller."

It's possible to find a 457 or T1x that shoots in the .400s and get an Anschütz that tops out at .500s to use Killough's numbers. There are few guarantees. In part, you see something of a division in the precision rimfire online forums. You have shooters who buy inexpensive guns and work on them relentlessly to get them to shoot. You have another group that buys and tests every new rifle, prospecting. Then you have the "buy once, cry once" group that puts out for a very high-end rifle and is done with it.

These factors lead me to believe budget and shooter personality are the best criteria for selecting a new rifle — not precision, not accuracy. If you have $500 and like to tinker, it's hard to beat a CZ with the wide world of aftermarket parts and the online brain trust of CZ shooters who know how to make them precise. (See the CZ Forum on rimfirecentral.com.) If you don't like to tinker and have the same $500 to spend, the Tikka, to my mind, is very hard to beat. If

you have $1,200, or $2,000 to $4,000, that recommendation changes.

When shopping, it's also essential to consider the optic, mounts, and ammunition. In NRL22-style shooting, where targets are inside 100 yards, *the optic is more important than the rifle.* I repeat: *The optic is more important than the rifle.* That means most factory rifles, even the inexpensive ones, are accurate enough to connect on the typically 2 MOA targets inside 100 yards. Cheap scopes, not so much. With a cheap, blurry scope, it's difficult to see a ¼-inch target at 25 yards. As a general rule, spend equally for optics and rifle — and half that for ammunition. If you plan to spend $500 on a rifle, drop another $500 for the scope and mounts and $250 more to buy ammo. Every real competitor out there would take a Tikka with a mid-tier Vortex shooting Center-X over a Vudoo with a Tasco shooting bulk pack. When it comes to precise and accurate rimfire shooting, optics and ammunition are equally important — if not more important — than the rifle itself. When considering precision and accuracy, you must think about the total rifle system, not just the bare rifle on the gun shop wall.

Universal Rifle Setup

Suppose you've read this far, grew inspired, and bought a new rimfire rifle, optic, and mounts. To set it up correctly is not difficult. It requires a torque wrench (like a set of Fix It Sticks), some bubble levels, a basic rifle cleaning kit, and a cradle or vise. In a pinch, it's possible to level a rifle on bags. Then:

Clean the rifle. Rifles do not come clean from the factory. There is often left-over compound in the bore from the manufacturing process. To remove it, run an oiled patch down the barrel with a cleaning rod, then follow with dry patches until they come out clean.

Remove the barreled action from the stock. Often there's grit and other manufacturing grime you can wipe off the action's underside and in the stock. Inspect and assess the quality of the bedding during this process.

Check the recommended torque for the action screws, which you'll typically find in the owner's manual. If not, you can find it easily online. Re-install the barreled action to the recommended torque. With some rimfire rifles, group size will change based on the torque, so it's good to know your starting torque value. If the recommended torque is a range, say 35 to 45 in-lbs, I tend to start on the high end and work backward if needed.

Level the rifle at the receiver in a cradle or vise. There are scope leveling kits widely available for this job, but a two-pack of inexpensive bubble levels works just as well in most cases.

If you bought a Picatinny rail or another base, install it to the leveled receiver with a drop of Loctite 242 (blue) in the screw holes. Torque it down to what the rail manufacturer recommends or 25 in-lbs. Give it a little time to dry.

Loosely attach the rings to the scope, if vertical rings like Warnes, or the bottom half of the horizontal rings to the Pic rail. The scope rings should be snugged forward on the Pic rail or base while tightening down in both cases. (The recoil impulse of a rifle pushes the action and optic forward, not backward.)

Tighten the rings to the base or rail to the recommended torque, and the scope rings to the scope just enough to hold it in place.

Confirm proper eye relief by shouldering the rifle with the scope at its highest power. You should be able to comfortably see through the scope without excessive shading or moving your head out of its most natural position.

Put the rifle back in the cradle or vise, level the receiver, then level the scope by resting a bubble level on the elevation turret. Turn the scope in the rings until the scope level matches the receiver level.

Alternate tightening the screws in a crisscross pattern, i.e., bottom left screw, top right, etc., and don't tighten them down in one go. Snug them all hand tight and ensure the gaps in the rings are similar on all sides. Continue to tighten them in this crisscross pattern until you hit the recommended torque. For scope rings, that's usually between 15 and 25 in-lbs but always follow the scope manufacturer guidelines.

Now you're ready to sight in the rifle. Most NRL22 shooters zero at 50 yards, as that equates to a dead-center hold on targets between 25 and 55 or 60 yards with match ammunition. Others advocate for 25 to 35 yards as that zeros the optic at the peak of the bullet's trajectory. There are pros and cons to each method. I zero all my .22 LRs at 50 yards, .17 Mach 2s at 30 yards, and magnum rimfires at 100 yards.

With a bolt gun and a normal-sized target, it's easy to get on paper. Remove the bolt and secure the rifle in a cradle or on bags. Look through and center the bore on the target. While looking through the scope, carefully turn the elevation and windage turrets until you center the reticle on the target. This procedure almost always gets you on paper. You can then zero the rifle at your desired yardage.

Rimfire Barrel Break-In

Breaking in a rifle barrel through a routine of shooting, then cleaning, then shooting some more is either a required step for a precision rimfire rifle system or not necessary at all, depending with whom you talk.

The more accurate answer to rimfire barrel break-in is, "it depends."

First, consider the caliber. A .22 LR shooting lead bullets may require a different process than a .17 HMR or .22 WMR that shoots jacketed bullets. Lilja Rifles, Inc., no stranger to precision shooting, says, "Rimfire rifle barrels are different from centerfire barrels in that they require minimal cleaning and essentially no break-in procedure." Then they go on to state, "The .22 WMR and .17 HMR cartridges are rimfires, but they fire a jacketed bullet and therefore centerfire cleaning, and break-in instructions apply." (See sidebar.)

An important note here, Lilja barrels — and Shilen, Muller, Bartlein, and other premium makers — are hand-lapped to a mirror polish. That means they remove any tooling marks left in the bore from the barrel-making process. That is not the case with factory barrels. With a borescope, you can see plain as day little ridges and nicks in many factory barrels. Those imperfections can be made smoother after shooting lead .22 LRs down the bore, as imperfections fill in with lead and lube, which slicks up the bore and makes for better groups. That is why so many factory rimfires seem to shoot better after many hundreds of rounds and why so many rimfire shooters seem allergic to ever cleaning their bores. However, there are downsides to an always dirty barrel — as we'll see in the chapter on cleaning.

It seems a factory or rough barrel can be broken in by shooting it a lot, whereas a hand-lapped barrel does not require this. Likewise, a hand-lapped premium barrel can be kept cleaner for longevity's sake, as it only takes half a box of ammo or less to "re-foul" the bore and for accurate shooting. In both cases, it is not as necessary to shoot, clean, shoot, clean using some prescribed protocol as it is for barrels that send copper-jacketed bullets downrange.

Box Testing

As a rule of thumb, a good thing to do while break-

The Lilja Break-in Procedure for Centerfire and Jacketed Rimfire Barrels

"We are concerned with two types of fouling: copper fouling from bullet jacket material in the bore and powder fouling. During the first few rounds, substantial copper fouling will coat the barrel. Remove this fouling thoroughly after each shot to help prevent a build-up later on. Powder fouling is ongoing but easy to remove. Do not use moly-coated bullets during the break-in procedure.

"For an effective break-in, you should clean the bore after every shot for the first 10-12 rounds or until copper fouling stops. Our procedure is to push a cotton patch that is wet with solvent through the barrel. This process will remove much of the powder fouling and wet the inside of the barrel with solvent. Next, wet a bronze brush (not a nylon brush) with solvent and stroke the barrel 5-10 times. Follow this by another wet patch and then one dry patch. Now soak the barrel with a strong copper-removing solvent, removing the blue mess from the barrel. The copper fouling will be heavy for a few rounds and then taper off quickly in just one or two shots. Once it has stopped or diminished significantly, it is time to start shooting 5-shot groups, cleaning after each one. After 25-30 rounds, clean at a regular interval of 10-25 rounds. Your barrel is now broken-in."

ing in or fouling a rimfire barrel is box testing the riflescope. The weak link in most rifle systems is the optic. More specifically, the way the elevation and windage adjustments in the scope track as they're changed. In other words, that 0.1-MIL click adjustment at 100 yards may be closer to 0.125 or 0.75 MILs in a poorly made or defective scope. These errors may not make a huge difference when shooting close, but they can compound and make shots way off at farther yardages.

Frank Galli of snipershide.com, who has forgotten more about precision shooting than most of us will ever know, has written that "It's typical to see a 2

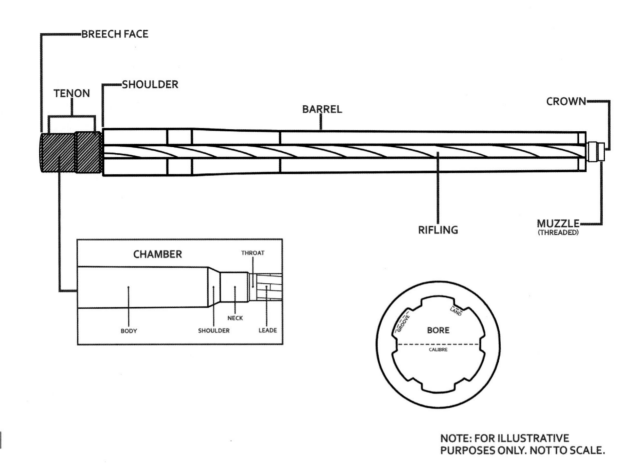

NOTE: FOR ILLUSTRATIVE
PURPOSES ONLY. NOT TO SCALE.

144

RIMFIRE REVOLUTION

percent error factor in scopes at or below [the $1,500] price point, and that has a cascading effect on accuracy results. If you're using any ballistic software, this is your most significant point of failure when the ballistic curve does not line up with your rig." [Editor's note: Galli is the author of *Precision Rifle Marksmanship: The Fundamentals – A Marine Sniper's Guide to Long Range Shooting*, available at GunDigestStore.com.]

A box test requires a 24- to 36-inch target at 100 yards. Lock down the rifle scope, either in a jig or with the rifle strapped into a heavy cradle. For rimfires, I do a watered-down live-fire version of this on my 50-yard home range. I sight in at 50 yards. Then I hang a tall sheet of paper downrange with a bullseye on the paper's bottom edge. I take a shot at 50, then spin up 1 MIL or 1 MOA of elevation (depending on the scope) and shoot another round. I do this until I run out of paper, which is typically 8 or 9 MILs. I then spin the

elevation back to zero, pick a bullet hole in the middle of the target, do the same thing with windage, add 1 MIL, shoot a shot, etc., moving both left and right while maintaining the hold on that center bullet hole. When at the extreme left and right edge of the paper, I track the elevation again.

The result is a big cross on the paper downrange with one to four small boxes. If there are no issues, I can see the bullet holes line up with the hash marks in my scope reticle. That is, the 2-MIL bullet hole lines up with the 2-MIL hash mark when I hold to that point of aim. This method is not as accurate as a test that runs through the entire usable range of the optic, but it lets me quickly know if something significant is off in the scope.

Barrels

A survey of rifle precision and accuracy would be

incomplete without a look at barrels. A rifle action's mechanical repeatability, lock time speed, trigger, and bedding quality, contribute to a precision rifle system. Still, no one variable is more important than the quality of the barrel.

Rimfire barrels are most often made of type 416 stainless steel or type 4140 chrome-moly steel. Chrome-moly is easier to machine, requires less lubrication, as it is less susceptible to galling. Stainless steel is better at resisting oxidation but contains carbon and will rust in bad conditions or left filthy in a moist environment. Barrels are rifled one of four ways:

• Cut or single-point cut rifling, cutting one groove at a time;

• Broached rifling, or cutting all the grooves at the same time, an uncommon practice these days;

• Hammer forging, or pounding the barrel over a tungsten carbide mandrel with the reverse image of the rifling;

• Button rifling, or pressing the grooves into the steel with a short carbide "button" with the rifling's reverse image pulled down the barrel's length with immense force.

Most barrel makers do one method or the other. There is a fierce debate over which approach makes the "most accurate" or "most precise" barrel. In the world of competitive rimfire benchrest, only two barrel makers are routinely winning these days, and both use a button rifling process — Shilen and Muller Works. Other close contenders, Benchmark, Broughton, and Douglas, are buttoned. Vudoo Gun Works uses single-point cut Ace Barrels, and Mike Bush has been vocal in his belief that the accuracy potential is every bit as good as the super-premium button-rifled barrels. He likens the dominance of button-rifled barrels in benchrest to their much wider use within that sport, sort of like why red sports cars get more speeding tickets — because there are more red cars on the road. As Vudoo's new single-shot benchrest action with Ace barrel sees time on the firing line at national-level benchrest matches, we will learn more.

Of the barrel makers popular with precision shooters, Bartlein, PROOF Research, and IBI use the cut method. Krieger offers both cut and buttoned barrels. Lilja, Hart, and Lothar Walther are buttoned. Anschütz, Bergara, and Savage button rifle their barrels. CZ, Ruger, and Sako/Tikka cold hammer forge.

Drawbacks: Some believe hammer-forged barrels are less precise, yet they're much less expensive to manufacture. Cut rifling is slow and costly and not conducive to mass production — as anyone who's tried to order a custom cut-rifled barrel quickly will tell you. Button-rifled barrels are accurate, cost-effective, and mass-produce quickly but *must* be appropriately heat-treated to relieve the stress induced by the rifling process. If not, the bore's internal dimensions can warp when the barrel is contoured or when you thread the muzzle for a brake.

Whatever the rifling process, they all ultimately do the same thing: Cut, press, or forge in the spiral lands and grooves inside the barrel. How much that spiral spins is called "twist rate," and for the longest time, the twist rate for .22 LR has been 1:16 or one full rotation over 16 inches of barrel. Some barrel makers tweak that up to 1:17 and down to 1:15. No one has any idea which is best. Generally, faster twists are better for longer, heavier bullets. Yet this is moot in a .22 LR landscape where 99 percent of precision shooters are shooting 40-grain match loads. The advent of cooper-solid extreme long-range rimfire ammunition may change that. The .17-caliber rimfires run almost exclusively with a 1:9 or 1:10 twist.

The number of lands and grooves — and the shape of the lands — can vary from maker to maker.

Rimfire Twist Rates
.22 LR – 1:17 to 1:15
.22 LR ELR – 1:7 or 1:12
.22 WMR – 1:16 or 1:15
.17 HM2, .17 HMR, .17 WSM – 1:9 or 1:10

For centuries, standard rifling was square with sharp corners. Rimfire specialists changed some of their rifling patterning over time, tapering the shape of the lands. The Shilen Ratchet is the most famous example of this. The 5R profile is another. As to an ideal number of lands and grooves, it pays to look at the world of benchrest.

The Shilen Ratchet is a four-groove. It also offers a standard eight-groove. Muller Works offers a 5R in four- or eight-groove. Douglas and Broughton, two other highly respected barrel manufacturers, use a four-groove rifle pattern. Benchmark has a two- and three-groove, and Lilja offers three-, four-, and six-groove depending on twist rate. The lands and grooves' internal dimensions also vary by manufacturer, but in all cases, they're appreciably tighter than the soft lead .224-diameter .22 LR bullet. Lilja, for example, writes on its website: "Our standard dimensions are a .2215 diameter groove and a .217 diameter bore. The `tight' barrels are .2200 by .215 diameters." Bore tightness affects squeezing or molding the soft lead bullet to the lands, which shapes each bullet more uniform, thereby more consistent and accurate — or so the thinking goes.

The best barrels are hand-lapped or hand-polished. No factory barrels are hand-lapped. It's a labor-intensive process, which is why custom barrels cost so much more. In the lapping process, you make a lead slug to the bore's internal dimensions for an exact fit. You then coat the lap with a gritty lapping compound and oil. It's pushed and pulled through the barrel many hundreds or thousands of times by hand. Lapping is a skill, and when the person on the lap "feels" they've completed the job, they stop. They then check the finish with a borescope and measure the lands, grooves, and bore diameter.

Traditionally, an "accurate" bore has the same diameter to 0.0001 of an inch from chamber to muzzle. Some manufactures grade their barrels with the most premium blanks running a uniform 0.0002 to 0.0001 inch the full length of the barrel. For some perspective, consider a sheet of paper. A piece of paper is around 0.002-inch thick, so hand lappers take these barrels to a tolerance of 20th of that! The benchrest shooter, gunsmith, and writer Bill Calfee pioneered the idea of lapping and cutting barrel blanks for "choke" or at a tight spot in a barrel. Calfee found tight areas in barrel blanks by pushing a lead slug down a blank and feeling where it hung up. He then cut the blank at that tight spot so the muzzle, or last point of contact between bullet and barrel, was a fraction tighter than the rest of the bore. This method, he believed, released the bullet at its best harmonic node. Calfee hung blanks and taped them like wind chimes to hear how they rang, homing in on these tight spots and their harmonic differences. His ideas are controversial in benchrest circles, but no one will argue his impact on the discussion of super accuracy in rimfire rifles. His book, *The Art of Rimfire Accuracy,* is well worth a read for those who want to wade deep into the weeds. The last essay in the book, *A Rifle's Tale* by Wallace Smallwood is the best thing I've ever read on how a custom rifle gets made.

Rimfire barrel lengths typically run from 16 to 24 inches for rimfires, and .22 LR bullet velocities tend to run consistently in good barrels from 16 to 20 inches. After that, in most cases, the barrel imparts "drag" on the bullet, slowing it down. For accurate shooting and tiny groups, this is a good or bad thing, depending on who you consult. Contours or shapes can be straight and heavy, like a bull or MTU. They can be spaghetti thin like a sporter or pencil contour. There is no definitive guide for length or contour related to the accuracy, but many have theories. It's worth noting that precision barrels tend to be heavier and longer. Tuners or devices that clamp to a barrel muzzle and adjust to tweak barrel harmonics generally work better on thinner, less heavy premium barrels. Tuners click to different lengths and move weight toward or away from the shooter, thereby changing the barrel harmonics. The general theory with tuners, and the entire process of matching ammunition to a barrel,

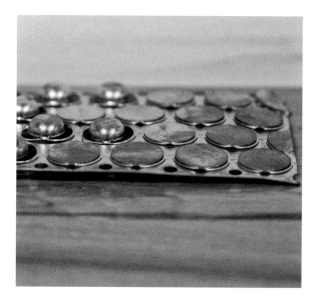

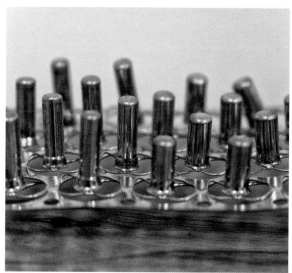

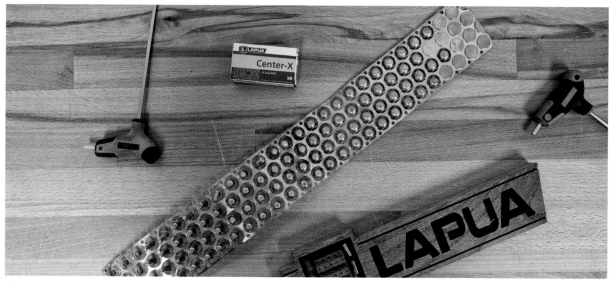

The steps by which ammo makers change brass sheeting into brass .22 LR cases.

arrives at the most repeatable, consistent harmonics, which translates — so the thinking goes — to the most consistent groups.

Chambers

Central to the success of a barrel is the chamber. The chamber is where the cartridge sits in the barrel when the firing pin strikes it. Tighter chambers are considered more accurate but within reason. Tight chambers can have drawbacks when it comes to extraction. There is no such thing as a "match" chamber. There are simply tighter, shorter, or angled chamber designs that are more conducive to match shooting. There is no consensus on the best type. Some believe they can tailor their chamber to ammunition, for example, an ELEY EPS chamber for ELEY Tenex ammo or the Vudoo Ravage chamber for Lapua. Other experts disagree with this.

One of the surest ways to make a factory barrel shoot better is to have the barrel "set back" and rechambered. A gunsmith removes a few millimeters from the breechface and barrel shoulder, then recuts

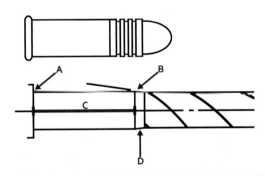

Common .22 Chamber Specifications

Pacific Tool & Gauge publishes a list of specs for the wide variety of chamber reamers it sells. You can find other specs online, and more still are considered propriety and closely held secrets. Combining all available sources, this is the best list I could come up with for .22 LR chamber specs. If anything, this list demonstrates how wide the variance in chambers can be.

the chamber with a more precision-focused design. Coupled with tweaking the rifle's headspace to match the desired ammunition's rim thickness can do wonders. Universally, precision chambers seat the .22 LR bullet into the lands of the rifling. That is the bullet nose presses into the lands and grooves, something you can check on any rifle by chambering a live round, then extracting it. The soft lead bullet will be marked or engraved with lines from the lands. As rimfire rifle shooters have grown more accuracy-obsessed, the big-time firearm manufactures are starting to cut chambers into their rifles that engrave bullets. The exception here is semi-automatics. The key to ensuring reliable extraction is to keep bullets off the lands in autoloaders.

Ammunition

Heraclitus famously said, "no man ever steps in the same river twice." You can say the same of barrels. No barrel maker ever makes the same barrel twice. Likewise, no lot of rimfire ammunition is the same.

Lot to lot, the powder charged in the loading machines may be slightly different on a minuscule chemical level. The lead alloy that makes the bullets may be fractionally harder or softer from shipment to shipment. The ductility of the brass can change from run to run. The temperature and humidity in the rooms where ammunition is loaded can change. The leading European ammo companies do their best

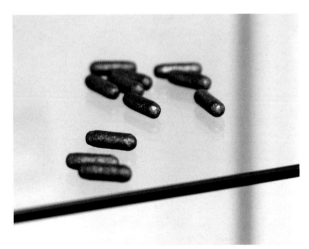

Lead slugs that are swage formed into shaped .22 LR bullets.

.22 LR Chamber Specifications

	A	B	C	D
Description	Diameter	Diameter	Length	Angle
.22 Bentz	.2278	.2264	.6787	1°35'
.22 Browning	.228	.226	.670	2°
.22 Butler Creek	.228	.225	.750	2°
.22 Chipmunk	.228	.226	.670	2°
.22 ELEY EPS Target	.2254	.2252	.617	1°30'
.22 ELEY Match	.2252	.2252	.590	1°
.22 ELEY SA Match	.2255	.2255	.595	1°30'
.22 Freeland MG	.2242	.224	.600	2°
.22 Lakefield	.229	.227	.700	2°
.22 Lilja	.2267	.224	.630	2°
.22 Meyers	.225	.2248	.600	1°30'
.22 PPG Match	.2269	.2256	.630	1°30'
.22 Rogue	.2225	.2242	.620	1°30'
.22 Stinger	.2275	.226	.735	1°30'
.22 Straight I	.225	.225	.600	2° or 2°30'
.22 Straight II	.2255	.2255	.600	2° or 2°30'
.22 Straight III	.2260	.226	.600	2° or 2°30'
.22 Time	.2262	.2248	.610	1°
.22 Ultimate EPS	.2252	.2252	.600	2° or 2°30'
.22 LR 547	.2261	.2251	.600	2°
.22 LR Anschütz	.2255	.2248	.619	1/2°
.22 LR Match	.2267	.2248	.600	5°
.22 LR Sporting	.2307	.227	.775	5°
Calfee I	.2255	.2255	.600	1°30'
Calfee II	.2255	.225	.600	2°
Win 52D Match	.2278	.225	.580	2°
.22 Short	.2291	.227	.431	5°
.22 Long	.2306	.227	.775	5°
.22 LR Shot	.2284	.2236	.871	30°

to control all these factors. Still, there is an array of microscopic factors that can make one lot of ammo perform differently than another — even within the very same barrel. That is why, for example, my CZ mentioned earlier showed a preference for Lot 23 of Lapua Center-X but didn't shoot Lot 13 worth a lick. Whatever magic happened in the making of Lot 23 matched that PROOF barrel.

Matching ammo to barrels is peculiar and necessary when chasing peak rimfire rifle precision. It's why Lapua and ELEY have test tunnels open to the public at a nominal cost. We mere mortals not associated with a national shooting team can make an appointment, bring our rifles, and have lot after lot tested, and — we hope — find that perfect match for our precision rifle.

You can also ship your rifles to these test facilities. Eley has a tunnel at Killough's in Winters, Texas. Lapua has two, Mesa, Arizona, near Phoenix, and Marengo, Ohio, at the Cardinal Shooting Center.

Lapua charges $50 a rifle, ELEY $45. Both wave the fee if you purchase a case of ammunition based on the testing. They do not charge for the test ammo. Both only test ammo they have in stock and ready to sell. In this recurring era of ammunition shortages, that is worth the price of admission alone. Not only are you certain you can find and buy the ammo, but you can purchase many thousands of rounds of it. Now, this is not inexpensive ammo. ELEY only tests Tenex, which runs around $19 a box. Lapua tests Center-X and Midas+, which run around $11 and $15 a box, respectively. So, for a case of 5,000 rounds, you're looking at a price between $1,100 and $1,900 — a significant sum of money, but worth it if you shoot a lot and peak precision is the goal.

ELEY vs. Lapua

The Brits and the Germans both make superb ammunition. It's a point of national pride. Both win medals. Combined, both companies win all the medals as the only real choice of Olympic-class shooters.

The ELEY Tenex bullet is a flat-nose with a tell-tale nipple or bump in the center. It was designed almost exclusively for 50-meter competition but performs very well at longer ranges, too. The ELEY primer system or EPS is among the best in the world, contributing to the very stable velocities for which Tenex and the less expensive Match line are known. ELEY also uses a unique beeswax lubricant on the Tenex line. The newer Semi-Auto Benchrest Precision ammunition is Tenex but with a petroleum-based lube that ELEY says cycles better in magazine-fed rifles.

Lapua X-Act, Midas+, and Center-X are all the same ammo. They use the same round-nose bullet, case, powder, and primer, but Lapua tests and sorts the most consistent lots and then brands the very best performers as X-Act. For a spell, Lapua claimed velocity standard deviations of 10 or less with X-Act, 20 or less with Midas+ and 30 or less with Center-X. These were generous, though it is

helpful to think of X-Act as plus 30 percent the performance of Center-X at about double the price.

Center-X has become something of the de facto precision rifle ammunition for PRS-style shooters in the United States. It is wonderfully accurate in many rifles and chambers. Vudoo Gun Works says it cuts its chambers for Lapua ammo, which has undoubtedly helped boost Center-X. Price is another major factor. You can get Center-X for about $11 a box, compared to the $19 or more for Tenex and $24 or $25 for X-Act.

The rim thickness of Lapua ammo is typically 0.043 inch, compared to 0.039 on ELEY, an advantage for many shooters as production rifles made in the USA must adhere to Sporting Arms and Ammunition Manufacturers' Institute or SAAMI guidelines on headspace. For .22 LR, that's a minimum of 0.043 inch. So, a factory rifle set with the minimum headspace — as many of them now are — lines right up with Lapua rim thickness. This matchup of headspace to rim thickness undoubtedly contributes to why Lapua shoots so well in such a wide variety of rifles.

Luke Johnson ammo testing one of the author's Vudoos at the Lapua Test Tunnel in Ohio.

Tunnel Testing

Early last winter, I visited the Lapua Performance Rimfire Center at the Cardinal Shooting Center in Marengo, Ohio. It's about 30 minutes north of Columbus and 1.5 hours south of Cleveland. Cardinal is a destination for shotgun shooters and hosts several major events. It has 52 trap fields, 14 skeet fields, two sporting clays courses, 5-stand, plus 14 pistol bays, a 3D archery course, and a new 100-yard rifle range — there is even a restaurant on-site, plus cabins, an indoor pool, and acres of RV campgrounds. Just off Interstate 71, there are several hotel chains within a 10-minute drive.

Luke Johnson met me at the new Lapua test tunnel, which opened its doors in March 2020. Johnson is the performance center manager for Lapua and a four-time NCAA All-American positional shooter for the University of Alaska, Fairbanks. Luke is a wealth of information on everything rimfire. It takes two to four hours to test a rifle, and I brought four, so we had plenty of time to discuss all things accuracy.

The test tunnel has Meyton Elektronik infrared targets at 50 and 100 meters and an Oehler-Research chronograph system. When I was there, unfortunately, the chronograph system was down. The optical target system records every bullet as its "breaks" the infrared screen of light and relays it back to a computer. Lapua's test procedure is one 10-round group per lot, with repeat 10-round groups with the better-performing ammunition. The facility tests Center-X and

Producer: Vudoo ▮▮▮▮   **TestNo.:**
Tester: **Date:** 27.08.2030
Remark: **Barrel length:** 0 mm

An example results sheet from the Lapua test tunnel.

Ammunition: CenterX2		Batch: #23-26555/603584
Hmax 11.84	Wmax 7.94	Sx 2.50 Sy 3.08
DHH-STD 2.77	DHH-Min 0.84	DHH-Max 11.33

#20   DHH 4.43   Ø18.20

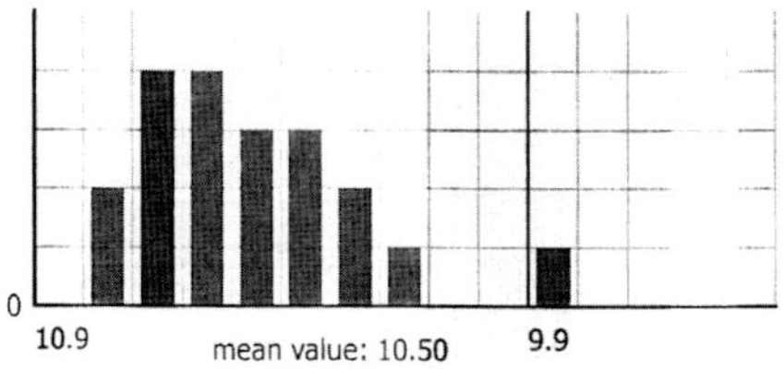

mean value: 10.50

Ammunition: Centerx-1		Batch: #13-26555/601195
Hmax 12.71	Wmax 4.22	Sx 1.61 Sy 3.48
DHH-STD 2.59	DHH-Min 0.71	DHH-Max 8.36

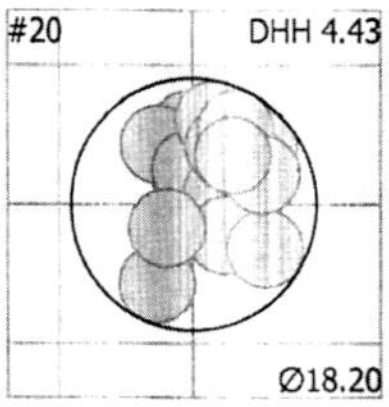

#10   DHH 4.64   Ø18.32

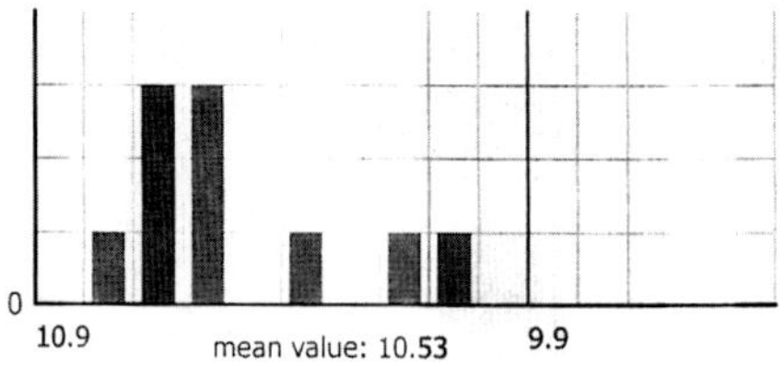

mean value: 10.53

Ammunition: Centerx`		Batch: #7-27555/603486
Hmax 10.25	Wmax 9.65	Sx 2.37 Sy 3.43
DHH-STD 2.33	DHH-Min 2.60	DHH-Max 9.98

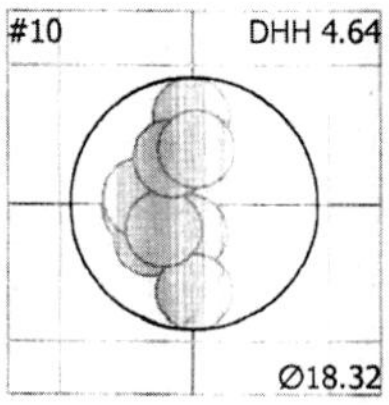

#10   DHH 7.00   Ø17.18

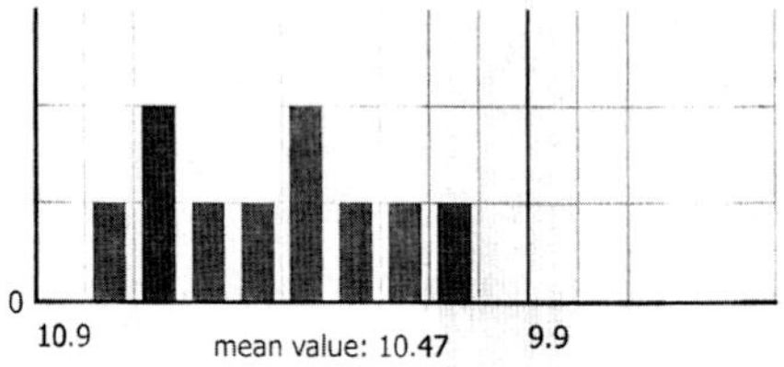

mean value: 10.47

Ammunition: CenterX2		Batch: #20-28555/603306
Hmax 15.96	Wmax 5.88	Sx 1.55 Sy 4.45
DHH-STD 3.49	DHH-Min 2.03	DHH-Max 13.98

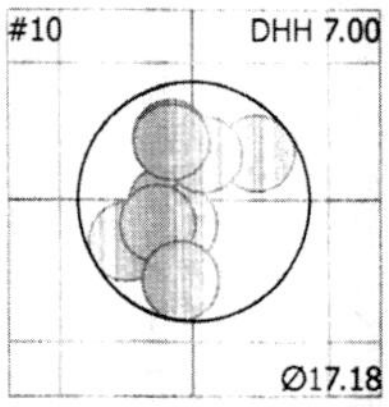

#10   DHH 5.55   Ø21.66

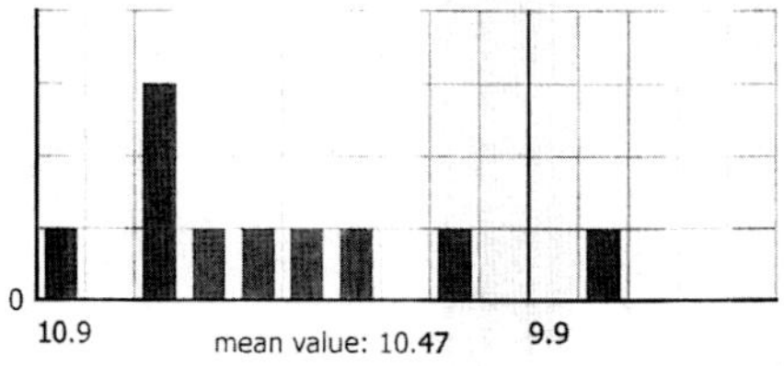

mean value: 10.47

Ammunition: Centerx`		Batch: #10-26555-601362
Hmax 9.05	Wmax 8.83	Sx 2.90 Sy 3.09
DHH-STD 2.54	DHH-Min 2.01	DHH-Max 8.71

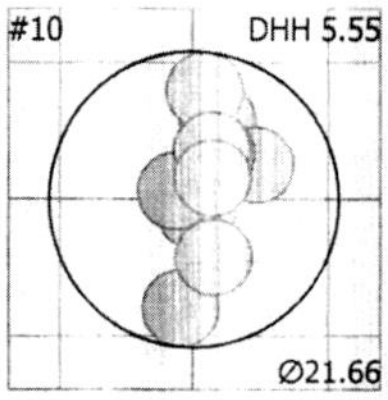

#9   DHH 5.57   Ø16.10

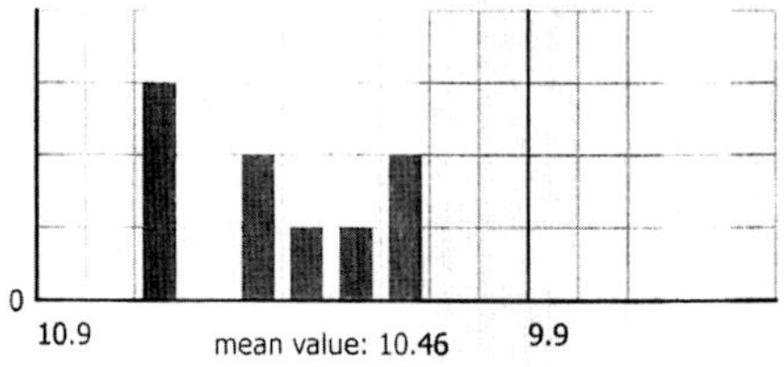

mean value: 10.46

Ammunition: Centerx-1		Batch: #15-25555/601266
Hmax 22.26	Wmax 9.43	Sx 3.28 Sy 5.93
DHH-STD 4.75	DHH-Min 2.81	DHH-Max 18.87

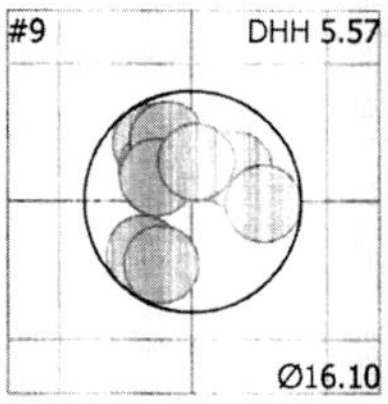

#10   DHH 6.39   Ø28.54

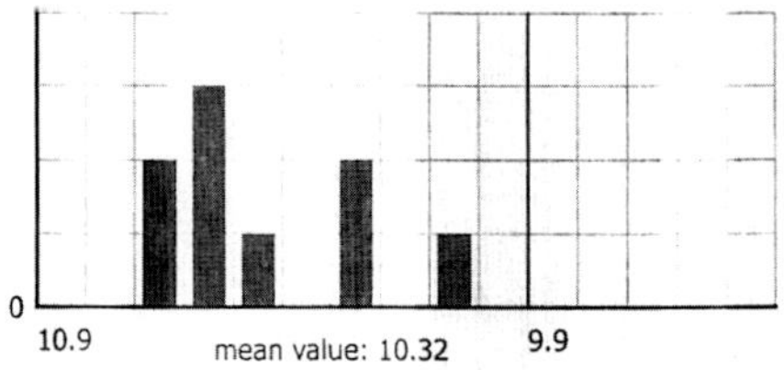

mean value: 10.32

Ammunition: Centerx`		Batch: #9-26555/603453
Hmax 10.52	Wmax 6.99	Sx 1.97 Sy 2.80
DHH-STD 2.55	DHH-Min 0.24	DHH-Max 8.88

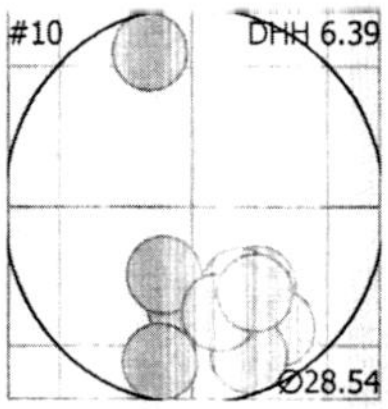

#10   DHH 4.70   Ø16.30

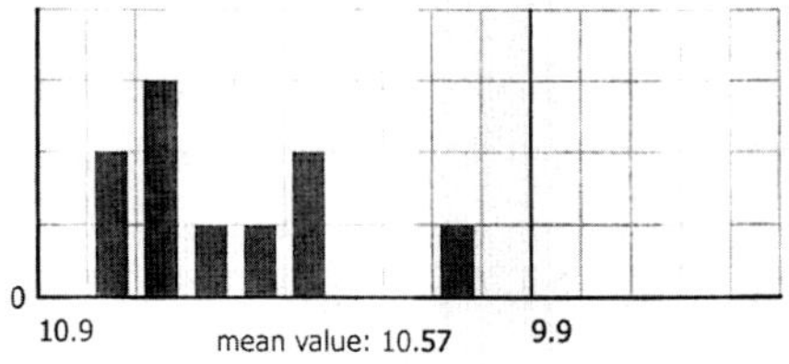

mean value: 10.57

Ammunition: CenterX2		Batch: #27-26555/601873
Hmax 15.73	Wmax 10.27	Sx 3.03 Sy 4.37
DHH-STD 2.34	DHH-Min 2.78	DHH-Max 10.09

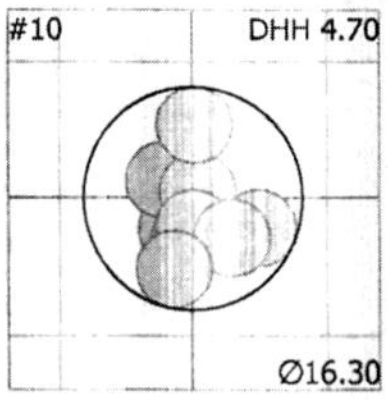

#10   DHH 6.70   Ø21.88

mean value: 10.36

10.9 ... 9.9

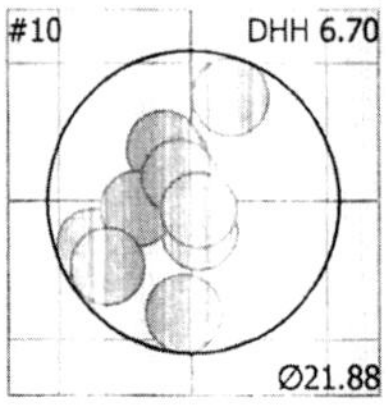

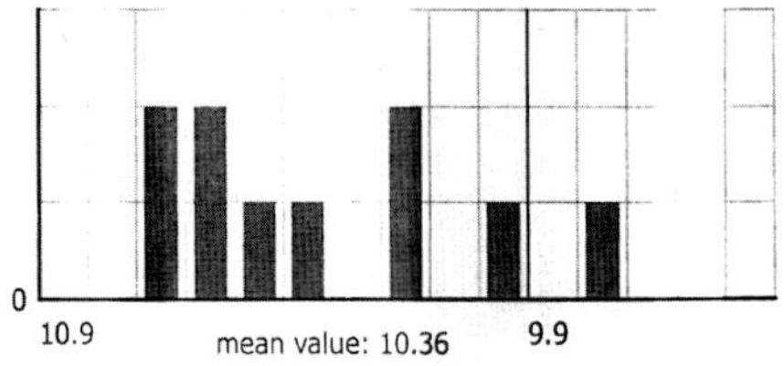

Midas+ or whatever ammo you want to bring (or ship to the facility). The optical targets record group data at 50 and 100 meters. The data includes:

- Dmax, or diameter max, or outside diameter, in millimeters;
- Hmax, or the height of the group, in millimeters;
- Wmax, or the width of the group, in millimeters;
- Sx, or standard deviation of the hit positions in the horizontal direction;
- Sy, or standard deviation of the hit positions in the vertical direction;
- DHH or distance hit to hit, the center point distance between two consecutive hits;
- DHH-STD, or the standard deviation of the DHH values of the consecutive hits of a series;
- DHH-Min, or the smallest DHH value of consecutive hits of a series;
- DHH-Max, or the largest DHH value of consecutive hits of a series;
- Mean Value at 50 meters, or ring mean, which replicates how the group would score in an Olympic-style positional match, with 10.9 being the highest possible value.

If this reads like a firehose blast of information, that's exactly how it feels during the testing process. More experienced, statistical-minded shooters, Johnson told me, often focus on the DHH measurement for its predictive qualities. For example, if nine shots make up a .350-inch group, and the tenth shot is a flier and blows the group out to 1 inch, that's a 1-inch group. In effect, that group measurement is simply the measure of the two widest shots. With DHH-STD and the corollary Radial Standard Deviation, which ELEY measures and computes, you're using information from every single shot. Shooters will also consider how the group looks with a preference for rounded, circular bullet groupings rather than vertical or horizontal strings — even if the latter registers smaller numbers.

To come away with numbers relevant to most shooters, I was most concerned having waded recent-

ly into the world of statistics, I was most concerned with outside diameter and how the 50- and 100-meter group sizes translated to 50 and 100 yards. This method helped my Imperial American brain translate what I saw at the test tunnel to all my previous experience shooting and measuring groups at 50 and 100 yards.

Converting millimeters to inches is easy enough: 1 millimeter = 0.0393701 inch. Converting meters to yards is straightforward. 1 meter = 1.0936 yards, or 50 meters = 54.6807 yards, 100 meters = 109.361 yards. I also typically measure outside diameter, then subtract .224 for the diameter of a .22 LR bullet to get a center-to-center measurement. Why? Because smaller numbers look and feel better. Honestly, under my current thinking, there is no reason to do this except for that's how I've always done it. So, to convert an outside diameter measurement in millimeters to a center-to-center measurement in inches, we need to do this:

(Group OD mm/25.4) − .224 = CTC in inches

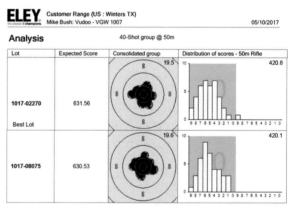

"40 - Shot score. Everything in green is a 10 with decimal at bottom. 10.0 is barely nipping the 10 ring. 10.9 is a center punch"

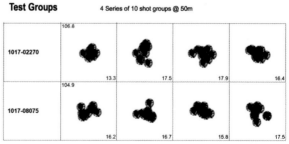

"Individual 10 shot groups with the group measurement in mm measured outside to outside"

An example results sheet from ELEY.

To then adjust it from 54.6807 yards to 50 yards requires this:

(CTC in inches * 50)/ 54.6807 = CTC in inches at 50 yards

Admittedly, this is weird science, and the result is theoretical. Bullets do funny things, and you cannot scale back a group from 54 yards or 109 yards to 50 and 100 yards with perfect accuracy. It is theoretical, not actual. It is helpful because it puts the results in an easy-to-understand format for regular shooters like me. It's also important to emphasize that these are 10-shot groups, not the 5-shot groups most gun writers and online reviewers report.

So, to flesh out my accuracy figures, if the Lapua tunnel reported: Group OD 15.66mm at 50 meters, by my calculations, translates to a Group CTC 0.393 inch at 50 yards.

A 0.393 group at 50 I can understand, whereas 15.66mm at meters I cannot.

At Lapua, we secured barreled actions into a fixture. Then we set the fixture in a vise. The vise recoils on slides, but the system is more accurate when fully locked down. The setup was one of the first projects Johnson explored when he started as a manager. With a Vudoo rifle, he tested return to battery and torque setting. He found an action torque of 65 in-lbs. to average 3mm better at 50 meters and 5mm better at 100 meters than when torqued 45 in-lbs. He found group sizes smaller at both torques when affixing the rifle in the vise rather than free recoiling on slides. Johnson recommends torquing actions to the fixture at the maximum recommended torque and lock the vise in place.

There are more than 30 fixtures at Lapua. The only hitch I encountered was with the Bergara B-14R. Mike Bush at Vudoo made the Remington 700 footprint fixture at Lapua. Unlike the Bergaras, Vudoos do not have a full-sized recoil lug, and the fixture reflects that. We could have barrel clamped the B-14, but that affects harmonics. Instead, we opted not to test it until someone could make a new fixture.

Example Lapua and ELEY box codes. Bring back velocity info, ELEY! Photo: Cosmo Genova

How to Read Lapua and ELEY Lot Numbers

The side of a box of Lapua and ELEY ammunition tells you quite a lot. Of most importance may be the tested velocity. Luke Johnson, the performance center manager for Lapua, told me the best thing to do when buying unknown lots of ammo is to match the velocity. For example, if you have a lot of Lapua that works well in your rifle with a box code that shows a factory velocity of 326 meters per second, look for a box code showing 326 meters per second when hunting for new ammo off the shelf.

Example, Lapua: 26555/603584

Put a 3 before the first two numbers to figure velocity as tested at the factory – 3-26 or 326 meters per second or 1069.55 fps.

The next number is bullet type. For Center-X, Midas+, and X-Act, that number is always 5.

The last two numbers are year of manufacture. 55 = 2020, 54 = 2019, 53 = 2018, etc.

After the slash (/) is the actual lot code.

So, Lapua lot number 26555/603584 is 326 meters per second, round-nose ammo manufactured in 2020.

Example, ELEY: 1019-03192

The first two numbers are the product, 11 is Match, and 10 is Tenex.

The second two numbers are year of manufacture, in this case, 2019.

The next two digits are the machine number, in this case, 03.

The last three are the lot run.

So, ELEY lot number 1019-03192 is Tenex, made in 2019 on machine No. 3. For a while, ELEY printed the velocity on the box in feet per second. Until 2020, it had a "lot analyzer" feature on its website that gave even more detailed information. We can only hope ELEY goes back to its old easy-to-read system.

The advantage of a test tunnel? With the rifle in the vise, you remove the human and optical elements from the equation. It's an accurate measure of mechanical accuracy — rifle action, barrel, and ammunition — instead of practical accuracy that includes factors such as optics, environmentals, shooter ability, etc.

All told, we tested:

RimX action with 16.5-inch Sendero contoured PROOF, assembled by the team at Zermatt, with a Timney HIT;

CZ 457 with a 20-inch PROOF drop-in, assembled by me, with factory CZ trigger;

Vudoo V-22 (Vudoo No. 1) with an 18-inch Kukri contour Ace barrel and Timney Elite Hunter, assembled by Vudoo;

Vudoo V-22 (Vudoo No. 2) with an 18-inch MTU-V contour Ace barrel and Timney Elite Hunter, assembled by Vudoo;

Almost universally, the rifles performed better with Center-X than Midas+. Also, note how large the spread within the same brand, from the same gun, with the only difference being lot — 0.825 inch with the CZ and Lot 23 at 100 yards compared to 3.5 inches at 100 yards with Lot 13.

Also, notice the quirky results between 50- and 100-yard data. It shows that bullets in flight do not

50 yrds		RimX		CZ		Vudoo No. 1		Vudoo No. 2	
		50 yrds	100 yrds	50 yrds	100 yrds	50 yrds	100 yrds	50 yrds	100 yrds
Center-X	Lot 23	0.425	1.505	0.509	0.825	0.515	0.855	0.450	0.692
Center-X	Lot 15	0.359	1.180	0.774	1.019	1.144	1.085	0.823	0.893
Center-X	Lot 10	0.591	1.288	0.522	0.867			0.375	0.923
Center-X	Lot 13	0.671	0.764	0.612	3.512	0.337	0.785	0.455	1.000
Center-X	Lot 07	0.612	1.445	0.638	1.356	0.450	0.726	0.414	1.142
Center-X	Lot 27		1.024			0.472	1.321	0.583	1.388
Center-X	Lot 20	0.631	1.767			0.428	1.274	0.575	1.462
Center-X	Lot 14	0.640	1.586	0.564	1.051	0.869	1.652		
Midas+	Lot 14	0.450	1.462	0.386	0.991	0.372	0.784	0.400	0.611
Midas+	Lot 10	0.915	2.242	0.513	0.846	0.365	0.808	0.455	0.734
Midas+	Lot 16	0.764	1.864	0.409	1.001	0.411	0.642	0.430	0.945
Midas+	Lot 02	0.646	1.644	0.539	1.157	0.453	1.209	0.422	1.041
Midas+	Lot 12					0.378	1.188	0.416	1.085
Midas+	Lot 14	0.454	1.030			0.558	1.290	0.425	1.214
Midas+	Lot 23	0.404	1.148	0.517	1.047			0.503	1.279
Midas+	Lot 07	0.454	1.105	0.695	1.466		1.386	1.266	2.636
Midas+	Lot 24	0.864	2.145	0.837	1.656		1.942		
Midas+	Lot 06			0.529	1.386				

Note: Lot numbers are not actual lot numbers but were used for testing purposes. Green highlights the best result for that rifle per brand. Red highlights indicate the worst result per rifle overall.

degrade at the same time. For example, with the RimX, Lot 15 shot an excellent 0.359-inch group at 50, which opened up to 1.180 inches at 100. Lot 13 almost doubled Lot 15 at 50 with a group size of 0.671 inch but held that group remarkably tight at 0.764 inch at 100 yards. (I figured this was an error and triple-checked it.) There are multiple other examples on the chart that show bullets doing well at 50 and less well at 100, and others doing so-so at 50, but exceptionally at 100. Rimfire precision does not scale well.

One of the best groups of the day, Lot 13 of Center-X in the Vudoo No. 1, stopped Johnson and me in our tracks. Eight shots into the 10-shot groups, he asked me, "Are you watching this?" On the computer monitor was a petal of a group smack in the bullseye and small. "If a Vudoo with an 18-inch barrel breaks the range record, I'm going to hear no end of it," he said. He shot again. And then the last shot. "Nope," he said. "But man, is that a good group. Benchrest guys would be high-fiving each other right now." That's the fun of tunnel testing: You shoot a lot and collect lots of data. And, hopefully, you find gold.

All told, the Vudoo No. 1 produced the best 50-yard group with Lot 13 of Center-X. The best 100-yard group

The Test Tunnel Top 10

ELEY and Lapua keep records of all the rifles tested in their tunnels. They keep this information close to their chest. Yet at the Winters Park test range, the No. 1 most precise rifle tested was a 2500X Action with a Shilen Ratchet barrel. At the Lapua Performance Rimfire Center in Ohio, the top 10 rifles tested in 2020 — the first year of operation — were:
- Turbo V1 with Benchmark barrel — 9.41mm 10-shot group at 50 meters, range record
- Stiller 2500x with Lilja barrel — 16.61mm 10-shot group at 100 meters, range record
- Stiller 2500x with Shilen barrel
- Stiller 2500x with Shilen barrel
- Stiller 2500x with Shilen barrel
- Anschutz 1913 with Kreiger barrel
- Vudoo V22 with 22-inch Bartlein barrel
- Vudoo v22 with 20-inch Ace barrel
- Walther KK500 with the factory barrel
- Stiller Trident with Muller barrel

It should come as no surprise that six of the 10 are custom single-shot benchrest actions, and five of those six are from benchrest guru Jerry Stiller.

It's important to know what your ammo will do when engaging a field of fire like this. Photo: Cosmo Genova

came from Vudoo No. 2 shooting Lot 14 of Midas+.

Ammo Testing At Home

There are various procedures posted online for lot or brand testing ammunition on your home range. None I've tested are bad. The important thing is to do it consistently. What follows is an ammo test protocol from personal experience and lengthy discussions with Dan Killough of ELEY, Luke Johnson of Lapua, plus the shooting instructors at Peacemaker National Training Center Gerradstown, West Virginia.

Have a rock-solid shooting bench or prone shooting position. Folding shooting tables are often wobbly. Concrete benches are the best.

Use good paper targets that cut well. Use the same target style for all lots tested. I'm partial to the USBR 50-yard target from American Target Company that has 28 2-inch bulls.

Pick a calm day, or have wind flags and know how to use them.

Choose a shooting distance that best matches your ideal competition or hunting shot distance. You will see more dramatic results the farther back you go.

When hanging the target, use a bubble level to level the target on the board. When you level your rifle on the bench, this ensures the target lines match horizontal lines in your reticle, which makes holding on the point-of-aim easier.

Ensure the rifle is clean.

Velocity is a crucial indicator of rimfire ammunition consistency. If you have a shoot-through or radar-based chronograph like a Labradar, record all shots by lot or brand. Chronographs that attach to barrels can affect barrel harmonics and, therefore, group size data.

Level the rifle on the bench in a secure shooting position using bags, bipod, or shooting rest. A bubble level in your stock or chassis or attached to the leveled scope comes in very handy.

Change the reticle point of impact so the bullets *do not* hit exactly where the crosshairs settle. That way,

you'll ensure a consistent hold point on the target. If you don't do this, it's possible to "shoot out" the bullseye and compromise your hold point's consistency. I will typically get zero on a bull, then up the elevation a click. Different ammo will often impact other places, too, which helps preserve the consistent hold.

Shoot well and know thyself. Personally, after 200 or 300 concentrated shots, I know my skills degrade, so I plan for this.

I shoot 5-shot groups. Others shoot 10. Others still shoot 20 to 50.

Regardless of how many shots you decide to shoot and measure, Killough recommends no less than one box or 50 rounds per lot tested.

When moving on to different ammunition brands, lightly clean the rifle and take several shots of that new brand to foul the bore with the new ammunition's lube. (For Lapua, Johnson recommends lightly cleaning a precision rifle after every 200 shots.)

When the best lots or brands of ammo are determined, Killough recommends testing no fewer than two ammo boxes to dial in the best of the best.

Velocity

Velocity may be the best indicator of consistency in a lot or brand of ammunition. Velocity consistencies become hugely important when shooting .22 LR at long range. There are many good chronographs on the market, though I'm partial to the Labradar system. Figures are recorded to a spreadsheet on an SD card within the unit that looks like this:

RimX, PROOF, ELEY Match, 50 shots:

Stats - Average	1109.98	fps
Stats - Highest	1128.61	fps
Stats - Lowest	1095.39	fps
Stats - Ext. Spread	33.23	fps
Stats - Std. Dev	7.78	fps

Input Parameters			
Ballistic Coefficient	0.172	Muzzle Velocity	1073 fps
Bullet Weight	40 grains	Zero Range	100 y
Bullet Diameter	0.224 inches	Sight Height	1.50 inches
Bullet Length	0.475 inches	Twist Rate	15.00 inches
Wind Speed	5.00 mph	Heading	0 degrees
Wind Speed	9.00 mph	Inclination	0 degrees
Pressure	29.92 inHg	Target Speed	0 mph
Humidity	0 % RH	Air Density	0.07654 lb/ft^3
Form Factor	0.662	Stability Factor (Sg)	1.484

Range Card							
Range (y)	TOF (s)	Mach (s)	Velocity (fps)	Energy (ft-lbs)	Elevation (inches)	Windage (inches)	Lead (inches)
0	0.000	0.96	1073	102	-1.50	0.00	0.00
50	0.145	0.90	1001	89	3.66	0.37	0.00
100	0.298	0.85	945	79	-0.22	1.79	0.00
150	0.461	0.80	899	72	-13.61	4.11	0.00
200	0.631	0.77	859	65	-37.74	7.31	0.00
250	0.809	0.74	823	60	-73.64	11.39	0.00
300	0.994	0.71	790	55	-122.34	16.36	0.00
350	1.187	0.68	760	51	-184.95	22.22	0.00
400	1.388	0.65	731	47	-262.61	29.01	0.00
450	1.597	0.63	703	44	-356.53	36.77	0.00
500	1.814	0.61	677	41	-468.03	45.54	0.00

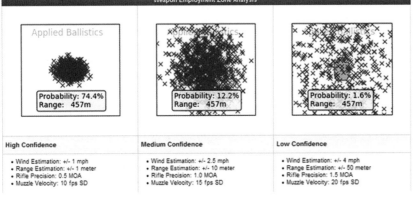

Weapon Employment Zone Analysis

Applied Ballistics — Probability: 74.4% Range: 457m

Applied Ballistics — Probability: 12.2% Range: 457m

Applied Ballistics — Probability: 1.6% Range: 457m

High Confidence
- Wind Estimation: +/- 1 mph
- Range Estimation: +/- 1 meter
- Rifle Precision: 0.5 MOA
- Muzzle Velocity: 10 fps SD

Medium Confidence
- Wind Estimation: +/- 2.5 mph
- Range Estimation: +/- 10 meter
- Rifle Precision: 1.0 MOA
- Muzzle Velocity: 15 fps SD

Low Confidence
- Wind Estimation: +/- 4 mph
- Range Estimation: +/- 50 meter
- Rifle Precision: 1.5 MOA
- Muzzle Velocity: 20 fps SD

The Applied Ballistics WEZ calculator can be found at http://appliedballisticsllc.com/ballistics/

ample, may have an SD over 50 fps. Shooting at a distance with a .22 LR, even at just 100 yards, you can see the effects of velocity swings like this on a target. Ammunition with a high SD will string out vertically — the rounds with more velocity striking higher than those with less. Many rimfire shooters care little about measured group size for extreme long-range shooting and instead focus on consistent velocities represented in low extreme spreads or SDs.

Applied Ballistics has an excellent calculator on its website that demonstrates the effects of velocity and wind on hit probability. When you input information for a Lapua .22 LR, at 500 meters with no wind and an SD of 10 fps, the hit probability is 62.4 percent. When the SD jumps to 20 fps and the wind to 4 mph, the hit probability drops to 1.4 percent. In the graphic below, note the vertical spread in the plot shots as the SD changes. Velocity changes everything.

This table shows the average, highest, and lowest velocity figures over, in this case, a 50-shot test. It also shows the extreme spread (the spread between the highest and lowest velocities) and the standard deviation. Standard deviation or SD shows consistency of muzzle velocity. If every shot launched with the same speed, the SD would be zero. The higher the SD, the more the velocities are spread out over a set. Single-digit SDs, like this example, are truly excellent in rimfire. Inexpensive bulk pack ammunition, for ex-

Ammunition Sorting

Sorting ammo by dimensions and weight is either the secret to world-class groups or a complete waste of time, depending on whom you ask.

Some shooters weigh rounds on a reloading scale and group like weights together. Others measure rim thickness and concentricity or bullet runout. Nielson Brothers Arms, Hornady, Raven Eye Customs, and others make a variety of gauges and tools that can help divide a brick of ammunition by a wide variety of

CCI V-MAX, 17gr.

Weight											
Grains	29.9	29.8	29.7	29.6	29.5	29.4					
Qty	2	0	35	2	8	3					
Seating Depth											
OAL	0.991	0.990	0.991	0.992	0.993	0.994	0.995	0.996	0.997	0.998	0.917
Qty	3	6	10	5	9	7	3	3	2	1	1

factors. With less expensive or hunting ammunition, I'm confident that sorting can improve groups. With top-tier ammo such as Center-X or Midas+, Tenex or Match, I am less sure. There is little consensus among experts or in my testing.

Dave Emary, the former ballistician for Hornady and creator of .17 HMR and .17 HM2, has post-retirement written about sorting rimfire ammunition for *Guns & Ammo*. He found significant gains when sorting CCI Mini-Mags by concentricity but told me he expects to see much less return on effort when sorting premium match loads. Likewise, Steven Boelter, in *The Rifleman's Guide to Rimfire Ammunition*, did an extensive review of sorting .22 LR and concluded that sorting improved lower grades, but higher-grade ammo proved inconclusive.

Firsthand, I've seen real improvements when sorting .17-caliber ammo, a tactic for wringing the best groups out of any .17 rifle. Like low- to mid-tier .22 LR, no one makes .17-caliber ammo to exacting "match" standards, so there is room for improvement.

I sorted a box of CCI V-MAX by weight and another box by Overall Length (OAL). Seating depth varied greatly round-to-round with the .17s. Spill a box of HMR or HM2 on your desk and look closely. You can see the variable seating depth with a naked eye. Those little bullets are simply difficult for the machines to load with high degrees of precision. Measuring OAL is a quick and dirty way to gauge seating depth and sort for variation.

The CCI was very uniform by weight, with 35 of the 50 rounds measuring to one-tenth of a grain, accord-

CCI V-MAX	Weight Sorted	Uniform OAL	No Sort
Avg. Velocity (fps)	2,077.94	2,128.79	2,122.04
Highest velocity (fps)	2,190.28	2,188.48	2,225.13
Lowest velocity (fps)	1,926.20	2,005.04	1,971.96
Ext. Spread (fps)	264.08	183.44	253.17
Std. Dev (fps)	71.50	52.97	53.83
Avg. Group (inches)	0.40	0.46	0.5711
Best group (inches)	0.27	0.36	0.361
Worst group (inches)	0.58	0.62	0.809

ing to my RCBS powder scale. There was a 0.5-grain extreme spread in weight over the 50 rounds, but 45 of those were within 0.2 grains of each other.

OAL was more divergent. Interestingly, the 10 rounds that measured 0.991 COAL varied in weight by +/-0.3 grains, so there doesn't appear to be any deep connection between seating depth and weight.

When we sent the sorted ammo downrange to 50 yards in 5-shot groups, the weight-sorted rounds proved the most accurate. That was an extremely limited two-box test. A better look would involve a brick, or multiple bricks, plus multiple rifles and shooters, *but* it does show that there's some value in sorting the .17s for weight and OAL if peak accuracy is the goal. [RR]

7

CLEANING, MAINTENANCE & CARE

When and how to clean rimfire rifles is a topic of some debate. There is no universally agreed-upon method or timetable. "Clean them when they lose accuracy" is probably the closest thing to a universal recommendation, but what that looks like to a benchrest shooter and a backyard plinker can be two vastly different things. Many have long said that more rifle barrels have been damaged by cleaning rods than accidents afield. Modern tools such as VFG pellets, coated Teflon rods, and bore snakes have cured some of this, but there is no cure for stupid to date. They all still must be used correctly, often as simple as reading and following the directions. Once, I watched a fellow at a public range take a mallet to the handle end of a cleaning rod to unstick a patch. He did not read the directions. That said, if you have a cleaning method that works, stick with it. If your cleaning method requires a mallet, keep reading.

When we talk about cleaning rifles, we mainly talk about cleaning bores or the inside of barrels. Actions, triggers, stocks, and chassis need to be cleaned, too, especially with semi-automatics that draw more fouling into the action. How you clean the bore of a .17 HMR or .22 WMR shooting copper-plated bullets differs from how you clean a .22 LR shooting lubed lead bullets.

Cleaning technology has come a long way since Hoppe's 9 but it's still an excellent solution for most shooters.

This jag is from one pass through a new rifle. You should clean a new rifle before you shoot it. Photo: Cosmo Genova

There are three basic types of cleaning:

• New rifle cleaning, which we covered in the previous chapter on accuracy

• Maintenance or light cleaning to remove fouling

• Deep cleaning to strip a fouled bore back down to the bare metal

Steve Boelter, a former rimfire columnist for *Precision Shooting* magazine and Custom Shop Director – Anschütz North America, wrote the best dissertation on the science of deep cleaning rimfires that I've read anywhere. You can find a version in Steve's book, *Rifleman's Guide to Rimfire Ammunition*, or a PDF of his 30,000-word essay online for the full treatment. Much of the information lined out here comes from Steve's work.

Why Clean Rimfire Rifles

A rifle barrel begins to lose its accuracy when the bore's lands and grooves get worn down, damaged, or filthy. Centerfire rifles lose accuracy from erosion, a process caused by the scorching-hot flame firing down the barrel with every shot. Each ignition acts like a millisecond blowtorch blast to the leade or the very start of the lands. Over time, this blast eats them away, literally burning up and eroding a few thousandths of bore material. The estimated barrel life for the popular 6.5 Creedmoor is between 2,000 and 2,500 rounds. The faster, hotter, 6mm Creedmoor may burn up closer to the 1,500-round mark. After 1,500 rounds, accuracy declines as erosion changes the distance between the start of the lands and the bullet.

Cal Zant of the very excellent precisionrifleblog.com has a rich article on measured erosion in popular PRS 6mm rifle calibers. He found 6mm Creedmoor eroded the lands on his rifle an average of 0.006 to 0.007 inch per 100 rounds. Variables such as barrel steel, chamber specs, and ammunition could alter this figure. While we can't make a universal claim on erosion for all 6mm Creedmoor rifles, it does demonstrate the accuracy-effecting change that erosion can make to a centerfire bore. It moves the rifling away from the chambered bullet over time.

Rimfire accuracy issues arise in almost the exact opposite way: Rimfire calibers, even the hot ones like .17 WSM, do not generate enough pressure or heat to erode barrels. That is why an accurate .22 LR from the 1960s remains accurate today. It's nearly impossible to wear out a rimfire barrel in a lifetime of shooting. Barrel maker Dan Lilja once noted that a competitive shooter put 200,000 rounds through one of his barrels before real accuracy loss. Others have reported strong accuracy to the 500,000-round mark. The secret

A felt jag with pelts. The system works well. Photo: Cosmo Genova

to long rimfire barrel life seems to be a cocktail of original build quality, ammo, and how it's cleaned. For most of us, an accurate .22 LR today will remain so for our grandchildren.

However, fouling and an effect known as "carbon ring" can cause rimfire barrels to lose accuracy. (As can damage by cleaning rod.) Imagine erosion in a centerfire bore loosening the bullet fit to the lands. Fouling from relatively dirty rimfire ammo does the opposite — it tightens the bullet to the throat. Match chambers in precision rimfire rifles are already tight. One way to see this is to chamber a .22 LR round, then extract it. The soft lead bullet's bearing surface should be engraved or marked from the start of the lands.

Now, consider what a .22 LR bullet does when fired: On ignition, the bullet separates from the case in the chamber under an expansion of hot gasses. You can see the residue of this not just in the chamber but on the spent case. Fired .22 LR brass often has black

marks around the case mouth from the scorching gas. These marks are more pronounced in inexpensive and high-velocity ammo compared to match loads. Over time, escaping gas builds up a carbon deposit ring in the chamber's throat near the case head. This buildup is called a "carbon ring." The ring itself is not uniform. Thanks to gravity, it tends to be thicker at the 6 o'clock position. Carbon rings left unchecked can put non-uniform pressure on the bullet as it presses into the lands, affecting how the bullet travels down the barrel and ultimate downrange accuracy. A perfectly spec'd chamber is knocked out of alignment, and the bullet sits off-center due to carbon buildup.

But fouling is not just carbon in the chamber. On ignition, while the bullet moves down the barrel, hot gasses nip at its heeled backside. Burned and unburned primer compound and gun powder make up the blast. Neither mixture completely burns off on ignition, even with the absolute best ammo. To

Burned cases. What is that doing to your chamber? Making a carbon ring, that's what. Photo: Cosmo Genova

see this in black and white, set up a rifle prone in the snow and send a few rounds. With bulk pack ammo and a short barrel especially, you'll see a Jackson Pollock form in the snow of primer and powder debris. It's not nearly as dramatic as doing the same test with a blackpowder .50-caliber muzzleloader, but it's visible. The shot leaves behind some unburned primer and powder in the bore and a light smoke or vapor from the gas burn. You can see this with the naked eye, too. Shoot a .22 LR bolt gun, then quickly remove the bolt and look down the bore. You won't see daylight through the smoke. Boelter and others have demonstrated that much of this is water vapor, and by chemical make-up, unburned primer compound draws moisture to itself. So especially in humid environments, this fouling is drawing moisture into the bore. Moisture, we know, is an enemy of steel as it creates corrosion and pitting.

Now, consider the bullet being pushed along by this cloud of hot gasses and burned and unburned powder and primer. Bullet-to-bore fit is tight, as we've seen in our engraved example, and under pressure and heat,

the lead further deforms to seal the bullet into the rifle's lands and grooves. As it spins down the bore, it leaves behind trace amounts of lubricant — either wax or petroleum-based oil, depending on ammo — and minor lead deposits. This fouling is a cocktail of carbon, unburned primer and powder residue, lubricant, and lead, built up in varying degrees from chamber to muzzle.

When I first learned about all this, I had a powerful itch to scrub all my rifle barrels clean, but that isn't necessarily the answer.

Not all rimfire barrels foul the same way. Fouling varies from rifle to rifle, barrel to barrel. High-quality match barrels like those made by Lilja, Shilen, and others are hand-lapped or polished to a mirror finish. This level of detail is what you're paying for with a high-quality barrel. The polished surface makes for less friction, so there's less surface area for lube and lead to collect in the bore. These barrels are usually easier to clean and "settle in" or return to good accuracy quickly after cleaning.

Mass-produced factory barrels have tooling marks

Rods and bore snakes are must-own kit. Photo: Cosmo Genova

and use lesser quality, softer steel. The softer the metal, the more barrels a gun drill can make before the tool head needs sharpening. Tool marks can be seen plain as day with a borescope. Imagine a block of clay. Now scrape the top of it lightly with a fine-toothed comb. Those tight, tiny ridges and valleys are like tool marks in a bore. When you fire the rifle, the tool marks pick up fouling like lint to a sweater. Over time, lesser barrels may shoot better as the lead bullets fill imperfections and smooth the ridges with lead and lube. That is why some rifles seem to shoot better with age — and why many shooters are so reluctant to clean their barrels. If the tooling marks are dramatic or grossly uneven down the bore, the rifle may shoot worse with age, as fouling buildup can magnify the nature of these imperfections. It's possible to lap such barrels with an abrasive compound, but that is not without the risk of ruining the bore completely.

Spotless clean .22 LR barrels tend not to shoot their best. Even mirror-finished bores need some fouling. In other words, it takes fouling to achieve peak accuracy.

Some believe that lube on .22 LR bullets coats the bore, reduces friction, and makes for more consistent bullet velocity shot to shot. How many shots it takes to foul a bore into better accuracy varies by the rifle. As for lube, the old saying goes that it takes one bullet for every inch of the barrel to get a proper lube. That can also vary. Knowing how many fouling shots a barrel needs requires shooting and testing.

In time, the effects of carbon ring buildup and barrel fouling will decrease accuracy, at which point it is time to clean again. This period when the barrel is shooting its best — between those first good shots from a freshly fouled barrel to an accuracy decline — is called the "accuracy window." For a benchrest shooter, that window is invariably much smaller than a Steel Challenge competitor running a tuned-up 10/22. A reasonable accuracy window may be several thousand rounds for some. For extreme precision shooters, it could be less than 100. The only way to know the accuracy window on a rifle is to shoot it, then measure and record results. Thus the very best shooters keep detailed notes on their rifles and ammo with meticulous round counts.

Visit any national-level benchrest finals or an ISSF 3-position match, and you'll see the best of the best cleaning their rifles before, after, and during the match. Luke Johnson of Lapua told me his cleaning protocol was, "After every practice session, or 200 rounds, or if I noticed an issue. Whichever comes first." Some shooters resist cleaning the bore but extend that accuracy window by cleaning the chamber more regularly. With solvent and a bronze or nylon chamber brush, it's not difficult to break down the carbon ring when staying off the lands and grooves.

Cleaning Tools

The tools used to clean a rifle are *more important* than the method. With the right tools, you're less likely to damage a bore. What order of dry patch, solvent patch, and oil patch you use are much less critical.

Rods and Snakes

The cleaning rod is the most critical piece of equipment in a rifle cleaning kit. There are several things to consider when buying one:

The rod must be one-piece. Jointed rods that snap or screw together have more flex than one-piece rods. They can also scrape the bore at the joints. The handle should have ball-bearings or some other means to spin the rod, jag, and patch with the rifling as it moves down the barrel. Fixed-handled rods tend to stick, skip, and jump in the lands and grooves.

Also, it should have a female-threaded tip. Some high-quality rods come either male- or female-threaded. The problem with male-threaded tips is most attachments require female-threading at the rod. That said, a male-threaded tip makes for a stronger attachment. If this motivates you, just make sure you can get all the attachments you need before committing. (I bought a nice male-threaded .17-caliber rod and struggled to find end pieces I wanted, and

when I did, they were much more expensive.)

You should size the rod accordingly for the bore. With rimfire, this means a .17- or .22-caliber rod. Generally, .17-caliber rods flex excessively in a .22-caliber bore, so if you have a rifle of each caliber, you need a rod for each. Also, read the fine print. Some .22-caliber systems are sized for centerfire .223 and don't work in rimfire rifles, such as the Otis. Many rimfire aficionados prefer .204-sized rods for their .22s. The thinking is, it puts more space between the rod and bore, so any debris on the rod won't rub the steel. It is not my custom to roll my rod around in the sand, then send it down my rifle barrel, so I don't quite follow this logic. Whatever the rod diameter, it's essential to keep the rod clean and polished. The first step in any cleaning should be wiping down the rod.

Rod material is of utmost importance. Aluminum has memory, so when an aluminum rod warps, it stays warped and is suitable for nothing save corralling chickens. Naked stainless steel rods are stiff and flex, but they're scary. Steel cuts steel, so if the rod is harder than the barrel and a mishap occurs in the bore, it's a tragedy. Coated steel prevents this, and many of the high-quality rods on the market have a tough but relatively soft polymer coating to avoid direct steel-on-bore contact. Carbon fiber is stiff, flexes, and resists warping. That said, carbon-fiber rods do seem to flex a touch more than coated steel ones, so it reasons you can put more pressure on steel.

Rod length is critical. You want the shortest rod you can get away with as a shorter rod will flex less. To find that magic length, add barrel length to action length or bore guide length, plus a few inches.

Tipton, Dewey, Bore Tech, and Montana X-Treme all make excellent rods that meet these criteria. My go-to is the Tipton Deluxe carbon-fiber rod. Good rods run from $45 to $85 each, or many multiples more than an all-in-one multi-caliber breakdown system in a cheap wood box, like those you can find at any big box store. Still, high-quality rods are very worth it. You're paying for a tool that won't ruin your bore.

A sample of rimfire jags.

You must hang rods to store them correctly. If you lean them against a shelf or flat on the ground, they'll warp over time. Good rods come in plastic tubes that can double as travel containers. Or a rod tube can be made with a length of 1.5-inch PVC pipe and threaded end caps.

Pull-through systems like bore snakes or worms, or cables also work well for regular or light cleanings. You can't quite put the power to them as you can with a rod, so they're not ideal for deep cleanings. Hoppe's BoreSnakes have an embedded bronze brush at one end followed by a few feet of thick, soft cloth that acts like a series of patches. They do a good job, but you need to wash them after the first few passes on a dirty rifle. Therefore many precision-minded shooters avoid them except in a pinch. (They're great in a range bag.) Without washing a bore snake, you're effectively sending the fouling you pulled from the bore back through it. When pulling the string through from the muzzle end, ensure you're pulling straight. If you yank it out at an angle, say over the 3 o'clock position on the muzzle, it'll wear at that spot. Once, or twice, or ten times this probably isn't an issue, but many hundreds or thousands of times over the life a rifle could cause problems.

To clean a cloth bore snake, soak it in warm water with a little laundry detergent. Massage the crud out of it under warm water in a sink and repeat if necessary. Squeeze it out and let dry. Alternatively, you can clean it in a washing machine or dishwasher. It may turn into a nasty tangle in the washing machine, so roll it up loosely and secure it with a rubber band for best results.

Jags

The round-nose Parker Hale-style jag is the longtime

gun-cleaning standard, but it seems to have lost ground to the more common spear-point or pierce-point jag. With a Parker Hale, you run the rod through the action, stop short of the chamber, line up the patch, and push it through. With a pierce-point, you spear the patch to the jag, then run the whole thing through the bore guide and barrel. That might seem like a minuscule difference, but attaching the patch to the jag saves much time and frustration when running a dozen or more patches through a rifle. Jags need to be straight and true. Boelter recommends putting them in an electric drill and spinning them, though a poorly made jag will wobble. I've done this and have yet to find a bad one but have probably only tested half a dozen or so. He also recommends sharpening the tip for cleaner patch spears.

Tipton, Dewey, Bore Tech, Pro Shot, and others make good jag spears. There are specialty jags for felt cleaning pellets. These are shorter than traditional pierce-point jags, but the point is elongated and threaded. The felt pellet goes over the point. Germans originally invented the system for cleaning air rifles — the felt pellets are shot through those guns. You can find VFG Felt Cleaners from Germany at shooting supplier Champion's Choice and Brownell's, but these imports are often out of stock. Tipton makes a similar system, and you can find Felt Cleaning Pellets on Amazon, which cost less and come with the jag. Both VFG and Tipton make all-felt pellets and abrasive pellets with bronze whiskers embedded. Both systems fit looser in a .22-caliber rimfire bore than a classic pierce jag and 1-inch circle patch. But, they're excellent for applying solvents, oil, and pastes such as J-B Non-Embedding Bore Cleaning Compound. The felt soaks up liquid and holds paste well.

Loop patches are just that, brass or plastic loops that

A sample of .22 LR bronze brushes, left, and nylon brushes, right. Photo: Cosmo Genova

you affix to the end of a cleaning rod. You can pull a patch through the loop and run it through the bore. They're not as thorough as a pierce jag and patch or felt pellet system. You can see this for yourself. Clean until happy with a loop jag, then run a piece jag and patch through the barrel. You'll find grime that the loop jag missed. Some think patches in loop jags do a better job of mopping solvents and oils into a bore, but they're not worth the trouble, as you can do it all with a pierce-point jag, patches, and a good set of brushes.

Brushes

Bore brushes come in two flavors: nylon or brass. Technically, there's a third, stainless steel, made by some sick sadist who wants people to ruin their rifles. Never use a steel brush anywhere on a rifle. Steel cuts steel, so by using one, you're not just asking for trouble — you're giving trouble red wine and a foot massage.

Nylon brushes have more bristles than brass and are softer and more flexible. They hold solvent well. Brass brushes are stiffer and do faster work on carbon rings and other stubborn fouling. You should not use them

with a copper solvent like Sweet's 7.62 as that strong cleaner will dissolve the brush.

Some shooters won't use brass brushes because they fear they will scratch the bore. This assumption doesn't track with basic metallurgy. Brass is a generic name for copper-zinc alloys, the most common being yellow brass or cartridge brass. Inexpensive tools like $3 brushes are made of yellow brass (or cheaper, softer "soft brass") for the fundamental economic reason that it costs less and is forged widely. On the Rockwell Hardness B-scale, yellow brass comes in at 55, while cold-rolled low-carbon steel measures 60. Gun barrel steels like Chromoly and stainless steels vary in hardness by the particulars of the alloy and manufacturing process but start around 88 for stainless and 92 for low-end 4130 Chromoly. By the nature of these materials, brass will not scratch steel, even cheap, low-quality steel. Maybe, heavy scrubbing with a brass brush could hasten the erosion of scorched and compromised centerfire lands, but I doubt it. Nevertheless, it's a nonissue with rimfires. Brass can't scratch steel.

Test this yourself on a piece of scrap steel. Clean the steel and polish it smooth. Take a brass bore brush,

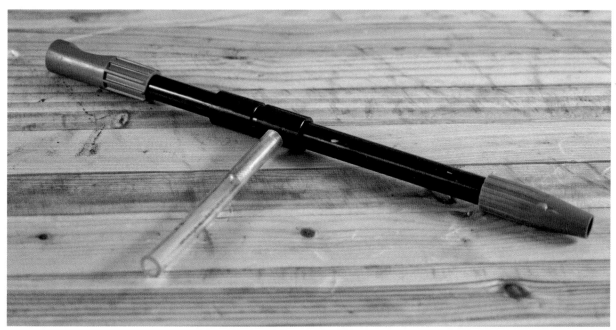

A universal bore guide. Action-specific guides work much better, especially for small-diameter rimfire receivers. Photo: Cosmo Genova

give it the old Kung Fu grip, and scrub the steel until the brush wears down to nothing. You'll see marks on the steel, but that's brass rub-off, not unlike a crayon on paper. Clean the marks off with some solvent and inspect. Put it under a microscope. You will find no damage to the steel.

Lilja Precision Rifle Barrels makes no bones about this on its website: "Some shooters and gunsmiths have the mistaken idea that a bronze brush will harm a barrel. It *will not cause any damage* to a barrel, and the use of a bronze brush *is necessary* to remove all fouling. Substituting a nylon brush *will not* remove fouling as effectively as a bronze brush."

Nylon brushes have a place as they're a softer touch than brass, but shooters who want clean rifles should not be afraid of brass ones.

A brass brush bent at a 90-degree angle makes a good chamber brush for scrubbing out carbon rings.

Patches

Cotton patches come sized for caliber, but most of them still need some work. The ¾-inch square patches generally fit .22 rimfire bores but sometimes need trimming. I've found the 1-inch squares fit, too, if you trim the corners liberally. When you cut them, square patches can fray and shed thin cotton strings. This problem bugs me as I imagine some coming loose in the bore, though I can't honestly say that's ever happened. I'm partial to Pro-Shot 1-inch round patches, which fit well, don't require cutting, and don't shed. These patches' cotton flannel seems to be of higher quality than the stuff used in bulk bags of square patches from Hoppe's and others. The upside of cutting square patches is you can often get a slightly tighter fit. You can also change the tightness of a square patch by where you spear it. Stick it closer to a corner and wrap the patch around the jag, and it

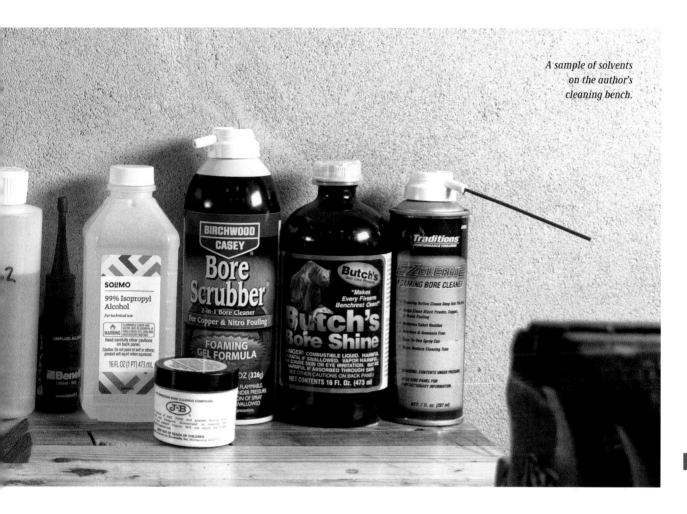

A sample of solvents on the author's cleaning bench.

will fit looser than a patch speared dead center.

Bore Guides

To properly clean a rifle, you need a bore guide. In a bolt action, simply remove the bolt and slot the guide in its place. You should be able to look through it from the back and see out the muzzle. Bore guides do several things. They ensure the rod is going into the bore centered, so there isn't uneven pressure exerted at the start of the lands and grooves, and they help ensure back and forth strokes aren't exerting any side-to-side pressure. Also, they keep solvents out of the action.

There are universal bore guides for not much money, but they don't work well in rimfire rifles' small actions. Bore Tech and Possum Hollow make good bore guides for various actions and calibers; Sinclair International has a great selection, plus an in-house guide. Killough Shooting Sports and Champion's Choice sell them for benchrest and ISSF rifle actions.

Solvents and Oils

There is no shortage of solvents, oils, and other cleaning liquids for firearms. They all work. We could argue all day about which work better, but short of agreeing to pay for some extensive laboratory testing, we wouldn't get very far. If you have a particular solvent you like, adequately stock it on your workbench. My preferences have changed over time and are primarily informed by asking accomplished shooters and barrel makers what they recommend. When it comes to solvents such as Butch's, Hoppe's, and the powerful stuff like Sweet's, I transfer them to squeeze bottles, simplifying barrel flushing. As you'll see below, I'm a fan of flushing bores with blasts of solvents and oil, as I learned at the Original

Pennsylvania 1,000 Yard Benchrest School. Here is my personal, and by no means inclusive, list of chemicals, in alphabetical order:

Birchwood Casey Bore Scrubber — This is a foaming gel cleanser that I squirt directly down the barrel, like the more popular and much more expensive WIPE OUT Bore Cleaner. Many benchrest shooters foam their dirty barrel and let it sit several minutes before getting after it with a bronze or nylon brush. It may be unnecessary for some rimfires as there's no copper fouling to soak out, so I reserve this step for the occasional deep clean.

Break-Free — You can find this ubiquitous brake and parts cleaner anywhere. The difference between the bottles marketed to firearms versa auto-repair is mostly price. Brake cleaner eats oil and might be one of the best degreasers on Planet Earth. A friend who was an armorer in the U.S. Army said they didn't use it since it strips oil off metal *too well*. Indeed, you should use it sparingly. And it's not for bore cleaning. I use it for small metal parts that resist other measures. It will strip paint or finish off a wood stock and discolor synthetics. Proceed with caution.

Butch's Bore Shine — This is a general-purpose bore cleaner, which Lilja recommends. It's hell on carbon and is an excellent solvent for regular and deep cleanings. I use Butch's more than anything on this list, but other widely acclaimed bore solvents, such as Montana X-Treme and Bore Tech, have rimfire-specific blends that don't have a cooper-eating agent included.

Hoppe's No. 9 — The classic, and it's still hard to beat as a general-purpose cleaning solvent.

J-B Non-Embedding Bore Cleaning Compound — If J-B's won't clean a barrel, then the barrel can't be cleaned. This mild abrasive paste blows out carbon and other deep, stuck-on fouling. Some love it. Some feel it's too harsh. The stuff is a centerpiece in my deep cleaning ritual. I think of J-B's like hitting the reset button on a bore. I'll also use it on a brand new barrel if common solvents and patches take too long to get manufacturing residue out.

Kroil Oil — The best of the penetrating oils for firearms and a standard for generations. Along with Butch's, this is my standard solvent and oil combo.

Rem Oil Wipes — Rem Oil has a mixed reputation

It's OK to clean an autoloader such as the Ruger 10/22 from the muzzle, provided you remove and thoroughly clean the action, and take care not to ding the muzzle. The Ruger 10/22 Takedown, shown here, can be disassmbled and cleaned chamber to muzzle.

mainly because some think it eats plastic, such as polymer handgun frames, and others think it's too thin and runny for a gun oil. Maybe, but the tub of oiled wipes is very convenient for wiping rifles after a damp morning in the squirrel woods.

Super Lube — Bolt actions and semi-autos like 10/22s (think AR-15s) have multiple points that need grease for peak performance. My go-to is Super Lube because it has such a low freeze point and a thick, viscous nature that sticks and doesn't run. It's also inexpensive and available to everyone. Tony Kidd uses Mil-Comm TW25B Gun Grease in his shop, and he builds some of the best semi-auto rimfire rifles money can buy. Many of the benchrest competitors I know use Pro-Shot Pro-Gold or Shooter's Choice. For Super Lube, I buy packs of plastic dental syringes with the curved tip and fill them with the stuff for easy application.

Sweet's 7.62 Solvent — The great destroyer of copper. It's so good it can destroy a barrel, too. Sweet's is ammonia-based, and ammonia can pit barrels, so you must follow the directions on the bottle carefully and not leave it in the bore longer than 15

minutes. Of course, .22 LRs don't need this level of copper-blasting, even if you use copper-plated ammo. Copper-removing agents in solvents like Butch's are enough. The low-speed, low-pressure of .22 LR doesn't put down enough copper in a bore to warrant such extreme tactics. I have used it successfully on .17s and .22 WMRs that eat copper-plated V-MAX and VNT bullet debris. You can tell it's working by the bluish/purplish stain of dissolved copper it leaves on a patch, but all that said, it's overkill even for the .17s and magnums. Sweet's will eat a bronze brush. Nylon only. And the smell can knock a cat off a fence. Use outside.

Zippo Lighter Fluid — For flushing triggers clean.

How To Clean

Like the type of tools and solvents used to clean a rifle, opinions on using them range far and wide. What follows is not some perfect methodology, but what I've pieced together through talking with experts — a deep cleaning method for bringing a bore down to the bare metal — hitting the reset button. I do this once a year, typically in late fall after hunting season, to get my rimfires ready for a winter of ammo testing, tinkering, and general weathered-in dabbling.

Shoot the rifle, if possible. It's easier to clean a warm barrel than a cold one. I typically send ten shots down my home range to heat things.

Remove the bolt and install the bore guide.

Apply bore foam, Bore Scrubber, Wipe Out, or even a muzzleloader-specific foam like CVA Barrel Blaster.

Push a dry patch through and inspect. Keep sending patches until they come out dry, showing that the foaming cleaner is all out. Note, the patches are likely still dirty at this point.

With the Butch's or another solvent in a squeeze bottle, squirt it in the bore guide and down the barrel until it drips out the muzzle end.

With a nylon or bronze brush, run it down the barrel and back in a sawing motion, but at low speed, making sure the rod spins with the rifling. Take it easy — six to ten strokes.

Run three or four patches soaked in Kroil down the bore and inspect. If they still look filthy, move on to the abrasives.

Cover a felt pellet or patch with J-B compound and run it up and down the bore five to ten times.

With the solvent in a squeeze bottle, squirt it in the bore guide to flush out the compound. As a benchrest shooter told me, "Use it like someone else bought it."

Send a dry patch down the barrel, alternating with Kroil oil patches until the dry patch comes out clean. If I expect the rifle to sit in the safe for a while, I'll conclude with an oiled patch as I live in a humid environment.

With an old .22 that you've never cleaned well, this may not destroy the carbon ring, at which point I'll use a bronze brush and solvent on a short pistol-length cleaning rod to scrub out the back few inches of the bore.

When cleaning .17s or magnums that shoot copper-plated bullets, look for blue tinting on the patches after running a solvent like Butch's. That would be a sign of the copper fouling breaking down. Make sure by the end of your deep-clean process that a Butch's

patch shows no blue.

Every 200 to 400 rounds, I'll give my precision .22s a light version of this cleaning by running a Butch's solvent patch, then a dry patch, then three or four patches of Kroil, followed by three or four dry patches.

For semi-automatics like Ruger 10/22s and Savage A-series rifles, I clean the bolt and receiver every time I clean the barrel. Blowback semi-automatics and delayed blowbacks like the Savage draw fouling from the chamber back into the action as they cycle, so they get much dirtier in the fire control mechanisms than bolt-action rifles.

It's possible to drill a cleaning hole in the back of a 10/22 receiver with a jig. For 10/22s with super-premium barrels, I recommend the cleaning hole. Otherwise, I clean them with rods from the muzzle end or with bore snakes. Cleaning a rifle from muzzle to action is not the end of the world, as some shooters surmise. It's problematic mainly because it's pushing dirty patches and gunk into the rifle action, not out of it, and if you're not careful, you can damage the crown. But on a system like a 10/22 — where you remove the trigger and bolt for cleaning — you can easily clean the receiver after the bore.

Triggers, Actions, and Bolts

Triggers, actions, and bolts collect gunk over time, and eventually, you need to clean them. That is especially the case with rimfires, as the ammo tends to run dirtier than centerfires. Precision triggers are especially prone to fouling and can cause misfires when dirty, especially open trigger works like those found on Anschutz and CZ rifles. Contained trigger systems collect gunk, too, but less so. In both cases, the cleaning process is the same and bone simple: flush with lighter fluid. Let it evaporate and air dry. Oil or grease if the trigger system calls for it — many new triggers don't. Compressed air from an air compressor works well, primarily when used in conjunction with lighter fluid. Compressed air in a can, not so much. It doesn't have enough force and leaves a thin residue.

A 12- or 20-gauge nylon bore brush does wonders for getting in an action and scrubbing it out. Metal dental picks and long-handled wooden Q-tips can get in little crevasses like eject cuts in a breechface. Mild solvents such as Hoppe's works well. After cleaning, I tend to oil with Kroil, let the rifle sit, and then wipe it all clean with a dry lint-free rag and reassemble before the next outing.

To clean a bolt, disassemble it per manufacturer instructions. With a solvent like Hoppe's or, in some cases, Break-Free, I'll soak and then scrub with an old toothbrush or nylon brush. It's easy to see carbon buildup on a bolt face and extractors, and you can tell when they're sparkling clean. I will polish and dry with a soft cloth, oil, and reassemble. With Super Lube in a dental syringe, I'll lightly grease the raceway for a smooth action.

How Clean is Clean?

It's easy to get carried away and want every millimeter of a rifle to shine spotless, to have the white cotton patches pull through clean and crisp as mountain air. If that's your jam, more power to you, but rifle cleaning shouldn't make you crazy or ruin a whole afternoon.

As we know, fouled bores shoot better than pristine ones. So, how clean is clean? My favorite answer to this is in the FAQ section on Shilen Rifles' website. Shilen has made more world-record rimfire barrels than anyone. Shilen geared its statement toward centerfire, but if you're a .22 LR precision shooter, swap out "cooper" for "lead and lube," and the conclusion still holds:

"We get this question many times and have a great deal of difficulty helping some customers understand that a rifle barrel does not have to be spotless to shoot great. Many times, more harm than good is done in trying to get it that way. Picture a car's fender. If the fender has a small dent in it, then professional application of body putty fills the dent. When painted over, the dent becomes unnoticeable, and the surface of the fender is smooth and consistent. The same thing happens in a rifle barrel on a microscopic level. Removing this small trace of copper puts you right back to square one. The next bullet that crosses that area will, again, leave a small trace of copper. Similar to patching a pothole. All successful benchrest shooters shoot one or more 'fouler' shots down the barrel before going to the record target. This is not to warm up the barrel. They are resurfacing it on the inside. Benchrest shooters clean between relays to get the powder fouling out, not the copper. However, since copper usually comes out with the powder, they know that it must be replaced to get 'back in the groove.' I've had shooters tell me they 'cleaned their rifle for 3 hours to get all the copper out of it.' Their next statement is almost invariably that they had to shoot 4-5 rounds through it just to get it back to 'shooting' again. This tells me that in order for the rifle to shoot well again, they had to replace the copper they worked so diligently to remove. I have a 7x08 Improved that shoots the same 1/2 MOA after 15 minutes of cleaning or 3 hours of scrubbing and de-coppering. Personally, I prefer shooting to cleaning. The gist of this is to set a regular cleaning regimen and stay with it. If the accuracy of the rifle is acceptable with a 15 min. cleaning, why clean longer? I would much rather have people admiring the groups I shot than marveling at how clean my barrel looks on the inside." RR

8

CUSTOMIZATION, UPGRADES, AND REPAIR

Tin·ker \ 'tiŋ-kər \
    verb: to work in the manner of a tinker *especially*: to repair, adjust, or work with something in an unskilled or experimental manner: FIDDLE
    noun: a: a usually itinerant mender of household utensils b: an unskillful mender: BUNGLER

    Gunsmiths love Dremels, or so the saying goes, because after someone works on their rifle with a Dremel, they need to pay a gunsmith to fix it. That never dissuaded me from firing up a rotary tool. Thankfully, the gunsmith bills haven't been too costly. I'm a tinkerer at heart. I enjoy working on rifles almost as much as I enjoy shooting them. And I am not alone. Spend any time on the shooting forums online, and you'll see the same questions pop up repeatedly.

A supressed Vudoo in an ultra-light carbon stock. Photo: Mike Semanoff.

The author's first (poor) bedding job, top, compared to Sitman's professional work at bottom. Photo: Cosmo Genova

There is something profoundly American about not leaving well enough alone. The gun industry knows this. The gun industry has responded.

Modularity is not a new concept. ArmaLite introduced the AR-15 in 1957 and 1958, Ruger the 10/22 in 1964. Part of the universal success of these platforms is user serviceability. Should something jam, break, or otherwise screw up, the knowledgeable shooter can likely diagnose and correct it with minimal tools. Both platforms birthed vibrant aftermarkets.

In the last few years, rimfire manufacturers have doubled down on modularity and aftermarket sup-

port in a nod to tinkerers and the money they spend. Anschütz, Bergara, CZ, RimX, Ruger, Sako, T/C, Tikka, and Volquartsen all have new rifles with replaceable barrel systems. Most also have replaceable trigger groups. Companies such as CZ-USA are actively working to build a rimfire aftermarket, working with the likes of Area419, Diversified Innovation Products, Inc., and other performance shops. Bergara, RimX, and Vudoo smartly tapped into an existing aftermarket by building their rifles on a Remington 700 footprint.

Nearly all these companies are working with the best barrel markers in the U.S. and Canada. For An-

a difference between actual gunsmithing and building a 10/22 or AR-15 from a parts kit.

In the United States, to work on someone else's firearms, you need a Federal Firearms License (FFL). Working on your guns generally does not require one, but that alone doesn't make one a gunsmith. I do most of my work myself, right down to experimenting with chambers, bedding, bolts, and trigger tuning. But I am not a gunsmith. I don't own a lathe. I take my metalwork to friends, usually Justin Potter of Valley Armament in Sayre, Pennsylvania, a trained machinist, and gunsmith. I'm an enthusiast. Justin is the gunsmith. He often refines my ideas, then executes them. To my mind, this is an important distinction to make as real gunsmiths deserve respect not so quickly afforded in our new DIY culture. Building a bolt-action rifle no longer makes one a gunsmith. The gunsmith did the real work of action blueprinting and thread timing, so a guy like me could screw it all together. So, while tinkering is educational and fun, it is not gunsmithing, and the deeper down the rabbit hole you go, you'll find points where it makes better sense to pay a gunsmith for professional work, even for the supposed "easy" jobs.

When the rimfire bug first bit me hard, I started bedding my wood and laminate sporter stocks. My projects came out well. I saw accuracy improvements across the board. Life got busy with work, and I had two special rifles I wanted to bed. I saved them for last because I wanted to practice on my lesser guns. I couldn't get to them with other commitments, so after a bit of research, I sent them to Alex Sitman of Master Class Stocks in Bellwood, Pennsylvania. Sitman is the best stock man in the United States. He does inletting and R&D work for McMillan and is a favorite on the benchrest circuit. Not only that, he has worked on numerous world champion rifles, such as Paul Philips' record-setting .416 Barrett. I packed up my rifles and sent them to PA.

When I got the rifles back, I pulled the action screws, and the actions wouldn't come out. They did

schütz, CZ, Ruger, Sako, and Tikka, most of the elite barrel builders offer drop-ins that the shooter can install at home without a lathe or other specialized tooling. Some of these new rifles can get a full caliber makeover at the kitchen table by changing out the barrel and bolt in a minute or two.

It's an exciting time for tinkerers. But you're limited without a lathe, a mill, and an experienced gunsmith to use them. As one manufacturer told me, "Mario Andretti didn't work on his own car." Indeed, across all shooting disciplines, most top competitors do not service their rifles. Real gunsmiths do that, and there's

Tweaking 10/22s is fun and addiciting. Before you know it, you'll have a benchtop like this.

with a little effort and an audible "pop" like they were vacuum-sealed in place. The lines underneath were crisp, sharp, with glass bedding compound only where it needed to be. It was a work of art unlike mine, which was like a crayon drawing by a four-year-old. I'm glad I bedded the rifles that I did, though, because I learned a lot in the process. But now I send all my rifles that need bedding to Master Class. It is not expensive to get a rifle bedded. It's a downright deal when you deduct the materials cost and time that a DIY project requires.

I've reshaped firing pins and stoned triggers, but I recognize the limits of my abilities and know when to call in the experts.

What follows is a look at tinkering with an eye toward performance: making rifles more accurate, more ergonomic, better shooting. Most are DIY affairs, but some require a competent gunsmith. We'll look at the most common platforms for customization, the 10/22, the CZ 455/457, along with Remington 700 footprint rifles and what you need to customize them. We'll also look at universal stock work, which every rifle needs.

Trigger Warning

Accuracy is expensive. Every rifle in this book can perform under MOA with suitable ammunition. Shaving those groups to the .300s or maintaining sub-MOA at 100 yards takes some doing. As the distance increases, it costs more to keep groups tiny. Bringing a rifle from a .400-inch performer at 50 yards to a regular .300-inch shooter isn't just difficult and expensive; it is often not possible. This dilemma opens up a discussion of cost versus performance versus value. That's a personal dilemma to ponder, so we're not going to get into it except to say that the cost of tinkering can escalate quickly.

Take the CZ 457, for example. It's possible to make a 457 every bit as accurate as an Anschütz or Vudoo. But, swapping the barrel, trigger, and chassis will cost as much as high-end custom. A tried-and-true tinkerer won't mind because it's *their rifle*, and the satisfaction of a successful DIY project makes it worth it. Others might wonder why not just buy that performance in a complete rifle in the first place? Neither option is better than the other. They're just different approaches.

If you're going the homebuilt route, you'll need some tools and a workspace — things you should not try to scrimp on. Precision rifles require precision work through every step of the process, which begins with a good torque wrench. You'll need a wide variety of bits and extensions. Sets are widely available online. Also, you should invest in a cleaning cradle to hold a rifle level and steady. Tipton, MTM, and Hyskore make them. You need a solid bench on which to work. A 4-inch vise with padded jaws and a barrel vise is a bonus. Your workspace should be clean and dust-free. Working on a rifle in a barn, woodshop, or garage that doubles as a cat hotel is less than ideal. If starting from scratch, adding all this to the cost of a CZ plus a PROOF or Bartlein or Lilja barrel, and a chassis-style stock, you'll likely have exceeded the upper limits of a Vudoo or a custom-built RimX. I'm not arguing against this path. Hell, one of my favorite rifles is a PROOF-barreled 457. Just be aware of how deep this water is before you jump. And please don't flail like a person sucking water when adding an $800 chassis, $500 barrel, and $200 trigger to a $400 rifle.

The 10/22 Platform

The OG of custom rimfire rifles, the Ruger 10/22, is one of the most popular and best-selling long guns worldwide. The Ruger patent on the 10/22 design long expired. At one point, more than a dozen smaller companies were selling 10/22 clones. The depth of aftermarket support, from action screws and iron sights to full receivers, bolts, and barrels, is only rivaled by the AR-15. Third parties make every component, right down to magazine springs. New, the rifles run from a sale price under $200 for a sporter in a birch stock to $2,200 for a kitted-out Volquartsen Inferno.

With so many part options available, many 10/22

nuts never buy a full rifle to start. They begin with a receiver — the only ATF-regulated item in a 10/22 build that requires an FFL — and build from the ground up. If you want to build a rifle, it's hard to beat the 10/22. They snap together like Lego blocks and require no special tooling. Assembling custom 10/22s was all the rage in the late 1990s and early 2000s, but they're back now with a vengeance as precision rimfire matches have gained traction. In a timed NRL22 match, you simply cannot beat the speed of an autoloader, no matter how fast you learn to run a bolt.

With a 10/22, the old saw that rifle accuracy boils down to "bullets, barrels, and bedding" couldn't be truer. Every 10/22 build should start and end with an ammo test. Group shooting can tell you what you need to change and what you have already improved. That said, if I'm tearing down a stock Ruger for a build and know I'll replace the barrel, I'll swap the barrel first, then shoot a variety of ammo as a baseline before moving to other upgrades. A chronograph is essential when working on a semi-automatic rifle. With consistent match ammo, you can identify ignition issues by watching velocities as well as groups downrange. If upgrading a rifle, it's immensely satisfying to shoot it as is, then test it when the upgrade is complete and compare targets.

What follows is a short guide on how to upgrade a Ruger 10/22. These are not just my in-depth thoughts on the subject from working on a dozen or more builds. The following comes from hours of discussion with three of the best 10/22 hands in the country: Tony Kidd of Kidd Innovative Designs; Joe Chacon, gunsmith and founder of the Auto Bench Rest Association; and Randy Carbine, of Connecticut Precision Chambering.

10/22 Barrels

No single upgrade will make more of an improvement to a 10/22 than a new barrel. "The main thing is the barrel," Tony Kidd once told me. "The first thing you'll need is a good barrel. We put a lot into our bar-

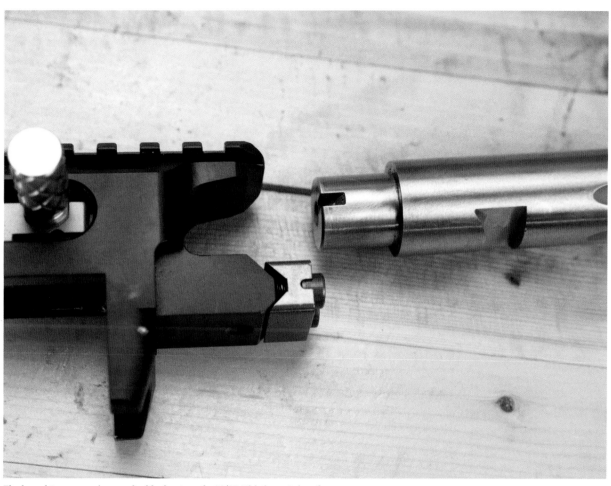

The barrel tenon, receiver, and v-block setup of a 10/22. This is an Azimuth receiver and bolt with a Green Mountain barrel. Photo: Cosmo Genova

rels, but there are plenty of other good ones out there. The market is big."

If building from scratch, the barrel is the first thing to consider. It's the heart and soul of an accurate rifle. When considering lengths and contours, it's best to think in terms of end-use. If the rifle is for squirrel hunting or Rimfire Challenge, a light sporter barrel will work great, and there are some excellent ones out there, like Green Mountain Rifle Barrels. 16 to 18 inches is a good, accurate barrel length. Shorter feels better when running suppressors. For precision games like NRL22 and benchrest, the trend is heavy and long — bull barrels with a straight .920-inch minimal taper in lengths from 20 to 24 inches. 10/22 benchrest founder Joe Chacon likes a 22-inch .920-inch counter barrel. Stainless is the current fad in barrels, but 4140

tool steel heat treats better with a harder finished product than stainless. For precision rifles that will be Cerakoted or dipped, 4140 is ideal.

There are many good 10/22 barrel makers, but "buying a barrel is hit or miss, from any company," Charon once told me. "Every company makes a bad one once in a while, but Shilen makes a lot less bad ones, and their good ones are the best." Shilen barrels hold a pile of benchrest and other precision records. So does Lilja. Both are button-rifled barrels. Bartlein does limited-run 10/22 barrels twice a year, and many consider them the best of the cut-rifled type, though they're hard to get as they sell out instantly. It's also possible to have super-premium 10/22 barrels produced by a competent gunsmith from .22 RF blanks, such as Muller Works, Kreiger, Hart, and others.

A few 10/22 stock options on the author's bench. Photo: Cosmo Genova

Some drop-in barrel builders of note include Kidd, Clark, and Fedderson. Whistle Pig barrels have good reviews, as do German-made Lothar Walthers, though Lothar seems to release its barrels in limited runs. Many smaller barrel builders such as Kidd start with Lothar blanks. Volquartsen makes some excellent ultra-light carbon-fiber tension barrels, as well. They're among my favorite for hunting builds. PROOF does as well, but they run double and triple the price of similar quality tubes, like the Volquartsen.

Nearly all good 10/22 barrel makers cut a Bentz chamber or some variation. These are tighter than Sporting and Universal .22 LR chambers but are only loosely considered "match" in tightness and inherent accuracy. The Bentz chamber's appeal is its relatively wider mouth at the breech end and tapered chamber walls that narrow more at the leade than a Sporting chamber. The broad backside facilitates easy extraction of spent cases by a blowback semi-auto bolt, while the tightness of the chamber neck and leade help accuracy.

Not all Bentz chambers are created equal. Some are tighter than others, probably by just a few thousandths, but that can translate to real functionality differences. For example, a new Green Mountain barrel with a Bentz chamber will not extract live rounds. It's just too tight when freshly cut, and they tell you so when ordering. For other barrels with Bentz chambers, this is not the case. Nor is it necessarily a bad thing, as all other things being equal, a tighter chamber generally makes for a more accurate rimfire.

For 10/22 barrels with Sporting chambers, a knowledgeable gunsmith can shorten them on the lathe by taking 0.060 to 0.080 inch off the breechface. Makers can shorten Bentz chambers this way, too, but that may create feed issues.

10/22 Stocks and Chassis

The best barrel in the world won't shoot straight if it's not bedded correctly to a quality stock or chassis. To start, consider the stock. There is no lack of quality 10/22 stocks on the market, but beware of the current

Timney 10/22 aftermarket trigger.

trend toward ridged aluminum chassis if your goal is ultimate accuracy with a semi-auto. "Wood and fiberglass, their hybrids, they all dampen vibration," Chacon says. "And think about how much vibration happens when a 10/22 fires. That bolt is slamming back and forth. Put that on top of metal, and you have a giant vibrator. It kills barrel harmonics."

On the high-end, Chacon likes McMillan and custom laminate stock builder Tony Mele. Boyds Gun Stocks are top-rated in the 10/22 world. You can make significant accuracy improvements by dropping a factory 10/22 in a Boyd's or similar laminate stock. The Magpul Hunter X-22 is an excellent synthetic stock. It says something that Kidd puts most of his rifles in Magpuls. The tolerances stock-to-stock are fantastic. The Victor Titan, which has an anchor for a rear tang and second action screw, is popular in the NRL22 world, though many semi-auto shooters have moved toward a new crop of 10/22-specific chassis.

Kinetic Research Group or KRG released a version of its popular Bravo chassis for the 10/22. It has a full-length aluminum backbone or bedding block that runs the chassis' length for peak rigidity. The block is polymer overwrapped, so it's quiet, doesn't get cold on the hand like metal, and most importantly, for 10/22s — absorbs vibration and keeps barrel harmonics happy. The length-of-pull is adjustable, a feature oddly missing from many 10/22 stocks. It's compatible with a Kidd rear tang for two action screws. There are endless attachment points with sling studs, sling cups, and M-LOK slots throughout the chassis, plus a flat forend for attaching an ARCA rail for even more options. Like all KRG chassis, your imagination is the only real limit to what you can hang off it.

ORYX, a division of MDT, has a similar 10/22, but it has no rear tang feature. Manners is developing a long-delayed 10/22 chassis, too. It's worth noting that other chassis builders have wrestled with long 10/22 development timelines. Others, like MDT, have made and sold 10/22 systems, only to abandon them later. Much of that is due to fitment. Aftermarket 10/22 receivers are not all spec'd the same, and many of the

An aftermarket 10/22 reciever by Azimuth, the author's current favorite.

better actions are a touch larger than the factory Ru-gers. The older factory Rugers are slightly larger than the newer ones. You may need to do some inletting, either trimming out some polymer sidewall or beefing it up. A Remington 700 footprint is a beautiful thing because the specs, action-to-action are identical, so various stocks and actions snug together perfectly. 10/22 receivers only seem universal until you get the micrometer out and measure different ones. Then it's clear they're all over the place. Companies making precision chassis must contend with this, which ex-plains why there are so few options compared to other rifle platforms.

In the early days of NRL22 competition, Kidd rifles were always top contenders. The 2020 National Match was the first year that no shooter shot a 10/22 clone. I expect the new crop of chassis like the KRG to change that.

10/22 Triggers

For a precision 10/22 rifle, let's save some time. Buy a Kidd trigger. Kidds come two-stage or single-stage, with pull weights from 6 ounces to 2.5 pounds. The internal parts geometry is what makes them so unique. It is not a Ruger design with slicked-up parts, but you can feel a real design improvement in every pull. If your project doesn't require this performance level, the Ruger BX Trigger is better than it used to be. But not all BX triggers are created equal. Go to a big box or gun store, and try each one on the shelf. The BX trigger packaging allows you to feel the trigger pull without taking it out of the box. It's possible to find a gem by pulling them all. The Calvin Elite from Timney has great ergonomics with adjustable length of pull, cast, and height. Set at 2 lbs. this is my go-to small game hunting and Rimfire Challenge race-gun trigger. Brimstone Gunsmithing and Randy at CPC will also tune a stock Ruger trigger for around $100, or you can work on it yourself with a parts kit from Volquartsen. Lawyers prevent book writers from getting specific on the how-to of trigger work, but all the information needed is widely available online. Or, you just hit the easy button and buy a Kidd trigger. They are worth it.

10/22 Receivers

If you're upgrading a 10/22, the receiver is the last thing you should worry about. Stock Ruger receivers do the job and can easily be slicked-up internally with a green Scotch-Brite pad and some elbow grease. If you're building fresh, you have many options that you can reduce to two: steel or aluminum. Steel options include the Elite 22 from Tactical Innovations and the gorgeous nickel-bronze receiver from Fedderson. Both have machined-in Pic rails, which are great unless you want to shoot long distances and need an MOA rail. (The one workaround here is the Burris Xtreme Tactical rings with the plus 5 to 40 MOA ring inserts.)

For aluminum, you can get stripped Ruger receivers from S&P Outfitters for cheap or go with the Brownell's BRN-22, though you may need to file the inside rail to get the bolt to fit. That issue plagued early runs of the Brownell's. Like those from Tactical Innovations, Kidd, and others, anodized aluminum receivers will generally run better than raw or rough aluminum. The anodizing process hardens and slicks the action, so there's less friction as the bolt moves back and forth.

A new company, Azimuth Precision, now makes 7075-T6 aluminum receivers and barreled actions. 7075 is much stronger than the 6061-series aluminum used by most others. Unlike steel, they do not weigh 1.5 pounds. Its AZTP-22 has a dual bolt rail — something Ruger discontinued after three years, which Azimuth says eliminates bolt canting under pressure. A zero-degree Pic rail is milled right into the top of the receiver. The fit and finish are impeccable.

Of receivers, there are two real upgrades to con-

Installing a Rear Tang

The rear tang keys into a shallow groove that you mill into the receiver's backside. A skilled DIY'er can do this with a drill press. The rear tang's keyed front face is .250-inch wide. There's a .125-inch radius on both ends, with an overall length of .625 inch. The key stands .051-inch proud of the surrounding surface.

To align correctly on the receiver's back, use a jig of the Gunsmither tool designed for cutting a cleaning hole in the back of a 10/22 receiver. The key's top rounded end snugs into the top of the cleaning hole. Then drill a 3/16-inch hole for the tang's retaining screw .375 inch below the cleaning hole center. It holds the tang to the receiver. Mill out a 051-inch deep channel between the two holes for the key. On the inside of the receiver, countersink to match the retaining screw head. With the right tools, none of this is challenging work.

sider. A cleaning hole drilled in the back to run a rod down the action and barrel without taking the barrel off the receiver; and a rear tang for a second action screw. Cut cleaning holes on a drill press with an inexpensive guide solder by Gunsmither Tools. The rear tang requires a little more machining work.

Some view the rear tang as the best thing to happen to 10/22s since CCI Standard. For others, it's a waste of money. Stock Ruger 10/22s and their clones have one takedown screw located behind the v-block that holds the barrel to the action. Some believe this isn't enough to prevent the action from seesawing in the stock with that one touchpoint, especially if the barrel is free-floated.

Tony Kidd pioneered a rear tang, and many quality stock and chassis makers, including McMillan, Victor, and KRG, have inletted for the second screw. While this undeniably makes the connection between the action and stock stronger, Chacon and Carbine say it does not help accuracy one bit, assuming you have

A lineup of custom 10/22 bolts.

correctly bedded the rifle.

For intense competitions such as 3-Gun or NRL22, during which you may be dropping rifles hard on a barricade, a rear tang makes a lot of sense. I use it and have never met anyone with a rear tang in their 10/22 who didn't like it. It makes the rifle feel more solid in hand. With a good drill press or a mill, installation is not complicated, but nearly every Ruger 'smith you can find online will install one affordably. Kidd sells the tang for $22.

10/22 Bolts

Bolt tuning for optimal ignition and extraction can get complicated, but it's possible to do much of the work yourself. For starters, put some white grease on the bolt, then run it a few times by hand in the receiver. Pull the bolt, and you'll see where it rubs the receiver — polish those touchpoints with a green Scotch Brite pad for a slicker action. Volquartsen sells a popular Bolt Tune-Up kit with a wide, hardened firing pin, a hardened and sharpened extractor, plus

springs. Kidd sells excellent bolt handles and guide rod springs. (The heavier plus-10 percent spring is a must if you want to shoot high-velocity ammo regularly.) If you need to buy a bolt outright, the Kidd and Volquartsen ones are excellent, or you can go with the JWH Custom, which Chacon likes and comes in a variety of engraving options. Though many world-class 10/22s use tuned-up stock Ruger bolts, gunsmith Carbine will do it for about $50 — see below.

With the right tools, 10/22 bolts can be trued by entirely straightening the bolt's inside edge with a jig and grinder or mill. With that straight edge, the gunsmith squares the bolt face perfectly to the breechface. You must do this carefully, as it can affect the recess for the rim (the headspace) in the bolt face. Lapua rim thickness runs .043 inch, Eley is .039 inch. I do this truing process to all my bolts and check the recess with a mic depth gauge, making sure to keep them all at .043 inch to be safe. Most 10/22 gunsmiths will do this for you affordably.

It's good to have options.

Small 10/22 Parts

Volquartsen, Tandemkross, Raven Eye Custom, and Gunsmither all make small parts like trigger parts kits, action screws, pins, and springs for the 10/22. Oversized trigger pins are highly recommended for precision builds. For buffer pins that run through the receiver and stop the bolt, I buy .25-inch Delrin rods and cut them to size. Kidd and others sell plastic coated pins as well. Anything is better than the stock Ruger steel pins that make noise and shock rather than absorb it.

10/22 Assembly

Remove the original barrel, if necessary, by loosening the two socket cap screws with a 5/32-inch Allen wrench. Slide the dovetail v-block out and fit the new barrel into the receiver. If the barrel tenon is slightly oversized (a good thing), a few taps on the back of a receiver with a dead blow hammer can encourage a proper fit. Another method to make tight parts fit is to heat them gently in an oven or chill them in a freezer.

These methods terrify me, frankly. If the fit is loose (a bad thing), consider a newer receiver or tighten the barrel to receiver fit with some Loctite 609 compound. Many 10/22 gunsmiths do this as a practice to ensure things remain right. Ruger recommends 20 in-lbs, but Tony Kidd takes his to only 10 in-lbs. "All you want that v-block to do is keep the barrel from coming out," he says. Excess torque on the v-block screws induces stress in the metal and can affect the chamber.

Next, install the charging handle and spring in the receiver, followed by the bolt. I like to put a touch of Super Lube or TW25B grease along the bolt rails and at the receiver's top. Secure the trigger group with two oversized pins.

I'm partial to Raven Eye Custom titanium takedown screws. I typically start with 20 in-lbs, but this is highly dependent on the stock and bedding. Kidd torques all his Magpul-stocked rifles to 30 in-lbs. I have a hard laminate stock with aluminum pillars and a good glass bed with 40 in-lbs that does well. Many shooters on rimfirecentral.com — an excellent resource for

Another view of the 10/22 receiver-to-barrel connection.

everything 10/22 — swear by a hair's breadth of 10 to 15 in-lbs. Every action/stock/chassis combination is different. It's shocking how action toque can affect group size in a 10/22. For a quick trial, shoot groups with your rifle stock torqued to 15 in-lbs, then jack it up to 40 in-lbs if your stock can handle it, then shoot again.

Once you assemble the gun, make sure the barrel is free-floated. Many old-timers will say a 10/22 needs a "pressure pad" toward the stock's tip, but as Chacon, Kidd, Carbine, and other experts have told me, this is malarkey. Some talk about "barrel droop," claiming the receiver's connection isn't strong enough to prevent the barrel from sagging due to hard use and gravity. For a spell, this leads to some 10/22 receivers with threading for a threaded barrel tenon. Chacon has tested these various combinations of the barrel-to-action connection and has found no one more accurate than any other. Experts conclude that barrel droop, though it sounds plausible, is also malarkey

talked up by OCD non-experts. If the barrel doesn't float in a wood or laminate stock, wrap sandpaper around a 7/8-inch dowel and work the channel until four thicknesses of printer paper easily slip between barrel and stock. A dollar bill width isn't enough.

Safety check the trigger, then shoot your best ammo on hand. If the groups aren't in the .300-inch range with match ammo, play with action torque. If the action feels less than perfectly slick, work over the receiver internals and bolt some more with a Scotch-Brite and give it a quick blast of Hornady One-Shot dry lube. With the right parts, good ammo, and some common sense, it's possible to get barn-burner accuracy out of the humble 10/22.

10/22 Function Issues

The vast majority of 10/22 function problems can be traced back to two things: a filthy barrel or a bad magazine. To correct, first do a deep cleaning with particular emphasis on the chamber, as outlined in

10/22 Gunsmiths

A Joe Charon custom 10/22. Custom builder Tony Mele makes the stock. Photos: Cosmo Genova

Building custom 10/22s is fun, will teach you the basics of how autoloaders work and can be a less expensive path to a very accurate rifle. Or it can be a money pit, a waste of time and resources in an endless quest for smaller and smaller groups that just won't materialize. At that point — or hopefully, well before it — you may need professional help. When that happens, these are the men to call.

The Tune-Up

You can get the best deal in the entire 10/22 universe at a quiet machine shop in suburban New England. Connecticut Precision Chambering or CPC (ct-precision.com) offers a 10/22 accurizing package that includes a barrel, bolt, receiver, and trigger work. The appropriately named proprietor, Randy Carbine, left a career at barrel maker Wilson Arms in the early 1990s as the 10/22 craze hit peak fad but quickly made a lasting name for himself as one of the best smallbore Ruger 'smiths in the country. The full tune-up runs around $200 and includes a ¼-inch barrel setback, re-chamber, and chamber polish. Carbine hand-laps the barrel and re-crowns it concentric to the bore. He cuts the barrel tenon oversized for a perfect receiver fit, then deburrs and squares the receiver, recutting the barrel hole straight. Randy squares the bolt and headspaces, then cuts radiuses along the back side's edges for better cycling with subsonic loads. He polishes contact points on the bolts and pins the firing pin to prevent any vertical movement. He wraps up with a trigger job that takes a stock Ruger trigger group and makes it a crisp, clean 2.5-pound break — all for less than you'd pay for a decent aftermarket trigger. CPC did a similar tune-up on a 77/22 magnum for me, and the previously piss-poor rifle now shoots quarter-sized groups at 50 yards. Someone should canonize the man.

A Complete Rifle

The most accurate stock Ruger 10/22 was the now-discontinued LVT, though you can still find them online if you look hard enough. In the $500 to $1,000 bracket, the Bergara BXR with a world-class Bergara barrel and stock is an incredible value at $600. The T/CR22 from Thompson/Center is a fantastic shooter. In the $1,000 to $2,000 range, you get to the rarified air of Kidd Innovations and Volquartsen. Every tolerance on these rifles is to the ten-thousandth, and you feel it. If you want something different, consider Volquartsen's straight-pull bolt-action 10/22 — the Summit. Suppressed with subsonic ammo, it's something special.

The Full Custom

Joe Chacon builds the most accurate 10/22s in the world. Except for the magazine, nothing about his guns are normal. Chacon swaps even the magazine release springs. The benchrest shooter and gunsmith from the Texas Hill Country usually starts with a stainless steel Elite 22 receiver from Tactical Innovations, matched to a JWH Custom bolt, and fitted with a two-stage Kidd trigger. But assembling that list of parts alone does not make a Chacon rifle. Instead of using drop-in barrels, he turns, chambers, laps, and fits four-groove ratchet blanks from Shilen. Then he goes to work on the small parts, tuning and polishing for perfect ignition before test firing in the ammo tunnels at Lapua in Mesa, Arizona, and Eley in Winters, Texas. He beds most of his rifles in custom Tony Mele benchrest stocks, but he's working on a new design for tactical precision rimfire shooting and NRL22 now. When you buy one of his guns, which start around $2,000, you get lot numbers for the best ammunition and lifetime customer service. He'll also work on any dysfunctional 10/22 DIY projects that may have gone wrong. He's a world-class talker, too. Block out two hours, give him a call, and prepare to learn more about the 10/22 than you ever thought possible. The man is full of tips, tricks, and accuracy-inducing advice.

the chapter on cleaning. Clean the bolt and action, too. When you touch a round off in a semi-auto, there's an explosion underway in the chamber, and for a millisecond, the bolt is back, opening the receiver to fouling. Autoloaders need a more thorough cleaning than bolt actions. While the rifle is apart, scuff up the inside of the action with a green Scotch-Brite or fine steel wool until the bolt runs in the receiver slick as snot.

If that doesn't fix things, try a new magazine. The Ruger 10/22 rotary magazine is the best of its kind, but some are dysfunctional when they come off the production line. I buy 3-packs of BX 10-rounders often, and every ninth one seems to have issues. If running into problems, try a new magazine or disassemble and thoroughly clean your old ones. New magazines correct more 10/22 feed problems than anything else.

Action-to-stock fit can throw things off, too, as it can affect the magazine feed geometry. If a new magazine doesn't correct the issue when shooting standard-velocity ammo, play with action torque, starting at 15 in-lbs and work up to 40 in-lbs. If the fit feels loose even at higher torques, you can shore it up with some aluminum foil tape, the kind used for HVAC repairs. This mod is rarely necessary with modern stocks and chassis but can be a lifesaver for an older sloppy rifle.

DIY firing pin shaping. Note the filed striker, right, compared to the factory model at left. Photo: Cosmo Genova

High-velocity ammunition can throw off bolt timing as well, creating issues. The solution is a Kidd heavy bolt spring. If the problem is poor extraction, the bolt kit from Volquartsen can help.

The CZs

CZ rifles have long been considered the best value in bolt-action rimfires. They were also among the first big manufacturers to take PRS-style precision rimfire shooting seriously. The 60-degree bolt throw of the 457 action is faster than the 90-degree throws of the better machined Bergara, RimX, and Vudoo rifles. With the right barrel and gunsmith, a CZ can be made as accurate, too — benchrest accurate. But that's a process that requires real work, not a simple assembly of premium parts like building out a 10/22. A superb, well-fitted barrel is what makes accuracy. The rub with CZ is the "well-fitted" part.

CZ Barrel, Headspace, Chamber, and Fit

CZ 455/457 actions have a drop-in barrel system. The barrel tenon has two v-cuts that contact grub screws on the underside of the receiver. Generally, the fit is not nearly as tight as premium 10/22 parts. It is very much a slip fit. Of the two 457 actions I've worked on the most, one is noticeably looser than the other, so there's tolerance variation from action to action. The best barrels in the world will not shoot worth a lick if this connection to the receiver is poor, or the headspace isn't correct, or it has a sloppy chamber. Those issues corrected — barrel, headspace, chamber, and fit — and you can have a barn-burner of a CZ .22 LR, but to do it right requires a lathe and some expertise. A kitchen table barrel install with a FAT wrench just can't accomplish what you need to make a CZ sing.

Don Smith (djdilliodon on snipershide.com and rimfirecentral.com) makes CZs more accurate than

A lineup of CZ barrels, from left, PROOF, two stock CZ barrels, and a Lilja. Photo: Cosmo Genova

anyone. Much of my understanding of how to tune them comes from his writings. He worked directly with Carson Lilja on Lilja's shim system for properly headspacing CZs. Indeed, the fastest way to tick off three of the four things needed to make CZs excellent (premium barrel, headspace, and chamber) is to write a check to Lilja.

Caveat: Not every Lilja (or Bartlein, or Muller, or Shilen, or Benchmark) is an excellent barrel that will throw .200-inch groups, but the odds of getting a great barrel from a premium builder is significantly better than anything mass-produced in a gun factory. Bill Calfee, the great rimfire benchrest 'smith, and other excellent benchrest builders, all buy premium barrel blanks and slug them, checking for imperfections and choke, then cut those barrels at the best possible spot, harmonically speaking. According to them, one in ten premium blanks has the stuff to make a world-class barrel. So, buying a Lilja, as an

example, does not guarantee greatness but gives you better odds of excellence, assuming all other factors (and there are many) are top shelf and professionally done. On the other end of the spectrum, you may hit the lottery and get a world-class shooter right from CZ, but it's unlikely. I know great CZ barrels happen (or I think I know because everything on the Internet is true, right?), but I have not found one or seen one firsthand.

So, step one of accurizing a CZ is getting a premium barrel. Next is making sure you headspace the barreled action correctly. Don Smith and Lilja came up with an innovative system to tune headspace by using shims.

The barrel tenon on a Lilja for a 455 or 457 is 1.200 inches long. On a factory CZ barrel — including the PROOF I have on hand — the tenon is 1.190 inches long. The more extended tenon on the Lilja barrel means if you install it on an action *without shims*, it

Lilja barrel shims make for more exact headspacing on the CZ platforms.

will not fire, or more specifically, there is not enough headspace to close the bolt. Lilja provides shims that go over the tenon and snug on the action face from .001 to .005 inch in .001-inch increments. By adding shims, you get enough distance to seat a cartridge and fire properly.

With this system, you can tune your rifle's head-space to the ammo's rim thickness you want to shoot, for example, 0.043 inch for Lapua or 0.039 inch for ELEY. This process might sound complicated, but in practice, it's straightforward. As Lilja explains:

1. First you will need to measure your headspace. The most accurate way to do this is by using a depth gauge, and measuring from the receiver face, to the bolt face recess while the action is cocked. Let's say you get a mea-surement of 1.235 inches and you want your headspace at .043 inch. That means you need a shank length of 1.192 inches. (1.235 – .043 = 1.192)

2. Every barrel will have a shank length of 1.200 inches. So now we know to shim the barrel .008" to ob-tain proper headspace. (1.200 – 1.192 = .008)

3. Now that we know how much we need to shim the barrel, we can use a .005-inch shim and a .003-inch shim stacked together to obtain headspace. You can use any combination you'd like, but try to use the least amount possible.

4. Slide the .005- and .003-inch shim onto the barrel shank, making sure they are fit up tight against the bar-rel's shoulder.

5. Slide the new barrel, with shims up firmly against the shoulder into the new action, being careful to align the ridge of the cuts for the set screws at the 6:00 posi-tion. Tighten the two set screws equally, pulling the barrel into the receiver. Recommended torque is 35-40 in-lbs.

To test your work, chamber a live round and close the bolt. (Do this with the barrel pointed in a safe direction in case you inadvertently crush a rim and set off the round.) If the bolt doesn't close, go up another .001 inch. If it closes too easily, go down .001 inch. You know you've found the sweet spot when

there's a touch of resistance in the bolt handle. That resistance is the bolt face compressing the rim of the round against the breech face in the chamber. Most agree that headspace set at the exact rim thickness, or .001 inch less than, makes a more accurate rifle. Once headspace starts to exceed rim thickness, group sizes grow exponentially. Like most useful solutions, this one is simple and works. I don't know why other CZ barrel builders haven't moved to it.

With a lathe, you can add a shim system to any factory or drop-in CZ barrel by turning the shoulder down until the tenon runs 1.200 inches (for shims) or to cut the barrel to the exact depth of your re-ceiver plus the required headspace. For example, if the receiver depth to bolt runs 1.235 inches and a new drop-in barrel tenon is 1.190 inches, it makes for a headspace of 0.045 inch. (1.235 – 1.190 = .045). By removing .002 inch off the barrel shoulder, the tenon would lengthen by .002 inch and give a headspace of 0.43 inch (1.235 – 1.190 = .043). In most cases, exact headspacing at the shoulder like this is preferable to shims.

Lilja will sell you shims, or you can order Ring Shims online from McMaster-Carr. McMaster needs an internal dimension of ¾-inch to fit over the tenon and an outer diameter of the barrel's width where it con-nects to the receiver.

While planning out this work, it's essential to consider the barrel chamber. Many premium CZ drop-in barrel builders chamber their tubes with Bentz chambers. As we've seen, these are ideal for autoload-ers, but dimensionally they're too wide and long for peak precision in a bolt action. By comparison, Vudoo bases its Ace barrel chambers on a variation of the Winchester 52 D Match chamber, which is almost a tenth of an inch shorter than a Bentz. That is why, even when headspaced correctly, many premium CZ drop-ins do not engrave bullets. The chambers are too long to seat the bullet into the lands. Lilja cuts its proprietary Lilja 2 chamber in its CZ .22 LR barrels. That chamber is tight and engraves bullets, which is why I say putting Lilja barrels on CZs clears up three of the four critical factors in making them shoot. They're premium barrels that Lilja correctly headspaces, with a sufficiently tight chamber.

It's possible to shorten a Bentz chamber with a lathe or mill, as mentioned in the section on 10/22s. Chamber length to the leade or angle on a Bentz is 0.679 inch compared to 0.600 inch of the Calfee chambers and 0.580 inch of the proven Winchester 52 D Match chamber. Keep in mind the leade angle is different in these chambers, too. The Bentz runs 1-degree, 35-minutes, while the 52 D is 2 degrees. Whatever amount you take off the breechface, you should remove the same from the barrel shoulder to preserve headspace.

It's also possible to shave more off the breechface and "set the barrel back" then rechamber with a proper precision reamer. That is about as far as you can push a drop-in barrel with a lathe. The question

becomes, is it worth the time and money? If you have a lathe or a friend with one and are into this stuff as I am, it's interesting to tweak, shoot, and learn. But if you're paying a gunsmith an hourly rate for this work, a full custom barrel is a better investment. It will fit the receiver better and likely shoot better. Don Smith did this while still in business and long guaranteed his CZs to lay down 0.200-inch groups at 50 yards with the right ammo.

A full custom barrel corrects the CZ barrel swap system's big rub: the barrel-to-receiver fit. A good 'smith can true the action face, and the receiver's inside diameter and cut a barrel tenon to match it. Makers work these barrels down from premium blanks, so drop-in is not part of the equation.

For DIY'ers using premium drop-in barrels, the only real solution to fitment is Loctite 609 or gluing the barrel into the receiver. I can't say whether this helps or not.

CZ 457 barreled action.

CZ Bolt Work

Once you address the barrel and barrel-to-receiver connection, the next point of focus for CZ customization is the bolt.

You can alter headspace by putting shims on the bolt forward of the bolt handle to increase its overall length. This tactic seems a temporary or experimental solution, to my mind, as thin metal shims will inevitably wear with each bolt rotation when you cycle the action. Changing the bolt length can also affect the trigger and safety mechanism. Some aftermarket trigger makers state specifically not to shim bolts with their products.

Polishing bolt internals is well worth doing. CZ gets kicked online for rough machining with tool marks left behind on the bolt face, bolt housing, etc. While photos don't lie, I've yet to encounter that in person. All the bolts in my collection came from the factory clean. But that is not to say they're without burrs and rough patches barely detectable to the naked eye. To correct these, first disassemble the bolt:

- Remove the bolt from the rifle.
- Decock it by pushing down on the bolt handle.
- Remove the c-clamp with a dental pick or small flathead screwdriver.
- Remove extractor and retainer — they will fall free on a clean bolt.

- Hold the bolt face down on something soft, like a towel or mousepad at a desk or workbench, then press down to compress the striker spring.
- Push out the retaining pin with a 1/8-inch brass punch.
- The bolt body will come apart in two pieces, plus the handle, and you can quickly get at the springs and striker.

To polish the striker, take 400 grit wet sandpaper and work over the bottom and sides. Get in the channel in the bolt where the striker rides. Remove any burr or sharp edge on the striker or in the channel. Next, take a Dremel with a soft polishing tip and apply a bit of jeweler's compound like Red Rouge. Polish the striker and channel. Smooth out any tooling marks on the bolt body or bolt face. Polish the side and bottom rails where the bolt runs in the raceway. Clean, then oil everything, making sure it's completely wiped and dry. A little dry lube like Hornady One-Shot on the pin's sides and in the channel finishes the process. There should be no wet oil anywhere as it will only collect fouling and gum things up.

Another possible modification is reshaping the firing pin to a chiseled point for more concentrated impacts. Filing the rectangle down to a square or small circle makes for deep, more focused hits. Be

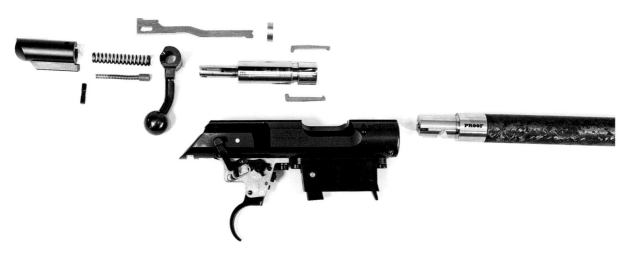

A broken down CZ 457 bolt.

careful. You can take this too far. I've filed firing pins on several rifles, and while others have reported more consistent SDs with reshaped strikers, I have not personally seen that. I have noticed fewer marks on the breech above the chamber when you file the top of the sticker pin back a few thousandths so that it is just under even with the bolt face. When tightening headspace, the striker can make hard contact with the breech when firing or dry firing.

With the bolt apart, you can upgrade to an Extra Power Firing Pin Spring as sold by DIP Inc. and others. This stiffer spring gives the striker a little more speed for harder impacts at the case head. DIP also sells an Aluminum Magazine Well for the 455/457 to replace the thin plastic well that comes stock with these rifles. These improve magazine fit — and there's something to be said for replacing the only cheap plastic component in an otherwise all-metal action. DIP, Area 419, and many others also sell screw-on bolt knobs to replace the factory round ball. Some of these are just cosmetic, but others, like the Area 419 hourglass design, make for easy bolt handling. With the hourglass, you can effectively run the bolt with just your index finger and thumb.

Rough cycling was an issue with older CZs but has mostly gone away with the smooth-operator 457. If the bolt cycles rough, put it in your lap one evening while watching a movie and cycle it a few hundred times. I've read of people putting J-B compound or even toothpaste into the action for their abrasive properties. I don't recommend that. If your action is so rough that it needs toothpaste after a few hundred cycles, I'd send it back and let the manufacturer deal with it.

CZ Triggers

As with CZ barrels, you could hit the lottery with a 457 trigger. My first one, a 457 Varmint MTR, had an excellent bang switch. Adjusting sear engagement, travel, and weight worked down to a wonderfully crisp 10-oz. pull. It was an exceptional single-stage with no creep or overtravel. The next two 457s in my collection, a Premium and Varmint Precision Chassis, didn't get close to that. The lightest I could get them was 2.2 and 2.0 lbs., respectively. The only difference in these triggers was the blade's color — some ship black, others silver. Mechanically, they all work the same. For a long while, I thought the MTR trigger might get some special attention in the factory, but that is not the case. It's the luck of the draw — or the parts pulled from bins while assembled on the factory floor.

You can get 455/457 direct replacement triggers from Timney, Rifle Basix, and part-time machinist and CZ trigger guru Bill Scaramuzzo, who works under the name Triggers by BScar. The single-stage Timney runs to 2 lbs. and the single-stage Rifle Basix adjusts down to 10 oz. The two-stage BScar can hit 3 oz./3 oz. and is the choice of benchrest shooters trying to make CZs win. A trigger is more than pull weight, and all three options are a significant improvement over a run-of-the-mill stock one. They just feel better. But do not be afraid to work on a CZ trigger. They tune up well.

YoDave makes a spring kit for 455s and 457s that will take a trigger with a 2 lb. low-end and shave it down to 1 lb. or less. McMaster Carr also sells springs that will work and for less cost (#9657K612). DIP sells an adjustable sear for the 455. CZ triggers also respond well to honing, but proceed with caution as it's easy to push the sear too far.

Before doing any work, the best way to see a stock trigger's limits is to bring it down correctly. To do this, cock the bolt and turn out the sear engagement screw on the trigger's underside in front of the blade. Keep turning until the firing pin drops, then bring it back ¼ to ½ a turn. Next, remove the locking nut over the trigger pull weight screw and back it out. If this process brings the trigger under 1 lb. you know you've scored a winner. More likely, it'll be in the 1.8- to 2.2-lb. range.

Make sure you can get spare parts before polishing the sear should things go wrong. CZ-USA parts seem to swing in and out of stock. Sometimes they remain

A Lilja .17 HM2 barrel for a CZ 455/457 action.

out of stock for many weeks or months. Always make sure a light trigger does not go off with the safety on and passes the "bump test." Cock the rifle, then bump the rifle butt on a hard surface like a workbench or floor with the safety off. If the trigger goes "click," the trigger is not safe.

Finally, you break triggers in as you use them. It's not a bad idea to leave it alone over the first couple thousand rounds while the barrel breaks in, then adjust it as the last step in your precision rifle tuning process.

Chassis and Stocks

CZ wood stocks are outstanding. The walnut Premium and MTR stocks come with composite pillars installed. The Varmint Precision Trainer comes in an excellent Manners composite stock. The CZ-made chassis for the Precision Varmint Chassis is excellent. However, it's dimensionally smaller compared to similar centerfire and Remington 700 footprint chassis.

PDC Customs, Masterpiece Arms, MDT, MDT Oryx, XLR, Kinetic Research Group, and Accurate Rifle Systems make other popular chassis for CZ precision rifles. Chassis with built-in Swiss ARCA rails along the forend for adjustable mounting options have become increasingly popular, such as the PDC Customs. However, you can easily add a full-length ARCA rail to any chassis or stock with a straight, flat forend.

The advantage of a chassis over wood or synthetic stock is weight — they're heavier and can be made very heavy with a weight kit. Heavy rimfire rifles better match the centerfire guns they're often built to mimic. Weight can also help a rifle sit steadily on an awkward barricade and keep a recoil-sensitive shooter in the scope between shots. Chassis are often more ergonomic with multiple point-of-contact adjustments between shooter, rifle, and bag or barricade. They also have near-endless accessory and attachment point options. They make terrible hunting rifles, though, save for bench-bound varmint shoot-

The CZ 457 chassis.

ing. Chassis don't make a rifle any more accurate than a quality pillar-and-epoxy bedded stock. They look cool or resemble an abomination, depending on your perspective. Chassis are purpose-driven tools. There's a reason they've taken over the precision shooting rimfire world.

At the 2020 NRL22 National Match, 17 of the 71 shooters that completed the gear survey shot a CZ. Of those, seven used a Manners stock, four factory wood or Boyd's synthetic stock. Two used Masterpiece Arms, two an MDT, and one the Precision Varmint Chassis with an XLR buttstock.

For barrels, nine reported using a factory CZ, four

a Lilja, two Bartlein, one a PROOF, and one a factory Anschütz barrel recut and re-chambered.

For triggers, one ran a Timney, the rest went with the stock trigger, with four indicating they installed YoDave springs.

Remington 700 Footprint Rifles

Vudoo, RimX, and Bergara .22 LRs are vastly different animals from the Rugers and CZs discussed above. The first two are custom rifles. Vudoo makes its rifles in St. George, Utah to order. Zermatt only makes RimX actions. Some homebuilders are putting RimXs

A CZ 455 in an MDT chassis. Photo: CZ-USA

together with timed pre-fit barrels, while a small collection of high-quality gunsmiths currently assembles most RimX rifles.

These premium rimfire platforms aren't like the Remington actions that came before them. Traditionally, Remington actions have been "blueprinted" for concentricity and tolerances within 0.001 inch. That process involved putting the action in a fixture on a lathe and truing the receiver face. Machinists cut the receiver threads into perfect alignment with the trued receiver's axis, threading the barrel squarely into the receiver — so the receiver, bore, and bolt aligned. Gunsmiths machined the recoil lug true to the receiver face and lightly faced back the receiver ring to match it, making for a perfect mating of the recoil lug and the bearing surface at the barrel shoulder.

With mass-produced Remington actions that were lathe-cut and heat-treated (read: warped) as a last step in the manufacturing process, this was essential for creating a precise union of receiver, bolt, and barrel. With modern CNC machine-cut actions like the Vudoo, RimX, and Bergara, blueprinting is unnecessary.

The tolerances off the line now are in the 0.001-inch neighborhood. This level of machined-in precision is why half a dozen premium barrel companies can make timed pre-fits that attach to a RimX without lathe work — and they shoot lights out, without a Savage-style barrel nut. Traditional accurizing does not apply to modern .22 LR actions of the Remington 700 footprint. If they do need tweaking by a skilled gunsmith, they cut very little metal.

With a Ruger, CZ, Tikka, and other popular precision rimfire rifles, the first giant leap in accurizing is swapping for a better barrel. Vudoo discourages this and currently sells its benchrest action with Ace or Shilen barrels and the repeaters with just Ace. In a sign of the new dominance of precision rimfire shooting, every single quality barrel builder working today now makes .22 LR pre-fits for RimX rifles.

Vudoo, RimX, and Bergara all have innovative ways to headspace their bolts. By comparison, to make a CZ sing — barrel, chamber, headspace, and fit — happens at the point-of-sell with these new school Remmy footprint rifles.

Vudoo single-shot action.

The author's RimX barrel action with a 16-inch PROOF, Timney HIT, and Vortex Strike Eagle.

For the time being, performance tuning and tinkering with Vudoos, Bergaras, and RimXs are not much of a thing. I'm sure some kindred spirits are toiling away on basement lathes working to make them even better, but thus far, no real workflow has come to light. Tweaking them is simply a matter of swapping parts — changing triggers, chassis, and other accessories. In that way, they're almost like a less-intensive 10/22.

The Aftermarket

There's no lack of parts suppliers for these rifles. The table below is not a complete list, but it's close and does show the most relevant precision aftermarket suppliers in the space.

When you get in the weeds on accessories, so much of what separates one manufacturer from another is subjective. Honestly, I cannot feel the difference between a tuned Bix'n Andy, Jewell, or Tubbs trigger. They all feel like the best trigger I've ever shot.

The best rifle component analysis, in my opinion, is the gear surveys published by competitive shooting orgs or national matches. Cal Zent of the Precision Rifle Blog has long published a survey, *What the Pros Use*, covering the centerfire PRS circuit. The National Rifle League posts a gear survey online, revealing the shooters' gear in its annual NRL22 National Match. The American Rimfire Association (ARA) lists equipment in its match results. If you want to know what gear is winning trophies, it's all online for the taking.

For rimfire, the ARA results are fascinating. For example, of the 78 competitors at its national match at Chickenfoot, 40 used Shilen barrels. The next closest was Muller, with 20 shooters running them. On triggers, 32 ran Bix'n Andy while 19 used Jewel. When it comes to stocks and chassis, precisionrifleblog.com has a survey that lists winning gear in the centerfire PRS world: 27 percent ran a Masterpiece Arms Competition Chassis, and 17 percent shot a Manners Com-

objectively. Likewise, when asked about affordable optics for NRL22, I recommend the Athlon Argos BTR Gen2. It is not because I love that scope — I don't — but because the vast majority of successful base class NRL22 competitors use it.

Stock Work

A rifle stock needs to be rigid to promote accuracy and stable to yield consistency. It must be impervious to weather. The natural swelling and shrinking of wood due to humidity and temperature are mostly why competitors no longer use natural wood stocks on top-tier precision rifles. Like those made by Boyd's, laminate wood stocks are different, as epoxy soaks through the wood, making it impervious to mother nature. A laminate stock is more glue than wood. "Synthetic" is mainly a catch-all term. The most premium stocks, such as Manners and McMillan, are made of fiberglass composite.

posite Stock. According to NRL22 results, 31 percent of shooters had Vudoos.

This data all tells me that the ceiling, or the *crème de la crème* precision rimfire rifle at this moment, looks something like a Vudoo, with a Shilen, and Bix'n Andy, in an MPA chassis or Manners stock. (If you want to buy *that* rifle, get your checkbook ready.) That's not to say *that it is the best rifle.* Not at all. It is a thought experiment, something shooters can and should debate. It's also a clear-eyed way to look at components

Barrels	Triggers	Chassis & Stocks
Bartlein	AMP	Accurate Rifle Systems
Benchmark	Bix'n Andy	Ashbury Precision Ordnance
Douglas	CMC	Bell & Carlson
Green Mountain	Geissele Automatics	Boyd's
Hart	Elftmann Tactical	Cadex Defense
HLR	Flavio	Foundation
International Barrels	Huber	Grayboe
Krieger	Jewell	GRS
Lilja	Rifle Basix	H-S Precision
Match Grade Machine	Timney	J. Allen Enterprise
Muller Works	Trigger Tech	JP Rifles
Pac Nor	Tubbs	Kinetic Research Group
PROOF		Magpul
Rock Creek		Manners Composites
Shilen		Masterpiece Arms
Walther Lothar		McMillan
Whistle Pig		MDT
		Sabre Tactical
		Woox
		XLR

You could throw this RimX bolt across the room, and the round wouldn't pop out.

Overall, rifle consistency and accuracy correlate to stock durability, rigidity, and stability. Stock quality consists of three things: material, design, and bedding.

Stock Materials

Hardwood – The most traditional material. Many gun buffs believe nothing looks nicer than finely grained and whorled walnut. That may be so, but it can swell and shrink as the weather changes and easily dents and scuffs with hard use. Still, wood makes for great small game stocks. Most of the rimfires in my safe with the most sentimental value to me have hardwood stocks.

Laminated – Laminate stock makers use thin strips of wood epoxied together into a block, then cut to shape, usually on a milling machine called a stock duplicator. The wood is often died in different colors before stacking, which leads to wild color possibilities. Laminates are probably the most stable of the less expensive stocks and come in a vast assortment of designs. See Boyd's website. Inletting can be hit or miss as these stocks are rarely hand-inletted, so to buy one may mean some Dremel work to make it perfectly match your barreled action.

Synthetics – This is mostly a catch-all term for injection-molded polyester-based stocks that are inexpensive to manufacture. Quality varies widely, from the outstanding Magpul rimfire stocks to factory-made ones from the big gun companies that bend and twist at the forend like a wet noodle. Some are "overmolded" with a soft plastic material for comfort, such as the Hogue or factory Remington SPS stocks.

A PROOF-barreled 457 work in progress.

Inletting is generally loose, and they benefit significantly from bedding, but the inner action surface needs to be aggressively marked and nicked to ensure epoxy adhesion.

Fiberglass Composites — Arguably the best stock material for a precision rifle (not considering chassis) because they're remarkably ridged and, by manufacturing process, come with tight, well-fit inletting. Unlike synthetics, fiberglass composite material adheres well to bedding epoxy. Most of the good ones have an aluminum bedding rail baked in, too.

Carbon Fiber — The lightest stocks out there use carbon-fiber shells, and they're ideal for centerfire mountain rifles or ultra-light small game setups. Want to build a 4-lb. squirrel gun? Carbon fiber is your jam.

Precision Stock Design

The best stock design is the one that fits you best. That said, several design factors are generally agreed upon to aid accurate shooting through stability, rigidity, and consistency, mainly when shooting in a PRS-style match format. These include an open barrel channel for a free-floated barrel, a beefy forend that resists flex, and a vertical grip — or more upright than a classic sporter stock — for increased trigger control. Most precision stocks also have an adjustable cheek riser to bring the eye in line with the riflescope and an adjustable length-of-pull to size the rifle to the shooter correctly. The forend's bottom line often runs parallel to the barrel, too, unlike a traditional American sporter rifle forend that tapers toward the barrel.

The modern classic of this precision rifle design is the McMillan A3 and A4, which the United States Marine Corps adopted and have gone on to be one of the most-issued tactical stocks to police and military units worldwide. They combine benchrest lines with adjustability and an all-around ruggedness thanks to the rigid fiberglass composite.

Bedding

"Rifle bedding is fundamental to rifle accuracy," writes New Zealand firearms researcher Nathan Foster. "The term bedding refers to the fit and stability of a barreled action within the rifle stock. If the metalwork's fit and stability with the stock are poor, the rifle will be inaccurate. Bedding a rifle with epoxy resin is the optimum method of obtaining a correct fit, long-term stock stability, and optimum rifle accuracy."

It would be best if you bedded all stocks, even those with CNC-machined aluminum bedding blocks. Some experts disagree with this, but you do not need to look at many bedding blocks and actions to see how most do not fit together perfectly without the benefit of glass bedding. Joseph Von Benedikt, Richard Mann, and a handful of other notable gun writers have published reports on stocks with bedding blocks, showing group size before and after epoxy bedding. In every case, glass bedding improved accuracy. Foster, who sells epoxy, has oodles of research worth looking at on his website ballisticstudies.com. In some instances, all-aluminum chassis can be improved with bedding, too.

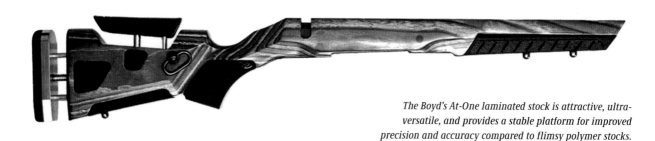

The Boyd's At-One laminated stock is attractive, ultra-versatile, and provides a stable platform for improved precision and accuracy compared to flimsy polymer stocks. This model is the Shady Camo scheme. Photo: Boyd's

You can vastly improve an inexpensive plastic stock like those that come standard with Tikka and Savage by glass bedding. If the stock does not have metal or hard composite pillars through which the action screws run, you should install them in the glass bedding process. This process is called pillar bedding.

To understand why bedding is so helpful, imagine a rifle like a sandwich. The top piece of toast is the barreled action. The bottom piece of toast is the bottom metal of the triggerguard and mag well. Between them is the warm swiss cheese and tomato. When you squeeze the action and bottom metal, it compresses the stock like a sandwich. Stock materials can help. Aluminum and composite are less gushy, but pillars are best.

Pillars take all the pressure of the torqued action screws, so it's metal on metal. Epoxy ensures 100 percent contact between pillar and stock inletting to the action and bottom metal. It's like smearing butter over toast. It fills in all the tiny dings and divots and imperfections in the action and stock you cannot see with a naked eye. When broken down and re-torqued, it compresses the same way every time.

Pillar bedding and glass bedding generally works like this:

• You drill out the action screw holes in the stock and fit them for pillars.

• Shape the top of the pillars to match the bottom of the rifle action perfectly.

• Coat the pillars with epoxy, then square and secure them in the stock.

• Make small cuts or remove pockets from the stock material under the action to provide a mechanical lock for the epoxy.

• Heavily tape the stock to control epoxy flow.

• Coat the action in a release agent.

• Fill the inletted stock with epoxy at points where it contacts the action.

• Sink the action in the epoxy and torque it down.

This process creates a "bed" of "glass" or epoxy perfectly fit to the action and the stock's specific contours. Devcon and Marine-Tex are standard epoxies for the job. Brownell's and Wheeler's sell glass bedding kits that provide all the materials and come with more specific instructions. Brownell's ArcaGlass kit is particularly good.

Perhaps the best directions come from Richard Franklin of Richard's Custom Rifles as found on accurateshooter.com under the title, *Stress-Free Pillar*

The Ruger American Rimfire is available in a laminated stock, which provides a more stable platform than the line's typical black plastic stock. Photo: Ruger

Bedding. Franklin builds and beds stocks for centerfire benchrest shooters, and it's clear the man knows his work. Before bedding your first stock, read and reread Franklin's essay.

Some other points to consider before bedding a rifle:

Pillar kits for Remington 700 footprints, CZs, Rugers, and every other action out there are available online and tailor the pillars to the action easier. You can find all diameter and length pillars you'd ever need through McMaster Carr. For straight-end pillars, it's an excellent and inexpensive resource.

Generally, only bed the action at the first inch or chamber section of the barrel, but refer to established best practices, which you can find online for most actions.

Be generous with the release agent. If it fails — or more likely it was not applied correctly — and the action cannot be removed from the bedding, put the whole rifle in a chest freezer. The metal will contract and pull free. Or so I've read.

Stock Stabilization

You can also use epoxy to make stocks more ridged. My Lithgow LA101, for example, was extremely ac-curate out of the box, regularly laying down sub-MOA groups with Wolf and CCI ammo. I shot it nearly exclusively seated off a stable bench. When I put it on a bipod and went prone, accuracy suffered. It was easy to see why. The plastic, synthetic stock flexed at the forend, and by weighting the bipod while shooting prone, I had put the otherwise floated barrel in contact with the stock. Groups fell apart. Factory Savage composite stocks nearly always flex like this, too. Tikka and Ruger American Rimfire stocks are stiffer and still flex, but much less.

Stiffening a Tupperware stock with epoxy is straightforward. Simply put the stock in a vise, level it, and make small relief cuts in the plastic. The cuts allow the epoxy to create mechanical locks and take purchase. It's crucial to keep epoxy out of the recoil lug recess, and you can use modeling clay to build a dam. Likewise, sling stud and QD mount holes that need to be left open can be plugged with clay or otherwise epoxied in place. I used my Lithgow stock's stiffing as an excuse to install female QD swivel mounts and a 6 o'clock Pic rail for a bipod.

For incredibly flimsy stocks that can crack when epoxied (we're looking at you, Savage), aluminum or steel bar stock, round files, even cut arrow shafts

The Ruger American Rimfire comes with a lightweight polymer stock that is not a total loss if you epoxy bed it. Photo: Ruger

can be set in place to add more stiffness. For match rifles where more weight is advantageous, pour lead shot – the smaller the better, like No. 12s directly into the forend channel before you epoxy it over. Whatever way you go, it's a simple, inexpensive fix that does not require buying a new stock. Just keep expectations in check. A synthetic factory stock will never be a McMillan, no matter how much effort and epoxy you put into it.

In all cases, when bedding a rifle, the barrel should be fully free-floated. The standard test of running a dollar bill between the action and stock is not enough to prevent harmonic contact. Four thicknesses of printer paper will give you the right amount. Fold a sheet in quarters, and if that runs the length of the barrel without touching, you're good to go. You should do this before you lay any epoxy. There are special tools for hogging out wood stocks, but a wooden dowel with some sandpaper wrapped around it works well. Factory synthetic stocks can be sanded like this, too. If the stock is wood, make sure to weather seal it before laying down an epoxy bed.

Proper barrel floating and bedding can do magical things. My dad bought a Ruger American Rimfire on sale one year for less than $200. It shot okay, but after an easy trigger job, hogging out the barrel channel, and bedding it, the groups shrunk to half. He's never and will never shoot rifles competitively or even go squirrel hunting, but the rifle still did its job. It knocked the socks off the other old guys at his gun club. RR

9

RIMFIRE SHOOTING & SPORT

In his classic 1971 book, *The .22 Rifle*, Dave Petzal summed up good shooting and our national disposition for it better than anyone:

"ERNEST HEMINGWAY once wrote of a rifleman freezing himself into 'that impersonal state you shoot from.' At the time I read this, it did not register especially hard, but now I can see that Hemingway knew what he was talking about.

"I have had the privilege of associating with some

truly marvelous shots, and all of them, without exception, freeze themselves into that impersonal state. I do not mean that they turn themselves into unbreathing statues. Rather, they are able to concentrate themselves so totally upon the act of hitting their target that all else fades into the background. Watching one of these men, you get the impression that you could set off a cherry bomb in his hip pocket and he would pay it no notice until after the shot was away.

A 3P match in the UK. Photo: ELEY

"Papa" Hemingway understood shooters and good shooting better than most.

"If there is a secret to good shooting, concentration is it. Not great eyesight, not fast reflexes, not superb coordination – although all these things help. I know men and women who have all these attributes, yet are mediocre marksmen, and always will be. Once in a while they make a fine shot, or they may even get hot for a stretch and do amazing things with a gun, but it will never last long.

"All the really excellent marksmen I have known have three things in common: they understand their guns and ammunition thoroughly, and know exactly what various firearms can and cannot do. They have practiced, endlessly, until the knowledge of how to shoot is no longer in their minds, but in their muscles. And finally, they are able to obliterate everything from their minds except the act of shooting. They shoot coldly and precisely, most of them taking little time to aim or get set, seemingly careless, but with the carelessness born of complete mastery.

"If you ask the average big-game guide his opinion of his clients' marksmanship, he'll answer that a few of them are very good, but most of them are just plain lousy. They are not familiar with their equipment and they don't practice. Presumably they hope that when the time comes to take that one shot on which a trophy rides, they will summon up the spirit of Davy Crockett to aid them, and the bullet will connect.

"There seems to be a notion that we are indeed a nation of riflemen, that the ability to handle a gun is bequeathed to us at birth. The spirit of the frontier, of the Minutemen at Concord, of Sergeant York mowing down half the Kaiser's army with his Springfield, all persist, and may account for this deer hunter who fires his gun once a year. When I was a marksmanship instructor in the Army, I got a good look at what a cross-section of America can do with a rifle, and I think that Sergeant York would not approve."

It turns out that dead-eyed marksmanship is not a national instinct we freedom-loving Americans inherit at birth. It's a perishable skill that requires practice and concentration, along with deep familiarity with the rifle.

But how should you practice? How do you develop concentration? That first question is more comfortable to answer because you can let competition guide you.

My first NRL22-style precision rimfire match was

NRL22 matches test stable shooting positions by using unlikely barricades, like this step ladder. Photo: ConX Media

rough because rather than practice shooting off barricades and from unstable shooting positions, I only trained off a bench at 50 and 100 yards. I thought my ¾-inch groups at 100 were something special. They got me nowhere fast in that first match, save the warm-up prone stage.

I've since seen the same thing happen to half a dozen new shooters at my monthly NRL22 match. They know their rifles inside and out. They can shoot bughole groups at 50 and have memorized bullet drops to 200 yards. They have the best bags, bipods, and slings, and their optics cost two months' mortgage plus a car payment. They're active Internet forum experts. You can see the pride creep into their face when they place that shiny new rifle on the bench. But they've never shot off a tank trap or even thought much about it. So focused on gear, they're like a motorcycle mechanic building a dream bike and showing up on the line, having never taken it out of second gear. In the match, the tank trap takes their lunch money. Some shooters are so embarrassed they never come back for a second match. A few get inspired. These guys usually text me pictures a week or so later of the

tank trap they've built in their backyard. I know these guys well because I was one of them.

Nothing helps power a red-blooded American through a learning curve like a healthy dose of humiliation. After my disastrous first match, I spoke with Greg Hamilton, one of the top endurance precision rifle competitors in the country and a weapon test specialist at PROOF Research. "You have to get off the bench," he said. That advice is as true for the squirrel hunter as it is for the precision rifle competitor. A true rifleman or riflewoman can shoot with accuracy from various positions under a variety of stressful conditions. Success is not a gift. As Petzal pointed out all those years ago, it's a combination of practice and concentration.

Guys and gals not interested in formal competition but who hunt with a rifle — or want to improve their general marksmanship — should keep reading, too. Though it is my deep belief that every hunter should compete because it's the only thing that remotely replicates the high-stakes pressure of drawing a bead on a living creature. Plinking soda cans in the backyard just doesn't summon the seriousness of steadying the

Photo: ConX Media

crosshairs on a bushy tail's eyeball from 100 yards distant. Looking like a jackwagon in front of your friends can create that stress level.

What follows are most of the ways we Americans compete with rimfire rifles. There's something for everyone. The best competition isn't the newest or coolest, but the one you'll attend. That might be the one closest to your home. The National Shooting Sports Foundation (NSSF) has an online tool to find ranges and competitions. The app Practiscore is excellent, too. All of the organizations listed below post online match locations and dates.

NRL22 & NRL22X Competitions

NRL22 and NRL22X, along with PRS Rimfire and who knows how many unsanctioned outlaw precision rimfire matches, have taken off quickly. The success of these matches and the growing public appetite for this style of shooting has led to our current rimfire renaissance.

NRL22 was started in 2017 by Tyler Frehner and Travis Ishida of the National Rifle League as a minor league training camp to the centerfire majors. They

didn't foresee that the rimfire participation levels would far surpass centerfire a few years later. The game has spread like wildfire, thanks to the relatively low cost of entry compared to centerfire events and the ingenious open-source competition system that Frehner and a handful of dedicated NRL match directors dreamed up.

Every month, a standard course of fire is posted online at nrl22.org, and any club or range can run a match. All it takes is a few steel targets and some barricades. NRL22 uses the term "club" loosely, so any group from a sportsman's organization to five guys with a hayfield can download the monthly course of fire and hold a match. The target distances are never more than 100 yards, so any safe spot with that modest distance can be the playing field.

Match directors are encouraged to set up longer bonus stages if they have space. In 2020, Ishida launched NRL22X, where the only limit is the match director's imagination, but those regional shoots are more of the centerfire NRL-style sanctioned and approved events. They're all slated to a competition calendar a year in advance.

Shooting bags make all the difference. Photo: ConX Media

Anyone can hold an NRL22 match. By registering for the free event, a club can purchase an official target pack. It's a sweet deal on some steel — you get 16 targets and ten hangers for less than $350. There are also plans online for self-starters who want to build their targets. The course of fire always includes two prone stages, one positional and one barricade. Directions on building the barricades are online, too, along with Home Depot SKU numbers. Many barricade items are things a club or range are apt to have on hand, such as a 6-foot step ladder, a 5-gallon bucket, or a folding metal chair.

Because the course of fire is standardized, the NRL22 team can post shooter rankings from around the globe online. They hold monthly awards and prize drawings on Facebook Live. To be in the running, clubs need to submit scores to NRL headquarters at the cost of $35 a match, and the shooters need to buy an $85 annual NRL22 membership. (You're not required to purchase a membership to shoot a match, only to have your scores submitted to the national ranking.) NRL22 is a 501c3 nonprofit with the stated goal of growing shooting sports. Buying a member-ship helps them do that.

NRL22 matches have six classes: Open, which allows any .22 LR rifle and optic regardless of cost; Base, which sets a limit of $1,050 (MSRP) for rifle and scope; Ladies; Young Guns, for shooters age 8 to 16; Old Guns for 60-year-old shooters and older; and Air Rifle. In each case, you need a bipod for prone stages, and you're allowed one bag and a sling for barricade and positional shooting.

The official season runs June through February, and the best shooters in the country attend the National Match by invitation, traditionally held in May. The course-of-fire changes monthly — one month, you may be shooting off each spire of the tank trap. The following month you might be doing the same thing, but after racing to touch a brick behind the shooting position or doing a few jumping jacks to get your heart rate up. The following month might be a step ladder.

The positional stage includes the common positions like standing, sitting, and kneeling and off-side shooting or shooting with your non-dominate side. For a right-handed shooter, this means shouldering the rifle

Want to shoot a .22 LR from mountain ridge to mountain ridge? You'll need a Charlie TARAC. Photo: Mike Semanoff

left-handed and aiming with the non-dominate eye. To call this a challenge is an understatement. It takes my lunch money every damn month.

Practice wins NRL22 matches, but that doesn't mean this new sport hasn't set off an arms race for better and more accurate .22s. Vudoo Gun Works has dominated the Top 10 slots for the last two years in the Open Class. Savage controlled Base class in 2019, but in 2020 the top rifle was a Tikka, followed closely by CZ, then Savage. For the complete gear surveys, see the Appendix.

Extreme Long Range

Why would anyone want to shoot a 40-grain .22 LR bullet 400 yards or more? For the very same reason that shooters push centerfire rounds to the 1,600-yard mark and beyond. Extreme Long Range or ELR .22 is a burgeoning rimfire discipline popping up at shooting hotspots worldwide. It's an ideal new pursuit for shooters, ranges, shooting centers, and sportsman's clubs that want to capitalize on the trend in long-

range precision shooting but don't have thousands of yards at their disposal. With ELR, a 500-yard range feels like 2,000 — and 1,000 yards makes King of Two Miles look short. How is this possible? Let's take a look at the math.

Take a diminutive 40-grain .22 LR match load with a velocity of 1,050 fps traveling through a 90-degree full value 10 mph wind. At 100 yards, that wind pushes the little bullet 3.8 inches off course.

Now, consider a modern precision centerfire cartridge, like the cartridge *du jour* 6mm Creedmoor with a 103-grain pill and a 3,000-fps muzzle velocity. That sleek bullet won't drift 3.8 inches in a 10-mph crosswind until the 250-yard mark. Stretch the shot farther, and that same rough 2.5x multiplier for wind generally holds. At 400 yards, the .22 LR bullet drifts 52 inches, whereas it takes 850 yards to move the 6mm that much.

Trajectory comparisons yield similar results. With a .22 LR zeroed at 100 yards, the shooter needs to spin 7 MILs of come-ups to connect at 225 yards. With the

A Charlie TARAC from tacomHQ sits on a rail forward the optic. Photo: Mike Semanoff

6mm, 7 MILs of adjustment puts the bullet on target at 950 yards. If we push the .22 LR to 400 yards — a very attainable long rimfire shot — the shooter needs to adjust by 19.3 MILs. To work a scope turret that much with a 6mm Creedmoor build, the shooter would need a range of at least 1,560 yards.

The ballistic wizards at FinnAccuacy have developed a scaling tool that you can download in Microsoft Excel format to see how your centerfire rifle scales specifically to a .22 LR build. Through that work, it concluded that "If typical .22 LR drop is compared to typical .308 Winchester drop, [the] ratio is roughly 25 percent. The .22 LR rifle bullet drop is same 10mrad 25 percent of distance where bigger caliber drop is same 10mrad. This is valid with 25m and 100m zero ranges."

With that scaling tool, it's possible to line up and determine proportional wind corrections, too. When combined with down-sized 25-percent scale targets, things can get interesting.

"If perfect fit scale factor turns out to be, say, 25 percent to match both drop and wind, target is scaled to one quarter," according to FinAccuracy. "22 LR shooting is then done 25 percent of actual distances: Large caliber charts will match to scaled 22 LR drops with 25 percent ratio. Also, angular dimensions to scaled targets are identical through [the] scope, drop is same, wind same click amount in same actual/true measured sidewind."

This training scenario is ideal for centerfire shooters who don't have a long-distance range at which to practice but have a .22 LR.

Most shooters using .22 LR rifles for centerfire tactical training don't push the parallels this tight, but it demonstrates the utility of shooting rimfire rounds long. For most recreational U.S. shooters, finding a 1,500-yard range is almost impossible. But 400 yards? Not so much.

You can make any sub-MOA rimfire rifle shoot long, but shooting a group inside an inch with a .22 at 100 yards can be a tall order. That said, most of the rifles mentioned early in this book can do it with a bit of work. Sub-MOA rimfire is very achievable with a flat wind, a quality rifle, and — most importantly — good ammunition.

Beyond 100 yards — and definitely beyond 200 yards — things go sideways fast. Ammunition becomes the critical factor in getting hits. I've shot ammo that printed one-hole groups at 50 yards and quarter-sized groups at 100 but then went to hell at 150 and missed the target entirely at 200. The bullets simply went wild after 100 yards.

The only way to know if a rifle-and-ammo combination will keep cool on a long flight is to shoot it. As we saw in the Precision & Accuracy chapter, consistent velocities, standard deviation, and extreme spread ("waterline" as centerfire reloaders call it) matter. That is why serious, extreme long-range rimfire shooters spend the money on Lapua X-Act and RWS 100. The standard deviations are the lowest available in .22 LR and limit vertical stringing caused by inconsistent velocities.

Chronographing lots of ammunition — lots of lots of ammunition — is the best way to determine the best ammo-to-rifle fit. If that sounds daunting, you can send your rifle to Lapua or ELEY and have them do testing. They record shots at 50 and 100 meters.

After finding consistent ammunition for your rifle, the next challenge with ELR rimfire is building an optics platform that will let you correct for oodles of bullet drop.

Most 30mm scopes have around 18 MILs of total elevation adjustment, as we saw in the Optics chapter, whereas 34mm tubes hover about 30 MILs. But if you zero the scope at the center of its elevation adjustment, you'll only have half that total figure in come-ups — 9 and 15 MILs, respectively. To bottom out the scope, so the zero is at the low range of adjustment, it takes a canted rail, typically between a 30 and 60 MOA with 30mm and 34mm optics.

With a 34mm scope, 60 MOA of taper is the way to

The author sighting in rifles. A 50 or 100 yard zero must be dead nuts for any ELR shooting to work.

go for a dedicated ELR build. Nightforce makes one, as does Sphur with a one-piece base and rings system. Burris Extreme Tactical Rings that come with plastic MOA shims are another way to add even more cant. With 10 MILs in the reticle, plus some additional hold-over, these platforms will make the optics package capable of the roughly 42 MILs required to connect with a .22 LR at 600 yards. With lots of taper, a good 34mm scope, and using all of the reticle, 600 yards is about the limit you can push most .22 LR rigs without specialized equipment. With these massive scopes and 0 or 20 MOA rails sighted at 50 yards, 400 to 500 yards is a more common limit.

To get enough DOPE to connect after 600 yards requires a unique device, the Charlie TARAC from tacomHQ. This little black box that connects to the scope's objective lens or forward of the scope via forend rail optically adds elevation up to an additional 250 MILs. The device works very much like a peri-scope, using mirrors to shift the point-of-aim higher, reflecting light, so the target image stays bright and optically centered in the scope. The Charlie TARAC is what A.J. Stewart used to make his 1,000-yard and 1,200-yard .22 LR shots (see sidebar) and what King of Two-Mile centerfire competitors use to send .50 BMGs well past 3,500 yards.

I've never seen someone squirrel hunt at 1,000 yards. You may be thinking the same thing. However, that's missing the point. Like its centerfire brother, ELR rimfire shooting is the Space X of long-range small arms precision — a program and practice operating on the outer edge of possibility. Advances learned in ELR inevitably trickle downward, such as we've seen in the last ten years with the rush of modern high BC bullets, and bipod systems, and rangefinding and wind-reading technology. Long-range fanatics shooting at unreasonable distances proved the ideas and technologies that many hunters and target shooters now lean on.

The author's first real ELR22 outing, and connections at 460 yards, in 2018 at Peacemaker.

A.J.'s Long Shot

A.J. Stewart had dropped three .22 LR shots onto a steel target at 825 yards — and into a group about the size of a Copenhagen can. Now, with a ridiculous 120 MILs of elevation doped into his rig, he sent it to 1,000. But it wasn't going well.

The splashes landed in front of the 30-inch square steel plate that Stewart had set in the sandpit he shoots at near Mobile, Alabama. He spun up more elevation. "With .22 LR, at that distance, to get it to travel another five yards, you need a whole MIL of elevation," Stewart told me. "That's how steep the bullet is coming down. One meter of elevation for five meters of distance." He went to 122, 123, 124, 125. Still, no hits.

"Aw hell," said his friend and shooting partner Chad Long, "I'll go down there."

ELR shooters make regular use of forward observers. Long knew this and took his truck to 1,000 yards and got safely behind some heavy construction debris. Yes, that goes against pretty much every gun safety rule taught to us as kids, but it's the standard operating procedure at the outer limits of long-distance shooting.

Long made safe off to the side and behind the giant excavators. He radioed back to Stewart, and Stewart shot. "You're 35 feet or so behind the target," Long radioed back. Through the spotting scope, Stewart and Long saw the splashes under the steel target, not in front of it as they first thought. The shots looked like they were landing short from 1,000 yards away, but Long could see Stewart was well over it.

Stewart walked the elevation down. When he got to 113 MILs, he shot and waited. A full 5.5 seconds later, the 40-grain lead round-nose connected. A few seconds after that, prone on his shooting mat,

Stewart heard a faint but distinct ding. "That," he told me, "was the best sound in the world." Stewart shot again. "Hit," Long radioed back. "Hit. Hit." Four in a row. They had solved the 1,000-yard .22 LR puzzle.

Stewart used a Vudoo Gun Works rifle with its in-house ACE barrel in MTU contour and a Trigger Tech Diamond sitting in a Cadex Defense chassis to make the shot. He topped the rifle with a Nightforce ATACR 7-35x56 F1 optic and a Charlie TARAC prism. The Charlie allowed for that insane 113 MILs of reticle adjustment. Stewart was shooting Lapua X-Act ammo but has since moved on to RWS 100, which has a slightly higher velocity while staying subsonic with very good SDs.

He's since connected with his .22 LR regularly at 1,252 yards. That, he says, is the outer possibility of the rimfire cartridge with the current generation of shooting technology. New advances in bullet design and new faster twist rates could change that, and he's one of the first guys to experiment with new handloaded copper-solid rimfire .22s, like those from Badlands Precision.

The physics-based range limitation of the .22 LR is undoubtedly well past 1,200 yards. SAMMI lists the extreme range at 1,800 yards. C. Rodney James, in his book, *Small-Bore Rifles*, reports on a 1930s ballistic test on a beach in Florida. They set the rifle at 30 degrees to shoot for distance and measured the crater 1,325 feet from the bore. Getting to the magic 1,760 yards in one mile, or SAMMI's broad-brushed 1,800, is likely possible with modern rifles and ammunition. Doing it with any repeatability is an entirely different story. If and when it happens, I'm sure Stewart will let us know.

Smallbore F-Class

Centerfire F-Class is the brainchild of the late Canadian rifleman George "Farky" Farquharson, for whom the discipline is named. All that's required is a scoped rifle, shooting mat, front rest or bipod, rear bag, and ammo. It is shot prone at ranges from 300 to 1,000 yards, with 600 and 1,000 being the most common. The target is paper with a ½ MOA x-ring and 1 MOA 10-ring.

The much newer smallbore F-Class follows the same guidelines, but you must chamber the rifle in .22 LR, and the distances are 50 meters and 100 yards. Like the centerfire version, there are two classes, Open or F-O and Target Rifle or F-TR. Open rifles cannot weigh more than 8.25 kilograms or 18.18 pounds, and you may fire it off a front rest. F-TR rifles have the same 18.18-pound weight limit, but you can only fire it from a bipod, with or without a sling. It is governed and run by the NRA and detailed on page 65 of the official NRA Smallbore Rifle Rules book.

Smallbore Benchrest

Benchrest is home to the most accurate rifles in the world. Unlike F-Class that is shot prone or precision rimfire matches like NRL22 that you shoot from various positions, benchrest is a one-position game — off the bench.

Unlike the modern tactical-style precision rifles, competitive benchrest guns are 100 percent custom rifles built by a small cadre of elite gunsmiths. Factory guns cannot compete against the customs. Vudoo Gun Works has recently got in the game with its first benchrest action. Anschutz 54 actions were once competitive. Today, gunsmiths churn out the most winning rifles at small-run boutique shops like the Turbo, the 10x, Stiller Precision's 2500x, and the Hole Shot Tridents. These winning single shots are often paired with Shilen, Muller, and Benchmark barrels and blueprinted and assembled to tolerances to the ten-thousandth (0.0001) inch. The barrels are capped with tuners that "click" in different settings, chang-

ing the barrel's harmonics, further "tuning" it to the ammunition. The tunnel records at ELEY and Lapua — that is, the most accurate groups ever fired in those facilities — are always held by benchrest guns.

The 704-page tomb *The Art of Rimfire Accuracy* by Bill Calfee is the closest thing we have to a complete dive on all things benchrest rifles. Calfee is a somewhat controversial figure thanks to his strong ideas on what makes an accurate rifle, but few can argue with his results. He is probably the greatest benchrest gun builder of all time. The book is a collection of Calfee's *Precision Shooting* magazine columns, and while not an easy read, it's packed with nuggets of gold that rimfire nerds can't resist.

Benchrest lacks the field-practicality of tactical-style precision and positional shooting, but a laser-beam rifle alone won't win a match. Matches are held outside, and successful wind-reading is paramount to success. Shooters dot their lanes with dozens of planted wind flags to get an edge on mother nature. Before a match, the work is in tuning a rifle to a good performing lot of ammunition and wind practice. During a match, it's all about the wind.

The largest of the smallbore leagues is the American Rimfire Association or ARA, where the only gear restriction is the rifle needs to be .22 LR. The 50-yard paper target has 25 bulls, with one shot taken per bull. With 100 points per bull, there is a maximum score of 2,500. There is now a new ARA Factory class where the MSRP of the rifle cannot exceed $1,000. Killough Shooting Sports, owned by ELEY, runs the ARA and sells a "Factory Class Rifle Kit" built around a CZ 457 Varmint and a Sightron 36X scope.

The offshoot Professional Shooting League puts on more competitive regional ARA-style benchrest matches and awards cash to winners. It scores targets the same way, but there's also an X count to the scoring so that a perfect target would be 2,500-25X.

The IR 50/50 organization hosts similar matches with various rifle weight classes. The United States Bench Rest League or USBR also sanctions matches

Team USA's Virginia "Ginny" Thrasher won a gold medal at the Rio Olympics in air rifle. Photo: Ginny Thrasher

similar to ARA, but it operates on a much smaller scale. The new Bullet Pro 150, started by Ivan Wells and Mike Bush of Vudoo, is now taking off.

Finally, there is the Auto Bench Rest Association, or ABRA, founded by 10/22 wizard Joe Charon. This group is a semi-automatic .22 LR benchrest league where the rifles are almost all Ruger 10/22 clones customized. ABRA has two main classes: Unlimited, where anything goes except the rifle must be a semi-auto with the round fed from a magazine; Factory, where the same rules apply and the barrel diameter cannot exceed .750 inch at the muzzle. Recently it added similar outlaw bolt-gun classes. Charon is a wealth of information on rifle accuracy.

Positional & ISSF Shooting

Positional rifle shooting goes back to the flintlock days but took off post-Civil War in the U.S. and Britain. From the turn of the century through the 1960s, it was a popular pursuit. In the US, it has since dwindled in the general public and shooter consciousness. Positional or International Shooting Sports Federation shooting is an Olympic event and an NCAA sport. No talented young rifle shooter will win a Nike sponsorship, but they very well could earn a college scholarship.

You shoot matches at 50 meters or yards and 100 meters or yards, depending on the match type and sanctioning body. Long-range 200- and 300-yard .22 LR matches were common until they vanished in the late 1960s and 1970s. Positional shooters make use of special clothing that helps stiffen their bodies for more solid holds. They also use "rolls" that are very much like shooting bags, but rather than stabilize the rifle, they're used to stabilize the shooter in the kneeling position. That "impersonal state you shoot from" that Hemmingway wrote about might be best typified in positional shooters. The 2016 Rio gold medalist Ginny Thrasher told me that while most Olympic sports cultivate action, power, and speed, shooters

On the left, a shooter in the unsupported prone position. On the right, the author shooting supported prone, off a bipod.

seek "stillness." (See the Q&A with Thrasher at the end of the book.)

There are four basic positions. The NRA describes them as such. Note, prone does not include a bipod. This position is often called "unsupported prone" in the NRL/PRS world.

"Prone – Body extended on the ground, head toward the target. The rifle will be supported by both hands and one shoulder only. No portion of the arms below the elbows shall rest upon the ground or any artificial support, nor may any portion of the rifle or body rest against any artificial support. The forearm supporting the rifle shall form an angle with the line from the point of elbow contact to the target of not less than 30-degrees.

"Sitting – Weight of the body supported on the buttocks and the feet or ankles, no other portion of the body touching the ground. The rifle will be supported by both hands and one shoulder only. Elbows may rest on the legs at any point above the ankles.

"Kneeling – Buttocks clear of the ground, but may rest on one foot. The rifle will be supported by both hands and one shoulder only. The elbow of the arm supporting the rifle rests on the knee or leg. The elbow of the trigger arm will be free from all support. One knee must be touching the ground or shooting mat. The shooter may be on all, partially on, or all off the shooting mat. A roll may be placed under the instep provided the foot is placed toe down at an angle not greater than 45 degrees from the vertical. Only the trousers and underclothing

may be worn between the shooter's buttocks and heel. The jacket or other article may not be placed between these two points. If the kneeling roll is not used, the foot may be positioned at any angle, to include placing the side of the foot and the lower leg in contact with the ground.

"Standing – The shooter shall stand free with both feet on the ground or a thin mat without any other support. The rifle shall be held with both hands and the shoulder (upper right chest) or the upper arm near the shoulder, the cheek and the part of the chest next to the right shoulder. However the rifle must not be supported by the jacket or chest beyond the area of the right shoulder and right chest. The left upper arm and elbow may be supported on the chest or on the hip. In the free rifle events, a palm rest may be used in this position. The use of the sling is prohibited for all rifles. (Left-handed shooters reverse these descriptions).

Three-position shooting is an Olympic sport and the most popular of the positional games. In the ISSF match qualification round, 40 shots are taken in the prone position, 40 standing, and 40 kneeling at a 50-meter target. The 10-ring is 0.41 inch, the bullseye or X is about the period's size at the end of this sentence. The competitors have 2 hours and 45 minutes to make their shots in the qualification round. The top eight shooters move on to a final of 15 shots kneeling, 15 standing, and 15 prone. Directors time the shot strings with the last five fired on command within 50 seconds.

The only other ISSF/Olympic event is the 10-meter

standing air rifle. Many close watchers of the International Olympic Committee believe air rifle is the only rifle event with a real future, unfortunately. Outside of the United States, powder-burning firearms are so heavily regulated and so politically divisive, many feel three-position Olympic contests, as well as Biathlon, Trap, and Skeet are destined to be dropped. It says something, too, that even here in the U.S., new events like snowboarding and kayaking get national television coverage. While the shooting sports that have been a part of the Olympic games since the very beginning are black-balled — even though more Americans shoot than play golf.

Positional rifles are highly sport-specific. For ISSF matches, they cannot exceed 8 kilograms or 17.6 pounds and must have metallic or iron sights. The stocks are highly adjustable with hook-type butt plates, palm swells, and more. (See the section, Other Rifles, in Chapter 4, Precision Rimfire Rifles.) You could argue that advances in positional rifles don't revolve around the action, barrel, trigger, or any part of the ignition system, but in ergonomics, how well does the gun fit the shooter. In many ways, this separates positional shooting from many other shooting sports. The rifles and ammo are so refined for that set 50-meter distance that the deciding factor in elite competitions like the Olympics and the World Cup has little to do with gear. There's no way to chisel a few points by spending more money. Persistent practice and a perfect day make gold medals.

In the U.S., the very best international shooters come out of a handful of Division 1 NCAA schools, such as the University of West Virginia and the University of Alaska, Fairbanks, along with the elite U.S. Army Marksmanship Unit based out of Fort Benning, Georgia. Since 1956, AMU members have earned 24 Olymfic medals.

Metallic Silhouette

Metallic silhouette or "*siluetas metalicas*" dates to Mexico in the early 1900s, where competitors staked live animals at varying distances as targets. Drawing blood was considered a hit, and as the game evolved, shooters would aim low for a higher odd shot that dirt, gravel, or rock would cut the animals' feet, or so the story goes. By the 1940s, metal cutouts of the

The kneeling position in ISSF or Olympic-style smallbore shooting. Photo: ELEY

animals were used instead of livestock, with the first documented match held in Mexico City in 1948. In 1967, the first U.S. silhouette range went in at Nogales, Arizona. It's grown into a popular NRA shooting discipline with multiple classes, from handgun to high-powered rifle, to lever guns and pistol caliber carbines.

The targets are the *gallina* or chicken, *jabali* or pig, *guajalote* or turkey, and *borrego* or ram. Distances vary by caliber and match type. In smallbore, match directors set the chicken at 40 meters, the pig at 60, the turkey at 77, and the ram at 100. They set ten of each target on a metal rail, and you shoot in banks of five. Hitting the target isn't enough — the shot needs to tip the metallic critter over. You do all the shooting

standing without a sling. No special gloves or shooting clothing are allowed.

It is exceedingly difficult, and only a handful of competitors have ever shot perfect matches. It is amusing, too, with instant feedback in knocking over the metal targets. But lord, is it difficult.

There are two classes: Silhouette Rifle and Hunter Rifle. Silhouette-class rifles cannot exceed 10 lbs. 2 ounces with the scope and a "traditional" stock, i.e., no butt hooks or other ergonomic aids like those found on a positional rifle. The same rules apply to Hunter-class rifles, except they cannot exceed 8.5 pounds, and you may not set the trigger less than 2 lbs. Many active smallbore silhouette shooters use the same bolt gun in both classes. On the high end, An-

schütz rifles in fiberglass stocks like those from McMillan are popular, but so are less expensive CZs, Rugers, Savages, and Remingtons. It's such a challenging match to shoot well that hyper-accurate rifles are only buying forgiveness. A talented rifleman with a cheap gun will outperform a poor or mediocre shot with a great rifle. For many, this is part of the silhouette appeal.

A good optic with turrets is required. Some shooters use fixed-powered 36x target scopes like the now-discontinued Weaver T36. More common is optics with a 16x to 24x top end. A talented shooter in my club uses a 12x. More critical than magnification power is figuring the rifles' hold point and DOPE for 40, 60, 77, and 100 meters. Many shooters will hold low on the chickens at 40, dead-on or high on the pigs at 60. At 77 and 100 yards,

Take range notes. It will make getting on target faster the next time out.

Biathlon is a significant sporting event in Western European and Scandinavian countries that combines .22 LR rifle shooting with cross-country skiing. Photo: International Biathlon Union

they click in the final adjustments. Also important is remembering what you clicked into your scope and not shooting chickens with your 100-meter elevation. Don't ask me how I know this.

Biathlon

Biathlon is a Winter Olympic event that combines cross country skiing and rifle shooting. It's popular in Germany, Scandinavia, and Russia but has never gained a real American foothold. There are five men's events, five women's events, and a mixed team relay with race distances from 10 to 20 kilometers and smallbore targets at 50 meters. The U.S. has never won a medal.

Biathlon boils down to a ski race plus a high-pressure shooting match. It is a major sporting event with the target shooting and penalty laps playing out in big stadiums before large audiences and broadcast on major television networks across Europe. For every target a competitor misses, they must ski a penalty lap. The fastest time wins. Some variations are dependant on the circuit. In certain events, missed targets add time rather than laps. In others, the penalties only stack if shooters burn through all their ammo.

The first Olympic biathlon event happened in the 1960 Winter Olympics at Squaw Valley, California, but its roots stretch back much further. The Norse God Ullr represented both skiing and hunting. In the snow-blanket countries of northern Europe, the connection is ancient and militaristic. Scandinavian armies have used skiing with rifles as a tool of hunting and war for 200 years. Modern biathlon is a variant of old Nordic military exercises. According to the Norwegian skier and writer Einar Bergsland:

"Norwegian skiing regiments organized military skiing contests in the 18th century, divided in four classes: shooting at mark while skiing at top speed, downhill race among trees, downhill race on big hills without falling, and a long race on flat ground while carrying rifle and military pack. In modern terminology these military contests included downhill, slalom, biathlon, and cross-country skiing."

In the first Olympic events, competitors shot center-fire rifles in the military calibers of .30-06 Springfield and 7.62 NATO. The event standardized the .22 LR in 1978. The rifle used since the 1980s is almost exclusively the Anschütz 1827 Fortner straight-pull biathlon rifle designed by Peter Fortner, as described in the

Greg Hamilon, left, and Sean Murphy—two of the winningest precision shooters in a decade. Photo: Greg Hamilton

Anschütz section in Chapter 4.

Biathlon never has, and never will be popular in the United States, where so few people ski and shooting hotspots are in places like Texas and Arizona. But modern tactical shooting can learn from the sport and the gear. It might be the original endurance tactical sport. Competitors' heart rates are often through the roof because they've been racing flat-out on skies, then they must compose and collect enough to make a winning shot at a 1.7-inch target. In that respect, endurance sniper matches and newer 5k and 10k run-and-shoot events are very much in the spirit of the old god Ullr.

Sporter Rifle & Challenge Matches

There are many other kinds of shooting competitions that use .22 LR rifles, but they begin to stretch the definition of precision. Sporter Rifle postal matches are still prevalent in my home state of New York, shot indoors over the winter. You stand and shoot at a paper target 50 feet downrange with a scoped rifle

weighing no more than 7.5 pounds.

Challenge matches like Rimfire Challenge and Steel Challenge are more popular. They have pistol and carbine classes and have mostly grown out of practical shooting. It's a speed game, with human-sized paper cutouts engaged from spitting distances. The rifles are very cool, often highly modified Ruger 10/22s with irons or red dots.

Practice

In the world of precision endurance rifle shooting, Greg Hamilton dominates. With his teammate Sean Murphy, Hamilton has won the Mammoth Sniper Challenge, one of the country's premier precision rifle matches, three years in a row. Over three days, competitors hike, camp, and shoot a 30-mile course, engaging dozens of targets with centerfire rifles from 250 to 1,000 yards.

Hamilton does all of his rifle training for the centerfire events with a .22 LR on his 50-yard backyard range. "Whether you're plinking with a .22 or big game hunting with a magnum rifle, the skills are all the same," he says. "There's tons of value in training small."

Here's Hamilton's advice on building a range and developing a shooting routine to boost general marksmanship. These tips will help hunters, whatever caliber you shoot, and is a recipe for getting good at precision rimfire games like NRL22.

• Build a range. Hamilton uses a simple know-your-limits plate rack with eight spinner targets that start at 2 inches and go down to a minuscule ¼ inch. At 50 yards, that ¼-inch target equates to ½ MOA or a 2-inch target at 400 yards, so if you can reliably punch it, you're doing great. Hamilton will start a training session in a new shooting position on the 1 incher, then work down until he's "found his limit," then he drills there. The plate rack packs flat and is easy to move, so if you don't have 50 yards of backyard with a good backstop, it's easy to set up and takedown at your local shooting club.

• Sight in. Hamilton shoots two bleeding-edge rifles that run north of $4,000 each, but he feeds them CCI Standard ammo, which you can find at Walmart for less than $4 a box, or at least you could in the Before Times. "It's economical and accurate at 50," he says. Hot rod rifles are fun, but any .22 that will reliably print a 1-inch group at 50 yards will work. If that's a stumbling block, move the target closer and use the

gun you have, he says.

• Stand, kneel, sit, shoot. Hamilton focuses on a handful of shooting positions, namely standing off-hand, sitting, kneeling, prone, and off a tripod from Really Right Stuff. The idea is to replicate field conditions the best you can. Take your time. Focus on getting stable and comfortable and breaking the trigger cleanly. Set and reset your position every few shots.

• Get fast. Once you've drilled a stable shooting position into muscle memory, it's time to get into it quickly. Hamilton does this with a shot timer, but a stopwatch or kitchen timer will work, too. Start standing with your rifle slung over your shoulder as if walking afield. Put 30 seconds on the stopwatch, get into a shooting position, and break two clean shots. When that's easy, cut 5 seconds off the clock and do it again. Then cut another 5 seconds and another.

• Embrace the wind. To train for unknown wind conditions, Hamilton recruits his understanding wife. Ask your partner — in life or shooting — to spin a few MOA of windage into your .22's scope turret without you looking at it. On your first shot, the bullet will be way right or left. Practice calling how far off that shot was, mentally marking it, then follow up with a second shot, making the "wind" correction with the scope's reticle. This drill simulates an unknown amount of downrange wind. [RR]

Hamilton and Murphy are no stranger to centerfire trophies and barricades. Yet most of their training is done with the humble .22 LR.

10

HUNTING WITH RIMFIRES

Many shooters — whether newbies or ardent target competitors — eventually want to test their skills afield. That's when they take up rimfire rifle hunting. My interest in precision rimfires worked in the other direction. It grew out of love for hunting and a quest for an ever-more accurate rifle platform.

My introduction came when my friend Will Brantley, the hunting editor at *Field & Stream*, gave me a last-minute assignment to interview Kentucky squirrel hunter Ricky King for a small game story. King hunts everything but is best known in his home state for sniping gray squirrels at 100-plus yards with a rimfire.

King is paraplegic. He got his start at long-range squirrel hunting almost 40 years ago, after a severe three-wheeler accident left him paralyzed from the waist down. He refused to let that keep him out of

Status update: limits.

the woods and learned how to navigate the timber on an ATV, but the machine's limited mobility and noise made getting close to the bushy tails tricky. When he did set up close early enough in the morning not to spook them, it didn't take long for the squirrels to spot his ATV and booger off.

So, King adapted. He'd scout the woods the day before by ATV and find a pignut or hickory that the squirrels were hitting. The following day, he'd roll in before sunrise and park about 100 yards or so from that hot tree. Then King would wait.

He made shooting bags for the handlebars and front rack of his quad, so his rifle was bone steady. He kept a tripod at the ready in case the squirrels flanked him, and he'd have to adjust. As the sun came up, he would sit in silence and watch. With his rifle and scope, if he could see a squirrel, he could kill a squirrel — 80-, 90-, 100-yard headshots were his thing.

I'd shot .22s. I'd even shot .17s. But a 100-yard head-shot on a 2-inch squirrel noggin? I couldn't believe it. The secret, I came to find out, was in his setup.

King shot an out-of-production Anschütz Model 1502 Heavy-Barrel Classic in .17 Mach 2 — that little bullet rises and falls 2 inches to about 130 yards. The trajectory is laser flat. He topped the rifle with a Leupold VX-3i 6.5-20x40mm EFR scope with an adjustable objective lens for parallax correction. I'll never forget what he said when I asked him why he needed all that magnification. "I like to count their eyelashes." He zeroed his .17 Mach 2 dead nuts at 25 yards. That way, it hit a ½ inch high at 50 yards, a fuzz north of that at 75, and would center-punch the X again at 100. If the squirrel felt close, he'd hold dead-on. In the more common 40- to 75-yard shot range, he'd put the reticle right on the squirrel's chin or neck. Way out there, he held dead-on again. No rangefinder required.

I was hooked.

After I hung up the phone with Ricky, I got on Gunbroker, found an Anschütz 1502, and snapped it up. (It was the first of what would be several Anschütz

rifles in my safe. Please do not tell my wife.) I'll never forget the first time I sighted it in at 25 yards. I shot, and it was high, so I spun the turrets and shot again. Bullseye. I shot again. No hole. *Huh*, I thought. I shot again. No hole. *What's going on*, I thought. I knocked on the scope, turned the elevation up a few clicks, then back down. Reshot. No hole. *How was it possible I was missing the paper at 25 yards?* When I walked up on the target, I realized it wasn't one shot that made the hole. Every shot was going in the same hole — a single hole a few fractions wider than the .17-caliber bullet itself. Man, was I thrilled.

My home office sits in an outbuilding 80 yards or so behind our house. Every spring, there's a war of attrition against chipmunks that chew our siding and get in the attic. I believe that when you shoot a chip-munk, two more instantly materialize at their forward operating base. Nevertheless, I shoot them, trap them, curse them, and keep up a spirited fight. A few days after sighting in the .17, I was in my office and spotted a chipmunk up by the house on the woodpile. I put the reticle on his toes, and that little bullet cut the bugger in half. It was a 73-yard shot. Reaching out and touching tiny targets with miniature bullets felt something like a religious experience. Where the heck was this my whole life? To call sniping like this fun is a gross understatement.

That year, squirrel hunting ruined my deer hunt-ing, duck hunting, and almost my marriage when the wife clued in to what I was spending on rifles and hard-to-find (expensive) .17 Mach 2 ammo. Precision rimfire matches soon followed. Then I was running them. Once a month through the spring and summer, I began directing a local NRL22 match. But when Sep-tember came, I was a ghost, either hunting my home woods or making the trip down south to squirrel hunt with Brantley and friends in what's become an annual bushy tail camp.

Hair-splitting accuracy isn't necessary for most small game hunting — but man, does it help. Most small game hunting with rimfires is all about preci-

The author getting stable on a carbon fiber tripod with HOG saddle head.

sion shooting, whether the quarry is tree squirrels or varmints. One scoped rifle can do it all, but there are some critical differences between competition and hunting guns and squirrel versus varmint rifles.

Hunting Rifles, Calibers & Maximum Point Blank Range

The critical difference between competition and hunting is that you know the target's distance when target shooting. Or you can use a rangefinder for ranging it. For example, the silhouette turkeys are at 77 meters. The NRL22 course-of-fire has targets at 60 and 90 yards. That squirrel at the top of an old white oak? It's guesswork.

You can use a laser rangefinder to ping an exact distance, sometimes, but they don't tend to work well through tree branches, and by the time you figure the distance, the squirrel might be gone. When small game hunting, you need to guess distance with a reasonable degree of accuracy, and the flatter the bullet's trajectory, the more wiggle room you have. If the 2-inch kill zone of a squirrel's head is at 75 yards, but you guess it at 50 and use the 50-yard hash in your scope zeroed at 25, you will miss that squirrel if you're

Will Brantley, Ryan McCaferty, and the author with limits of bushy tails on Kentucky Lake.

shooting standard-velocity .22 LR. However, with the faster, flatter, .17 Mach 2, you'd smack him in the face. The same smackdown would happen with a .17 HMR and .22 WMR. Velocity flattens trajectory.

Thus, hunters have largely moved toward high-speed and hyper-speed .22 LR loads or the even faster .17s. They help immensely with figuring distance and hold. That all said, nothing trumps developing the skill of accurately calling yardages by sight. It separates the good rifle hunters from the greats. One way to develop this skillset, which I did when I first started

bowhunting, is to put a laser rangefinder on a lanyard around your neck when doing yard work. Mowing the grass, ask yourself, *How far to that stump?* Take a guess, then range it to confirm. Technology and gear go a long way with life and hunting, but there is still no replacement for hard-earned skillcraft.

Any modern rimfire sporter can make a good squirrel rifle. My Kentucky squirrel hunting buddy Ryan McCafferty lays them down with a Ruger American Rimfire in .22 WMR and a cheap Walmart scope that he bought used in a gas station parking lot for $200.

The CZ 457 lineup is also excellent, but I'm partial to the thoroughly modern Volquartsen Summit in .17 Mach 2. With the tensioned carbon barrel and Magpul Hunter stock, it's impervious to the elements. The Annie's are shooters, no doubt, but I get irrational when it starts pouring rain on them.

Varmint rifles are heavier. Let's face it: They're target rifles. The shooting is typically from prone or off a trailered bench. Any modern precision rifle in a hot caliber like .17 HMR or .17 WSM can work, depending on the expected distance. For varmints like prairie

dogs where distances exceed 100 yards, most sight-in their rifles at 100 yards, figure the ballistics and drop, and have at it. It's not hard to use a laser rangefinder and range bands of distance over the prairie, so you know that a given spot is about 150 yards, another is 200, and farther back is 250, for example. With a fast, flat-shooting round like the .17 WSM, good drop data with a rough known distance can add up to a bloody day in dog town.

For inside 100-yard shooting, like most tree squirrel situations, it gets more complicated. A .17 HMR or .22

Will Brantley demonstrates the body position of this old school squirrel hunter's treetop shooting form. Always make sure you backstop the shot by a branch or tree trunk.

WMR, as two of my good squirrel hunting buddies shoot, zeroed at 50 yards, will knock the sauce out of a bushy tail at any distance you can see in the timber with your naked eye. The magnums, though, will render a squirrel nearly inedible with a body shot. Anything less than a headshot, and there's too much meat damage to salvage a carcass. With the .17 Mach 2, the opposite is true. If you gut shoot a squirrel and the little bullet doesn't connect with bone and explode, you'll lose that squirrel. For both reasons, the .17s and the magnums are for headshot specialists only.

In all these cases, you set the rifle and optic for Maximum Point Blank Range (MPBR), or the total distance over which the bullet will travel without flying above or below the vital zone — in this case, a 2-inch squirrel head. You can input a "vital zone radius" into many ballistics calculators, which lets you quickly see the max distance at which a dead-center hold will work. With the app and some knowledge of expected hunting ranges, you can tune your zero point, requiring little mental drop calculation in the field.

For .22 LR, many small game hunters use a hybrid combination of MPBR and known drop. With a 50-yard zero, a standard-velocity .22 LR drops about an inch at 10 yards and about 2 inches around 70 yards. So, for zero to 60 or 65 yards, you can hold dead-on, then figure out where the corresponding bullet drop is at 70 to 100 or your max distance. As mentioned in the chapter on optics, BDC reticles work very well here, especially when keyed to high- and hyper-velocity ammunition. That said, subsonic to hyper-sonic, round-nose, or hollowpoint, the .22 LR is a squirrel killing son-of-a-gun. Target loads will knock them flat as fast as hunting loads. The .22 is loved because it does the job on head and body shots without a gross amount of meat damage. Not only that, but it's also possible to "bark" squirrels with the slow-moving 40-grainers. If a squirrel is lying flat on a tree branch and you can't see enough head or heart to make a killing shot, you can shoot the "bark" of the branch under the squirrel's head. This shot often creates a concussive wave that kicks the squirrel off the limb, falling dead. It works

The author sees dumplings in this squirrel's future.

with the slow, heavy, solid bullet of a standard-velocity .22 LR, but not the hyper-fast varmint bullets designed to explode on impact, like the .17s.

Once the zero-point is determined, the final step is to shoot at known distances and look at the actual bullet drop. To do this, pick your zero distance and shoot it, say 50 yards. Next, bring the target into 25 yards. Without adjusting the scope or changing your aim point, shoot another group, holding dead center. Go to 75 and 100 yards and do the same thing. The result will be a single piece of paper with a vertical string of bullet groupings showing your bullet's flight from 25 to 100 yards. Alternatively, you can shoot the same-sized bull with an identical hold at different distances and line up your targets side to side. Doing so illustrates the rise and fall of the bullet to varying distances with a fixed hold.

If you don't like what you see, adjust the zero. You can zero hyper-velocity .22 LRs at 70 or 75 yards as that can still put the little 32-grainers in the kill zone at 15 paces. As you dial in, play with target distances, and see what it's doing at 10 yards and 60. I guess that 99.9 percent of rimfire-shot bushy tails die between 10 and 60 yards. Shoot these distances. Know what your bullet does.

One season, I switched my .17 Mach 2 zero to 50 yards thinking it'd work better. I missed more squirrels up close than all previous seasons combined, so I switched back to King's 25 yards. Adjust and tweak the zero until it works for your setup. Once it works, don't touch it.

Tree Squirrel Hunting

There are two dominant approaches to tree squirrel hunting: Run through the woods behind dogs, and when a freaked-out bushy tail makes for a treetop escape, swing on him with a shotgun and blast away. Or, slip through the woods unseen, toward the sound of squirrel teeth cutting tree nuts, build a position unnoticed, draw a bead on those gnarly buckteeth with a scoped rimfire, and squeeze.

Hunting with shotguns and dogs is akin to a fire team kicking in a door and blasting. It's loud kinetic work, the element of surprise be damned. Scoped rifle

The author's squirrel rig, a Volquartsen Summit in .17 HM2.

hunts are a sniper's work — the solitary but satisfying job of precision shooting. I've listened to a squirrel cut on a pignut for 30 minutes before it moved enough that I could get a visual and shoot.

Shooting sticks or a tripod help when building a steady shooting position in the woods. Often, you're sitting or kneeling on the ground, aiming up at an acute degree. Straight-up shots are not uncommon. For that, the classic squirrel hunter's back position works well.

The tripod Trigger Stick from Primos works excellent. It's light and easy to deploy. So does a hog saddle on a lightweight photography tripod — my go-to rig. Brantley and McCafferty and I hunted four mornings along the shores of Kentucky Lake at our first squirrel camp — boating in under the cover of dark and watching the sunrise over the timber, listening for the sound of cutting bushy tails. We knocked 52 down in four days — and ate a pile of squirrel fajitas. With the hog saddle tripod setup, my Volquartsen barely moved on the report. I don't clamp the rifle in but use the saddle as a rest.

Midsouth squirrel hunting is like nothing I've ever seen in the Northeast. Every squirrel for miles, it seems, will mob one pignut, beech, or hickory, barking each other down, tussling, then finding a branch to settle in and eat. Shoot one off a tree and be patient. In a few minutes, they'll all come charging back to feed. One morning, I shot six from the same tree. It was great fun, precision long-range hunting, all within 100 yards. In much of the Northeast, squirrel hunting requires more walking. There aren't the numbers like in the south, but they're adapted for cold and are much bigger.

Deer hunting is fun. Duck hunting is great. But if all I could ever do were go squirrel hunting with a scoped rimfire rifle, I'd be okay. It's hard to beat cool September mornings after a rain when the ground is quiet and the air is still.

Rabbits

At one time, cottontails were the most popular small game species in the country. They are great fun to hunt behind beagles or with a pack of friends jumping on brush piles. Shotguns work best, but take a Ruger 10/22 or lever-action Henry in .22 LR to up the ante. It's a riot. Take precaution, though, when shooting around dogs and other hunters, especially if they're accustomed to only working with shotguns. Bullets ricochet. Be safe.

Varmint Hunting

Varmints, or pest and nuisance animals that we hunt but generally do not eat, may range from small ground squirrels damaging cow pasture in the West to big coyotes hammering the fawn population in the Northeast. The .22 WMR and .17 WSM are viable short-range coyote medicine but serious 'yote hunters move up a size-class to the light centerfires for dedicated predator rifles. Likewise, some people hunt woodchucks or groundhogs with rimfires. Rural woodchuck shooting is a relic of the past, at least in the Northeast, as modern farm practices have cleared them from the landscape. Old-time New York hunters talk about shooting them up like prairie dogs. I haven't seen or heard of that done in my lifetime. In many of the classic pre-war books on rimfire, there are long digressions on woodchucks. It's fun to read about, gone as woodchucks mostly are now. **RR**

11
PARTING SHOTS

I'm a gearhead. Much of my drive to write this book was as an excuse to nerd-out full-time on all the cool rifles, optics, ammo, and assorted doodads that comprise precision rimfire shooting.

If you survey my desk, there are signs of this everywhere: a Vudoo magazine next to my coffee cup, a Tenex box, and Center-X nearby. There is a RimX bolt, a Bergara bolt, and a Ruger 77/17 bolt, next to some 10/22 and Savage B-22 magazines, two aftermarket 10/22 bolts with assorted springs, a Timney trigger pull scale, and a pile of oddball ammunition — Aguila 5mm Remington, .22 WRF, and half a dozen others. My desk looks out a window, and if I turn around to face the office, there's a Vudoo in a JP APAC at arm's reach and another on a nearby table in pieces, plus a Ruger American stock I just swapped out for my dad. There are six other rimfire rifles in eyeshot, from an old Savage to a new Annie, and books and

targets and printed out pieces of paper everywhere. Whoever said, "messy desk, clean mind" must have meant the entire office. At least, I hope so.

Gear is interesting. And fun. It has consumed me for the better part of a year writing this book, but the equipment is not shooting. One of my favorite things about hosting an NRL22 match, bad as it might be to admit this, is watching someone show up with a new Vudoo or Anschütz, only to get smoked by my buddy Mike and his beat-up Savage Mark II. Mike prints out the monthly course of fire as soon as NRL posts it and shoots every night after work. That kind of dedication will make anyone a better shot. Time at the range drilling unlikely shooting positions with an old rifle will outperform writing a big check or doing some deep-dive rifle modification the cool kids are talking about on the internet.

I write this because I don't want people to take away from this dive on gear a sense that you *need* to spend thousands to shoot and shoot well or that you need to tinker all night for a rifle to shoot competitively. There's nothing wrong with having a healthy budget to pursue shooting or playing with action torques for weeks. But if you are spending money that hurts, know it's unnecessary. If you're losing sleep thinking about this stuff (as I have), know there's a better way. Shoot the gear you have until that gear keeps you from winning. Perfect practice makes perfect shots.

It's important to remember this stuff should be fun, too. When I was trying to drum up interest in my then-new NRL22 match, I was at a nearby range and pitching precision shooting to an old group of silhouette shooters. I emphasized the fun aspect of it,

of shooting from more than one position. Maybe I was too enthusiastic for them. One old-timer looked at me dead in the eye and said, "I don't do this for fun."

Wow, I thought, he must be *really* good. I asked a friendlier shooter about Mr. Frowns A Lot, and he shrugged. Yes, he's good, he said, "but it's not like he's winning at Ridgeway." For him, the shooting had become work, and work wasn't going so well. Such thinking can happen to any of us who takes what we do too seriously. There were times when writing this book where I thought, "I'm never going to shoot a .22 LR again." I took a break, and a few days later, I was back to shooting and writing here at my home office range. But when it becomes too much like work, it's time for a break.

It's tempting at the close of a project like this to think, "What's next?" Where will precision rimfire shooting lead us? I'm confident we will see more, better rifles in the next few years — some at price points almost every kid in American can afford, and others will cost more than a good motorcycle. The firearms industry is wide awake to the juggernaut that is accurate rimfire rifles and the people who love them. The industry is responding. That said, the most significant innovations in rimfire will likely come in ammunition. Sure, the new copper solids, which are already out and shooting well, but also new lead-core bullet designs, more and better pre-primed rimfire brass options, and faster rifle twists at very long barrel lengths. The magnums and hollowpoint hunting loads will get more accurate, too, as shooters demand better non-match ammo. It's an exciting time for rimfire shooters, but we're only just getting started. **RR**

12

Q&A WITH RIMFIRE THOUGHT LEADERS

Mike Bush, Founder and Lead Engineer at Vudoo Gun Works
Mike Bush has had a long and successful run in the firearms industry, but nothing has caught fire like his full-sized .22 LR rifle with a Remington 700 footprint. The V-22 action in no small way kicked off the precision rimfire revolution in American shooting. Yet Bush isn't finished. Here we discuss what made Vudoo possible and where it's going.

Q: What are the key ingredients in your mind for peak rimfire precision?

A: Peak rimfire precision, in any platform, is going to come down to a combination of these two things: timing and tuning. In order to have a platform that can be properly timed and properly tuned, you have to start with sub-assemblies, such as the action, and then there's a whole cascade of things to get into as it relates to the action. But

Mike Bush of Vudoo Gun Works.

you have to create the ability to bring every piece together in what is a truly functional assembly. Every little thing you do is going to make a big difference and how it contributes to precision. Overall, what we're looking for is the absolute best downrange performance as defined by whatever that particular discipline of shooting, whether it's benchrest, or F-class or PRS, or NRL, or even a hunting rifle. But the key ingredients are the ability to properly time and properly tune the platform.

Q: So, how do you do that? I think of magazine geometry, the lack of lug ways in the Vudoo's case, I think of barrel quality, headspace. So, what are all the steps on your checklist that make that well-timed and tuned system?

A: First of all, you have to properly feed the round into the chamber. And you know, that by itself is a huge ordeal as it relates to the .22 LR cartridge. So, if we focus on higher quality match ammunition that the Vudoo was designed around, getting that round effectively into the chamber without damaging the soft lead bullet is the first part. In order to do that, there's a cascading effect of all the things that are necessary as part of the functional system to allow you to do that — in a repeater. As it relates to our single shot, the V-22s, it emulates the same type of loading. It's not a controlled-round system because it doesn't have to be, but the angle of entry into the chamber is the same. But, with repeaters, once the bullet is properly chambered — in a proper chamber — then you have ignition, and the consistency of ignition is one of the biggest detractors to precision performance. When you properly ignite good ammunition, then you have a huge accomplishment and are well on your way to performing downrange.

Q: So, what makes proper ignition?

A: Proper ignition occurs from a fire control system that every time you press the trigger, that firing pin and the amount of kinetic energy delivered to the rim

of the case does so in the exact same way, every time. So, the trigger has to be very finely tuned. How the spring in the cocking piece rides has to be incredibly consistent. The pin needs to hit the exact same spot on the case head every time. Once you get that, it's up to the barrel to do its job.

There are a lot of really, really good performing chambers out there, so we'll just assume that we have a good chamber. Now, here's where the ability to now properly time and tune the rifle comes into play. You chambered the round, so you have no damage to the bullet, and you provided good ignition or superior ignition. So now, the velocity of the internal ballistics (the bullet in the bore) should be incredibly consistent. So, bore geometry is incredibly important. This is where taper lapped bores and things like that come into play.

Q: Are you guys lapping taper into your Ace barrels?

A: Well, there was never a need for taper-lapped pores in our repeaters because of the shooting disciplines those are geared for. Now, we do use an MI or minimally invasive style of rifling in our barrels on our repeaters, but in order to achieve what is a specific velocity at a specific point in the barrel, that's where taper lapping can come into play. We're not tapering our factory hotrod barrels, the Ace barrels, for our V-22s. But we have worked out some expectations with Shilen in the barrels that we received from them. They have very stringent requirements on what the bores of these barrels should look like. So, our Shilen barrels used on our V-22s are taper lapped from Shilen. We're not doing any taper lapping in-house, but we are slugging barrels to validate condition to the bore before we build a rifle. And that's for all our barrels now. That's not just Shilens.

Q: Interesting. Are you doing that on the repeaters as well, or just the single shots?

We are now slugging the repeaters, yes. That's a new part of the process within the last year or so. The data from that feeds my lean-forward process for the development of new products. So, there's information I'm looking for, that, well – it's designed to obviously serve the customer to make sure that we're delivering rifles that are incredibly consistent rifle to rifle. That's a big part of that, but as I worked on the V-22s and understanding the customer base more so than I ever have, not being a benchrest shooter myself, and learning what's important to these guys to be competitive in the American Rimfire Association or the Professional Shooting League, and now working with Ivan Wells to bring Bullet Pro 150 online, we've developed some new ideas. So this data project is a way to help better satisfy this group of shooters. So, yes, we are slugging Ace barrels now, as well as any other barrels we use. But as you know, we'll only use barrels from manufacturers we've validated. That's not to say if we're not using a barrel, it's no good. It just means we haven't validated it yet. There's Benchmark and a few other manufacturers that I really want to dig into, but for me, it's a bandwidth thing. I do expect to bring a lot more quality barrels to the mix at Vudoo this year.

Q: That brings up an interesting point. You guys seem resistant – "resistant" might be too strong a word – but you tell people flatly not to re-barrel your actions. This is curious because it is a Remington 700 platform, and lots of people are very proficient at re-barreling that system. Why is that?

A: So, this is a very good question. I'm not going to worry about being careful here. First off, I would love it, truly love it, if there were more people out there that were able to barrel the V-22. And I say that because there are so many that have attempted it, without asking questions, without asking for the right information that we supply, and they do it on their own based on either what they know, or what they thought they knew, or what so and so said, or what they read on the Internet, and ultimately it does not work. When they do it wrong, they blame the action for it because it could not have possibly been that

they didn't do it correctly. Ultimately, we end up seeing these rifles when they don't work. We get a phone call. We're so adamantly passionate about how we treat our customers that we send out a shipping label right away. Then we receive the rifle back and find out someone else put the barrel on. Remember, we're talking about a functional system. Everything about how the V-22 works as a system. That includes the way the barrel breech is designed.

Q: What makes it more unique than timed threads and torque and proper extractor cuts?

A: Well, we have protruding extractors. So, we have extractor cuts in the breech of the barrel. Those extractor cuts are an engineered part of the system. Many people just assume that their clearance cuts allow the protruding extractors a place to go. That's not true. The extractor cuts are actually part of the timing, to open those extractors as you're closing a bolt. Then as you open the bolt, the radius of those extractors and where they fall relative to the centerline of the bore is what allows those extractors to properly close on the case head and provide effective extraction. So, it's a process to do those extractor cuts, and it's not for the faint of heart. Guys guess at it. They assume that the extractors are on the centerline, the horizontal centerline, when in fact, they're not – they're 0.0024 above centerline. So, they put the extraction cuts in the wrong place, they use the wrong diameter tool so that the radius is not correct. That radius does not match the profile of the extractors, and the extractor doesn't open properly, they don't close properly and grip the case head. So, when you press the trigger on the chambered round, there's no support for the back end of the case, and then the back end of the case blows out. It's not that we're resistant to people re-barreling. We're resistant to those that assume they know how to do it, do it improperly, then tell us there's something wrong with their rifle. We pay to ship this back. Then we stop production to put a new barrel on the action. There's this long trickle-down effect. Now that all said, I'm not opposed to pre-fit barrels. And quite frankly, I developed the ability to have pre-fit barrels on a Vudoo quite some time back. I have several pre-fits here in the lab, and I put them on various actions to test guns. So, it is hugely possible to do a pre-fit to a Vudoo, but to just turn that information out there and not have it used correctly, absorbs a lot of time to deal with and can affect our ability to make rifles. We're very careful how we manage our time. I don't want to sound smart, or arrogant, or egotistical. I'm just being honest with what we experienced, and we want people to realize it isn't something you can just throw on a lathe and do.

Q: I love the idea of a Vudoo pre-fit. What's that going to look like?

Well, actually, it's the exact same barrel we're doing right now. It is the same action. It's the same barrel breech design. Everything is the exact same. But there is a formula to properly placing the extractor cut relative to ... the thread timing, plus barrel torque. That's it. It's a mathematical problem, and that mathematical problem has been solved. It's repeatable within a few ten thousandths. All that's required is altering barrel torque a few ounces outside of nominal. There's a tolerance band. And, when you properly clock the barrel, the major thing, of course, is headspace. But the consistency of our components, action to action, is within 0.001. So, that's highly controllable.

Q: Why not just send that formula to Benchmark and PROOF and Bartlein and all the rest? I imagine all these guys would trip over themselves to make Vudoo pre-fits.

A: They would. I'm quite certain. But again, that's a huge thing to manage. It's an enormous thing to manage. So, I'm starting small with people that I've known for a long time. The guy I'm starting with ... is Josh Kunz at Patriot Valley Arms. I've known Josh for a long time. He's a highly accomplished mechanical engineer. He has built quite a business on being able

to do pre-fits, and it's all based on his process engineering. It's dialed so tightly it's like, 'You know what, Josh, you'd be the perfect guy to hand this off to.' Josh is now working on the first Vudoo pre-fits for the V-22.

Q: I want to preface this next question by saying I know a lot of people with Vudoos. Everyone is very happy with them. They rave about the customer service, but all that said, there have been some issues. I'm thinking about the fitment issue with some of the magazines and chassis. The crescent-shaped firing pin, when first launched, created misfires for a lot of guys. These things have all been addressed, but how do you square that with this need, this desire, to build a precise timed and tuned rifle platform.

A: Well, we could be defensive, be negative, but we look at this all as an opportunity to really perform as a company, to really be transparent about what we're trying to do at Vudoo. All those issues you mentioned, every bit of those things boils down to the complexity of rimfire as it relates to centerfire. Centerfire is so easy because there's a lot of forgiveness. With rimfire, it's tons harder for a number of reasons, which we don't have to get into, but in all those cases, it launched big investigations on our end, so because of who we are, and because its rimfire, little things get a lot of attention.

When I talked about ignition earlier, the crescent-shaped impact on the case head no longer striking across the rim is a better, more consistent ignition system. Striking across the rim creates the result, it creates ignition, but understanding how primer compound works, the burn rate of that compound, how to get more consistent ignition on that column of powder that lays horizontal in the bottom of the case, because the case is nowhere near full of powder. So, we're addressing this with the crescent pin, and a word comes up — variation. What the SAAMI drawings say, relative to the dimensions of the .22 LR case versus what's actually being produced, does not match. There were a whole lot of things that came to the forefront once those pins got out in the world and where you used them in a wide variety of situations. Magazines, it's similar in that there's huge variation across different stocks and chassis. A lot of these systems are reverse engineered through parts that are already produced, not the root information that came from Accuracy International. So, I provided that root information to the chassis makers that were interested enough, humble enough, to say, 'Yeah, we'll take a look at that.' MDT was awesome to deal with. JP enterprises with the APAC chassis were awesome to deal with. Others were not, and they're still having issues. You know, it's not always an easy road to hoe. The result we're after is not always easy. It's always a work in progress. And we do lean-forward a lot as to what we provide the customer and how we provide it, and how we continue to push the envelope. What started this whole conversation was precision. Changing the firing pin tip is all about precision. Changing the fire control systems all about precision. Designing our own trigger in coordination with Flavio Flare out of Italy is all about precision. That's not always easy or perfect.

Q: Following the shooting space pretty closely, I've come to think of Vudoo as a tech company rather than a firearms manufacturer, like a software company working through bugs in real-time and making significant leaps fast. The whole "move fast and break stuff" model. Does that sound fair to you?

A: It sounds awesome. That's a perspective I haven't thought of before. From what I know about tech companies, I think that's a pretty insightful perspective, actually. We work with our customers that way. One of the things I really enjoy is working with our customers. One of the things I truly enjoy — my wife not so much — is I'm damn near 100 percent accessible. Before I deleted Facebook, people would reach out on Facebook Messenger, and I always got back within minutes. So, I reached out and said, "Hey, I'm deleting my social media, but this is how you get in touch with me. These are the forums, etc." After I knew most people had a chance to see that, I deleted my accounts, and you know what, I didn't miss a lick. I'm getting emails. I'm getting PMs on the forums. All our customers have a direct line to me or a direct line to St. George, so no one ever feels like they're in this situation where they spent all this money and need something and get crickets. That happens way too much in the gun industry. Vudoo is not going to be crickets. There's a thread on Sniper's Hide that I started in August 2017, and it's 140 pages long. People get on there and ask a question, and I answer, and it's public, and it's all incredibly transparent. If something is broken, I'm going to talk about it right there in front of everybody. It's just how we work. I think it's been a huge eye-opener. Not just to the buying community but other manufactures in the industry. I see more companies take this radically open approach. For those that are unwilling to do it, it has become completely unacceptable, publicly, for them to be unwilling to participate in the shooting community. We are a community, and it's been a cool thing to watch. It's been a cool thing to be a part of.

Steve Boelter

Steve Boelter, Director of Product Development for Tactical Solutions, former Custom Shop Director, Anschütz North America

Steve Boelter has been a longtime fixture in the rimfire world. He wrote about rimfire for the excellent and sadly defunct *Precision Shooting Magazine* and authored The Rifleman's Guide to Rimfire Ammunition. A longtime competitive benchrest and silhouette shooter, he went on to serve as the president of Anschütz North America, where he spearheaded its Las Vegas custom shop. He's opinionated, brusque, and one of the sharpest thinkers in precision rimfire shooting.

Q: Your book, The Rifleman's Guide to Rimfire Ammunition, *is one of the most comprehensive works on rimfire accuracy out there, and it's all about ammo. Can you characterize the difference between the European rimfire ammo – the ELEY, Lapua, and RWS – versus the American brands?*

A: The biggest difference is attention to detail. There are some nuances in terms of how the machines are designed, how they make their bullets, but those processes are somewhat insider information. But generally, a great way to understand ammunition is to look at it like wine. A jug of wine, cheap wine, could be $10 for a gallon, or you could spend $200 on a regular bottle of quality wine. When you look at the conceptual differences in a grade of wine, very good wine, the grapes are picked by hand, sorted by hand, there are no stems, no leaves, they're washed, they're picked just at the right time. There's a lot more hands-on work. High-end European ammo goes through the same thing. The lead is of higher quality. The alloys are much tighter within a spec. The brass is tighter. The loading machines run slower. The lot sizes are much, much smaller. They get a more intensive QC process every step of the way. That extra labor and process are really built into the price of the ammo. If you take an ELEY Tenex or R-50 or Lapua Midas+ on the high end of the spectrum and you pull them apart

and look at all the different aspects — how well was it lubed, how evenly is the powder, you pull the bullet, and see how well is the primer placed. Then do the same with a Winchester Wildcat or CCI Blazer or Remington Golden Bullet on the low end of the spectrum, and you can clearly see the difference in attention to detail in an assembly. You'll also see a difference in the quality of components. If you have the ability to test the lead alloy and see how much tin, how much antimony in it, you'll see the European ammo holds a much tighter spec. The alloy is much more homogenous, and the tin and antimony are much more evenly blended in the lead. This matters because as the bullet flies through the air, if it's not perfectly made, the center of gravity is off, and it wobbles. The loading process is different. When they're actually loading the finished bullets into cases, are they being bounced around in a big metal tin or a hopper or a bucket, and the heels are getting dented, or are they very carefully handled? One of the most critical areas of accuracy in a .22 bullet is a place that you and I cannot see. That's the heel. You only know if the heel is made right after you fire or if you rip it apart. But either way, you cannot preemptively sort based on how well the heel is because it's hidden inside the case. Those are the differences between them. There's not a magic accuracy dust.

Q: Why is the heel so important to accuracy?

A: A couple of things. A lot of people think that the primer sets the powder on fire, and the powder burns and launches the bullet down the barrel. That's true, to a point. There's enough pressure from the primer going off to get the bullet moving down the barrel. Look at Aguila Colibri that is a 20-grain bullet, short case, no powder, just primer, and it shoots. The point is the bullet gets moving before the powder builds up and goes through full combustion. So, the bullet gets going with gas pushing on the back of it. If the heel is not perfectly symmetrical around, it will push harder on one side than the other — if there's a dent or a ding. It's almost like having a plunger in a toilet and having it off-center, and water comes shooting out one side. There's less resistance on one side. If the bullet starts and the heel isn't perfectly formed, it gets pushed off-center, now your bullet isn't symmetrical anymore, and your center of gravity is off, and you go back to the wobble. Anytime the bullet enters the rifling not perfectly straight, it negatively affects accuracy. This is why in the (Anschütz) Custom Shop when we're chambering guns, we were extremely adamant about getting the chamber perfectly concentric to the grooves of the barrel, not the lands. With everything perfectly straight, concentric, rings within rings, and the bullet launches with a good heel, you have the best opportunity for accuracy. If you fail on the chambering process or the bullet heel is off, the bullet starts slightly crooked, and the pressure swages the bullet to one side of the bore. It's like someone throwing a football, and it wobbles.

Q: I've heard it said that at national match-level benchrest, or Olympic-level international shooting, the guns have all become almost mechanically perfect, by that I mean the gun is no limiting factory in wins or losses, but that mechanically the weak link in the chain is the ammo.

A: That's exactly right. And most people do not have the knowledge or the financial resources to really test ammo. I shot with a benchrest shooter, and for years he was untouchable. He would test no less than 60 or 70 lots a year. He'd match 10 lots of ammo a year to his bench gun. He was always testing ammo. This is known in benchrest very well. If you're not taking the time to match ammo, you're not going to win. I won't say the rifle doesn't matter, but I'd take a less quality rifle with matched ammo over pouring endless amounts of money in a rifle and shooting whatever ammo ELEY or Lapua or RWS gives me. Give me that secondhand rifle and a month to spend at Lapua. Every gun likes different ammo. Lapua, or ELEY, or RWS doesn't have the secret sauce. It's what does that gun like.

Q: What about chambers cut for particular ammo, like the ELEY EPS chamber for Tenex, for example?

It's a neat idea, but it doesn't really pan out. When I was at Anschütz, we had 167 years building rifles, and if that worked, I promise you we'd have done it. There's just too much variance in even the best ammo lot to lot. Consider a 50 meter .22 LR rifle. Have you seen a .22 LR in a vise at 50 meters put 60 shots in the same hole? Of course not. With a 10-meter air rifle in a vise, I can do that all day. Tuning a chamber to ammo is extremely hard because the ammo manufacturers cannot hold the tolerance needed to let that make a difference. Ammo changes. Bullet dies change. Bullet dies don't last forever. They wear out. New bullet dies are made and finished by hand. All those variables stack, and to say a tiny little variance in a reamer is going to make an appreciable difference, well, it just doesn't.

Q: You wrote an essay on cleaning rimfire rifles and a follow up on cleaning suppressors with a level of detail that's, well, impressive–

[Laughs] The first version of that was 38,000 words. Now, what's interesting is, I've had some newer thoughts about cleaning, but I have not had the time to have a laboratory analyze some of my thoughts and findings.

Q: That was my question. Has your thinking on cleaning rimfires changed?

A: Moisture plays a much bigger role in barrel damage than we originally thought. I think ambient moisture is a bigger player than we ever realized in how it corrodes steel.

Q: So, what does a shooter do with that? Does it change the way we should clean our rifles?

A: Well, the solution is still going to be the same. You should never put a gun away dirty. The people who said, "Well, you want to leave it dirty because that seals the barrel" — that's all bullshit. You should never put a rimfire away dirty because the powder, the fouling, is hygroscopic — it absorbs moisture. So, I'm in Las Vegas right now, and we average about 11 percent humidity, whereas if you're in Georgia, that's a totally different animal, right? So, if I put my gun away dirty, I could give you all this anecdotal information on how it never affects me, but if you do that in Georgia, I could find pits in the barrel in six months. So not only should you never put your gun away dirty, but I believe everyone needs to find the accuracy window of their barrel. It's like lot testing. It's essential. Once you understand your accuracy window, it will help you decide when to clean, but still, you should never put a gun away dirty. If you're in a situation at a match where you can't foul the barrel however many shots you need, you're going to have to figure something out.

Q: That's interesting because it's pretty much the opposite of what so many rimfire people say. I've heard guys say, "clean it at the end of the season" or "clean it when accuracy drops off."

A: Here's another way to look at it. You go to an optometrist to get your eyes checked. The equipment they use to check eyes is super clean. There's zero dust, lint, as it has to be because they're working at a high level of precision. Then with your new glasses, go to Home Depot and look at the community rip saw in the back. Look how clean that blade is. It's there to rip MDF boards. It's not a precision machine, so the cleanliness doesn't really matter.

A low-quality barrel with poor dimensions and shoots bulk ammo probably doesn't need to be cleaned every outing because it's not a precision machine. So, cleaning isn't one-size-fits-all. You have to treat a precision rifle like a precision tool if you want precise results.

Ginny Thrasher.

Ginny Thrasher, Team USA Rifle Shooter, 2016 Rio Olympics Gold Medalist

Team USA rifle shooter and Olympic gold medalist Ginny Thrasher first picked up a rifle at 14 years old on a hunting trip with her grandfather. She enjoyed it and, as a freshman, tried out for the West Springfield High School Rifle Team in Springfield, Virginia. In her sophomore year, she joined a travel team, the ACORNS of Arlington, and began competing across the country. In Ginny's senior high school year, she qualified for her first international match and committed to attending West Virginia University, the country's top NCAA rifle team.

Ginny's first year at college was particularly notable. She won NCAA individual titles in both rifle events, the air rifle and three-position smallbore – the first-ever freshman in history to do so. West Virginia University won the Team Championship. Three weeks later, she won the Olympic Trials as an underdog, and on August 6, 2016, after a summer of international match success, she shocked the world by winning a gold medal in air rifle at the Rio Olympic Games. This shooting prodigy was just 19 years old and had been shooting seriously for only five years. The average age of the Olympic rifle shooters in Rio was 31.

In May 2019, Ginny graduated Summa Cum Laude with a bachelor of science in Biomedical Engineering, 12 All-American Honors, 4 NCAA Individual Medals, and 2 NCAA Team Titles. Soon after, she moved to the U.S. Olympic Training Center in Colorado Springs to pursue international riflery full-time. She was on-track to make the 2020 Tokyo Olympic Team before the global coronavirus pandemic delayed the games. Team USA Olympic trials were postponed, as well. At the time of this interview, she was No. 1 in the point standings to make the Olympic team in three-position smallbore. The Tokyo Olympic Games are scheduled to open on July 23, 2021.

Q: You went from picking up a rifle for the first time to winning a gold medal in the Olympics in *almost exactly five years. That's amazing. Are there any other sports where that's even remotely possible?*

A: It's unusual. And not just for any sport, it's very unusual for rifle shooting, too. This is not the typical path. A lot of people see me, and see my journey, and think, Oh, anyone can do it. It's always a little awkward because my success is not because rifle shooting is easy. For a little perspective, when I went to the Olympics in 2016 and won in air rifle, there was a qualification match where everyone shoots 60 shots. Then they take the top eight athletes from there and do an elimination final. You take a few shots, then they say, Eighth place, sit down. Shoot a few more shots. Seventh place, sit down. So, when I made that final, for the top women in the world in the Olympics, the average age was 31 – the average. So, in my case, I've had lots of early success, but what's most exciting is that there's that kind of longevity in my sport. I know I can keep competing as long as I want.

Q: That also speaks to the talent, and I imagine the intensity of the training you put into it at 19.

A: I've always worked really hard, I still do, and it wasn't accidental. I definitely surprised some people and was an underdog going in. But shooting isn't like some Olympic sports, like swimming or gymnastics, where you pretty much know who's going to win or come very close. Shooting at this level, you could hold the match ten different times and have ten different winners. Shooting is a mental game. I think it's very similar to golf, and when you get to the Olympics or an international match, the top 10 or 15 shooters in the world all have the same physical ability. Everyone is shooting the same scores. But it's who can and is going to do it that day. It's a pressure cooker scenario.

Q: It's interesting that you didn't mention the gear. You didn't mention the rifles as a deciding factor. There are a handful of manufacturers of Olympic-caliber .22s, and I've heard it said that there's no single dominant platform – that the rifle systems and ammunition are so accurate at that 50-meter distance that the gear is never a limiting or deciding factor in competition.

A: I would agree but add if you have the best equipment on the market, then the accuracy of the gun isn't holding you back at all. There are definitely athletes with equipment that is not quite as good, for whatever reason, and that could hold them back, but at my level, it's definitely a technique game and mental game. But there are definitely phases where one gun gets really popular and a lot of people winning have it, but at the end of the day, some of it comes down to personal preference. You can replace barrels. You can do things to make your gun shoot a little better, you can find a batch of ammunition that really works for your rifle, but at the end of the day, it comes down to … do you like the gun you're shooting. For air rifle, I shoot Feinwerkbau. I love my Feinwerkbau, obviously. I won a gold medal in the Olympics with it. But the reason I picked one up in the first place is because that's what my junior club had to rent us. So, when the time came for me to buy my own, that's all I knew. It was a great decision. They have a great history internationally, but that decision came down to personal preference.

Q: What smallbore setup are you running now?

A: A Bleiker, from Switzerland. In my opinion, they make the best precision smallbores on the market right now. Most of the companies that make these rifles are European, three companies from Germany, Bleiker, and there is an American company now, Turbo, that makes a precision-style three-position rifle. A teammate here at the Olympic Training Center has a Turbo and really likes it.

Q: What barrel maker and ammo are you using?

A: Bleikers all come with Lilja barrels, and the national team shoots ELEY ammunition. Our rifles are lot tested at their factories. My gun has been to a few different places, actually. ELEY has a test range in England, Texas, and Germany. My gun has been to all

three. We can also lot test ammunition at the Olympic Training Center here in Colorado.

Q: What does a typical training day look like at the Olympic Training Center?

A: The Training Center is a great place to live and work because it has all the resources an athlete needs to compete at this level in one place. It's almost like a very small college campus. There's a rifle range. Ours is two stories, and both levels are identical. Shooting one direction across the range, you can shoot air rifle, or you can shoot lengthwise down the range and practice 50-meter smallbore. One range is usually set up for air rifle, and the other for smallbore. They also have a sports medicine facility and a gym, a sports psychologist and nutritionist, and a big cafeteria, and dorm rooms, swimming pools, basketball courts. It's been really great to live here, and Colorado is just gorgeous. A typical day of practice for me involves getting to the range around 8 a.m. and doing a full warmup routine. There are so many variables in shooting; you want to mentally and physically warm up the same way every day, so you're always starting from a consistent place. It's a process, but by the time I've gotten the gun ready, warmed up, and started shooting, it's about 9 a.m., and we'll shoot until a late lunchtime, then I pack up and workout at about 1:30 p.m. After that, there's some sort of meeting, whether that's with a sports psychologist or media interviews or what have you.

Q: What kind of workouts do you focus on to help your shooting?

A: We do a lot of targeted strength work and focus on injury prevention. We want strong core and lower back muscles so we can prevent injury when in the crazy positions we're holding for four hours a day. Another thing we work on is balance. We also want to build in as much stamina and endurance as needed to train as long as possible, so on long competition days, we don't fatigue out. The other thing we look at is heart rate. The lower your resting heart rate is, the more that can help your hold. So, I do a lot of strength-based training. Two days a week, I do cardio, whether High-Intensity Interval Training or longer steady-state cardio work, like a hike. The goal is to work down that resting heart rate. My fifth day is active recovery, stretching, mobility, core workouts, and the like.

Q: Just how important are heart rate and breath control to shooting well?

A: So, when you're in a competition, you're nervous. There's no getting around that. Your heart is going to be pounding a little bit faster. You can feel that pulse in your body, and you can see it in your sight picture in your holds. So, sometimes when we get to the competition, our holds are bigger because of our heart rate,

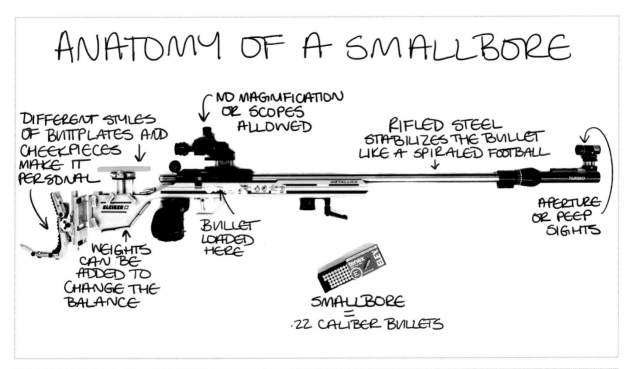

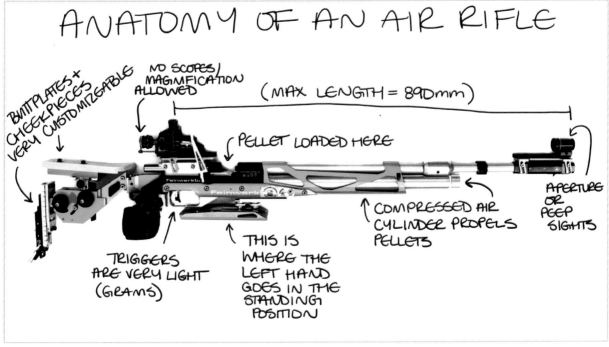

because we're super excited to compete, so we work on ways to keep our heart rate more controlled. One of the ways to do that is breathing. Different athletes have different breath techniques and practices that they'll use in the middle of a competition or before a competition. Those can be really effective. Another one, like how we train, is to lower your resting heart rate: the lower your resting heart rate, the less it's going to rise. So, if your resting heart rate is 70, it might be rising to 120. If your resting heart rate is 40, it might rise to 90, and that will make for a smaller hold when your heart rate is up. In my style of shooting, you're trying to be as slow and smooth and steady as possible. You're trying to achieve stillness. That's really hard to do, so you're working with yourself to control your body, to control your mind, to manage your body's reaction to stress in a very competitive environment.

Q: That's fascinating. So, how does the shooting training work? How does it build toward that stillness?

A: I would say we have four different areas. This is how I personally like to categorize it. First, you have positional. This is how you hold the gun. Our guns are very adjustable, so where does the cheekpiece go? Where does your hand go? Where do your feet go? That's the positional aspect of it, and it's needed for a great foundation. The next part is the technical aspect. How do you pull the trigger? What is your breathing process through the shot like? From what area do you approach the target? A lot of my training is on technique, whereas for a young shooter, it's very much about finding the right positions. A position is never perfect, but as it gets better, the other aspects become more important, like technique. The third aspect is mental. This is what you're saying to yourself. This is how you think about the competition, how you handle the pressure. The fourth is strategy. So, in a competition, where do you take your breaks. How do you shoot in the wind? When do you talk to your coach? It's the strategy of how you're going to shoot the match.

Q: I'd say your strategy is working.

A: [Laughs] I'd say I've found my passion. I tried so many sports. Most people who get to the Olympic level start their sport at three, four, five years old. I tried so many sports, musical instruments, languages, and I never found what I was passionate about. But I kept trying until I found shooting, and I love it.

Dave Emary, Creator of the
.17 HMR and .17 HM2

Dave Emary spent 24 years with Hornady Manufacturing Company, where he led one ground-breaking ballistics project after another, including the creation of the wildly successfully .17 Hornady Magnum Rimfire.

Yet his early work was decidedly larger. After earning a degree in physics at Bowling Green State University in Ohio, he joined the Air Force, where he managed large-scale test projects, such as 5,000-ton anti-nuclear weapon effect testing at White Sands Missile Range. After picking up an aeronautical engineering degree at the Air Force Institute of Technology at Wright-Patterson Air Force Base, he moved to the civilian sector, soon after landing at Hornady.

At Hornady, he was instrumental in the design of the 6.5 Creedmoor, the A-MAX and Varmint Express bullet lines, LEVERevolution, Critical Defense and Critical Duty, the Superformance lineup, and the rimfire .17s – the HMR and Mach 2. He's currently working a "retirement job" as Director of Engineering

for New Mexico Institute of Mining and Technology's Energetic Materials Research and Testing Center – the largest test range in the U.S. outside of the federal government – with a focus on 8-inch howitzers and 120mm ordinance. He also writes a regular column for *Guns & Ammo* magazine.

Q: How did the idea of necking down a .22 magnum to a .17 come about?

A: I have to give Steve Hornady credit. He really opened up to my ideas and would say, Yeah, go run with it. So, at the time, I didn't know anything about the work that Federal had done. Jamison and Federal had messed around with it in the late 80s, but of course, back in that time, they didn't have the propellants that we had in the early 2000s. I started out around 1999. My dad was getting pretty elderly, and he always liked to snipe woodchucks, and he had a .22-250, and he said, I just don't really want to shoot this thing much anymore. So, I decided I was going to make a really, really nice shooting .22 magnum. I completely redid a Marlin bolt action in .22 magnum and got the thing to shoot under minute-of-angle. I was messing around with that, and we were in between projects at work, and I wondered, what would happen if we neck down this .22 magnum case to .17 caliber, and that's kind of where it went from there. It was probably six or seven months of just messing around on weekends or lunch breaks with the concept. I started getting good results and brought it to Steve, and he said, Okay, go build a test barrel and do this legitimate like everything else, and it went from there. He approached CCI to load the stuff, and everybody's estimates of what the first-year sales would be were off by several orders of magnitude.

Q: Why do you think it became so popular? What need did it fill?

A: It really caught fire in the gun industry because they could take every .22 magnum platform they had and simply re-barrel them, which was a no-brainer. And it took rimfire into the realm of the lower-end centerfire calibers in terms of capability and performance. You can't say that the .17 HMR is a .22 Hornet, but it starts getting into that regime. That's to say, you've now got a rimfire that's accurate enough and effective enough to take small game at 150 to 175 yards. That's way outside the envelope of what anybody would have ever expected out of a rimfire cartridge. The other thing, too, we put a premium from the get-go on accuracy. This thing had to be highly accurate. Everybody then was used to .22s that weren't that accurate, so we wanted something with legitimate accuracy, centerfire-type accuracy, which we put into the design of the chamber, with the really high-quality jacketed bullets. That combination of performance and the low-cost platforms that it could go in were why I think it took off as it did.

Q: I've heard it said that the .22 magnum's reputation for poor accuracy was due to wide chamber specs, so custom builders could make them very accurate by working the chamber, but it was always an issue for factory guns.

A: Yes, the chamber design is not the best for accuracy. The old school blackpowder 15-degree throat they put in these things, you need to do the conventional 45-degree taper into a half the bullet diameter throat and get enough jump, so the pressure is the same, and these things can drive tacks. But you also have to remember that these guys at the time [when the .22WMR was developed in the 1960s] were not putting any kind of premium on the bullets they were making. They were just hammering out bullets on a header and thought, if it shoots two inches, that's good enough. Now, certainly, since 2013 when Hornady started putting that 30-grain V-MAX ammo in .22 mag ammo, you had high-quality, high-accuracy bullets instead of stuff just slapped together. It dramatically upped the game for the .22 magnum.

Q: So, when the .17 HMR came out at SHOT Show, it was a huge success and was quickly followed by the .17 Mach 2. Was the idea there simply, it worked for .22 Mag, so let's neck down a .22 LR?

That came about as a number of people tried to get the .17 HMR to work in semi-autos, and it just wouldn't work. The dwell times were too long, and the cases weren't strong enough. So, the .17 Mach 2 was primarily done to get these new high-velocity .17 rounds in a blowback semi-auto. Marlin had that 717 for a couple of years. I don't know why they discontinued it. It must not have sold, but that's a great shooting rifle.

Q: What's next for rimfire? Where do you see the space developing?

A: I think it's largely being driven toward people wanting better and better accuracy out of their gun-ammunition combination. It's all about precision. The future will be guns and ammunition that push the envelope of accuracy and performance. People want more and more out of rimfire now, and the manufacturers are going to have to answer that.

Steve "22Plinkster" Nash.

YouTube Rimfire Ambassador 22Plinkster

Steve "22Plinkster" Nash grew up in Tennessee and was taught to shoot by his father, a qualified U.S. Army Expert Marksmen in rifle and pistol. They loved squirrel hunting, and he'd often watch his dad drop bushy tails from the treetops with headshots from an iron-sighted handgun. A premium was put on accuracy in the Nash house, so when Dustin Ellermann won Top Shot season 3 in 2011 with a 100-yard .22 LR golf ball shot, Plinkster thought, I can do that.

He uploaded the video to YouTube to share with a friend and made the shot with a scoped pistol, rather than the Volquartsen rifle Ellerman used. The rest is history. He went on to be one of YouTube's top trick shooters and remains one of the largest firearm content creators and influencers on social media. He is currently sponsored by CCI, Henry, and Volquartsen.

Q: What's the full origin story? How did you get started as 22Plinkster?

A: It got started by accident. I didn't know You-Tube was a thing, or you could make money at it. But there was a television show many moons ago, called Top Shot. It was a shoot competition, and I was a big fan. In season 3, there was this contestant Dustin Ellermann, and I was pulling for Dustin. There were all these professional shooters, and Dustin was just the good old country boy who taught himself how to shoot. Well, to win the season, Dustin hit a golf ball at 100 yards with a Volquartsen rifle. I had never heard of Volquartsen back then, and now I shoot for them, so it's come full circle. Well, the next day, my buddy in the Navy who was stationed in Florida, we chatted once or twice a month. We grew up together. Childhood friends. Well, we get talking about Top

Shot, and he says, That was the luckiest shot I've ever seen in my life. And I'm like, No, with the right setup, the right shooter, it's possible. And he's like, No way. I've shot enough .22s. They're not accurate out to 100 yards. And I'm like, They very, very much are. And he was like, Well, do you think you could do that? And I say, You've seen me shoot, you know I can do it. So, he's like, Prove it. And I said, Okay, but I'm going to do it with a pistol. So, I got home and grabbed my phone, which was the only camera I had — a Droid, the first Droid, that filmed in 720p, and back then, that was the stuff. It's the most boring video you'll ever see … I said what I was going to do, backed up to 100 yards. Second shot, the golf ball goes flying, walk back, I forgot to hit the record button. So, I had to shoot it over, put the golf ball back up at 100 yards, shot it again, but on the third shot. I upload it to YouTube because you can't send a 5-minute video via text, so I upload it to YouTube so he can watch it. And so, I did that. He watched it. We laughed about it. We talked about it. That was it. That's all I wanted YouTube for was that one stinking video. I didn't even watch gun videos on YouTube. So, I guess it was about two months later, I got an email. This was back when YouTube first started, and every time someone commented on a video, they would send me an email notification. Well, I looked at that comment, and someone wrote, nice shot. I looked at the video had 74 views. I remember thinking to myself, 74 people wasted their time watching the most boring video ever made. Well, a couple of weeks later, people started asking if I could do other things, so I started doing 20- and 30-second clips of other trick shots, not even talking in the video, and it just kind of escalated from there.

Q: All these years later, a 100-yard .22 LR pistol shot is still a helluva shot. Where'd you learn to shoot?

A: I have my dad to thank for that. And he has my grandmother to thank for that. My grandmother taught my dad how to shoot, and he taught me. My dad was an Expert Marksmen in the Army, both rifle and pistol. I was amazed watching my dad shoot when I was younger, shooting squirrels out of the top of the trees with a .22 pistol from 60, 70 yards, and calling headshots. I remember seeing that, and not till probably my teenage years when I started shooting a pistol did I find out not everyone can do that. I had a semi-gift when I was younger, but it took years to develop that skill. But with my dad, there was no such thing as recreational shooting. You couldn't just grab a box of ammo, go out in the backyard, and shoot. That was a waste of ammo, and you are not allowed to do it. Say, for instance, I'd go squirrel hunting at 11 or 12 years old with the .22, he'd give me 10 rounds of ammo. And for every squirrel I missed, that was one day I couldn't hunt. If I brought home five squirrels and missed five times, that was five days I could not hunt, and you might as well have given me a whoopin' cause that wasn't worse than not being able to go hunt.

Q: He really drilled the importance of accuracy into you.

A: Yes. Breathing, cheek weld, trigger control. I can still hear his voice on our back porch when I was first learning to shoot a BB gun.

Q: So, until very recently, a lot of kids would start with BB guns, move into .22s, then in those late teenage years or early 20s graduated out into bigger calibers. What's kept you anchored in rimfire?

A: Well, probably 90 percent of everything on my channel is rimfire related. 10 percent is other calibers. The funny thing, what a lot of people don't understand, is I probably shoot as much centerfire as I do rimfire. I shoot a lot of centerfire. However, my channel is predominantly rimfire because if I shot everything, how would that make me any different than all the other Joe Blow gun channels out there? Now, people do often graduate out of the .22, but people also find themselves later in the years, in their 50s,

60s, 70s, 80s, going back to rimfire. I don't know why, but in parts of the Second Amendment community, it's almost like you're not a man if you don't shoot something big, and that's just so not true. You develop so many bad habits, from flinching to poor trigger control if you're shooting big stuff all the time. Then these guys wonder why they can't hit the broad side of a Jenny Craig patient. They've developed horrible habits. There's nothing un-masculine about shooting rimfire. It will help you be a better shooter all the way around, no matter what you pick up. I can't tell you how many thousands and thousands of people have told me, I never considered buying a .22 until I came across your channel, and now I own ten of them. That makes me happy.

Q: That's fantastic. And with your success, with NRL22, with the rise of Vudoo and inexpensive precision rifles that drive tacks, it feels like we're in a rimfire renaissance, so to speak, right now.

A: We are in a rimfire era like this world has never seen. So many companies, whether it be ammunition companies, pistol companies, rifle companies, they're all building the most accurate firearms because, with technology, accuracy has been brought down to a science. Not in a million years did I think a .22 LR has the capability to hit a target pretty consistent at 1,000 yards. That blows my mind. But they're

making it now, and it's just a great time to live in. And it's not just one company. Every year it feels like 15 or 20 new .22s come out, and most of them are really good now. It is the most popular caliber in the world for a good reason.

Q: Where do you see the rimfire space going? What's the next chapter?

A: In the next couple of years, rimfire will grow in leaps and bounds. There are over a million new gun owners in 2020. And a lot of those gun owners, they bought a 9mm or a .380 or a .38 Special for self-defense. After they shoot those, they're going to find out if they like shooting or not, and most will like it, and the second thought will be, it's expensive to shoot. A lot of people are going to buy that second gun, and it's going to be a .22 LR. I get direct messages on a daily basis from people asking exactly this. They have fallen in love with shooting, but they don't like going to the range and spending $40 to shoot only 100 rounds. For $40, you can shoot 800 or 900 rounds of .22 LR and get that practice in. The economics of it — especially in the face of new firearms and ammunition shortages — is going to bring more people into the rimfire space. That's great for shooting. Honestly, I just want to get as many people involved with shooting, not necessarily just rimfire shooting, but all shooting, as I possibly can.

Travis Ishida.

Travis Ishida, Founder and President of the National Rifle League and NRL22

Like so many of us, Travis Ishida fell down the precision shooting rabbit hole. A native of Yorba Linda, California, just southeast of Los Angeles, he had a successful career in photography and marketing. He started shooting rifles in addition to cameras, and very quickly, his wife hit him with a question many of us have heard before, "Why are you spending so much money on guns?"

Ishida committed to making firearms his career. He started a marketing firm ConX Media, aimed squarely at the firearms industry. His first client US Optics led to others, including a gig filming then-new Precision Rifle Series matches. The videos of sniper dudes doing sniper stuff went viral, but when PRS ownership changed hands, it took its marketing in a different direction. Undeterred, Ishida and a few shooting industry veterans started the nonprofit National Rifle League — and rolled out matches up and down the West Coast. Then in 2017, they struck on the idea of a .22LR-only league — no need for a ton of money in gear and a 1,000-yard shooting range. Just a few years later, NRL22, and the precision rimfire shooting movement it spawned is the fastest-growing shooting discipline in the world.

Q: Unlike most centerfire precision shooting, it's not uncommon to see base-class NRL22 shooters with sub-$1,050 rigs score right up there with the best open-class shooters. How is it that NRL22 has leveled this playing field when it comes to gear?

A: That's a tough question. When you have a new sport and a shooting community that has grown so fast and so large as we have, you always have shooters who want to push the boundaries on gear. We've tried to really restrain that so NRL22 doesn't become a gear race, a money race. That's what happened in the [centerfire] NRL and PRS. The rifles that those champions are using aren't practical for anything but NRL and PRS. They're purpose-built race guns. A lot of the stuff you see in NRL22 is becoming that way, but it doesn't have to be. We often see base-class shooters beat open-gun competitors. You can see a guy with a $1,000 rifle/optic platform go out there and totally beat up a guy with a $3,000 Vudoo. It's not about the gear. It's about fundamentals. We like it that way, and the course of fires are designed that way. If you come to NRL22 with good marksmanship fundamentals, you're going to do way better than the shooter that just goes out and buys a fancy race gun. Some guys want the race gun, they want to work on and develop their rifle/optics platform, they want to shoot past 100 yards, and that's cool. That's why we developed NRL22X.

Q: What is NRL22X?

A: Well, the biggest gripe we heard was people wanted to use whatever gear they wanted. They also wanted to shoot farther than the 100 yards that is a standard NRL22 course of fire. In NRL22, you're generally limited to a bag, bipod, and sling. If we opened that up to tripods and plates or whatever, we'd be changing the whole purpose of NRL22, which is an entry-level way to get shooters into the sport. If it were just a gear race, people wouldn't be interested, wouldn't want to spend the money to get started. But shooters like toys, shooters like spending money, so we started NRL22X to allow competitors to run whatever they want as long as it was deemed okay by the match director. This allows more freedom to the match director to design and create his own course of fire and allows the competitors the freedom to use whatever gear they felt necessary. Now we see NRL22X targets out past 400 yards.

Q: What separates NRL from all the other precision shooting leagues out there?

A: We're a nonprofit. The others are for-profit. There are big differences in the way we calculate our scores, with ours done off of points and rankings. We think this is a better show of skill than that one lucky day or a home-range advantage. We're not trying to be the biggest, hold the most events, get the most shooters, either. Our big goal was, and is, to include as many shooters as possible, especially new shooters. We want to have absolutely the best shooting event experience anywhere. We know this sport is male-dominated, too, so we want to get as many females and youth shooters involved as possible. And at least one member of our executive team attends every NRL and NRL22X match, so we're very present. NRL22, of course, is different as we have anywhere from 50 to 90 clubs a month hosting a match and submitting their local scores.

Q: It's crazy how that's blown up, even in just the last couple of years since we first met. Do you ever look at the submitted scores and think, 'Good lord, what did I create?'

A: [Laughs] We're not surprised it's such a success anymore, but sometimes we still pinch ourselves. One thing that happened: the market really responded, which we're grateful for. The .22 LR market was really tough before NRL22. There wasn't a lot of innovation, not many options, so there was a lot for people to be tentative about. Some guys had super-accurate .22s, but others had rifles that couldn't hit a soda can at 50 yards. Now, there are great, accurate rifles out there for not a lot of money. More and more manufactures are coming out with modern precision .22s every year. It's a good time to be a shooter, and NRL22 with that kind of market support is facilitating it. We're making more shooters. I mean, you know what it's like. It's addicting. You get on the line and shoot and hear that steel ring eight times of 10. You stand up, and the first thought is 'I know I can hit that 10 times in a row.' Man, it's just fun. It's awesome. It's not a surprise that so many people love it. RR

APPENDIX I

Further Reading

There are many books on rimfire rifles. Most of them are outdated or not particularly good. That said, there remains a small shelf of classics that stand the test of time, along with a few high-quality modern offerings. The books listed below have been instrumental in my thinking about rimfire :

22 Caliber Rifle Shooting by C.S. Landis (1932), Sportsman's Vintage Press, 2013

Rimfire Rifleman by Edwards Brown Jr., Firearms Classic Library, 2007 (reprint)

Ruger and His Guns: A History of the Man, the Company & Their Firearms by R. L. Wilson, Skyhorse, 1996

Small-bore Rifle Shooting by Edward C. Crossman, Firearms Classic Library, 2003 (reprint)

Small-Bore Rimfire Rifles by C. Rodney James, Skyhorse Publishing, 2018

The .22 Rifle by David Petzal, Winchester Press, 1973 (out of print, but available used online)

The Art of Rimfire Accuracy by Bill Calfee, AuthorHouse, 2011

The Rifleman's Guide to Rimfire Ammunition by Steven Boelter, Zediker Publishing, 2006

The Ruger 10/22 Complete Owner's and Assembly Guide by Walt Kuleck, Scott Duff Publishing, 2015

Walnut & Steel II: More Vintage .22 Rifles by Bill Ward, Palmetto Publishing Group, 2018

Walnut & Steel: Vintage .22 Rifles by Bill Ward, Author House, 2014

Books on Shooting

Shooting well is a skill developed on the range through work. The following two books explain the *why* behind the work — deep dives on long-range and accurate shooting concepts to better inform the training. Whether just starting your marksmanship journey or looking to review the fundamentals, these two books provide sound, engaging information for beginners, intermediate, or advanced shooters interested in modern precision shooting.

Long Range Shooting Handbook: The Complete Beginner's Guide by Ryan M. Cleckner, CreateSpace, 2016

Precision Rifle Marksmanship: The Fundamentals by Frank Galli, Gun Digest Books, 2020

Online Resources

The Internet is a beautiful place full of equal parts expertise and bullshit. It's on the reader to figure out which is which, but you can slant the odds in favor of reality by carefully picking your sources. These three online forums are where most of the serious rimfire discussions happen. They're also wonderful resources if you have technical questions about the operation, repair, or maintenance of a specific firearm. Lunatics abound online, but less so at these websites. Bonus: All have excellent classified sections.

• *Sniper's Hide*, https://www.snipershide.com/shooting/

Vudoo Gun Works' birthplace is the leading discussion board and clearinghouse for everything in modern precision shooting. The talent pool of posters skews young and opinionated. Strong language warning. Lots of great information on centerfire PRS and NRL shooting, too.

• *RimfireCentral.com*, https://www.rimfirecentral.com/forums/

The best resource online for everything Ruger, particularly 10/22s. It features excellent information on older firearms as well. The talent pool is more senior and mostly not tactical. Lots of DIY gunsmithing articles for kitchen-table rifle builders. Lots of insight into NRA-type shooting disciplines.

• *Rimfireaccuracy.com*, http://www.rimfireaccuracy.com/

Jerry Stiller is the preeminent benchrest rifle action builder alive today, and he also runs this information-rich benchrest shooters' forum. It's the best place to get match information or schooled in the world of pinpoint rifle accuracy. Numerous "sticky" threads go deep on what it takes to be a competitor.

APPENDIX II

Manufacturers of Note

RIFLES, ACTIONS & BARRELED ACTIONS

10x Custom Rifles
977 18th Avenue SW
Vero Beach, FL 32962
330-242-5605
www.10XCustomGuns.com

Anschutz (North America)
7661 Commerce Lane
Trussville, AL 35173-2837
205-655-7500
205-655-7502
www.anschutznorthamerica.com/
@anschutznorthamerica

Azimuth Technologies
10130 Market Street
Naples, FL 34112
239-352-0600
239-352-0665
www.azimuthtechnology.com/
@azimuthtechnology

Bergara
1270 Progress Center Ave.
Suite 100
Lawrenceville, GA 30043
877-892-7544
www.bergara.online/us/
@bergara_rifles

Browning
One Browning Place
Morgan UT, 84050
800-333-3288
801-876 2711
www.browning.com/
@browningfirearms

Chiappa Firearms
Italia | Headquarter
Chiappa Firearms Srl
Via Milano, 2
25020 Azzano Mella (Brescia)
Italy
+39-030-974-9232
USA | Distribution
Chiappa Firearms USA, Ltd.
1415 Stanley Avenue
Dayton, OH 45404
937-835-5000
www.chiappafirearms.com/
@chiappafirearms

Christensen Arms
550 N Cemetery Rd
Gunnison, UT 84634
435-633-4667
christensenarms.com/
@christensenarms

CMMG Manufacturing
PO Box 68
Boonville, MO 65233
660-248-2293
cmmginc.com/
@cmmginc

Cooper Firearms
3662 Hwy 93 North
Stevensville, Montana 59870
406-777-0373
cooperfirearms.com/
@cooperfirearms

CZ-USA
PO Box 171073
Kansas City, KS 66117
800-955-4486
cz-usa.com/
@czusafirearms

Dakota Arms
1310 Industry Road
Sturgis, SD 57785
605-347-4686
www.dakotaarms.com/
@dakotaarms_official

Feinwekbau
Neckarstraße 43
78727 Oberndorf/Neckar
+49 7423/814-0
www.feinwerkbau.de/willkommen
@feinwerkbaugmbh

Franklin Armory
2246 Park Place Suite B
Minden, NV 89423
775-783-4313
franklinarmory.com/
@franklinarmory

GSG Imports
231 Deming Way
Summerville, SC 29483
800-290-0065
www.americantactical.us/
@americantactical.us

Hall Manufacturing
142 County Road 406
Clanton, AL 35045
205-755-4904
www.hallmfg.com/

Henry
59 East 1st Street
Bayonne, NJ 07002
866-200-2354
www.henryusa.com/
@henry_rifles

Holeshot Arms
118 Regency Drive
Wylie, TX 75098
214-773-9010
holeshotarms.com/

Howa
4674 Aircenter Circle
Reno, NV 89502
800-553-4229
www.howausa.com/
@legacysportsint

Kel-Tec
1505 Cox Rd
Cocoa, FL 32926
321-631-0068
www.keltecweapons.com/
@keltecweapons

Keystone Sporting Arms
155 Sodom Road
Milton, PA 17847
1-800-742-0455
www.keystonesportingarmsllc.com/
@ksallc1

KIDD Innovative Designs
2633 Terminal Loop Rd
PO BOX 1039
McQueeney, TX 78123
830-557-4487
www.kiddinnovativedesign.com/
@kiddinnovativedesign

KRISS
912 Corporate Lane
Chesapeake, VA 23320
855-574-7787
kriss-usa.com/
@krissusainc

Legacy/Lithgow/Howa
4674 Aircenter Circle
Reno, NV 89502
775-828-0555
www.legacysports.com/catalog/
lithgow/
@legacysportsint

Magnum Research
12602 33rd Avenue SW
Pillager, MN 56473
508-635-4273
magnumresearch.com
@magnumresearchinc

Marlin
1-800-544-8892
www.marlinfirearms.com/
@marlinfirearms_official

Mossberg
7 Grasso Avenue
North Haven, CT 06473
203-230-5300
www.mossberg.com/
@mossbergcorp

New Ultra Light Arms
438 Miranov Street
Granville, WV 26534
304-292-0600
newultralightarms.com/

Patriot Ordnance Factory
623-321-1680
877-561-9572
pof-usa.com/
@pofusa

Radical Firearms
4413 Bluebonnet Suite 8
Stafford, TX 77477
www.radicalfirearms.com/
@radicalfirearms

Remington
1816 Remington Circle SW
Huntsville, AL 35824
1-800-243-9700
www.remington.com/
@remingtonarmscompany

Rossi
100 Taurus Way
Bainbridge, GA 39817
229-515-8707
rossiusa.com/
@rossiusa

Ruger
271 Cardwell Road
Mayodan, NC 27027
336-949-5200
ruger.com/
@rugersofficial

Sako/Tikka
17601 Beretta Drive
Accokeek, MD 20607
www.tikka.fi/en-us
@tikka_international

Savage
100 Springdale Road
Westfield, MA 01085
800-370-0708
www.savagearms.com/
@savagearms

Smith & Wesson
2100 Roosevelt Avenue
Springfield, MA 01104
1-800-331-0852
www.smith-wesson.com
@smithandwessoninc

Steyr Arms
2530 Morgan Road
Bessemer, AL 35022
205-417-8644
www.steyr-arms.com/us/
@steyrarms_us

Stiller Actions
543 N 5th St
Garland, TX 75040
972-429-5000
stilleractions.com/
@stilleractions

Tactical Solutions
2772 S. Victory View Way
Boise, ID 83709
866-333-9901
tacticalsol.com/
@tacticalsol

Thompson/Center (Smith & Wesson)
2100 Roosevelt Avenue
Springfield, MA 01104
866-730-1614
www.tcarms.com/
@tcarmsco

Turbo Actions
32 Silver Lake Road
Harrisonburg, VA 22801
540-438-1870
www.turboaction.net/
@turbo_rim_fire_actions

Ultimatum Precision
778-786-3582
www.ultimatumprecision.com/
@ultimatumprecision

Volquartsen
24276 240th Street
Carroll, IA 51401
712-792-4238
volquartsen.com/
@volquartsen_firearms

Vudoo Gun Works
4012 So. River Rd. Ste. 4-F
Saint George, UT 84790
435-359-2890
vudoogunworks.com/
@vudoogunworks

Walther USA
7700 Chad Colley Blvd
Fort Smith, AR 72916
479-242-8500
waltherarms.com/
@waltherarms

Winchester
275 Winchester Avenue
Morgan, UT 84050
800-333-3288 & 801-876-2711
www.winchesterguns.com/
@winchesterrepeatingarms

Zermatt Arms/Bighorn RimX
100 Monroe St.
Bennet, NE 68317
402-782-2884
bighornarms.com/

BARRELS

Bartlein
W208N16939 N. Center St
Jackson, Wisconsin 53037
262-677-1717
bartleinbarrels.com/
@bartleinbarrelsinc

Benchmark
1105 Pioneer Highway East
Arlington, Washington 98223
360-652-2594
www.benchmark-barrels.com/
@benchmarkbarrels

Brux
917 Development Drive
Lodi, WI 53555
608-592-3324
www.bruxbarrels.com/

Douglas Barrels
5504 Big Tyler Road
Charleston, WV 25313-1398
304-776-8560
www.douglasbarrels.net/

F.J. Feddersen
7501 Corporate Park Drive
Loudon, TN 37774-5609
fjfeddersen.com/

Green Mountain Rifle Barrel Co.
PO Box 2670
153 West Main St
Conway, NH 03818
603-447-1095
www.gmriflebarrel.com/
@gmriflebarrel

Hart Barrels
1690 Apulia Road
Lafayette, NY 13084
315-677-9841
www.hartbarrels.com/

IBI Barrels
604-674-6972
internationalbarrels.com/
@internationalbarrels

Krieger Barrels
2024 Mayfield Road
Richfield, WI 53076
262-628-8558
kriegerbarrels.com/
@kriegerbarrels

Lilja
81 Lower Lynch Creek Road
Plains, MT 59859
406-826-3084
riflebarrels.com/
@Lilja_rifle_barrels

Muller
mullerworksinc.com/

PROOF Research
10 Western Village Ln
Columbia Falls, MT 59912
proofresearch.com/
@proof_research

Rock Creek
PO Box 330
101 Ogden Ave
Albany, WI 53502
608-862-2357
608-862-3688
www.rockcreekbarrels.com/

Shilen
2501 North Interstate Highway 45
Ennis, Texas 75119
972-875-5318
www.shilen.com/
@shilenrifles

Walther Lothar
3425 Hutchinson Rd.
Cumming, GA 30040
770-889-9998
www.lothar-walther.com/
@lotharwalther_usa

Whistle Pig Gun Barrel Co.
PO Box 418
Aurora, OR 97002
971-808-1022
www.wpgbc.com/

TRIGGERS

Bix & Andy
Gewerbepark Süd 5
6330 Kufstein
+43/(0)5372/22/447
bixn-andy.at/en/
@bixnandy

Brimstone
4857 NW Lake Road
Suite #115
Camas, WA 98607
360-210-5403
brimstonegunsmithing.com/
@brimstonegunsmithing

CMC
5597 Oak Street
Fort Worth, TX 76140
817-563-6611
www.cmctriggers.com/
@cmctriggers

Elftmann Tactical
2401 West Phelps Ste. D
Phoenix, AZ 85023
602-441-5007
www.elftactical.com/
@elftactical

Jewell
3620 North State Highway 123
San Marcos, TX 78666
512-353-2999
jewelltriggers.com/
@jewelltriggers

Rifle Basix
PO Box 49064
Charlotte, NC 28277
704-499-3087
riflebasix.com/

Timney Triggers
2020 West Quail Ave.
Phoenix, AZ 85027
866-484-6639
timneytriggers.com/
@timney_triggers

Trigger Tech
24-26 1200 Aerowood Dr
Mississauga, On
L4W 2S7, Canada
1-888-795-1485
triggertech.com/
@trigger.tech

STOCKS & CHASSIS

Accuracy International
3410 Shannon Park Dr #100
Fredericksburg, VA 22408
540-368-3108
www.accuracyinternational.com/
@accuracyinternational

Ashbury Precision Ordnance
84 Business Park Circle
Ruckersville, VA 22968
434-296-8600
www.ashburyprecisionordnance.
net/
@ashburyprecisionordnance

Bell & Carlson
101 Allen Road
Dodge City, KS 67801
620-225-6688
www.bellandcarlson.com/
@bellandcarlson

Boyds Gun Stocks
25376 403rd Avenue
Mitchell, SD 57301
1-605-996-5011
www.boydsgunstocks.com/
@boydsgunstocks

Cadex Defense
755 Avenue Montrichard,
Saint-Jean-sur-Richelieu, QC
J2X 5K8
450-348-6774
888-348-6774
www.cadexdefence.com
@cadexdefence

Grayboe
6027 N 57th Dr
Glendale, AZ 85301
623-200-6440
www.grayboe.com/
@grayboe

GRS
900 Overlander Rd
Emporia, KS 66801
800-835-3519
620-343-1084
grs.com/
@grstools

H-S Precision
1301 Turbine Dr.
Rapid City, SD 57703
605-341-3006
hsprecision.com/
@officialhsprecision

J. Allen Enterprises
#726 100 Cherry St.
Sumas, Washington 98295
604-393-0800
www.jaechassis.com/jae_us/
@jaeglobal

JP Rifles
PO Box 378
Hugo, MN 55038
651-426-9196
www.jprifles.com/
@jprifles

Kinetic Research Group
372 S. Eagle Road Suite 342
Eagle, ID 83616
kineticresearchgroup.com/
@krg_ops

Magpul
8226 Bee Caves Rd.
Austin, TX 78746
877-462-4785
magpul.com/
@magpul

Manners
1232 Swift Ave
Kansas City, MO 64116
816-283-3334
mannersstocks.com/
@mannersstocks

Masterpiece Arms
4904 Hwy 98 East
Comer, GA 30629
706-395-7050
masterpiecearms.com/
@masterpiecearms

McMillan
1638 W Knudsen Drive
Phoenix, AZ 85027
623-582-9674
mcmillanusa.com/
@mcmillan_stocks

MDT
1-7949 Venture Pl
Chilliwack, BC V2R 4H5
604-393-0800
mdttac.com/us_en/
@mdttac21

PMACA
1340 N Dynamics St Ste K
Anaheim, CA 92806-1902
888-758-1022
pmacamfg.com/

Victor Co.
2629 Foothill Blvd #360
La Crescenta, CA 91214
323-419-1595
@victorcompanyusa

Walther Lothar
3425 Hutchinson Rd.
Cumming, GA 30040
770-889-9998
www.lothar-walther.com/
@lotharwalther_usa

XLR
2323 Grand Park Drive
Grand Junction, CO 81505
970-241-1807
xlrindustries.com/
@xlrindustries

PARTS & ACCESSORIES

Area 419
10110 Yawberg Rd
Grand Rapids, OH 43522
419-830-8353
www.area419.com/
@area419official

Armageddon Gear
29 Airport Rd.
Buena Vista, GA 31803
229-314-9059
www.armageddongear.com/
@armageddongear

Atlas Bipods
PO Box 771071
Wichita, KS 67277
316-721-1021
www.accu-shot.com/
@btindllc

DIP Inc.
PO Box 1687
Post Falls, ID 83877
208-660-9974
www.diproductsinc.com/

Fix It Sticks
4021 N Ravenswood Ste. A
Chicago, IL 60613
872-802-3110
store.fixitsticks.com/
@fixitsticksshooting

Garmin
1200 E 151st St
Olathe, KS 66062
913-397-8200
www.garmin.com/en-US/
@garmin

Harris Bipods
203-982-7844
www.harrisbipods.com/
@harrisbipods

J&P Custom Products, LLC.
PO Box 5947
Brookings, OR 97415
www.jnpgunsprings.com/

JWH Custom
6155 S. Eastern Ave.
Commerce, CA 90040
310-600-0281
www.jwhcustom.com/
@jwhcustom

Kelbly's Inc.
7222 Dalton Fox Lake Rd
North Lawrence, OH 44666
330-683-4674
www.kelbly.com
@kelblyrifles

Kestrel Ballistics
21 Creek Circle
Boothwyn, PA 19061
800-784-4221
kestrelballistics.com/
@kestrelballistics

Labradar
2455 Rue de l'Industrie,
Trois-Rivières, QC G8Z 4T1,
Canada
316-866-2525
mylabradar.com/
@mylabradar

Long Range Arms
5272 E. 49th N.
Idaho Falls, ID 83402
406-640-4302
long-range-arms.myshopify.com/
@long_range_arms

Longshot Cameras
1835 County Rd 130
Pearland, TX 77581
281-205-8134
www.longshotcameras.com/
@longshotcam

MagnetoSpeed
8801 Tara Lane
Austin, TX 78737
512-284-8161
magnetospeed.com/
@magnetospeed_llc

MCARBO
5601 116th Ave N
Clearwater, Florida 33760
727-223-1816
www.mcarbo.com/
@mcarbotriggers

Raven Eye Custom
5885 Allison Street #2215
Arvada, CO 80004
www.raveneyecustom.com/

Reactor
7835 E Gelding Dr Suite E
Scottsdale, AZ 85260
480-702-1482
reactorusa.com/
@reactorusa

S&P Outfitters
9500 Feather Grass Ln
Ste 120 Box 102
Fort Worth TX 76177
469-609-7273
sapoutfitters.com/

Short Action Precision
2501 N Hopi Ln
Chino Valley, AZ 86323
www.shortactionprecision.com/
@shortactionprecision

Side-Shot
495 South Main Street
Providence, UT 84332
385-312-0602
www.side-shot.
com/
@sideshotscopecam

SIG Sauer
72 Pease Boulevard
Newington, NH 03801
603-610-3000
www.sigsauer.com/
@sigsauerinc

Tandemkross
490 South Stark Highway
Weare, NH 03281
603-369-7060
www.tandemkross.com/
@tandemkross

Wheeler Gunsmithing
833-784-5522
www.wheelertools.com/
@wheelertools

Wiebad
12901 State Highway 30
College Station, TX 77845
979-314-3679
wiebad.com/
@wiebadgear

TacomHQ
PO Box 10507
Fort Smith, AZ 72917
833-822-6647
tacomhq.com/
@tacomhq

AMMUNITION

Aguila
888-452-4019
www.aguilaammo.com/
@aguilaammo

Armscor
150 North Smart Way
Pahrump, NV 89060
775-537-1444
www.armscor.com/
@rockislandarmory

Browning
One Browning Place
Morgan UT, 84050
800-333-3288
801-876 2711
www.browningammo.com/
@browningammo

CCI
2299 Snake River Ave
Lewiston, ID 83501
800-948-1356
www.cci-ammunition.com/
@cciammunition

ELEY
5999 US Highway 83
Winters, Texas 79567
325-754-5771
www.eleyammunition.com/
@eleyusa

Federal
900 Bob Ehlen
Anoka, MN 55303
800-831-8100
www.federalpremium.com/
@federalpremium

Fiocchi
6930 N Fremont Rd
Ozark, MO 65721
417-725-4118
fiocchiusa.com/
@fiocchi_ammunition

Geco
geco-munition.de/
@gecohunting

Lapua/SK
PO Box 5 / Patruunatehtaantie 15
FI-62101 Lapua, Finland
www.lapua.com/
@lapua_ammunition

Magtech
Av. Humberto de Campos, 3220
09426-900 – Ribeirão Pires /
SP – Brazil
magtechammunition.com/
@magtechammunition

Norma
Jägargatan
S-679 40 ÅMOTFORS
SWEDEN
+46 (0) 571-315 00
www.norma-ammunition.com/
en-us
@normahunting

Remington
1816 Remington Circle SW
Huntsville, AL 35824
1-800-243-9700
www.remington.com/ammunition/
@remingtonarmscompany

RWS
rws-ammunition.com/en/
@rwshunting

Winchester
275 Winchester Avenue
Morgan, UT 84050
800-333-3288
801-876-2711
www.winchesterguns.com/
@winchesterrepeatingarms

Wolf
PO Box 757
Placentia, CA 92871
wolfammo.com/
@wolfammo

CUSTOM WORK

Alex Sitman/Master Class Stocks
611 East Second Street
Bellwood, PA 16617
814-742-7868
www.masterclassstocks.com/

Connecticut Precision Chambering
1548 Saybrook Rd
Middletown, CT 06457
860-343-0552
ct-precision.com/

Hill Country Rifles
5726 Safari Dr
New Braunfels, TX 78132
830-609-3139
www.hillcountryrifles.com/
@hill_country_rifle_co

Joe Chacon, ARBA
505 Redwing Dr.
Bandera, TX 78003
830-796-0815
abra.22lr@yahoo.com
www.autobenchrestassociation.
com/

Keystone Accuracy
PO Box 612
Waverly, PA 18471
610-272-2511
keystoneaccuracy.com/
@keystoneaccuracy

TS Customs
907 E 4th St
Miller, SD 57362
605-870-1567
www.tscustom.com/
@tscustomrifles

RANK	SHOOTER	CLASS	RIFLE	STOCK/CHASSIS	BARREL	TRIGGER	RIFLESCOPE	AMMO
1	Paul Dallin	OPEN	Vudoo	XLR	Ace	Tubbs T7	Nightforce mil c	Lapua center x
2	Justin Carbone	OPEN	Anschutz 64	Anschutz Trainer	Shilen Ratchet 22 inch	Anschutz factory 5098	Nightforce ATACR 7-35 Mil-XT	Federal UltraMatch
3	Chris Simmons	OPEN	Vudoo	MPA BA Comp	Ace 20"	Triggertech Diamond	Us Optics ts20x jvcr reticle	Lapua center x
4	Vance koehn	OPEN	CZ 455	MPA BA Comp	anschutz cut for cz	factory with yo dave trigger kit	nf atacr 7-35 moa with moar reticle	rws r50
5	Allison Zane	YOUNG GUNS	Vudoo	MPA BA Comp	Vudoo Ace	Huber 2 stage	Vortex AMG with 7c reticle	Lapua Center X
6	Jason McBride	OPEN	Vudoo	MPA BA Comp	Bartlein	Timney Calvin Elite	Vortex Razor G2 / EBR2C - MOA	Lapua Center X
7	Mike Suttle	OPEN	Vudoo	MPA BA Comp	18" Ace , Kukri contour	Trigger Tech Diamond	Vortex Razor 4.5-27 x 56 Gen II HD, EBR7-C	Lapua Center -X
10	Trever Johnson	OPEN	Vudoo	MDT ACC	Vudoo	Trigger tech	Nightforce Atacr / milXT	Lapua center x
12	Larry Orines	OPEN	Vudoo	Manners	Ace	Hubert	Vortex gen2 3-18 ebr7c	CenterX
13	Justin Mehs	OPEN	Bergara B14R	MDT ACC	Factory Bergara	Triggertech Special	Athlon Midas TAC with APRS3 MIL recticle	Lapua Center X
14	Tyler Frehner	OPEN	Anshutz	Kelbly	Anshutz	Anshutz	Nightforce ATACR 7-35 mil-c	Lapua Center X
15	Kacen Gubler	OPEN	Vudoo	Grayboe	Preferred Barrel Blanks	Trigger Tech Dimond Flat	Vortex PST Gen 2 MRAD	SK Standard Plus
16	Terry Conaway	OPEN	Bergara B14R	Bergara	bergara	trigger tech	Kahles 5-25 skmr3	Lapua center x
17	Justin Topel	OPEN	Vudoo	MPA	Vudoo Ace	Trigger Tech Diamond	Z Comp MPCT2	Eley Tenex
18	Joe Maehs	OPEN	Vudoo	Foundation	ACE	Trigger Tech	Athlon Chronos	lapua X-act
21	Richard Rogers	OPEN	RimX	Grayboe Renegade	Shilen	Trigger Tech Diamond	Vortex Gen II Razor EBR-2C	SK Long Range
24	Ryan Curry	OPEN	CZ 457	Manners Composite Stocks	Bartlein	CZ 457 (Stock)	Nightforce ATACR, Mil-XT	Lapua Center-X
25	Levi Sanderson	BASE	Tikka T1x	Factory	Factory	Factory	Athlon Argos BTR 8-34x Gen 2	Center-X
26	Megan Pakradooni	LADIES	Vudoo	MPA	Ace 18" Kukri Contour	Timney Calvin Elite	Vortex Viper PST, EBR-7C	Lapua Center X
27	Lauryl Akenhead	YOUNG GUNS	CZ 457	Manners	Lilja	factory	steiner M7XI Tremor 3	SK
28	Michael Glander	BASE	Ruger American Rimfire	Factory stock	Factory barrel	Factory trigger	Vortex diamondback tactical 6-24 ebr2c mrad	SK Match
30	Victor Vuong	OPEN	Vudoo	MDT ACC	ACE 18" Kukri	Huber 2-Stage 1.5lb	Vortex Razor HD AMG - EBR 7B (MRAD)	Lapua Center-X
33	Boyd Linder	OPEN	Tikka T1x	Oryx	Factory	Timney	Vortex viper pst Gen 2 ebr7c	Eley tenex
34	thaddeous wilson	OPEN	Bergara B14R	Accurate Rifle Systems	bergara	trigger tech diamond	leupold marked cch	lapua centerx
37	Nate Kreimeyer	BASE	Ruger Precision Rimfire	Factory stock	Factory barrel	Factory trigger	Athlon Argos BTR Gen 1	Eley Target
38	Joseph Ogden	OPEN	Vudoo	Masterpiece arms	Bartlien	Jard triggers	Trijicon Tenmile 4.5-30x56 mil Christmas tree	Sk long range match
39	Josh Failes	OPEN	RimX	MPA BA Competition	HLR	TriggerTech Diamond	Vortex Gen 2 Razor EBR-7c	Eley Club
40	Johann Boden	OPEN	Vudoo V22	KRG Bravo	Vudoo Kukri (Bartlein)	TriggerTech Diamond	Vortex Viper PST Gen II, MRAD	Federal Ultramatch
43	Joey McConnell	OPEN	RimX	MDT ACC	Proof stainless prefit	Timney HIT	Vortex Razor HD Gen2 EBR-7C MRAD	Lapua Center-X
44	Greg Roman	OPEN	Vudoo	Manners PRS-1 W/Mini Chassis	20" Ace	Triggertech Diamond 2-Stage	ZCO 5-27 MPCT-2 Reticle	Lapua Center-X
46	Reese Boze	YOUNG GUNS	CZ 457	Manners	Factory	Stock	Bushnell HDMR II	Lapua center X
47	Alberto Perez	OPEN	CZ 455	Manners	Lilja	Stock Trigger - Yo Dave Trigger Kit	Vortex Razor Gen ii 4.5-27 - EBR7C Reticle	SK Standard Plus
48	Travis walla	OPEN	Vudoo	XLR Envy	Bartlein	Timney	Athlon Cronus mil reticle	Sk long range match

BIPOD	SPOTTER	MUZZLE DEVISE	BALLISTIC APP	BAG	SLING	How many hours a month do you practice?
Ckyepod	Leupold	None	Kestrel	Game changer	Sap	5-10
Cyke-pod	Buschnell LMSS	N/A	Kestrel 5700	OG game changer	Rifles Only	20/month
Atlas PSR	Bushnell Tactical 15-45	None	Kestrel w/AB	Bison Tactical Udder	Tab gear prs	12/week
atlas cal gen 2	bushnell forge 10×42 binoculars	na	kestrel with applied ballistics	waxed canvas gamechanger	Armageddon gear	22 and centerfire combined probably 10 hours a month.
MDT Cypod	Vortex UHD 18 x binos	None	Kestrel 5700 elite	Armageddon Gear pint size game changer	Armageddon Gear	2 hours dry fire per week plus matches on weekends
Atlas CAL	Vortex Kaibab 18x Binoculars	N/A	Istrelok Pro	Pint Size Game Changer / Heavy Fill	N/A	8 hours per week
Accu-Tac	Vortex Razor	None	Kestrel / Applied Ballistics	WieBad fortune cookie	SAP	2-3 hours a month
Evolution	Leupold Mark 4	None	Kestrel	Weibag fortune cookie	Rifles only	1/ month
Atlas	Swaro	None	Kestrel	Wiebad	Rifles Only	1
Atlas			Strelok Pro	Armageddon Gear pint size sticky gamechanger	Short Action Precision Positional Sling	5-10 hours per month
Skypod	Swarovski 15 binos	Silencerco sparrow	Shooter	SAP Solo Sac	SAP	0
Atlas	Vortex Fury 5000	None	Strelok	Game Changer	Home made	Once a month
atlas bt10		none	hornady	game changer	none	3 hours a week dryfire 1-2 hours live
Ckyepod		None	Kestrel	Gamechanger	Crosstac	2 hours month
Accu-Tac	Athlon	None	Kestrel Applied Ballistic	Pint Size wax canvas game changer	SAP	2-3 per week
Cyke Pod		N/A	Ballistics AE	Game Changer	Rifles Only	20
Atlas PSR		NA	Strelok Pro	Armaggedon Gear Game Changer	Armaggedon Gear	8
Accutac	Vortex Diamondback 12x56 Binoculars	TBAC 22 Takedown	Strelok Pro	Weibad mini fortune cookie and weibad pump pillow	SAP Sling	Once a week at local matches.
Accutac	Vortex Razor	None	Kestrel	Wiebad Mini Fortune Cookie	SAP	A few hours, not as much as I should.
atlas	Bushnell	N/A	Kestrel 5700	Armageddon gear- pint size game changer waxed canvas heavy fill	sharps mountain -- SIMPLE COMPETITION RIFLE SLING	3 to 4
Harris swivel	Vortex diamondback 12x binoculars	N/A	Kestrel	Armageddon gear gamechanger	Standard GI swivel	3-4
MDT Ckye Pod - PRS Short	Sig Kilo 3000 BDX	None	Kestrel 5700 Elite	Wiebad Charlie MFC	SAP	2 Hours / Week
Atlas	Vortex razor hd	OSS Suppressors rad22	Applied ballistic	Armageddon gear shmedium gamechanger	SAP	10-15 per month
utg	athlon	none	strelok	smedium gamechanger armageddon/area 419	SAP	10
Harris BRM-S 6-9"	Vortex Fury 5000 binos	None	Kestrel 5700 Elite	SAP WC Solo Sack	SAP Positional sling	
Atlas PSR		None	Applied ballistics	Weibad whiskey charlie mini fortune cookie	SAP	20/month
Atlas CAL	Bushnell Forge 15x binoculars	N/A	StrelokPro	WieBad Fortune Cookie	Short Action Precision	Less than one
Atlas		N/A	Applied Ballistics	Armageddon GameChanger	Magpul	2hrs/wk
MDT double pull ckyepod	Vortex viper HD R/T binos	Griffin armament revo45	Kestrel 5700 Elite	Original Waxed canvas gamechanger	SAP	5hr/week
Warne Skyline w/RRS head			Kestral W/AB	Tab Gear Str8Laced	SAP Sling	5-10 a month
Warne	Vortex binoculars		Ballistic AE	Armageddon Gear pint size game changer	Armageddon gear	8 hours week
Harris			Shooter	Home Made Sand Bag	SAP Sling	Just the Monthly NRL Course of Fire
Atlas			Kestrel with AB	Mini fortune cookie	None	10 hours per month

RANK	SHOOTER	CLASS	RIFLE	STOCK/CHASSIS	BARREL	TRIGGER	RIFLESCOPE	AMMO
49	Wini Bezold	BASE	Tikka	Tikka Factory	Tikka Factory	Tikka Factory	Cabela's Covenant 7 5-35	Lapua CenterX
50	Patrick Griffn	OPEN	Vudoo	Manners PRS-2	Kukri Contour	Timney Calvin Elite	Vortex Razor Gen II	SK Long Range
53	Doug Lynch	OPEN	RimX	KRG Whiskey	Proof	Unknown	Burris XTR3 3-18x SCR2	SK Rifle Match
54	Andrew DeMaranville	OPEN	Bergara B14R	Bell and Carlson 700 Competition	Factory	Timney HIT	Bushnell engage 3-18 deploy MIL reticle	SK rifle match
55	Erik Severson	OPEN	Vudoo	MDT ACC	Ace	TriggerTech Diamond	Kahles 5-25 SKMR 3	Lapua Center X
56	Micah Kuhn	BASE	CZ 457	Stock rifle stock	Stock barrel	Stock trigger	Vortex diamondback tactical w/ EBR-1C	Sk
57	Russ Ring	BASE	Savage	Factory boyds	Factory	Factory	Bushnell match pro, Mill reticle	SK Match yellow box
58	Tyson Spohn	OPEN	Rim X	Foundation	HLR	Triggertech diamond pro	Valdada, Recon G2, Mil	SK Long range
60	Stefan Leimer	OPEN	Tikka T1x	KRG Bravo	Stock	Stock	Vortex Strike Eagle 5-25 Milrad	SK St+
61	Neel Burnett	OPEN	Vudoo V22	XLR Industires Gen I Element	Vudoo MTU- ACE	Timney Calvin Elite	Nightforce NX8 4.5x32	Lapua Center-X
62	Ruth Soucie	LADIES	Anschutz 64	Anschutz Trainer	Factory Anschutz 1903	Factory Anschutz 5098	Nightforce NX8 4-32 Mil-XT	Federal UltraMatch
63	Bill Micke	OPEN	Ruger Precision Rimfire	Ruger	International Barrels Inc	Ruger	Vortex PST Gen 2 EBR2-C	SK Match
65	Janae Frehner	LADIES	Vudoo	XLR element	Vudoo	Timney Calvin elite 2 stage	Vortex 3x18 gen 2 razor	Lapua center X
66	Mitchell Tromberg	BASE	Savage MKII	Factory Wood Stock	Factory Savage Barrel	Factory Savage AccuTrigger	Vortex Diamondback Tactical 4-16 FFP MOA	Lapua CenterX
67	Cody Brink	BASE	CZ 457	Factory Walnut	Factory Varmint	Factory	Athlon Argos BTR GEN2 6-24×50 APLR2 FFP IR MOA	Lapua Center X
68	Alvin Sowers	OPEN	CZ 455	MDT ACC	Bartlien	Factory	Athlon Argos MIL FFP Gen 2	SK Biathlon
70	Christopher Swimm	OPEN	CZ455 Precision Trainer	Manners	CZ factory 16" threaded heavy barrel	Factory trigger with Yo Dave trigger kit	Vortex Viper PST 4-16x50 FFP MIL/MIL	SK rifle match
71	Jason Majors	OPEN	Vudoo	MPA BA Comp	Ace	TriggerTech Diamond	Vortex Razor HD AMG EBR-7B MRAD	Lapua Center-X
72	Dominic Thompson	OPEN	CZ 457	MPA	Lilja	yoDave Trigger	Kahles 525i with SKMR3 reticle	Lapua Center X
74	David Swedberg	BASE	CZ 457	CZ 457 OEM Varmit Stock	CZ 457 OEM Varmit Barrel	CZ 457 OEM trigger	Vortex Diamondback tactical EBR-2C	SK Rifle Match
77	Kyle Terhune	BASE	Ruger	Ruger	Ruger	Ruger	Cabelas MOA 6-24	Cci standard
79	Keith Rogers	BASE	CZ 457	Factory Boyd on CZ	Factory CZ	Factory CZ	Vortex diamond back 4-16	Sk and Lapua
80	Michelle Schroeder	LADIES	Ruger Precision Rimfire	Ruger Precision Rimfire	Ruger	Timney	Athlon Ares BTR	Eley Target
81	Joe Cornell	BASE	Ruger Precision Rimfire	Ruger	Ruger	Ruger	Vortex Diamondback Tactical 4-16 EBR-2C	Lapua Center X
82	Christopher Rische	OPEN	CZ 455	Factory	Stock barrel	Stock trigger	Vortex Viper PST Gen Ii	SK Rifle Match
83	Dennis Brierly	OPEN	Bergara B14R	MPA BA Comp	Bergara	Timney CE	Vortex strike Eagle ebr 7 moa	Sk standard plus
84	John McQuay	OPEN	Tikka T1x	MDT ACC	Lothar Walther	Tikka T1x	Athlon MIDAS TAC FFP APLR4	Lapua Center-X
85	Alexis linder	LADIES	Tikka T1x	Factory	Factory	Timney	Vortex viper pst gen 2, EBR 7C	Eley Tennex
86	Leif O'Brien	OPEN	CZ 457	Manners PRS1	CZ	CZ	Trijicon Accupower 4.5-30x56 MOA	Lapua Center X
87	Marcus Cisper	OPEN	CZ 457	CZ-USA chassis with XLR buttstock	Proof	CZ factory	Night force NX8	CCI standard
88	Joshua Keefer	OPEN	Tikka T1x	XLR Envy	Lilja	Tikka factory	Vortex pst gen 2	Lapua biathlon extreme
91	Aaron Gifford	OPEN	Anschutz 54	Anschutz bench rest	Anschutz	Anschutz	Vortex Gen 2 Razor, EBR 2C	Lapua Center X
93	Todd Sanders	OPEN	Cz 457	Manners	Lilja	Factory cz	Crimson trace 5 series 3x24x56	Lapua center x
94	Tara Landt	LADIES	CZ 455	MDT	CZ	Timney	ATHLON ARES moa	SK Standard plus
96	David Thornton	AIR RIFLE	FX Impact	Sabre Tactical	600mm .25 superior slug liner	AMP	Athlon ares 4-27 Christmas tree reticle	FX Hybrid slugs .25

BIPOD	SPOTTER	MUZZLE DEVISE	BALLISTIC APP	BAG	SLING	How many hours a month do you practice?
Atlas Cal Gen2	Swarovski STS 80HD 20-60	Silencerco Sparrow SS	Strelok PRO	Armageddon Gear sticky pint size gamechanger heavy	Rifles Only Tactical sling	10-15
Harris	Vortex Razor		JBM Ballistics	Game Changer	SAP Sling	3 hours a week
Ckye Pod	Burris	Thunderbeast	Shooter	Wiebad Mini Fortune Cookie	SAP	2 hours per week
Atlas CAL	Bushnell forge 15x binos		BulletDrop	Waxed canvas mini fortune cookie from weibad	None	Couple hours a week
Ckye Pod	Vortex Razor		Ballistic ARC	Schmedium Gamechanger	Short Action Precision	6 hrs/week
Accu-tac			Kestrel with applied ballistics	Wiebad	Sap sling	2-4 a week
Harris		Suppressor	Shooter	Rear bag homemade, barricade bag weibad fortune cookie heavy	Magpul	One to four hours a month
Atlas			Kestrel and Strelok Pro	Armageddon game changer sticky	None	Less than 2
Generic Harris			Strelok Pro	Homemade	Magpul Rifleman	~15 per month
Harris with RRS Adapter	Vortex Optics Viper 10x50 Binos	TBAC 22TD	Kestrel 5700 Elite	Armageddon Gear Gamechanger	SAP	2-3 hours per week
Cyke-pod	Buschnell Forge 15X binos		Ballistics Arc	Wiebad WC Mini Fortune cookie + OG Game Changer	SAP	2-3
Atlas	Vortex Binos		BallisticsARC	Wiebad Mini Fortune Cookie	SAP	2-4 hours per week
Ckye pod		Liberty mystic suppressor	Kestrel	Solo sack	SAP	Zero
Harris	Vortex Razor HD		Hornady 4DOF	Home-made	Unknown	3-4 hours a week
LRP	Athlon Cronus 20-60x86 UHD		StreLok Pro	Warhorse Development Clede	SAP	5-10 hrs a Month
Accu-tac	Bushnell		Kestrel 5700 Elite	Armeggdon Wax Game Changer	Hog Saddle Loop Sling	3-4
Atlas	Leupold MK4	YHM Stinger suppressor	KAC Bullet Flight military version	Wiebad Tactical mini fortune cookie	Homemade	10hrs/week
MDT Ckye Pod	Nikon Laserforce		Kestrel 5700 AB	Tab Gear	SAP	2-3 per month
Atlas	Swarovski STR80		Kestrel 5700 Elite	Wiebad waxed canvas MFC	SAP	6 hrs month
Harris			Strelok Pro	Armageddon Gear Pint-Sized Sticky Gamechanger	Short Action Precision	1-2 hours per week
Atlas		Spectre ii	Strelock	SAP	SAP	2
Accu-tac	Bushnell	Thunder beast	Applied Ballistics	Wiebad mini fortune cookie	Sap	Try to get in 2 hours
Harris			Kestrel	Schmedium Game Changer	SAP sling	3ish
Magpul		Dead Air Mask	Applied Ballistics	Pint Sized gamechanger	SAP Positional Rifle Sling	5 hours/week
Harris 6-9	Forge binoculars		Kestrel elite with applied ballistics	Pint sized game changer	SAP sling	10 hours + a month
Accu-tac	Hensdolt 45		Stelokpro	Armageddon mini coated	None	5-6 hours per month
Warne Skyline	Vortex Razor HD		Kestrel 5700AB	Reasor Precision Pint Size Gamechanger	TAB PRS	8/WK
Atlas				Wiebad mini fortune cookie	SAP sling	3 hours a week roughly
Atlas		YHM Stinger	Strelok	Armageddon Gear Sticky Game changer	SAP	45min/wk
Atlas	Bushnell forge binos		kestrel	Armageddon gear	SAP	12
Atlas		Sig srd22 suppressor	Strelockpro	SAP	SAP	3 a week
Ckye Pod and Harris			Shooter	Solo Sack	Short Action Precision Positional Sling	With Covid, no practice
Accutac	Athlon	Harrell precision tuner	Strelock	Area 419 smedium	Sap sling	20 -30 hours a month
LPR	Athlon cronos		Strelok pro	War horse	SAP	1-2 hours a month besides match
Accutac		Donny FL Sumo	ChairGun	Solo Sac	Vickers	2 hours a week

APPENDIX IV

Common DOPE

These charts are no substitute for checking the exact velocity for your load and rifle, but these common DOPES can get you moving in the right direction. All data computed in the very good Ballistics AE smartphone app.

.22 LR ELEY MATCH

BC	Bullet Weight	Muzzle Velocity	Zero Range	Sight Height	LOS Angle
0.150 G1	40 gr.	1,085	50	1.9 in	0°

Altitude	Pressure	Temp	RH	Wind Velocity	Wind Angle
1581	29.79 Hg.	63.0 °F	0%	6.5	193

Zero Altitude	Zero Pressure	Zero Temp	Zero RH	Min. PBR	Max. PBR
1535	29.79 Hg.	63.0 °F	0%	0	73

Bullet Trajectory

Range (yards)	Drop (in)	Drop (mrad)	Wind. (in)	Wind. (mrad)	Veloc. (fps)	Energy (ft-lbs)
0	-1.88	0	0	0	1,091	106
25	0.05	0.05	0.04	0.04	1,046	97
50	0	0	0.01	0.01	1,008	90
75	-2.17	-0.8	-0.07	-0.03	975	85
100	-6.62	-1.84	-0.22	-0.06	946	80
125	-13.49	-3	-0.41	-0.09	920	75
150	-22.92	-4.24	-0.65	-0.12	896	71
175	-35.04	-5.56	-0.94	-0.15	874	68
200	-50	-6.94	-1.28	-0.18	853	65
225	-67.94	-8.39	-1.66	-0.2	833	62
250	-89.01	-9.89	-2.08	-0.23	815	59
275	-113.34	-11.45	-2.55	-0.26	797	56
300	-141.09	-13.06	-3.07	-0.28	780	54
325	-172.42	-14.74	-3.63	-0.31	763	52
350	-207.47	-16.46	-4.22	-0.33	747	50
375	-246.41	-18.25	-4.85	-0.36	732	48
400	-289.41	-20.1	-5.49	-0.38	717	46
425	-336.63	-22	-6.16	-0.4	703	44
450	-388.26	-23.97	-6.84	-0.42	689	42
475	-444.47	-25.99	-7.52	-0.44	675	40
500	-505.46	-28.08	-8.19	-0.46	662	39

.22 LR LAPUA POLAR BIATHALON

BC	Bullet Weight	Muzzle Velocity	Zero Range	Sight Height	LOS Angle
0.172 G1	40gr	1,100	50	1.9 in	0°

Altitude	Pressure	Temp	RH	Wind Velocity	Wind Angle
1581	29.79 Hg.	63.0 °F	0%	6.5	193

Zero Altitude	Zero Pressure	Zero Temp	Zero RH	Min. PBR	Max. PBR
1535	29.79 Hg.	63.0 °F	0%	0	74

Bullet Trajectory

Range (yards)	Drop (in)	Drop (mrad)	Wind. (in)	Wind. (mrad)	Veloc. (fps)	Energy (ft-lbs)
0	-1.88	0	0	0	1,106	109
25	0.02	0.02	0.04	0.04	1,064	101
50	0	0	0.01	0.01	1,028	94
75	-2.19	-0.8	-0.07	-0.03	997	88
100	-6.3	-1.75	-0.19	-0.05	969	83
125	-12.84	-2.85	-0.37	-0.08	945	79
150	-21.81	-4.04	-0.58	-0.11	922	75
175	-33.33	-5.29	-0.84	-0.13	901	72
200	-47.53	-6.6	-1.14	-0.16	881	69
225	-64.52	-7.96	-1.48	-0.18	862	66
250	-84.42	-9.38	-1.86	-0.21	845	63
275	-107.37	-10.84	-2.28	-0.23	828	61
300	-133.48	-12.36	-2.73	-0.25	812	58
325	-162.89	-13.92	-3.22	-0.28	796	56
350	-195.73	-15.53	-3.74	-0.3	781	54
375	-232.12	-17.19	-4.29	-0.32	767	52
400	-272.2	-18.9	-4.86	-0.34	753	50
425	-316.11	-20.66	-5.44	-0.36	740	49
450	-363.99	-22.47	-6.02	-0.37	727	47
475	-415.99	-24.33	-6.61	-0.39	714	45
500	-472.26	-26.23	-7.2	-0.4	702	44

.22 LR CCI MINI-MAG

BC	Bullet Weight	Muzzle Velocity	Zero Range	Sight Height	LOS Angle
0.126 G1	36gr	1,280	50	1.9 in	0°

Altitude	Pressure	Temp	RH	Wind Velocity	Wind Angle
1581	29.79 Hg.	63.0 °F	0%	6.5	193

Zero Altitude	Zero Pressure	Zero Temp	Zero RH	Min. PBR	Max. PBR
1535	29.79 Hg.	63.0 °F	0%	0	79

Bullet Trajectory

Range (yards)	Drop (in)	Drop (mrad)	Wind. (in)	Wind. (mrad)	Veloc. (fps)	Energy (ft-lbs)
0	-1.88	0	0	0	1,292	133
25	-0.19	-0.21	0.06	0.06	1,204	116
50	0	0	0.01	0.01	1,130	102
75	-1.5	-0.55	-0.13	-0.05	1,070	91
100	-4.88	-1.36	-0.35	-0.1	1,021	83
125	-10.35	-2.3	-0.65	-0.14	981	77
150	-18.06	-3.34	-1.02	-0.19	946	72
175	-28.19	-4.48	-1.45	-0.23	915	67
200	-40.92	-5.68	-1.93	-0.27	887	63
225	-56.39	-6.96	-2.48	-0.31	861	59
250	-74.79	-8.31	-3.08	-0.34	838	56
275	-96.28	-9.72	-3.74	-0.38	815	53
300	-121.03	-11.21	-4.45	-0.41	794	50
325	-149.23	-12.75	-5.21	-0.45	774	48
350	-181.05	-14.37	-6.02	-0.48	754	45
375	-216.68	-16.05	-6.86	-0.51	736	43
400	-256.33	-17.8	-7.74	-0.54	718	41
425	-300.18	-19.62	-8.64	-0.56	701	39
450	-348.46	-21.51	-9.55	-0.59	684	37
475	-401.37	-23.47	-10.47	-0.61	669	36
500	-459.15	-25.51	-11.39	-0.63	653	34

.22 LR CCI Stingers

BC	Bullet Weight	Muzzle Velocity	Zero Range	Sight Height	LOS Angle	
0.103 G1	32 gr.	1,640	50	1.9 in	0°	

Altitude	Pressure	Temp	RH	Wind Velocity	Wind Angle	
1581	29.79 Hg.	63.0 °F	0%	6.5	193	

Zero Altitude	Zero Pressure	Zero Temp	Zero RH	Min. PBR	Max. PBR	
1535	29.79 Hg.	63.0 °F	0%	0	92	

Bullet Trajectory							
Range (yards)	Drop (in)	Drop (mrad)	Wind. (in)	Wind. (mrad)	Veloc. (fps)	Energy (ft-lbs)	Time (sec)
0	-1.88	0	0	0	1,661	196	0
25	-0.46	-0.51	0.06	0.07	1,510	162	0.04
50	0	0	0.01	0	1,375	134	0.08
75	-0.68	-0.25	-0.17	-0.06	1,256	112	0.13
100	-2.73	-0.76	-0.48	-0.13	1,156	95	0.19
125	-6.4	-1.42	-0.9	-0.2	1,078	83	0.24
150	-11.93	-2.21	-1.43	-0.27	1,018	74	0.31
175	-19.55	-3.1	-2.06	-0.33	970	67	0.37
200	-29.46	-4.09	-2.77	-0.38	930	61	0.44
225	-41.88	-5.17	-3.55	-0.44	894	57	0.52
250	-57.01	-6.33	-4.4	-0.49	862	53	0.6
275	-75.05	-7.58	-5.33	-0.54	833	49	0.68
300	-96.22	-8.91	-6.32	-0.59	806	46	0.76
325	-120.71	-10.32	-7.38	-0.63	781	43	0.85
350	-148.76	-11.81	-8.5	-0.67	757	41	0.94
375	-180.59	-13.38	-9.66	-0.72	734	38	1.03
400	-216.45	-15.03	-10.87	-0.75	713	36	1.13
425	-256.57	-16.77	-12.1	-0.79	692	34	1.23
450	-301.22	-18.59	-13.36	-0.82	672	32	1.33
475	-350.67	-20.51	-14.62	-0.86	653	30	1.43
500	-405.21	-22.51	-15.88	-0.88	635	29	1.54

.17 Mach 2 Hornady V-MAX

BC	Bullet Weight	Muzzle Velocity	Zero Range	Sight Height	LOS Angle	
0.125 G1	17 gr.	2,100	50	1.9 in	0°	

Altitude	Pressure	Temp	RH	Wind Velocity	Wind Angle	
1581	29.79 Hg.	63.0 °F	0%	6.5	193	

Zero Altitude	Zero Pressure	Zero Temp	Zero RH	Min. PBR	Max. PBR	
1535	29.79 Hg.	63.0 °F	0%	0	120	

Bullet Trajectory						
Range (yards)	Drop (in)	Drop (mrad)	Wind. (in)	Wind. (mrad)	Veloc. (fps)	Energy (ft-lbs)
0	-1.88	0	0	0	2,120	170
25	-0.66	-0.73	0.04	0.04	1,972	147
50	0	0	0.01	0	1,830	126
75	0.02	0.01	-0.1	-0.04	1,695	108
100	-0.72	-0.2	-0.29	-0.08	1,568	93
125	-2.34	-0.52	-0.57	-0.13	1,450	79
150	-4.99	-0.92	-0.95	-0.18	1,342	68
175	-8.84	-1.4	-1.44	-0.23	1,247	59
200	-14.08	-1.96	-2.02	-0.28	1,165	51
225	-20.91	-2.58	-2.71	-0.33	1,098	45
250	-29.54	-3.28	-3.49	-0.39	1,043	41
275	-40.15	-4.06	-4.34	-0.44	999	38
300	-52.93	-4.9	-5.26	-0.49	962	35
325	-68.05	-5.82	-6.25	-0.53	929	33
350	-85.67	-6.8	-7.29	-0.58	900	31
375	-105.96	-7.85	-8.37	-0.62	873	29
400	-129.09	-8.96	-9.48	-0.66	849	27
425	-155.23	-10.14	-10.62	-0.69	826	26
450	-184.53	-11.39	-11.77	-0.73	804	24
475	-217.17	-12.7	-12.92	-0.76	784	23
500	-253.33	-14.07	-14.07	-0.78	765	22

APPENDIX IV

.17 HMR Hornady HP XTP

BC	Bullet Weight	Muzzle Velocity	Zero Range	Sight Height	LOS Angle	
0.125 G1	20 gr.	2,375	50	1.9 in	0°	

Altitude	Pressure	Temp	RH	Wind Velocity	Wind Angle	
1581	29.79 Hg.	63.0 °F	0%	6.5	193	

Zero Altitude	Zero Pressure	Zero Temp	Zero RH	Min. PBR	Max. PBR	
1535	29.79 Hg.	63.0 °F	0%	0	138	

Bullet Trajectory						
Range (yards)	Drop (in)	Drop (mrad)	Wind. (in)	Wind. (mrad)	Veloc. (fps)	Energy (ft-lbs)
0	-1.87	0	0	0	2,396.00	255
25	-0.72	-0.8	0.03	0.04	2,237.00	222
50	0	0	0.01	0	2,084.00	193
75	0.23	0.08	-0.08	-0.03	1,937.00	167
100	-0.13	-0.03	-0.24	-0.07	1,797.00	143
125	-1.15	-0.25	-0.48	-0.11	1,664.00	123
150	-2.95	-0.55	-0.8	-0.15	1,539.00	105
175	-5.66	-0.9	-1.22	-0.19	1,423.00	90
200	-9.45	-1.31	-1.73	-0.24	1,319.00	77
225	-14.47	-1.79	-2.35	-0.29	1,226.00	67
250	-20.94	-2.33	-3.07	-0.34	1,148.00	58
275	-29.04	-2.93	-3.89	-0.39	1,084.00	52
300	-38.98	-3.61	-4.79	-0.44	1,032.00	47
325	-50.95	-4.35	-5.77	-0.49	990.00	43
350	-65.13	-5.17	-6.81	-0.54	954.00	40
375	-81.68	-6.05	-7.89	-0.58	922.00	38
400	-100.77	-7	-9.01	-0.63	894.00	35
425	-122.56	-8.01	-10.15	-0.66	868.00	33
450	-147.21	-9.09	-11.3	-0.7	844.00	32
475	-174.9	-10.23	-12.46	-0.73	822.00	30
500	-205.78	-11.43	-13.62	-0.76	801.00	28

.22 WMR CCI MAXI-MAG

BC	Bullet Weight	Muzzle Velocity	Zero Range	Sight Height	LOS Angle	
0.110 G1	40 gr.	1,910	50	1.9 in	0°	

Altitude	Pressure	Temp	RH	Wind Velocity	Wind Angle	
1581	29.79 Hg.	63.0 °F	0%	6.5	193	

Zero Altitude	Zero Pressure	Zero Temp	Zero RH	Min. PBR	Max. PBR	
1535	29.79 Hg.	63.0 °F	0%	0	107	

Bullet Trajectory							
Range (yards)	Drop (in)	Drop (mrad)	Wind. (in)	Wind. (mrad)	Veloc. (fps)	Energy (ft-lbs)	Time (sec)
0	-1.88	0	0	0	1,931	331	0
25	-0.59	-0.66	0.05	0.05	1,773	279	0.04
50	0	0	0.01	0	1,624	234	0.08
75	-0.22	-0.08	-0.13	-0.05	1,486	196	0.13
100	-1.43	-0.4	-0.39	-0.11	1,361	164	0.19
125	-3.81	-0.85	-0.76	-0.17	1,251	139	0.24
150	-7.57	-1.4	-1.25	-0.23	1,158	119	0.31
175	-12.94	-2.05	-1.85	-0.29	1,084	104	0.37
200	-20.15	-2.8	-2.55	-0.35	1,026	94	0.44
225	-29.42	-3.63	-3.33	-0.41	979	85	0.52
250	-40.94	-4.55	-4.2	-0.47	940	78	0.6
275	-54.91	-5.55	-5.14	-0.52	906	73	0.68
300	-71.51	-6.62	-6.14	-0.57	875	68	0.76
325	-90.95	-7.77	-7.21	-0.62	847	64	0.85
350	-113.41	-9	-8.33	-0.66	821	60	0.94
375	-139.08	-10.3	-9.5	-0.7	796	56	1.03
400	-168.16	-11.68	-10.71	-0.74	773	53	1.13
425	-200.87	-13.13	-11.93	-0.78	752	50	1.23
450	-237.4	-14.65	-13.18	-0.81	731	47	1.33
475	-278	-16.26	-14.43	-0.84	711	45	1.43
500	-322.88	-17.94	-15.69	-0.87	692	42	1.54